International Finance

MACMILLAN TEXTS IN ECONOMICS

Macmillan Texts in Economics is a new generation of economics
textbooks from Macmillan developed in conjunction with a panel of
distinguished editorial advisers:
David Greenaway, Professor of Economics, University of Nottingham;
Gordon Hughes, Professor of Political Economy, University of Edinburgh
David Pearce, Professor of Economics, University College, London
David Ulph, Professor of Economics, University of Bristol.

PUBLISHED

Understanding the UK Economy: Edited by Peter Curwen
International Finance: Keith Pilbeam

FORTHCOMING

Future Macmillan Texts in Economics cover the core compulsory and
optional courses in economics at first-degree level and will include:
Monetary Economics: Stuart Sayer
International Trade: Mia Mikic
Economics of the Labour Market: David Sapsford and Zafiris
  Tzannatos
Business Economics: Paul Ferguson and R. Rothschild
Development Economics: Ian Livingstone
Macroeconomics: Eric Pentecost
Environmental Economics: Nick Hanley and Ben White

INTERNATIONAL FINANCE

Keith Pilbeam

City University, London

MACMILLAN

First published 1992 by
THE MACMILLAN PRESS LTD
Houndmills, Basingstoke, Hampshire RG21 2XS
and London
Companies and representatives
throughout the world

ISBN 0–333–53130–2 hardcover
ISBN 0–333–54528–1 paperback

A catalogue record for this book is available
from the British Library.

Reprinted 1992, 1993, 1994

Printed in Hong Kong

Series Standing Order (Macmillan Texts in Economics)

If you would like to receive future titles in this series as they are published, you can make use of our standing order facility. To place a standing order please contact your bookseller or, in case of difficulty,write to us at the address below with your name and address and the name of the series. Please state with which title you wish to begin your standing order. (If you live outside the United Kingdom we may not have the rights for your area, in which case we will forward your order to the publisher concerned.)

Customer Services Department, Macmillan Distribution Ltd
Houndmills, Basingstoke, Hampshire RG21 2XS, England

To the children and workers
SOS Tibetan Children's Village, Pokhara, Nepal

Contents

PART 2 EXCHANGE-RATE DETERMINATION: THEORY, EVIDENCE AND POLICY

PART 3   THE POST-WAR INTERNATIONAL MONETARY SYSTEM

List of Figures

List of Boxes

List of Tables

Acknowledgements

In writing this book, I owe a heavy intellectual debt to the many people who have stimulated my interest and guided me through the field of international economics over the years; Ali El-Agraa, Tony Jones, Mike Stephenson, Theo Peeters, Loukas Tsoukalis, Jean-Paul Abraham, Paul De Grauwe, Alfred Steinherr, Emil-Maria Claassen and Wolfgang Gebauer. I am especially grateful to the series editor David Greenaway who read and commented on the entire manuscript. In addition, the comments and criticisms of four anonymous reviewers proved extremely helpful. Many thanks are due to the undergraduate students at City and participants in courses at the Management Development Centre. They were subjected to the contents of the book and their questions and demands for further clarifications significantly influenced the contents. Dion Glycopantis kept my teaching load down to a level which enabled the speedy completion of the manuscript. John Mark Downey of Cameron Markby Hewitt provided a lively discussion on the legal aspects of international finance. Finally, I should like to thank the commissioning editor Stephen Rutt for his enthusiastic and excellent support throughout the duration of the project.

KEITH PILBEAM

Introduction

■ *The subject matter of international finance*

The subject matter of international finance is, broadly speaking, concerned with the monetary and macroeconomic relations between countries. International finance is a constantly evolving subject that deals very much with real world issues such as balance-of-payments problems and policy, the causes of exchange-rate movements and the implications of macroeconomic linkages between economies.

Many economists had predicted that the adoption of generalised floating in 1973 would lead to a demise of interest in the subject. They believed that exchange-rate adjustments would eliminate balance-of-payments concerns. As is the case with many economists predictions, they were proved wrong! Floating exchange rates have not eliminated balance-of-payments preoccupations as the persistent concerns over the United States and United Kingdom current account deficits of the late 1980s and early 1990s have shown. Floating exchange rates have been characterised by high volatility and substantial deviations from purchasing power parities. Exciting new theories were developed to explain these phenomena and these theories have been subjected to close empirical scrutiny.

The quadrupling of oil prices at the end of 1973 and doubling in 1979 caused considerable turbulence to the world economy. There were dramatic divergences in economic performance; the United Kingdom and Italy experienced substantial rises in their inflation rates, while the Japanese and German economies managed to keep the lid on inflation. In such a turbulent world, a widespread desire to create a zone of currency stability between the currencies of countries belonging to the European Community led to the setting up of the European Monetary System in 1979. Contrary to much initial scepticism about its survival chances, it is now in its second decade of operation. In the 1990s, there is a considerable momentum for a European Monetary Union, that is, the creation of a single European currency.

A massive and sustained real appreciation of the dollar between 1981–5 was largely blamed on divergences in macroeconomic policies internationally. The United States had an ever-growing fiscal deficit with rising real interest rates while the European and Japanese economies were adopting much tougher fiscal policies. The resulting appreciation of the dollar led to trade frictions between the United States and its trading partners. To limit these damaging policy divergences, there were calls for a greater coordination of macroeconomic policies and much discussion in the economic literature over the potential gains to be had from such coordination. In August 1982 the international debt crisis exploded on the scene with the announcement of the Mexican moratorium. Since then the debt problems of numerous severely indebted countries have been at the forefront of concerns about the development of the world economy and stability of the international banking system.

Not surprisingly, in response to many of the foregoing developments, the literature and the importance of the subject has mushroomed. This is reflected in the fact that international finance is increasingly taught in universities and business schools as a separate course rather than as half of a course in international economics.

Although there are a number of very good texts covering many of these topics and developments, during my teaching of courses in international economics and international finance, it soon became evident that with so many developments it was extremely difficult to find a single core book to recommend. Some books are very strong on theory but pay little attention to empirical issues. Others are excellent on recent exchange-rate theory but presume a reasonable background in traditional exchange-rate and balance-of-payments theory. Older texts, while good on traditional theories, inevitably devote little space to much of the modern literature.

More generally, it was hard to find a text giving a reasonably extensive introduction to some of the most important recent topics such as international macroeconomic policy coordination, the European Monetary System, European monetary union and the international debt crisis. My discussions with others confirmed my feeling that there was an urgent need for an up-to-date text that gives a balanced introduction to the theoretical, empirical and applied topics in the field. In writing this book, I have attempted to provide a distinctive text that gives an accessible and up-to-date introduction to the field of international finance.

■ *Distinguishing features of this text*

The main distinguishing features of this text can be summarised as:

- The text presents both traditional and modern theories in the field. To the extent possible, the presentation follows a chronological order that gives students an impression of the development of the literature.

- The text is not purely theoretical and presents students with a reasonable overview of the empirical evidence relating to the theories discussed.
- The technical expertise required of students is kept to a fairly low level. However, rather than exclude some important topics that require a more technical exposition a basic knowledge of mathematics and statistics is assumed for some topics.
- Extensive use is made of diagrams, tables, graphs, and boxes to illustrate the arguments in the text.
- A number of important recent developments and subjects are given extensive rather than cursory treatment. Most notably, there are entire chapters devoted to international policy coordination, European monetary union and the European Monetary System, and the international debt crisis. Among the issues discussed are, *inter alia*, exchange-rate 'overshooting', the problem of time consistency and game theory.
- At the end of each chapter there is a selective list of further reading and references. It was felt that this would be considerably more useful to students and lecturers than a general bibliography at the end of the book. A list of very useful texts in the field is provided at the end of the book.

■ *Appropriate courses for the text*

The coverage and level of technical expertise expected of students makes the text suitable for use as a main text on a variety of degree courses. These include undergraduate and one-year postgraduate courses in international economics, international monetary economics and international finance. Much of the material covered makes the book particularly useful for the international finance component of MBA courses. Some of the chapters in the book are relevant to courses in intermediate macroeconomics and international relations.

■ *Presentation and contents*

In writing the text, it soon became apparent that there are a bewilderingly wide range of models that could be presented. At the same time it is extremely difficult to present the various theories as a subset of some general model, since that model would quickly become intractable. In the end, it was decided to concentrate on the models that have dominated the literature, even though the assumptions underlying the models in different chapters can differ greatly. It is hoped that the clear statement of the different assumptions underlying the theories at the beginning of each chapter and the contrasts drawn between the various models will facilitate student under-standing.

The book is divided into three parts each of five chapters. The opening part of the book is concerned with balance-of-payments theory and policy. The second part of the book is devoted to theories of exchange-rate determination and policy including an examination of the empirical exchange-rate literature. The final part of the book traces the evolution and development of the post-war international monetary system; the major features of the current system are analysed.

Broadly speaking an attempt has been made to present each part of the book in a chronological order that will give students a perspective on the development of the literature. A brief overview of the chapters is contained below.

Part I   Balance-of-payments theory and policy

The opening chapter provides an introduction to the foreign exchange market and provides an essential background to the study of the remaining chapters in the book. Chapter 2 provides an introduction to balance-of-payments statistics and their interpretation. Chapter 3 presents some natio-nal income and balance-of-payments identities and then examines the traditional elasticity and absorption approaches to devaluation that were developed in the 1930s to 1950s. Chapter 4 analyses macroeconomic policy in an open economy using the Keynesian IS–LM–BP model which domi-nated policy discussion in the 1960s. This framework is then used to examine the effectiveness of fiscal, monetary and exchange-rate policies in achieving internal and external balance. This is then followed in Chapter 5 by an examination of the distinctive monetary approach to the balance of payments which emerged in the late 1960s and early 1970s.

At the outset, it is worth noting that there are considerable differences between the Keynesian model of Chapter 4 and the monetary model of Chapter 5. The Keynesian model is based upon fixed domestic prices and assumes a horizontal aggregate supply schedule, so that variations in aggregate demand translate into changes in output and not prices. This contrasts with the monetary model, which assumes a vertical aggregate supply schedule at the full employment level of output so that changes in aggregate demand translate into changes in prices rather than output. The Keynesian model also takes a flow view of capital movements and assumes imperfect goods substitutability, whereas the monetary model takes a stock view of capital movements and assumes perfect goods substitutability.

Part II Exchange-rate theory, evidence and policy

Chapter 6 commences with the purchasing power parity (PPP) literature, which is one of the earliest theories of exchange-rate determination. PPP has not proved to be a reliable indicator of floating exchange behaviour and some of the explanations that have been put forward to explain its failure are discussed. In Chapter 7 there is an exposition of the modern monetary theories of exchange-rate determination that were developed in the 1970s; these emphasise the importance of monetary factors in explaining exchange-rate behaviour. We deal first with the 'flexible price' monetary model, followed by the 'sticky price' Dornbusch model and finally with the Frankel 'real interest rate differential model'. The portfolio balance exchange-rate model which was developed at the same time as the monetary models is discussed in Chapter 8. The portfolio balance model emphasises that risk factors and current account imbalances may have an important role to play in exchange rate determination.

In Chapter 9, the empirical literature on floating exchange rates which only really got under way at the end of the 1970s and mushroomed in the 1980s is discussed. Two major empirical issues are examined: the first is whether or not the foreign exchange market can be regarded as efficient; the second concerns whether modern exchange rate theories satisfactorily model observed exchange-rate behaviour. Chapter 10 concentrates on exchange-rate policy; it begins with a review of the traditional debate over the relative merits of fixed and floating exchange rates. This is then followed by an assessment using the more modern approach to analysing exchange-rate policy; this compares the stabilising properties of the two regimes within the context of a formal macroeconomic model.

Part III The post-war international monetary system

Chapter 11 provides an overview of the development of the post-Second World War international monetary system. It commences with the operation and eventual breakdown of the Bretton Woods system and then surveys the major developments since the adoption of generalised floating. Chapter 12 examines the functioning of and reasons behind the explosive growth of the eurocurrency markets and whether this growth was partly responsible for the upsurge in inflation during the 1970s. Chapter 13 provides an overview of the recent literature on international macroeconomic policy coordination, a topic on which there has been a great deal of research since 1985. Chapter 14 provides an analysis of a topic which will undoubtedly be at the centre of policy discussion in European countries throughout the 1990s, namely European monetary union. The European Monetary System is explained and appraised and the ways in which it may develop are discussed. The final chapter is devoted to an analysis of many of the issues raised by the international debt crisis, a problem that will no doubt continue throughout the 1990s.

■ *Use of the book*

The scope of the book is sufficiently wide that there is considerable flexibility for lecturers to design courses that reflect their own interests. Chapters 1–5 probably provide the backbone to most courses in this field. Chapter 6 on purchasing power parity is a core chapter on exchange-rate theory and floating exchange-rate experience. Thereafter, the degree to which modern exchange-rate theory is covered will be dependent on the length and priority of the course. Chapter 7 covers the modern monetary models. There is no doubt that the Dornbusch model of exchange-rate overshooting represents such a significant contribution to our understanding of exchange-rate behaviour that getting over its message is highly desirable. The problem is that a formal presentation is too advanced for some courses in international finance. For this reason, I have split up the presentation of the Dornbusch model into two parts: one is a simple explanation of the model without recourse to the use of equations. This is followed by a more formal presentation for more advanced classes. I hope that this approach enables most students to gain at least an intuitive grasp of the ideas underlying modern exchange-rate theory and at the same time satisfies the demands of more rigorous courses.

Chapter 8 on the portfolio balance model can easily be omitted if the course does not go into great detail on exchange-rate theory. With regard to the empirical evidence on exchange rates, it is quite possible to omit the coverage of exchange market efficiency tests and just recommend sections 9.6 to 9.8 for an overview of how well modern exchange-rate theories perform empirically. In Chapter 10 it is possible to cover the traditional debate on fixed and floating exchange-rate regimes without having to cover the more modern approach, although I have found the modern approach that compares the two regimes within an aggregate supply and demand framework to be very popular with students. Part III of the book offers a range of topics that can be chosen to reflect the emphasis of the particular course.

PART I
Balance-of-Payments Theory and Policy

■ *Chapter 1* ■

The Foreign Exchange Market

■ *1.1* Introduction

When studying open economies that trade with one another, there is a major difference in the transactions between domestic and foreign residents as compared with those between residents of the same country, namely, that differing national currencies are usually involved. A US importer will generally have to pay a Japanese exporter in yen, a German exporter in deutschmarks and a British exporter in pounds. For this reason, the US importer will have to buy these currencies with dollars in what is known as the foreign exchange market. The foreign exchange market is not a single physical place, rather it is defined as a market where the various national currencies are bought and sold. Exactly what factors determine how much domestic currency has to be given to obtain a unit of foreign currency, the behaviour of exchange rates and the impact of exchange rate changes is one of the major fields of study in international economics and are the subject matter of later chapters of this book.

In this chapter, we look at some preliminary issues. We examine the various participants in the foreign exchange market and the basic forces that operate in the market. We then examine the basic determinants of exchange-rate behaviour. The chapter proceeds to examine various exchange-rate definitions and their economic significance. We then look at the basic operational differences between fixed and floating exchange-rate regimes. The chapter finishes by examining the relationship between the spot and forward exchange rate.

■ *1.2* Exchange-rate definitions

The exchange rate is simply the price of one currency in terms of another. Since the exchange rate between two currencies is the price of one currency in terms of another there are two methods of expressing it:

1.   Domestic currency units per unit of foreign currency – for example, taking the pound sterling as the domestic currency, on 6 February 1991 there was approximately £0.50 required to purchase one US dollar.
2.   Foreign currency units per unit of the domestic currency – again taking the pound sterling as the domestic currency, on 6 February 1991, approximately $2 were required to obtain one pound.

The reader will note that second method is merely the reciprocal of the former. While it is not important which method of expressing the exchange rate is employed, it is necessary to be careful when talking about a rise or fall in the exchange rate because the meaning will be very different depending upon which definition is used. A rise in the pounds per dollar exchange rate from say £0.50/$1 to £0.60/$1 means that more pounds have to be given to obtain a dollar, this means that the pound has depreciated in value or equivalently the dollar has appreciated in value. If the second definition is employed, a rise in the exchange rate from $2/£1 to $2.10/£1 would mean that more dollars are obtained per pound, so that the pound has appreciated or equivalently the dollar has depreciated.

□ *Important note*

For the purposes of this chapter we shall define the exchange rate as foreign currency units per unit of domestic currency. This is the definition which is most commonly employed in the UK where the exchange rate is quoted as foreign currency (e.g. dollars, deutschmark and yen) per pound and is the definition most frequently employed when compiling real and nominal exchange rate indices (see **Section 1.6**) for all currencies. However, in other chapters of the book we shall normally be using the first definition because this is the definition most often employed in the theoretical economic literature. It is important that when reading newspapers, articles or other textbooks that readers familiarise themselves with the particular exchange rate definition being employed.

1.3 Characteristics and participants of the foreign exchange market

The foreign exchange market is a worldwide market and is made up primarily of commercial banks, foreign exchange brokers and other authorised agents trading in most of the currencies of the world. These groups are

Box 1.1   *Exchange rate quotations and the bid–ask spread*
The pound spot exchange rate against a variety of currencies at close of business on 8 October 1990.

	Foreign currency units per pound	Pounds per unit of foreign currency
	Bid–Ask	Bid–Ask
United States	1.9690–1.9825	0.5079–0.5044
Canada	2.2660–2.2875	0.4413–0.4372
Netherlands	3.39–3.445	0.2950–0.2903
Belgium	61.80–62.90	0.0162–0.0159
Denmark	11.4025–11.6525	0.0877–0.0858
Ireland	1.1260–1.1395	0.8881–0.8775
Germany	3.01–3.0525	0.3322–0.3276
Portugal	266.55–269.75	0.0038–0.0037
Spain	189.40–192.20	0.0053–0.0052
Italy	2245.5–2291.25	0.0004–0.0004
Norway	11.6225–11.7750	0.0860–0.0849
France	10.09–10.225	0.0991–0.0978
Sweden	11.07–11.22	0.0903–0.0891
Japan	257–259.25	0.0039–0.0039
Austria	21.20–21.50	0.0472–0.0465
Switzerland	2.505–2.545	0.3992–0.3929

Source: Financial Times, 9 October 1990.

The bid rate is the rate at which a bank will sell the currency of the country on the left hand column while the ask rate is the rate at which the bank will purchase the currency of the country on the left in exchange for pounds. The difference is known as the bid–ask spread and represents the gross profit margin of the bank. In the case of the dollar this spread was equal to $(1.982\,5–1.969\,0)/1.969 = 0.006\,86$ or approximately 0.7 per cent. The spread will vary from bank to bank, and from currency to currency and according to market conditions. Thinly traded currencies tend to have the largest spread and the spread usually increases if the risks of trading in a particular currency are perceived to have risen.

The quotation for the pound is usually made as foreign currency units per pound. However, the exchange rate of the pound can equally be expressed as pounds per unit of foreign currency. The equivalent bid–ask exchange rates for the pound using this method are shown in the far right hand column.

Table 1.1   *Currency composition of foreign exchange business. International comparisons (percentages of overall turnover)*

	London	Tokyo	New York
Dollar/Pound	27	4	15
Dollar/Deutschmark	22	10	33
Dollar/Yen	15	72	25
Dollar/Swiss Franc	10	4	12
Other	26	10	15

Note: The figures include cross-currency business.
Source: Bank of England Quarterly Bulletin, vol. 29 (Nov 1989), p. 533.

kept in close and continuous contact with one another and with developments in the market via telephone, computer terminals, telex and fax. Among the most important foreign exchange centres are London, New York, Tokyo, Zurich and Frankfurt. The net volume of foreign exchange dealing in these centres was in April 1989 estimated to be in excess of $450 billion per day, the most active centres being London with a daily turnover averaging $187 billion, followed by New York with $129 billion, Tokyo with $115 billion and Zurich $57 billion. **Table 1.1** shows the currency composition of business for the three major foreign exchange centres.

Easily the most heavily traded currency is the US dollar which is known as a vehicle currency – that is, a currency that is widely used to denominate international transactions. Oil and many other important primary products such as tin, coffee and gold all tend to be priced in dollars. Indeed, because the dollar is so heavily traded it is usually cheaper for a French foreign exchange dealer wanting Dutch guilders to firstly purchase US dollars and then sell the dollars to purchase guilders rather than directly purchase the guilders with French francs.

The main participants in the foreign exchange market can be categorised as follows:

Retail clients – these are made up of businesses, international investors, multinational corporations and the like who need foreign exchange for the purposes of operating their businesses. Normally, they do not directly purchase or sell foreign currencies themselves, rather they operate by placing buy/sell orders with the commercial banks.

Commercial banks – the commercial banks carry out buy/sell orders from their retail clients and buy/sell currencies on their own account so as to alter the structure of their assets and liabilities in different currencies. The banks deal either directly with other banks or more usually through foreign exchange brokers.

Figure 1.1   *The organisation of the foreign exchange market*

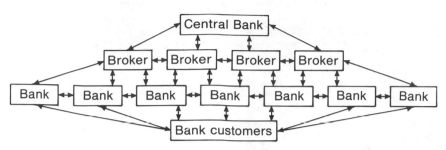

Note:

The boxes represent foreign exchange market participants and the lines are the business connections between them. Bank customers place buy/sell orders with their respective banks who balance the buy/sell orders that they receive and if they have insufficient or surplus funds they then place buy/sell orders with other banks or more usually with their brokers. The central bank keeps a daily watch on exchange-rate developments and intervenes to buy or sell its currency from time to time by placing buy/sell orders with its brokers.

Foreign exchange brokers – normally banks do not trade directly with one another, rather they offer to buy and sell currencies via foreign exchange brokers. Operating through such brokers is advantageous because they collect buy and sell quotations for most currencies from many banks, so that by going through a broker the most favourable quotation is obtained quickly and at very low cost. Each financial centre normally has just a handful of authorised brokers through which commercial banks conduct their exchanges.

Central banks – normally the monetary authorities of a country are not indifferent to changes in the external value of their currency and even though exchange rates of the major industrialised nations have been left to fluctuate freely since 1973 central banks frequently intervene to buy and sell their currencies in a bid to influence the rate at which their currency is traded. Under a fixed exchange rate system the authorities are obliged to purchase their currencies when there is excess supply and sell the currency when there is excess demand.

■ *1.4* Arbitrage in the foreign exchange market

One of the most important implications deriving from the close communication of buyers and sellers in the foreign exchange market is that there is almost instantaneous arbitrage across currencies and financial centres. Arbitrage is the exploitation of price differentials for riskless guaranteed

Table 1.2   *Foreign exchange cross rates on close of business, 8 October 1990*

	£	$	DM	Yen	F Fr	S Fr	H Fl	Lira	C $	B Fr
UK pound (£)	1	1.974	3.030	258.0	10.14	2.535	3.420	2273	2.275	62.35
US dollar ($)	0.507	1	1.535	130.7	5.137	1.284	1.733	1151	1.152	31.59
German mark (DM)	0.330	0.651	1	85.15	3.347	0.837	1.129	750.2	0.751	20.58
Japanese yen*	3.876	7.651	11.74	1000	39.30	9.826	13.26	8810	8.818	241.7
French franc (F Fr)*	0.986	1.947	2.988	254.4	10	2.500	3.373	2242	2.244	61.49
Swiss franc (S Fr)	0.394	0.779	1.195	101.8	4.000	1	1.349	896.6	0.897	24.60
Dutch guilder (H Fl)	0.292	0.577	0.886	75.44	2.965	0.741	1	664.6	0.665	18.23
Italian lira (L It)*	0.440	0.868	1.333	113.5	4.461	1.115	1.505	1000	1.001	27.43
Canadian dollar (C $)	0.440	0.868	1.332	113.4	4.457	1.114	1.503	999.1	1	27.41
Belgian franc (B Fr)*	1.604	3.166	4.860	413.8	16.26	4.066	5.485	3646	3.649	100

Note:
The exchange rate is the units of the currency in the top row per unit of the currency listed in the left-hand column, where the following applies to the units on the left-hand column.
* Yen 1000; French francs 10; lira 1000; Belgian francs 100.
Source: Financial Times, 9 October 1990.

profits. To illustrate what is meant by these two types of arbitrage we shall assume that transaction costs are negligible and that there is only a single exchange rate quotation ignoring the bid–ask spread (see Box 1.1).

Financial centre arbitrage – this type of arbitrage ensures that the dollar pound exchange rate quoted in New York will be the same as that quoted in London and other financial centres. This is because if the exchange rate is $2/£1 in New York but only $1.98/£1 in London, it would be profitable for banks to buy pounds in London and simultaneously sell them in New York and make a guaranteed 2 cents for every pound bought and sold. The act of buying pounds in London will lead to a depreciation of the dollar in London while selling pounds in New York will lead to an appreciation of dollars in New York. Such a process continues until the rate quoted in the two centres coincides at say $1.99/£1.

Cross-currency arbitrage – to illustrate what is meant by currency arbitrage let us suppose that the exchange rate of the dollar is $2/£1 and the exchange rate of the dollar against the deutschmark is $0.8/1DM. Currency arbitrage implies that the exchange rate of the deutschmark against the pound will be 2.5 DM/£1. If this were not the case, say there was 3 DM/£1, then a UK dealer wanting dollars would do better to firstly obtain 3 DM which will then buy $2.40, making nonsense of a $2/£1 quotation. The increased demand for deutschmarks would quickly appreciate its rate against the pound to the 2.5 DM/£1 level. **Table 1.2** shows a set of cross rates for the major currencies.

■ *1.5* The spot and forward exchange rates

Foreign exchange dealers not only deal with a wide variety of currencies but they also have a set of dealing rates for each currency which are known as the spot and forward rates.

□ *The spot exchange rate*

The spot exchange rate is the quotation between two currencies for immediate delivery. In other words, the spot exchange rate is the current exchange rate of two currencies *vis-à-vis* each other. In practice, there is normally a two day lag between a spot purchase or sale and the actual exchange of currencies to allow for verification, paperwork and clearing of payments.

☐ *The forward exchange rate*

In addition to the spot exchange rate it is possible for economic agents to agree today to exchange currencies at some specified time in the future, most commonly for 1 month (30 days), 3 months (90 days), 6 months (180 days), 9 months (270 days) and 1 year (360 days). The rate of exchange at which such a purchase or sale can be made is known as the forward exchange rate. Exactly why economic agents may engage in forward exchange transactions and how the forward exchange rate quotation is determined is a subject we shall look at later in this chapter.

1.6 Nominal, real and effective exchange rates

Policy makers and economists are very much concerned about analysing the implications of exchange-rate changes for the economy and the balance of payments. The exchange rate itself does not convey much information. To analyse the effects and implications of exchange rate changes economists compile indices of the nominal, real and effective exchange rates. Since most national and international authorities quote nominal, real and effective exchange rates as foreign currency per unit of domestic currency, we shall compile some hypothetical nominal, real and effective exchange rates using this definition. This means that a rise of the nominal, real or effective exchange-rate index represents an appreciation of the currency.

☐ *Nominal exchange rate*

The exchange rate that prevails at a given date is known as the nominal exchange rate, it is the amount of US dollars that will be obtained for one pound in the foreign exchange market. Similarly, if the deutschmark–pound quotation is 3 DM/£1, this is again a nominal exchange rate quotation. The nominal exchange rate is merely the price of one currency in terms of another with no reference made to what this means in terms of purchasing power of goods/services. The nominal exchange rate is usually presented in index form, if the base period for the index is $2/£1 and one period later the nominal exchange rate is $2.20/£1 the nominal index of the pound will change from the base period of 100 to 110, indicating that the pound has appreciated 10 per cent against the dollar. A depreciation or appreciation of the nominal exchange rate does not necessarily imply that the country has

Table 1.3   *Construction of nominal and real exchange-rate indices*

Period	Nominal exchange rate	Nominal exchange index	UK price index	US price index	Real exchange index
1	$2.00	100	100	100	100
2	$2.00	100	120	100	120
3	$2.40	120	120	120	120
4	$1.80	90	130	117	100
5	$1.60	80	150	160	75

Note:
The real exchange rate index is constructed by multiplying the nominal exchange rate index by the UK price index divided by the US price index.

become more or less competitive on international markets, for such a measure we have to look at the real exchange rate.

☐ *Real exchange rate*

The real exchange rate is the nominal exchange rate adjusted for relative prices between the countries under consideration. The real exchange rate is normally expressed in index form algebraically as:

$$S_r = \frac{SP}{P^*}$$

where S_r is the index of the real exchange rate, S is the nominal exchange rate (foreign currency units per unit of domestic currency) in index form, P the index of the domestic price level and P^* is the index of the foreign price level.

Table 1.3 depicts the compilation of hypothetical nominal and real exchange-rate indices for the pound. The table illustrates how the nominal and real exchange rate indices are compiled and what exactly changes in the real exchange rate measure. In the first period the real exchange rate index is set equal to 100. A basket of UK goods priced at £100 will cost a US resident $200, while a basket of US goods priced at $200 would cost a UK resident £100. Between period 1 and period 2 there is no change in the nominal exchange rate which remains at $2/£1; however, the UK price index rises while the US index remains the same. This means that there has been a real appreciation of the pound, UK goods now become relatively more expensive for US residents as they now have to use $240 dollars to purchase the original bundle of UK goods which now cost £120, the bundle of US goods still costs a British citizen £100. This decreased competitiveness is picked up by the real exchange rate appreciation from 100 to 120. Clearly, since the nominal exchange rate has remained at 100 it has failed to pick up the change in competitiveness.

Between periods 2 and 3 UK prices remain unchanged while US prices increase; however, the pound appreciates sufficiently that the UK gains no competitive advantage. Between periods 3 and 4 the UK prices rise and US prices fall but the competitive disadvantage to the UK is offset by a substantial depreciation of the pound, so that there is a real depreciation of the pound meaning an improvement UK competitiveness. Finally, between periods 4 and 5 UK prices rise much less than US prices and this is coupled with a nominal depreciation of the pound, this means that there is a substantial real depreciation of the pound. From this example it is clear that the real exchange rate monitors changes in a country's competitiveness. Real exchange-rate indices unlike nominal exchange-rate indices are not publishable on a daily basis because the price indices used are normally only published monthly.

Figures 1.2(a)–(c) show the evolution of the dollar–pound, deutschmark–dollar and yen–dollar nominal and real exchange-rate indices between 1973–91 compiled using quarterly data and wholesale price indices. The figures show that there have been very substantial movements in both nominal and real exchange rates since the commencement of generalised floating in 1973.

☐ *Effective exchange rate*

Since most countries of the world do not conduct all their trade with a single foreign country, policy makers are not so much concerned with what is happening to their exchange rate against a single foreign currency but rather what is happening to the exchange rate against a basket of foreign currencies with whom the country trades. The effective exchange rate is a measure of whether or not the currency is appreciating or depreciating against a weighted basket of foreign currencies. In order to illustrate how an effective exchange rate is compiled consider the hypothetical case of the UK conducting 30 per cent of its foreign trade with the US and 70 per cent of its trade with Germany. This means that a weight of 0.3 will be attached to the bilateral exchange rate index with the dollar and 0.7 with the deutschmark.

Table 1.4 shows the construction of a hypothetical effective sterling exchange rate based upon movements in the bilateral nominal exchange rate indices against the dollar and deutschmark. The US dollar has a 30 per cent weight and the German deutschmark a 70 per cent weight. Between periods 1 and 2 the pound appreciates 10 per cent against the dollar but depreciates 10 per cent against the deutschmark. Since the deutschmark has a greater weight than the dollar the effective exchange-rate index indicates an overall depreciation of 4 per cent. Period 3 leads to substantial appreciation against

Figure 1.2 (a) *The evolution of the dollar–pound nominal (——) and real (+++) exchange rate, 1973–91*

the US dollar and no change against the deutschmark, the resulting appreciation of the effective exchange rate is consequently less marked than the appreciation against the dollar. In period 4, the pound depreciates against both the dollar and deutschmark and consequently there is a depreciation of the effective exchange rate. Finally, in period 5 the pound depreciates against the US dollar and appreciates to a lesser extent against the deutschmark; however, the effective exchange rate depreciates only marginally because more weight is attached to the appreciation against the deutschmark than to the depreciation against the dollar.

While the nominal effective exchange rate is easy to compile on a daily basis and normally provides a reasonable measure of changes in a country's competitive position for periods of several months it does not take account of the effect of price movements. In order to get a better idea of changes in a country's competitive position over time we would need to compile real effective exchange rate indices. For this, we would first of all compile the real exchange rate against each of the trading partners' currencies in index form and then use the same procedure as for compiling the nominal effective exchange rates. **Table 1.5** shows the nominal effective exchange-rate indices for the major industrialised countries since 1975 which are derived from the International Monetary Fund's Multilateral Exchange Rate Model (MERM). **Table 1.6** shows the real effective exchange-rate indices for the

Figure 1.2 (b)   *The evolution of the deutschmark–dollar nominal (——) and real (+++) exchange rate, 1973–91*

major industrialised countries using wholesale price indices for calculation purposes.

1.7 A simple model of the determination of the spot exchange rate

Since the adoption of floating exchange rates in 1973 there has developed an exciting new set of theories attempting to explain exchange-rate behaviour, generally known as the modern asset market approach to exchange-rate determination. We shall be looking in some detail at these theories in Chapters 7–9. For the time being, we shall look at a simple model of exchange-rate determination which was widely used prior to the development of these new theories. Despite its shortcomings the model serves as a useful introduction to exchange-rate determination and is a prerequisite for the understanding of Chapters 1 to 6 of the book. The basic tenet of the model is that the exchange rate (the price) of a currency can be analysed like any other price by a resort to the tools of supply and demand. The exchange rate of the pound will be determined by the intersection of the supply and demand for pounds on the foreign exchange market.

Figure 1.2 (c)   *The evolution of the yen–dollar nominal (———) and real (+++) exchange rate, 1973–91*

Table 1.4   *Construction of a nominal effective exchange-rate index*

Period	Nominal exchange rate index of $/£	Nominal exchange rate index of DM/£	Effective exchange rate index of £
1	100	100	100
2	110	90	96
3	130	90	102
4	120	80	92
5	105	85	91

Note:
The effective exchange-rate index is constructed by multiplying the $/£ index by 0.3 and the DM/£ index by 0.7.

☐ *The demand for foreign exchange*

The demand for pounds in the foreign exchange market is a derived demand, that is, the pounds are not demanded because they have an intrinsic value in themselves, rather because of what they can buy. **Table 1.7** depicts the

Table 1.5   *Nominal effective exchange-rate indices, 1975–90*

	United States	Canada	Japan	United Kingdom	Germany	Italy	France
1975	100.0	100.0	100.0	100.0	100.0	100.0	100.0
1976	105.1	106.0	104.1	85.7	104.9	82.3	95.6
1977	104.6	98.0	115.1	81.2	113.0	75.5	91.3
1978	95.5	87.7	141.6	81.5	120.2	71.1	91.3
1979	93.5	84.3	131.4	87.3	127.5	69.4	93.3
1980	93.7	84.4	126.3	96.1	128.8	67.2	94.3
1981	105.6	86.9	142.9	95.0	119.3	58.3	84.3
1982	117.9	88.6	134.7	90.5	124.3	53.9	76.6
1983	124.7	91.4	148.3	83.3	127.2	51.2	70.0
1984	134.7	89.7	156.8	78.4	123.7	47.8	65.8
1985	130.0	93.3	160.7	78.1	123.6	45.0	66.5
1986	117.4	76.4	203.4	72.6	136.9	46.8	70.5
1987	117.0	67.4	219.9	72.4	147.3	47.6	72.2
1988	123.8	63.5	243.9	76.3	146.3	45.9	70.7
1989	131.3	66.3	233.3	73.6	143.7	45.8	69.0
1990	122.8	65.1	209.0	73.9	153.8	48.0	74.4

Notes:
A rise represents a nominal effective exchange-rate appreciation of the country's currency.
The above are the MERM nominal effective exchange rates derived from the International
Monetary Fund Multilateral Exchange Rate Model with the weighting system based on
1977 trade data.
Source: IMF, *International Financial Statistics.*

derivation of a hypothetical demand for pounds schedule with respect to
changes in the exchange rate. As the pound appreciates against the dollar the
price of the UK export to US importers increases, this leads to a lower
quantity of exports and with it a reduced demand for pounds. Hence, the
demand curve for pounds which is depicted in **Figure 1.3,** slopes down from
left to right.

In this simple model the price-elasticity of demand for pounds depends
upon the price elasticity of demand for UK exports. If the US demand for UK
exports is inelastic this means that an appreciation of the pound will lead to
a relatively small decrease in the demand for UK exports and hence a
relatively small decrease in the demand for pounds. Hence, the demand for
foreign exchange is more inelastic the more inelastic is the foreign import
demand. The more inelastic the demand for pounds the steeper the DD
schedule.

One of the key factors underlying the demand for pounds is the demand
for UK goods, any factor which results in an increase in the demand for UK

Table 1.6 *Real effective exchange-rate indices, 1975–90*

	United States	Canada	Japan	United Kingdom	Germany	Italy	France
1975	100.0	100.0	100.0	100.0	100.0	100.0	100.0
1976	102.7	104.8	103.2	94.3	101.6	93.5	96.5
1977	100.2	97.7	107.2	100.9	103.8	95.4	91.0
1978	92.5	90.7	120.4	105.1	104.5	93.7	93.4
1979	92.8	89.5	107.0	113.8	105.2	94.4	96.6
1980	93.7	89.1	104.2	127.4	100.4	96.4	101.0
1981	106.7	91.2	109.7	129.2	93.7	93.2	96.6
1982	114.8	94.0	99.6	124.8	97.3	93.1	92.8
1983	118.1	97.6	105.2	117.7	97.9	95.1	90.6
1984	125.8	96.1	107.7	114.3	94.3	95.6	89.4
1985	127.1	93.2	106.1	116.7	93.4	93.8	92.7
1986	101.4	88.1	124.0	113.9	100.2	95.6	97.7
1987	91.1	89.5	126.4	115.8	102.5	97.8	99.6
1988	87.7	94.9	134.3	125.0	100.9	96.8	96.4
1989	93.4	98.6	127.1	122.5	98.6	100.2	95.2
1990	88.6	95.9	111.4	125.0	102.3	104.4	100.0

Notes:
A rise represents a real effective exchange rate appreciation of the country's currency. The above indices are based on wholesale prices. The weights used for compiling the indices are based on disaggregated trade data for manufactured goods and primary products covering the three-year period 1980–82.
Source: IMF, *International Financial Statistics.*

Table 1.7 *The derivation of the demand for pounds*

Price of UK export good in £s	Exchange rate ($/£)	Price of UK export good in $s	Quantity of UK exports	Demand for pounds
10	$1.50	15	1 600	16 000
10	$1.60	16	1 550	15 500
10	$1.70	17	1 500	15 000
10	$1.80	18	1 450	14 500
10	$1.90	19	1 400	14 000
10	$2.00	20	1 350	13 500
10	$2.10	21	1 300	13 000
10	$2.20	22	1 250	12 500

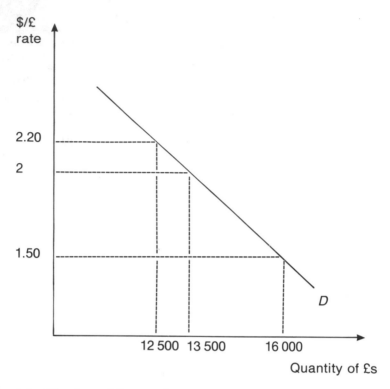

Figure 1.3   *The demand for pounds*

exports will result in an increased demand for pounds and a shift to the right of the demand curve for pounds. Among the factors that result in a rightward shift of the demand schedule for pounds are a rise in US income, a change in US tastes in favour of UK goods and a rise in the price of US goods. All these factors result in an increased demand for UK exports and hence pounds.

☐ *The supply of foreign exchange*

The supply of pounds is in essence the UK demand for dollars, **Table 1.8** sets out the derivation of a hypothetical supply of pounds schedule. As the pound appreciates the cost of US exports becomes cheaper for UK residents. As such, they demand more US exports and this results in an increased demand for dollars which are purchased by increasing the amount of pounds supplied in the foreign exchange market. In the example constructed this yields an upward sloping supply of pounds. It is possible that if the demand

Table 1.8   *The supply of pounds*

Price of US export goods in $s	Exchange rate ($/£)	Price of US export goods in £s	Quantity of US exports	Demand for dollars	Supply of pounds
20	$1.50	13.33	700	14 000	9 333
20	$1.60	12.50	800	16 000	10 000
20	$1.70	11.76	950	19 000	11 176
20	$1.80	11.11	1 100	22 000	12 222
20	$1.90	10.53	1 225	24 500	12 895
20	$2.00	10.00	1 350	27 000	13 500
20	$2.10	9.53	1 450	29 000	13 810
20	$2.20	9.09	1 550	31 000	14 091

for US goods is very inelastic the supply of pounds schedule may be downward sloping. For example, when the exchange rate moves from $2 to $2.10 if the quantity demanded of US exports rose from 1350 to only 1400 the demand for dollars would be $28 000 corresponding to a decrease in the supply for pounds from £13 500 to £13 333. We note but exclude this possibility in our exposition. **Figure 1.4** depicts the supply of pounds schedule derived from **Table 1.8.**

The elasticity of supply of pounds schedule depends upon the UK demand for US exports; the more inelastic UK demand for American exports the more inelastic will be the supply of pounds and the steeper the SS schedule over the relevant range. The position of the supply of pounds schedule will shift to the right if there is an increase in UK income, a change in British tastes in favour of US goods or a rise in UK prices. All these factors imply an increased demand for US goods and dollars which is reflected in an increased supply of pounds.

Since the exchange market is merely a market which brings together those people that wish to buy a currency (which represents the demand) with those that wish to sell the currency (which represents the supply) then the spot exchange rate can most easily be thought of as being determined by the interaction of the supply and demand for the currency. **Figure 1.5** depicts the determination of the dollar–pound exchange rate in the context of such a supply and demand framework.

Figure 1.5 depicts the supply and demand for pounds in the foreign exchange market. The equilibrium exchange rate is determined by the intersection of the supply and demand curves to yield a dollar–pound exchange of $2/£1. When the exchange rate is left to float freely it is determined by the interaction of the supply and demand curves.

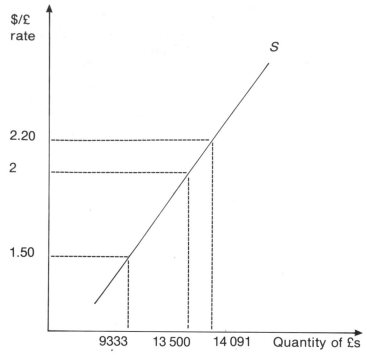

Figure 1.4   *The supply of pounds*

■ *1.8* Alternative exchange-rate regimes

At the Bretton Woods conference of 1948 the major nations of the Western world agreed to a pegged exchange-rate system, each country fixing its exchange rate against the US dollar with a small margin of fluctuation around the par value. In 1973 the Bretton Woods system broke down and the major currencies were left to be determined by market forces in a floating exchange rate world. We investigate these different historical experiences in some detail in Chapter 11 and examine the economics of the two regimes in Chapter 10. For the time being, it is important that the basic differences and operation of the two regimes be highlighted using the supply and demand framework.

□ *Floating exchange-rate regime*

Under a floating exchange-rate regime the authorities do not intervene to buy or sell their currency in the foreign exchange market. Rather, they allow the

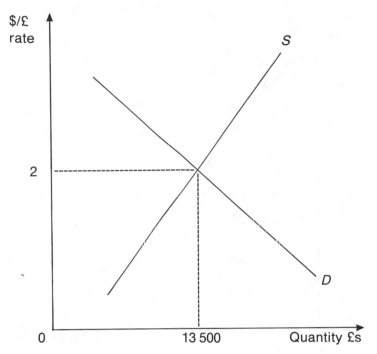

Figure 1.5 *Determination of the dollar–pound exchange rate*

value of their currency to change due to fluctuations in the supply and demand of the currency. This is illustrated in **Figure 1.6.**

In **Figure 1.6(a)** the exchange rate is initially determined by the interaction of the demand (D1) and supply (S1) of pounds at the exchange rate of $2/£1. There is an increase in the demand for UK exports which shifts the demand curve from D1 to D2. This increase in the demand for pounds leads to an appreciation of the pound from $2/£1 to $2.10/£1. **Figure 1.6(b)** examines the impact of an increase in the supply of pounds due to an increased demand for US exports and therefore dollars. The increased supply of pounds shifts the S1 schedule to the right to S2 resulting in a depreciation of the pound to $1.90/£1. The essence of a floating exchange rate is that the exchange rate adjusts in response to changes in the supply and demand for a currency.

☐ *Fixed exchange-rate regime*

In **Figure 1.7(a)** the exchange rate is assumed to be fixed by the authorities at the point where the demand schedule (D1) intersects the supply schedule (S1) at $2/£1. If there is an increase in the demand for pounds which shifts

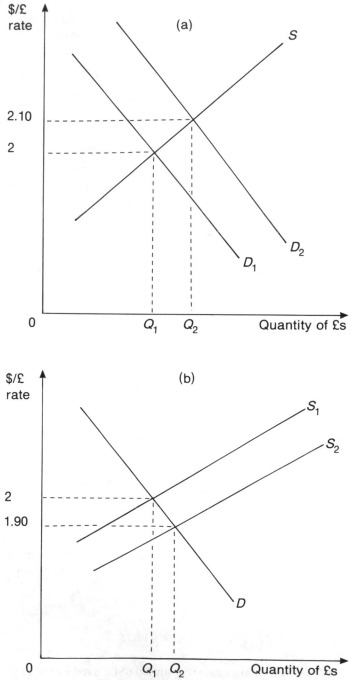

Figure 1.6 *Floating exchange-rate regime. (a) Increase in demand.*
(b) Increase in supply

the demand schedule from D1 to D2 there is a resulting pressure for the pound to be revalued. To avert an appreciation it is necessary for the Bank of England to sell Q1 Q2 of pounds to purchase dollars in the foreign exchange market; these purchases shift the supply of pounds from S1 to S2. Such intervention eliminates the excess demand for pounds so that the exchange rate remains fixed at \$2/£1. The intervention increases the Bank of England's reserves of US dollars while increasing the amount of pounds in circulation.

Figure 1.7(b) depicts an initial situation where the exchange rate is pegged by the authorities at the point where the demand schedule (D1) intersects the supply schedule (S1) at \$2/£1. An increase in the supply of pounds (increased demand for US dollars) shifts the supply schedule from S1 to S2. The result is that there is an excess supply of pounds at the prevailing exchange rate. This means that there will be pressure for the pound to be devalued. To avoid this, the Bank of England has to intervene in the foreign exchange market to purchase Q3 Q4 pounds to peg the exchange rate. This intervention is represented by a rightward shift of the demand schedule from D1 to D2. Such intervention removes the excess supply of pounds so that the exchange rate remains pegged at \$2/£1. The intervention leads to a fall in the Bank of England's reserves of US dollars and a fall (Q3 Q4) in the amount of sterling in circulation.

Having examined in a simple manner the determination of the spot exchange rate under both fixed and floating exchange rates, we now proceed to examine the relationship between the spot and forward exchange rate.

1.9 The determination of the forward exchange rate

The forward exchange market is where buyers and sellers agree to exchange currencies at some specified date in the future. For example, a UK trader who has to pay \$10 000 to his US supplier at the end of August may decide on 1 June to buy \$10 000 for delivery on 31 August of the same year at a 3-month forward exchange rate of \$2.05/£1. The question that naturally arises is why should anyone wish to agree today to exchange currencies at some specified time in the future? To answer this question we need to look at the various participants in the forward exchange market. Traditionally economic agents involved in the forward exchange market are divided up into three groups. These group classifications are distinguished by the motive for their participation in the foreign exchange market.

1.   **Hedgers** – these are agents (usually firms) that enter the forward exchange market to protect themselves against exchange-rate fluctuations which entail exchange-rate risk. By exchange risk we mean the risk of loss

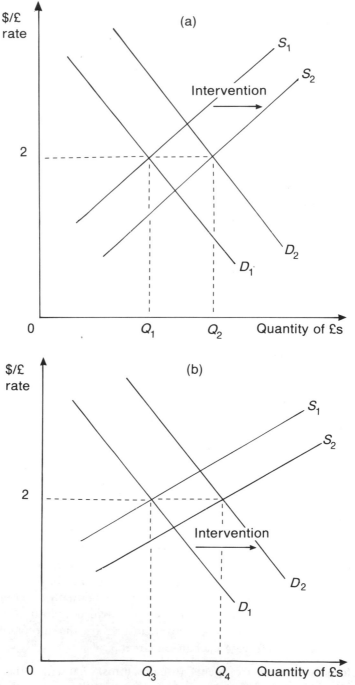

Figure 1.7   *Fixed exchange-rate regime. (a) Increase in demand. (b) Increase in supply*

due to adverse exchange-rate movements. To illustrate why a firm may engage in a forward exchange-rate transaction consider the example of a UK importer who is due to pay for goods from the US to the value of $4100 in three months time. Let us suppose that the spot exchange rate is $2/£1 while the three month forward exchange rate is $2.05/£1. By buying dollars forward at this rate the trader can be sure that he only has to pay £2000. If he does not buy forward today, he runs the risk that in three months time the spot exchange rate may be worse than $2.05/£1 such as $1.95/£1 which would mean him having to pay £2102.56 (4100/1.95). Of course, the spot exchange rate in three months time may be more favourable than $2.05/£1 such as $2.10/£1 in which case he would only have to pay £1952.38 (4100/2.1) which would *ex post* have been better than engaging in a forward exchange contract. By engaging in a forward exchange contract the trader can be sure of the amount of sterling he will have to pay for the imports. As such he can protect himself against the risk entailed by exchange rate fluctuations.

It may be asked why the importer does not immediately buy US $4100 dollars spot at $2/£1 and hold the dollars for three months. One reason is that he may not at present have the necessary funds for such a spot purchase and is reluctant to borrow the money, knowing that he will have the funds in three months time because of money from sales of goods. By engaging in a forward contract he can be sure of getting the dollars he requires at a known exchange rate even though he does not yet have the necessary sterling.

In effect, hedgers avoid exchange risk by matching their assets and liabilities in the foreign currency. In the above example, the UK importer buys $4100 forward (his asset) but will have to pay $4100 for the imported goods (his liability).

2. Arbitrageurs – these are agents (usually banks) that aim to make a riskless profit out of discrepancies between interest-rate differentials and what is known as the forward discount or forward premium. A currency is said to be at a forward premium if the forward exchange-rate quotation for that currency represents an appreciation for that currency compared with the spot quotation. Whereas a currency is said to be at a forward discount if the forward exchange-rate quotation for that currency represents a depreciation for that currency compared with the spot quotation.

The forward discount or premium is usually expressed as a percentage of the spot exchange rate. That is:

$$\text{Forward discount/premium} = \frac{F-S}{S} \times 100$$

where F is the forward exchange rate quotation and S is the spot exchange rate quotation.

The presence of arbitrageurs ensures that what is known as the **covered interest parity** (CIP) condition holds continually – the covered interest parity condition is the formula used by banks to calculate their forward exchange quotation and is given by the following formula:

$$F = \frac{(r^* - r)S}{(1 + r)} + S$$

(1.1)

where F is the one year forward exchange-rate quotation in foreign currency per unit of domestic currency, S is the spot exchange-rate quotation in foreign currency per unit of domestic currency, r is the one year domestic interest rate, and r^* is the one year foreign interest rate.

The above formula has to be amended by dividing the annualised three-month interest rates by 4 to calculate the three-month forward exchange rate quotation and dividing the six-month interest rates by 2 to calculate the six-month forward exchange rate (see Box 1.2).

Example calculation of the forward exchange rate: Suppose that the three-month dollar interest rate is 5 per cent, and sterling interest rate is 10 per cent and spot rate of the pound against the dollar is $2/£1. Then the three-month forward exchange rate of the pound is:

$$F = \frac{(0.0125 - 0.025)2}{1.025} + 2 = 1.9756$$

since

$$\frac{F - S}{S} = \frac{1.9756 - 2}{2} \times 100 = -1.22$$

The three-month forward rate of sterling is at an annual forward discount of 4.88 per cent (1.22×4).

To understand why CIP must be used to calculate the forward exchange rate consider what would happen if the forward rate was different from that quoted in the example, say it was $1.99/£1. In this instance, a US investor with $100 could earn the US interest rate and at the end of three months have $101.25 but by buying pounds spot at ($2/£1) and selling pounds forward (at $1.99/£1) he would have £50 earning the UK interest rate giving him £51.25 at the end of three months, which when sold at a forward price of $1.99/£1 gives $101.99. Clearly, it pays a US investor to buy pounds spot and sell pounds forward. With sufficient numbers of investors doing this, the spot rate of the pound would appreciate and the forward rate depreciate until such arbitrage possibilities are eliminated. With a spot rate of $2/£1, only if the forward rate is $1.9756 will the guaranteed yields in US and UK time deposits be identical since the £51.25 times $1.9756 equals $101.25. Only at this forward exchange rate there are no riskless arbitrage profits to be made.

Box 1.2 *The $/£ forward exchange quotations and UK and US interest rates on 8 October 1990*

	Dollar-Pound exchange rate	UK eurocurrency interest rate	US eurocurrency interest rate
Spot	1.974 0	14.00	8.125
1 month	1.964 5	14.00	8.187 5
3 month	1.947 5	13.75	8.187 5
6 month	1.924 9	13.437 5	8.125
12 month	1.89	13.0	8.187 5

Source: Financial Times, 9 October 1990.

Since the spot exchange rate was $1.9740 per pound.
The one-month forward exchange rate is calculated as:

$$\frac{[(0.081875 - 0.14)/12]}{(1 + 0.14/12)} 1.974 + 1.974 = 1.9645$$

The three-month forward exchange rate is calculated as:

$$\frac{[(0.081875 - 0.1375)/4]}{(1 + 0.1375/4)} 1.974 + 1.974 = 1.9475$$

The six-month forward exchange rate is calculated as:

$$\frac{[(0.08125 - 0.134375)/2]}{(1 + 0.134375/2)} 1.974 + 1.974 = 1.9249$$

The one year forward exchange rate is calculated as:

$$\frac{[(0.081875 - 0.13)]}{(1 + 0.13)} 1.974 + 1.974 = 1.89$$

Since the denominator in equation (1.1) is typically very small equation (1.1) can be simplified to yield an approximate expression for the forward premium/discount:

$$\frac{F - S}{S} \simeq r^* - r \tag{1.2}$$

This approximate version of CIP says that if the domestic interest rate is higher than the foreign interest rate then the domestic currency will be at a forward discount by an equivalent percentage, while if the domestic interest rate is lower than the foreign interest rate the currency will be at a forward premium by an equivalent percentage. In our example we would have the US interest rate of 5 per cent less the UK interest rate of 10 per cent giving an

---

Box 1.3 *Bulls and bears in the foreign exchange market*

Speculators are usually classified as bulls and bears according to their view on a particular currency. If a speculator expects a currency, e.g. the pound (spot and forward), to become more expensive in the future he is said to be 'bullish' about the currency. It pays the speculator to buy the pound spot or forward at a cheap price today in the belief that he can sell it at a higher price in the future. Such a speculator will take a **long position** on the currency.

   If a speculator expects the pound (spot or forward) to become cheaper in the future he is said to be 'bearish' about the currency. It will pay the speculator to take a **short position** on the currency, that is, to sell the pound at what he considers to be a relatively high price today in the hope of buying it back at a cheaper rate sometime in the future.

---

annual forward discount on the pound of 5 per cent which is an approximation to the 4.88 per cent of the full CIP formula.

Speculators – speculators are agents that hope to make a profit by accepting exchange-rate risk. Speculators engage in the forward exchange market because they believe that the future spot rate corresponding to the date of the quoted forward exchange rate will be different from the quoted forward rate. Consider, if the three-month forward rate is quoted at $2.05 and that a speculator feels that the pound will be $1.90 in three months time, in this instance he may sell £100 forward at $2.05 so as to obtain $205 and hope then to change them back into pounds in three months time at $1.90 and so obtain £107.89 making £7.89 profit. Of course, the speculator may be wrong and finds that in three months time the spot exchange rate is above $2.05 say $2.10 in which case his $205 are worth £97.62 implying a loss of £2.38.

   A speculator hopes to make money by taking an 'open position' in the foreign currency. In our example, he has a forward asset in dollars which is not matched by a corresponding liability of equal value.

1.10 The interaction of hedgers, arbitrageurs and speculators

The forward exchange rate is determined by the interaction of traders, hedgers and speculators. One of the conditions that must hold in the forward exchange market is that for every forward purchase there must be a forward sale of the currency so that the net demand for the currency sums to zero.

$$NDH + NDA + NDS = 0$$

where NDH is the net demand of hedgers, NDA is the net demand of arbitrageurs and NDS is the net demand of speculators.

The forward exchange rate and volume of forward transactions is determined by the actions of arbitrageurs, traders and speculators and is jointly determined with the spot exchange rate. This is illustrated in **Figure 1.8.**

Figure 1.8 depicts the simultaneous determination of the spot and forward exchange rate. **Figure 1.8(a)** shows the supply and demand situation in the spot market and **Figure 1.8(b)** the net supply and demand schedules in the forward market. The *A* schedule reflects the forward exchange rate consistent with CIP. In effect, this is the supply and demand of forward exchange of arbitrageurs for a given interest differential. Since the pound is at a forward discount the interest rate in the UK is above that in the US. The *Dh* schedule is the net demand of hedgers in the forward exchange market. As the pound depreciates in the forward market there is an increase in the net demand for forward pounds. This is indicated by the negative slope of the *Dh* schedule.

The *Ds* schedule is the *net* demand schedule for forward exchange of speculators, it cuts the vertical axis at $2.10/£1. This means that $2.10 represents the average forecast of speculators since at this rate speculators would be neither net purchasers nor sellers of forward pounds. However, because speculators on the average expect the pound to appreciate more than is indicated by the forward exchange rate they are net sellers of pounds forward if the rate is above $2.10 and net purchasers of pounds forward if the rate is below $2.10 (because they then expect to be able to sell in the future at a better rate than they purchased). The *D* schedule is the horizontal summation of speculators' and hedgers' demands for pounds. Where the *D* schedule cuts the *A* schedule yields the forward exchange rate of $1.95/£1. At a forward rate of $1.95/£1 the net purchases of speculators and hedgers of pounds are matched by net sales of arbitrageurs.

Speculators are at work in both the spot and forward exchange markets; if they decide that the current spot rate is overvalued they may sell spot so that the currency depreciates, if interest rates do not change then both the spot and forward exchange rates depreciate. Similarly, if speculators feel that the currency is overvalued forward then they will sell forward and both the forward and spot exchange quotations will depreciate. Hence, arbitrage ties the spot and forward exchange market quotations together via the CIP condition. Speculation may be thought of as determining the level of the spot and forward exchange quotations.

▪ *1.11* Conclusions

The need for a foreign exchange market arises because international trade in goods/services and financial assets almost always involves the exchange of

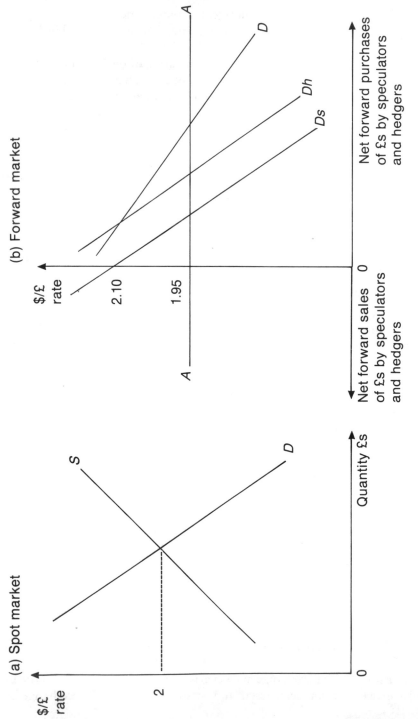

Figure 1.8   *The joint determination of the spot and forward exchange rate*

differing national currencies. Were the world economy to have a single currency then a foreign exchange market would not exist. The modern foreign exchange market is truly a global market and is characterised by a huge volume of daily transactions.

Much of the topic of international finance is about the forces that determine exchange-rate movements and on the implications of these movements for trade and economic growth and the development of the world economy. When conducting an economic analysis of the effects of exchange-rate changes, it proves useful to distinguish between the real and nominal exchange rate and between bilateral and effective exchange rates depending upon the purpose of the particular analysis being undertaken.

Although exchange rates may move quite substantially at times this is not necessarily disruptive to international trade as traders can protect themselves against exchange risk by hedging in the forward exchange market. For many countries, the depreciation/devaluation of their currencies is an important mechanism for maintaining their international competitiveness and trade volumes.

■ Selected further readings

Bank of England Quarterly Bulletin (1980) 'The Foreign Exchange Market in London', vol. 20, pp. 437–44.

Chrystal, K.A. (1984) 'A Guide to the Foreign Exchange Markets.' *Federal Reserve Bank of St Louis Quarterly Review*, vol. 66, no. 3, pp. 5–18.

Grabbe, J.O. (1986) *International Financial Markets* (New York: Elsevier).

■ *Chapter 2* ■

The Balance of Payments

■ *2.1* Introduction

In this chapter we look at one of the most important economic indicators for policy makers in an open economy, namely, the balance of payments. What is happening to a country's balance of payments often captures the news headlines and can become the focus of attention. A good or bad set of figures can have an influential effect on the exchange rate and can lead policy makers to change the content of their economic policies. Deficits may lead to the government raising interest rate or reducing public expenditure to reduce expenditure on imports. Alternatively, deficits may lead to calls for protection against foreign imports or capital controls to defend the exchange rate.

Before considering various policy options that may be devised to deal with perceived problems in the balance of payments, we need to consider in some detail exactly what the balance-of-payments figures are and what is meant by the notion of a balance-of-payments surplus or deficit. In this chapter, we shall look at what is contained in the balance of payments statistics, how they are compiled and at various possible economic interpretations of the statistics.

■ *2.2* What is the balance of payments?

The balance of payments is a statistical record of all the economic transactions between residents of the reporting country and residents of the rest of the world during a given time period. The usual reporting period for all the statistics included in the accounts is a year. However, some of the statistics that make up the balance of payments are published on a more regular monthly and quarterly basis. Without question the balance of payments is one of the most important statistical statements for any country. It reveals how many goods and services the country has been exporting and importing and whether the country has been borrowing from or lending money to the rest of the world. In addition, whether or not the central monetary authority (usually the central bank) has added to or reduced its reserves of foreign currency is reported in the statistics.

A key definition that needs to be resolved at the outset is that of a domestic and foreign resident. It is important to note that citizenship and residency are not necessarily the same thing from the viewpoint of the balance of payments statistics. The term residents comprises individuals, households, firms and the public authorities. There are some problems that arise with respect to the definition of a resident. Multinational corporations are by definition resident in more than one country. For the purposes of balance-of-payments reporting the subsidiaries of a multinational are treated as being a resident in the country in which they are located even if their shares are actually owned by domestic residents. Another problem concerns the treatment of international organisations such as the International Monetary Fund, the World Bank, United Nations and so forth. These institutions are treated as being foreign residents even though they may actually be located in the reporting country. For example, although the International Monetary Fund is located in Washington, contributions by the US government to the Fund are included in the US balance-of-payments statistics because they are regarded as transactions with a foreign resident. Tourists are regarded as being foreign residents if they stay in the reporting country for less than a year.

The criterion for a transaction to be included in the balance of payments is that it must involve a transaction between a resident of the reporting country and a resident from the rest of the world. Purchases and sales between residents from the same country are excluded.

 ## 2.3 Collection, reporting and presentation of the balance-of-payments statistics

The balance of payments statistics record all of the transactions between domestic and foreign residents be they purchases or sales of goods, services or of financial assets such as bonds, equities and banking transactions. Reported figures are normally in the domestic currency of the reporting country. Obviously, collecting statistics on every transaction between domestic and foreign residents is an impossible task. The authorities collect their information from the customs authorities, surveys of tourist numbers and expenditures, data on capital inflows and outflow obtained from banks, pension funds, multinationals and investment houses. Information on government expenditures and receipts with foreign residents is obtained from local authorities and central government agencies. The statistics are based on reliable sampling techniques but nevertheless, given the variety of sources, the figures provide only an estimate of the actual transactions. The responses from the various sources are compiled by government statistical agencies. In the United States the statistics are compiled by the US Department of Commerce and in the United Kingdom by the Department of Trade and Industry.

There is no unique method governing the presentation of balance-of-payments statistics and there can be considerable variations in the presentations of different national authorities. However, the International Monetary Fund provides a set of guidelines for the compilation of balance-of-payments statistics published in its *Balance of Payments Manual*. In addition, the Fund publishes the balance-of-payments statistics of all its member countries in a standardised format facilitating inter-country comparisons. These are presented in two publications – the *Balance of Payments Statistics Yearbook* and the *International Financial Statistics*.

In the US, the value of exports and imports is compiled on a monthly basis and likewise in the UK. The monthly figures are subject to later revision and two sets of statistics are published; the seasonally adjusted figure and the unadjusted figure. The seasonally adjusted figure corrects the balance-of-payments figures for the effect of seasonal factors which influence the balance of payments to reveal underlying trends.

2.4 Balance-of-payments accounting and accounts

An important point about a country's balance-of-payments statistics is that in an accounting sense it always balances. This is because it is based upon the principle of double entry book keeping. Each transaction between a domestic and foreign resident has two sides to it, a receipt and a payment, and both these sides are recorded in the balance-of-payments statistics. Each receipt of currency from residents of the rest of the world is recorded as a credit item (a plus in the accounts) while each payment to residents of the rest of the world is recorded as a debit (a minus in the accounts). Before considering some examples of how different types of economic transactions between domestic and foreign residents get recorded in the balance of payments, we need to consider the various sub-accounts that make up the balance of payments. Traditionally, the statistics are divided into two main sections – the current account and the capital account with each part being further subdivided. The explanation for dividing the balance of payments into these two main parts is that the current account items refer to income flows, while the capital account records changes in assets and liabilities.

A simplified example of the annual balance-of-payments accounts for Europa is presented in **Table 2.1.**

2.5 An overview of the sub-accounts in the balance of payments

☐ *The trade balance*

The trade balance is sometimes referred to as the visible balance because it represents the difference between receipts for exports of goods and expenditure on imports of goods which can be visibly seen crossing frontiers. The receipts for exports are recorded as a credit in the balance of payments, while the payment for imports is recorded as a debit. When the trade balance is in surplus this means that country has earned more from its exports of goods than it has paid for its imports of goods.

☐ *The current account balance*

The current account balance is the sum of visible trade balance and the invisible balance. The invisible balance shows the difference between revenue received for exports of services and payments made for imports of services such as shipping, tourism, insurance, and banking. In addition, receipts and payments of interest, dividends and profits are recorded in the invisible balance because they represent the rewards for investment in overseas companies, bonds and equity while payments reflect the rewards to foreign residents for their investment in the domestic economy. As such, they are receipts and payments for the services of capital that earn and cost the country income just as do exports and imports.

The reader will note that there is an item referred to as unilateral transfers included in the invisible balance, these are payments or receipts for which there is no corresponding quid pro quo. Examples of such transactions are

Table 2.1   *The Balance of payments of Europa*

Current account		
(1) Exports of goods	+ 200	
(2) Imports of goods	− 150	
(3) Trade balance	+ 50	rows (1) + (2)
(4) Exports of services	+120	
(5) Imports of services	− 160	
(6) Interest, profits and dividends received	+ 15	
(7) Interest, profits and dividends paid	− 10	
(8) Unilateral receipts	+ 30	
(9) Unilateral payments	− 20	
(10) Current balance	+ 25	sum rows (3)–(9) inclusive
Capital account		
(11) Investment abroad	− 35	increases in foreign assets
(12) Short-term lending	− 60	decreases in liabilities to foreigners
(13) Medium and long-term lending	− 90	
(14) Foreign investment	+70	decreases in foreign assets
(15) Short-term borrowing	+40	increases in liabilities to foreigners
(16) Medium and long-term borrowing	+30	
(17) Balance on capital account	− 45	sum (11)–(16) inclusive
(18) Statistical discrepancy	+ 5	0 − [(10) + (17) + (20) + (21)]
(19) Total currency flow	− 15	(10) + (17) + (18)
(20) Change in reserves rise (−), fall (+)	+ 10	
(21) IMF borrowing from (+) repayments to (−)	+ 5	

migrant workers' remittances to their families back home, the payment of pensions to foreign residents, and foreign aid. Such receipts and payments represent a redistribution of income between domestic and foreign residents. Unilateral payments can be viewed as a fall in domestic income owing to payments to foreigners and so are recorded as a debit, while unilateral receipts can be viewed as an increase in income owing to receipts from foreigners and consequently are recorded as a credit.

☐ *The capital account balance*

The capital account records transactions concerning the movement of financial capital into and out of the country. Capital comes into the country by borrowing, sales of overseas assets and investment in the country by foreigners. These items are referred to as capital inflows and are recorded as credit items in the balance of payments. **Capital inflows are, in effect, a decrease in the country's holding of foreign assets or increase in liabilities to foreigners.** The fact that capital inflows are recorded as credits in the balance of payments often presents students with difficulty. The easiest way to understand why they are pluses is to think of foreign borrowing as the export of an IOU. Similarly investment by foreign residents is the export of equity or bonds, while sales of overseas investments is an export of those investments to foreigners. Conversely, capital leaves the country due to lending, buying of overseas assets and purchases of domestic assets owned by foreign residents. These items represent capital outflows and are recorded as debits in the capital account. **Capital outflows are, in effect, an increase in the country's holding of foreign assets or decrease in liabilities to foreigners.** These items are recorded as debits as they represent the purchase of an IOU from foreigners, the purchase of foreign bonds or equity and the purchase of investments in the foreign economy.

Items in the capital account are normally distinguished according to whether they originate from the private or public sector and whether they are of a short-term or medium-to-long-term nature. The summation of the capital inflows and outflows as recorded in the capital account gives the total of investment and capital flows or capital account balance.

☐ *Total currency flow*

Given the huge statistical problems involved in compiling the balance-of-payments statistics there will usually be a discrepancy between the sum of all the items recorded in the current account, capital account and the balance of official financing (see below) which in theory should sum to zero. To ensure that the credits and debits are equal it is necessary to incorporate a **statistical discrepancy** for any difference between the sum of credits and debits. There are several possible sources of this error. One of the most important is that it is an impossible task to keep track of all the transactions between domestic and foreign residents; many of the reported statistics are based on sampling estimates derived from separate sources, so that some error is unavoidable. Another problem is that the desire to avoid taxes means that some of the transactions in the capital account are under-reported.

Moreover, some dishonest firms may deliberately under-invoice their exports and over-invoice their imports so as to artificially deflate their profits. Another problem is one of 'leads and lags'. The balance of payments records receipts and payments for a transaction between domestic and foreign residents but it can happen that a good is imported but the payment delayed. Since the import is recorded by the customs authorities and the payment by the banks, the time discrepancy may mean that the two sides of the transaction are not recorded in the same set of figures.

The summation of the current balance, capital account balance and the statistical discrepancy gives the total currency flow. The balance on this account is important because it shows the money available for adding to the country's official reserves or paying off the country's official borrowing.

☐ *The balance of official financing*

A central bank normally holds a stock of reserves made up of foreign currency assets, principally US treasury bills (the US authorities hold mainly deutschmark and yen treasury bills). Such reserves are held primarily to enable the central bank to purchase its currency should it wish to prevent it depreciating. Any total currency outflow has to be covered by the authorities drawing on the reserves, or borrowing money from foreign central banks or the IMF (recorded as a plus in the accounts). If, on the other hand there is a total currency inflow then the surplus can be covered by the government increasing official reserves or repaying debts to the IMF or other sources overseas (a minus since money leaves the country).

The fact that reserve increases are recorded as a minus, while reserve falls are recorded as a plus in the balance of payments statistics is usually a source of confusion. It is most easily rationalised by thinking that reserves increase when the authorities have been purchasing the foreign currency because the domestic currency is strong. This implies that the other items in the balance of payments are in surplus, so reserve increases have to be recorded as a debit to ensure overall balance. Conversely, reserves fall when the authorities have been supporting a currency that is weak, that is, all other items sum to a deficit so reserve falls must be recorded as a plus to ensure overall balance.

2.6 Recording of transactions in the balance of payments

To understand exactly why the sum of credits and debits in the balance of payments should sum to zero we consider some examples of economic transactions between domestic and foreign residents. There are basically five types of economic transactions that can take place between domestic and foreign residents:

(1)   An exchange of goods/services in return for a financial item.
(2)   An exchange of goods/services in return for other goods/services. Such trade is known as barter or countertrade.
(3)   An exchange of a financial item in return for a financial item.
(4)   A transfer of goods or services with no corresponding quid pro quo (for example, military and food aid).
(5)   A transfer of financial assets with no corresponding quid pro quo (for example, migrant workers' remittances to their families abroad, a money gift).

We now look at how each transaction is recorded twice, once as a credit and once as a debit. **Table 2.2** considers various types of transactions between the US and UK residents and shows how each transaction is recorded in each of the two countries balance of payments. The exchange rate for all transactions is assumed to be \$2/£1. The examples in **Table 2.2** illustrate in a simplified manner the double entry nature of balance-of-payments statistics. Since each credit in the accounts has a corresponding debit elsewhere, the sum of all items should be equal to zero. This naturally raises the question as to what is meant by a balance-of-payments deficit or surplus?

 ## 2.7 What is meant by a balance-of-payments surplus or deficit?

As we have seen in **Table 2.2**, the balance of payments always balances since each credit in the account has a corresponding debit elsewhere. However, while the overall balance of payments always balance this does not mean each of the individual accounts that make up the balance of payments is necessarily in balance. For instance, the current account can be in surplus while the capital account is in deficit. When talking about a balance of payments deficit or surplus economists are really saying that a subset of items in the balance of payments are in surplus or deficit.

When referring to a balance of payments deficit or surplus economists make a distinction between autonomous (above the line items) and accommodating (below the line) items. The autonomous items are transactions that take place independently of the balance of payments, whilst the accommodating items are those transactions which finance any difference between autonomous receipts or payments. A surplus in the balance of payments is defined as an excess of autonomous receipts over autonomous payments, while a deficit is an excess of autonomous payments over autonomous receipts.

Autonomous receipts > autonomous payments = surplus
Autonomous receipts < autonomous payments = deficit

The issue that then arises is which specific items in the balance of payments should be classified as autonomous and which as accommodating. Disagreement on which items qualify as autonomous leads to alternative views on what constitutes a balance-of-payments surplus or deficit. The difficulty over classifying items as autonomous or accommodating arises because it is not easy to identify the motive underlying a transaction. For example, if there is a short-term capital inflow in response to a higher domestic interest rate, it should be classified an autonomous item. If, however, the item is an

Table 2.2. *Examples of balance-of-payments accounting*

Example 1   The US exports $100 million of goods to the United Kingdom which is paid for by the UK importer debiting his US bank deposit account by a like amount.

US balance of payments		**UK balance of payments**	
Current account		*Current account*	
Exports of goods	+ $100m	Import of goods	− £50m
Capital account		*Capital account*	
Reduced US bank		Reduction in UK	
liabilities to UK residents	− $100m	residents' US bank	
		deposit assets	+ £50m

Example 2   The US exports $100 million of goods to the UK in exchange for $100 million of services.

US balance of payments		**UK balance of payments**	
Current account		*Current account*	
Merchandise exports	+ $100m	Exports of services	+ £50m
Imports of services	− $100m	Imports of goods	− £50m

Example 3   A US investor decides to buy £500 of UK Treasury bills and to pay for them by debiting his US bank account and crediting the account of the UK Treasury held in New York.

US balance of payments		**UK balance of payments**	
Capital account		*Capital account*	
Increase in UK Treasury		Increased bond liabilities	
bond holdings	− $1000	to US residents	+ £500
Increase in US bank		Increased US bank	
liabilities	+ $1000	deposit	− £500

Table 2.2 *contd.*

Example 4

The US makes a gift of £10 million of goods to a UK charitable organisation.

US balance of payments		UK balance of payments	
Current account		*Current account*	
Exports	+ $20m	Imports	− £10m
Unilateral payment	− $20m	Unilateral receipt	+ £10m

Example 5

The US pays interest, profits and dividends to UK investors of $50 million by debiting US bank accounts which are then credited to UK residents' bank accounts held in US.

US balance of payments		UK balance of payments	
Current account		*Current account*	
Interest, profits, dividends paid	− $50m	Interest, profits, dividends received	+ £25m
Capital account		*Capital account*	
Increased US bank liabilities	+ $50m	Increase in US bank deposits	− £25m

---

inflow to enable the financing of imports then it should be classified as an accommodating item. This difficulty of deciding which items should be classified as accommodating and autonomous items has led to several concepts of balance-of-payments disequilibrium. We shall now review some of the most important of these concepts and consider their usefulness as economic indicators.

2.8 Alternative concepts of surplus and deficits

☐ *The trade account and current account*

These two accounts derive much of their importance because estimates are published on a monthly basis by most developed countries. Since the current account balance is concerned with visibles and invisibles it is generally considered to be the more important of the two accounts. What really makes a current account surplus or deficit important is that a surplus means that the country as a whole is increasing its stock of claims on the rest of the world; while a deficit means that the country is reducing its net claims on the rest of the world. Furthermore, as we shall see in Chapter 3, the current account can readily be incorporated into economic analysis of an open economy. More generally, the current account is likely to quickly pick up changes in other economic variables such as changes in the real exchange rate, domestic and foreign economic growth and relative price inflation.

☐ *The basic balance*

This is the current account balance plus the net balance on long-term capital flows. The basic balance was considered to be particularly important during the 1950s and 1960s period of fixed exchange rates because it was viewed as bringing together the stable elements in the balance of payments. It was argued that any significant change in the basic balance must be a sign of a fundamental change in the direction of the balance of payments. The more volatile elements such as short-term capital flows and changes in official reserves were regarded as below the line items.

Although a worsening of the basic balance is supposed to be a sign of a worsening economic situation, having an overall basic balance deficit is not necessarily a bad thing. For example, a country may have a current account deficit that is reinforced by a large long-term capital outflow so that the basic balance is in a large deficit. However, the capital outflow will yield future profits, dividends and interest receipts that will help to generate future surpluses on the current account. Conversely, a surplus in the basic balance is not necessarily a good thing. A current account deficit which is more than covered by a net capital inflow so that the basic balance is in surplus could be open to two interpretations. It might be argued that because the country is able to borrow long run that there is nothing to worry about since the country is regarded as viable by the foreigners who are prepared to lend money long run to the country. Another interpretation could argue that the basic balance surplus is a problem because the long-term borrowing will lead to future interest, profits and dividend payments which will worsen the current account deficit.

Apart from interpretation, the principal problem with the basic balance concerns the classification of short and long-term capital flows. The usual means of classifying long-term loans or borrowing is that they be of at least 12 months to maturity. However, many long-term capital flows can be easily converted into short-term flows if need be. For example, the purchase of a five-year US treasury bond by a UK investor would be classified as a long-term capital outflow in the UK balance of payments and long-term capital inflow in the US balance of payments. However, the UK investor could very easily sell the bond back to US investors any time before its maturity date. Similarly, many short-term items with less than 12 months to maturity automatically get renewed annually so that they effectively become long-term assets. Another problem that blurs the distinction between short-term and long-term capital flows is that transactions in financial assets are classified in accordance with their original maturity date. Hence, if after four and a half years a UK investor sells his five-year US treasury bill to a US citizen it will be classified as a long-term capital flow even though the bond has only six months to maturity.

□ *The settlements concept*

The settlements concept focuses on the operations that the monetary authorities have to undertake to finance any imbalance in the current and capital accounts. With the settlements concept, the autonomous items are all those transactions that make up the total currency flow, while the accommodating items are those transactions that the monetary authorities have undertaken as indicated by the balance of official financing. The current account and capital account items are all regarded as being induced by independent households, firms, central and local government and are regarded as the autonomous items. If the total currency flow is negative, the country can be regarded as being in deficit as this has to be financed by the authorities drawing on their reserves of foreign currency, borrowing from foreign monetary authorities or the International Monetary Fund.

A major point to note with the settlements concept is that countries whose currency is used as a reserve asset can have a total currency flow deficit and yet maintain fixed parity for their currency without running down their reserves or borrowing from the IMF. This can be the case if foreign authorities eliminate the excess supply of the domestic currency by purchasing it and adding it to their reserves. This is particularly important when it comes to the United States since the US dollar is the major reserve currency. The United States can have a current account and capital account deficit which is financed by increased foreign authorities' purchases of dollars and dollar treasury bills – in other words increased US liabilities constituting foreign authorities' reserves. For this reason part of the official settlements balance records 'changes in liabilities constituting foreign authorities' reserves'.

The settlements concept of a surplus or deficit is not as relevant to countries that have floating exchange rates as it is to those with fixed exchange rates. This is because if exchange rates are left to float freely the balance for official financing will tend to zero because the central authorities neither purchase nor sell their currency and so there will be no changes in their reserves. If the sales of a currency exceed the purchases, then the currency will depreciate and if sales are less than purchases the currency appreciates. The settlements concept is, however, very important under fixed exchange rates because it shows the amount of pressure on the authorities to devalue or revalue the currency. Under a fixed exchange rate system a country that is running a total currency flow deficit will find that sales of its currency exceed purchases and, to avert a devaluation of the currency, authorities have to sell reserves of foreign currency to purchase the home currency. Whereas, under floating exchange rates and no intervention the settlements balance automatically tends to zero as the authorities do not buy or sell the home currency which is left to appreciate or depreciate.

Even in a fixed exchange-rate regime the settlements concept ignores the fact that the authorities have other instruments available with which to defend the exchange rate such as capital controls and interest rates. Also, it does not reveal the real threat to the domestic currency and official reserves represented by the liquid liabilities held by foreign residents that might switch suddenly out of the currency.

Although in 1973 the major industrialised countries switched from a fixed to floating exchange-rate system many developing countries continue to peg their exchange rate to the US dollar and consequently attach much significance to the settlements balance. Indeed, to the extent that industrialised countries continue to intervene in the foreign exchange market to influence the value of their currencies the settlements balance retains some significance and news about changes in the reserves of the authorities is of interest to foreign exchange dealers as a guide to the amount of official intervention in the foreign exchange market.

The IMF provides an annual summary of the balance-of-payments statistics using these alternative concepts of balance-of-payments disequilibrium, and the balance-of-payments statistics for the major seven industrialised nations in 1989 are presented in **Table 2.3**. **Table 2.4** summarises the main balance-of-payments disequilibrium concepts.

■ *2.9* Conclusions

From the discussion we can see that there are a variety of concepts of balance-of-payments disequilibrium. The very fact that there is no single agreed upon definition is not surprising. The choice of which concept is most relevant depends upon the exchange rate regime and the particular purpose of the analysis being undertaken. Each of the concepts has a different information content and taken together they provide an important indicator about the macro performance of an open economy. In the short run, however, it is inevitable the trade and current account balances capture the attention of macroeconomic policy makers because they are published so

Table 2.3   IMF balance-of-payments summary: the United States, Japan, Germany, France, Italy, Canada and the United Kingdom in 1989 (in billions of US dollars)

		U.S.	Japan	W. Germany	France	Italy	Canada	U.K
A.	Current account	-110.06	56.94	55.48	-4.30	-10.63	-14.09	-31.16
	Merchandise exports	360.46	269.59	324.48	171.32	140.30	123.22	151.31
	Merchandise imports	-475.33	-192.74	-247.77	-181.67	-142.29	-116.36	-189.26
	Trade balance	-114.87	76.85	76.71	-10.35	-1.99	6.86	-37.96
	Exports services	242.71	143.91	98.31	102.06	48.65	21.51	172.01
	Imports services	-223.14	-159.53	-101.13	-87.58	-55.05	-46.79	-157.79
	Private unrequited transfers	-1.33	-0.99	-6.17	-2.71	1.30	4.70	-0.49
	Official unrequited transfers	-13.43	-3.30	-12.24	-5.72	-3.54	-0.37	-6.93
B.	Direct investment and other long-term capital	87.93	-93.61	-11.65	7.03	15.30	19.68	-34.98
	Direct investment	40.50	-45.22	-6.99	-8.76	0.53	-0.81	0.23
	Portfolio investment	44.79	-32.53	-4.38	22.95	3.26	15.79	-43.17
	Other long-term capital	2.64	-15.86	-0.28	-7.16	11.51	4.70	-1.76
	Total Groups A plus B [Basic Balance]	-22.13	-36.67	43.82	2.73	4.67	5.59	-66.14
C.	Short-term capital	16.32	45.86	-56.75	-2.26	11.05	-0.40	27.53
D.	Net errors and omissions	22.60	-21.95	2.33	-2.94	-4.60	-4.90	24.55
E.	Counterpart items	1.55	-0.01	0.12	0.12	1.53	-0.03	-0.54
	Total Groups A through E [Official Settlements Balance]	18.33	-12.77	-10.49	-2.35	12.65	0.26	-14.60
F.	Exceptional financing	—	—	—	—	0.02	—	-1.94
G.	Liabilities constituting foreign authorities reserves	8.48	—	13.43	1.61	—	—	7.19
H.	Total change in reserves	-26.81	12.77	-2.95	0.73	-12.67	-0.26	9.34

Source: International Monetary Fund, Balance of Payments Yearbook (Washington, D.C.: IMF, 1990).

Table 2.4 *Summary of key balance-of-payments concepts*

Trade Balance

+ Exports of goods
− Imports of goods
= Trade Balance

Current Account

   Trade balance
+ Exports of services
+ Interest, dividends and profits received
+ Unilateral receipts
− Imports of services
− Interest, dividends and profits paid
− Unilateral payments abroad
= Current account balance

Basic Balance

   Current account balance
+ Balance on long-term capital account
= Basic balance

Settlements Balance

   Basic balance
+ Balance on short-term capital account
+ Statistical discrepancy
= Settlements balance

frequently. Furthermore, it is not what happens so much in any given quarter's balance of payments that is significant but what the statistics reveal over a period of time about the direction of an economy.

An important point to be borne in mind is that it is necessary to bring in a time dimension when analysing balance-of-payments statistics. A deficit is not necessarily a bad thing if it is likely to be followed by future surpluses and vice versa. In this respect, it can be argued that it is necessary to look at the composition of goods that a country is importing. If the imported goods are predominantly consumer goods like cars and consumer electronics then it might be argued that the deficit is more worrying than when the imports are plant and machinery that could be important in generating future exports.

Another point that needs to be borne in mind when considering if a current account deficit or surplus is a significant problem is whether or not the country concerned is a net creditor or debtor *vis-à-vis* the rest of the world. A current account deficit means that the country concerned is increasing its indebtedness or reducing its claims on the rest of the world. If the country is a net creditor it can usually afford to do this, whereas if it is a net debtor the deficit may be regarded as a more serious problem. This is why the deficits of the United States in the late 1980s and early 1990s have caused so much concern because the US has become the world's largest debtor. By contrast, there will be much less concern if German reunification results in German current account deficits because past German surpluses have made it a net creditor *vis-à-vis* the rest of the world.

When analysing a country's balance-of-payments statistics and attempting to assess whether the country is facing or is likely to face problems in the near future, it is important to remember that whatever concept of balance-of-payments disequilibrium is used it gives only a partial view of the economy. If a country has a current account deficit, high inflation and low economic growth then the balance-of-payments problem is more worrying than if the deficit is accompanied by high economic growth and low inflation.

■ Selected further readings

Kemp, D.S. (1987) 'Balance of Payments Concepts – What Do They Really Mean?', in *Readings in International Finance* (Chicago: Federal Reserve Bank of Chicago).

Meade, J.E. (1951) *The Balance of Payments* (Oxford: Oxford University Press).

Stern, R.M. *et al.* (1977) *The Presentation of the United States Balance of Payments – a Symposium*. Princeton Essays in International Finance No. 123, Princeton University.

Thirwall, A.P. (1986) *Balance of Payments Theory and the United Kingdom Experience* (London: Macmillan).

■ *Chapter 3* ■

Elasticity and Absorption Approaches to the Balance of Payments

■ *3.1* Introduction

In the opening two chapters we have introduced the exchange rate and the balance of payments. In this chapter, we investigate the relationship between the exchange rate and the balance of payments. In particular, we shall be studying two models that investigate the impact of exchange rate changes on the current account position of a country. These two approaches are popularly known as the elasticity approach and the absorption approach. Both models were designed to tackle one of the most perennial questions in international economics, will a devaluation (or depreciation) of the exchange rate lead to a reduction of a current account deficit? The answer to this question is of crucial importance because if an exchange rate change cannot be relied upon to ensure adjustment of the current account then policy makers will have to rely on other instruments to improve the position.

We start the chapter by examining some of the fundamental economic identities for an open economy. We then consider how changes in government expenditure and exports influence not only the level of national income of an open economy but also its current account position. The analysis then proceeds to examine the impact of exchange rate changes according to the elasticity and absorption models. The chapter concludes by analysing the similarities and differences between the two models.

Throughout this chapter, for simplicity, we shall ignore the complications of unilateral transfers and interest, profit and dividends on the current account balance and concentrate on the export and import of goods and services. **Throughout the chapter, the exchange rate is defined as domestic currency units per unit of foreign currency, so that a devaluation/depreciation of the currency is represented by a rise in the exchange rate.**

■ *3.2* Some open economy identities

In an open economy Gross Domestic Product (GDP) differs from that of a closed economy because there is an additional injection, export expenditure, which represents foreign expenditure on domestically produced goods. There is also an additional leakage, expenditure on imports, which represents domestic expenditure on foreign goods and raises foreign national income. The identity for an open economy is given by:

$$Y = C + I + G + X - M \tag{3.1}$$

where Y is national income, C is domestic consumption, I is domestic investment, G is government expenditure, X is export expenditure and M is import expenditure.

If we deduct taxation from the right hand side of equation (3.1) we have:

$$Y_d = C + I + G + X - M - T \tag{3.2}$$

where Y_d is disposable income.

If we denote private savings as $S = Y_d - C$ we can rearrange equation (3.2) to obtain:

$$(X - M) \; = \; (S - I) \qquad + \; (T - G) \tag{3.3}$$

Current balance	Net saving/ dissaving of private sector	Government deficit/surplus

Equation (3.3) is an important identity it says that a current account deficit has a counterpart in either private dissaving, that is, private investment exceeding private saving and/or in a government deficit, that is, government expenditure exceeding government taxation revenue. The equation is merely an identity and says nothing about causation. None the less, it is often stated that the current account deficit is due to the lack of private savings and/or the government budget deficit. However, it is possible that the causation runs the other way, and it is the current account deficit that may be responsible for the lack of private savings or budget deficit. The identity has been much talked about during the 1980s (see **Box 3.1.**).

Equation (3.3) can be re-arranged to yield:

$$I + G + X = S + T + M \tag{3.4}$$

This shows that the equilibrium level of national income is determined where injections (the variables on the left-hand side of (3.4)) are equal to leakages (the variables on the right-hand side of (3.4)). Injections are all those factors that work to raise national income, while leakages are those factors that work to lower national income. Equation (3.4) is an important identity to which we shall return in Chapter 4.

■ *3.3* Open economy multipliers

John Maynard Keynes in his classic work *The General Theory of Employment, Interest and Money* published in 1936 pioneered the use of multiplier analysis to examine the effects of changes in government expenditure and investment on output and employment. However, his work was concerned almost exclusively with a closed economy. It was not long, however, before the ideas of Keynes's work were applied to an analysis of open economies most notably by Fritz Machlup (1943).

The assumptions underlying basic multiplier analysis are; (i) both domestic prices and the exchange rate are fixed, (ii) economy is operating at less than full employment so that increases in demand result in an expansion of output and (iii) the authorities adjust the money supply to changes in money demand by pegging the domestic interest rate. This latter assumption is important; increases in output that lead to a rise in money demand would with a fixed money supply lead to a rise in the domestic interest rate; it is assumed that the authorities passively expand the money stock to meet any increase in money demand so that interest rates do not have to change. There is no inflation resulting from the money supply expansion because it is merely a response to the increase in money demand.

The starting point for the analysis is the identity of equation (3.1) repeated below as (3.5):

$$Y = C + I + G + X - M \tag{3.5}$$

Keynesian analysis proceeds to make assumptions concerning the determinants of the various components of national income. Government expenditure and exports are assumed to be exogenous, government expenditure being determined independently by political decision and exports by foreign expenditure decisions and foreign income.

Domestic consumption is partly autonomous and partly determined by the level of national income. This is denoted algebraically by the equation:

$$C = C_a + cY \tag{3.6}$$

Box 3.1   *Current accounts and government fiscal policies in the 1980s*

The fact that a country's current account is made up of the government budget surplus/deficit and net private savings/dissavings has led to very different perspectives on current account imbalances in the 1980s (see **Table 3.1**).

Table 3.1   *Budget deficits/surpluses and current account balances (percentage of GDP/GNP)*

Year	United States (T–G)	(S–I)	CA	United Kingdom (T–G)	(S–I)	CA
1980	−1.3	+1.3	0.0	−3.4	+4.8	+1.2
1981	−1.0	+1.2	0.2	−2.6	+5.3	+2.7
1982	−3.5	+3.2	−0.2	−2.5	+4.2	+1.7
1983	−3.8	+2.6	−1.2	−3.3	+4.5	+1.2
1984	−2.8	+0.2	−2.6	−3.9	+4.5	+0.6
1985	−3.3	+0.3	−3.0	−2.7	+3.5	+0.8
1986	−3.4	0.0	−3.4	−2.2	+2.2	0.0
1987	2.4	−1.0	−3.6	−1.3	+0.3	−1.0
1988	−2.0	−0.6	−2.6	+1.0	−4.2	−3.2
1989	−1.7	−0.4	−2.1	+0.9	−4.6	−3.7

Year	Germany (T–G)	(S–I)	CA	Japan (T–G)	(S–I)	CA
1980	−2.9	+1.2	−1.7	−4.4	+3.0	−1.0
1981	−3.7	+3.2	−0.5	−3.8	+4.2	+0.4
1982	−3.3	+4.1	+0.8	−3.6	+4.2	+0.6
1983	−2.5	+3.3	+0.8	−3.7	+5.5	+1.8
1984	−1.9	+3.5	+1.6	−2.1	+4.9	+2.8
1985	−1.1	+3.7	+2.6	−0.8	+4.5	+3.7
1986	−1.3	+5.7	+4.4	−0.9	+5.3	+4.4
1987	−1.9	+6.0	+4.1	−0.7	+4.3	+3.6
1988	−2.1	+6.3	+4.2	−2.1	+4.9	+2.8
1989	+0.2	+4.4	+4.6	−2.7	+4.7	+2.0

Source: OECD, *Economic Outlook.*

Interesting comparisons were made between the current account deficits of the US and the UK. Many economists blamed the rapidly growing US current account deficit from 1982 as due to the steep rise in the US budget deficit. The UK current account moved into heavy deficit from 1987 onwards. However, because the UK government was running a budget surplus, the deficit was seen as a private sector phenomenon. The contrasts naturally led economists to propose different solutions to the deficits in both countries. The US policy debate was concerned with measures to reduce the federal budget deficit, while discussion in the UK focused upon measures to encourage private sector savings (reducing private consumption).

Many economists believe that the reason why Germany and Japan have had such persistent surpluses in their current accounts is that they have had much higher savings ratios. At the end of the 1980s there is some evidence that the Japanese are saving somewhat less than in the past, while German reunification is likely to lead to much higher investment and much bigger government deficits. It will be interesting to see whether these trends translate themselves into smaller surpluses or even deficits in the 1990s.

where C_a is autonomous consumption, c is the marginal propensity to consume, that is, the fraction of any increase in income that is spent on consumption. In this simple model, consumption is assumed to be a linear function of income. An increase in consumers' income induces an increase in their consumption.

Import expenditure is assumed to be partly autonomous and partly a positive function of the level of domestic income,

$$M = M_a + mY \tag{3.7}$$

where M_a is autonomous import expenditure and m is the marginal propensity to import, that is, the fraction of any increase in income that is spent on imports. In this simple formulation import expenditure is assumed to be a positive linear function of income. There are several justifications for this; on the one hand increased income leads to increased expenditure on imports, and also more domestic production normally requires more imports of intermediate goods. Since we have assumed that domestic prices are fixed this means that income Y also represents real income. If we substitute equations (3.6) and (3.7) into equation (3.5) we obtain:

$$Y = C_a + cY + I + G + X - M_a - mY$$

therefore:

$$(1 - c + m)Y = C_a + I + G + X - M_a$$

Given that $(1 - c)$ is equal to the marginal propensity to save s, that is, the fraction of any increase in income that is saved, then we obtain:

$$Y = \frac{1}{s + m}(C_a + I + G + X - M_a) \tag{3.8}$$

Equation (3.8) can be transformed into difference form to yield:

$$dY = \frac{1}{s + m}(dC_a + dI + dG + dX - dM_a) \tag{3.9}$$

where d in front of a variable represents the change in the variable. From equation (3.9) we can obtain some simple open-economy multipliers.

□ *The government expenditure multiplier*

The first multiplier of interest is the government expenditure multiplier, which shows the increase in national income resulting from a given increase in government expenditure. This is given by:

$$dY/dG = 1/(s + m) > 0 \tag{3.10}$$

Equation (3.10) says that an increase in government expenditure will have an expansionary effect on national income, the size of which depends upon the marginal propensity to save and the marginal propensity to import. Since the sum of the marginal propensity to save and import is less than unity, an increase in government expenditure will result in an even greater increase in national income. Furthermore, the value of the open economy multiplier is less than the closed economy multiplier which is given by $1/s$. The reason for this is that increased expenditure is spent on both domestic and foreign goods rather than domestic goods alone and the expenditure on foreign goods raises foreign rather than domestic income.

Numerical example: Assume that the marginal propensity to save is 0.25 and the marginal propensity to import is 0.15. The effect of an increase in government expenditure of £100 million on national income is given by:

$$dY = \frac{1}{s+m} dG = \frac{1}{0.25+0.15} £100m = 2.5 \times £100m = £250m$$

Hence, an increase of government expenditure of £100m will raise eventual national income by £250m. This is because 60 per cent of the £100m will get spent giving a further £60 million increase in incomes of which 60 per cent will get spent giving a further £36 million increase in incomes and so on. The limit of such a series of expenditure rounds is £250 million.

☐ *The foreign trade or export multiplier*

In this simple model, the multiplier effect of an increase in exports is identical to that of an increase in government expenditure and is given by:

$$dY/dX = 1/(s+m)$$

In practice, it is often the case that government expenditure tends to be somewhat more biased to domestic output than private consumption expenditure, implying that the value of m is smaller in the case of the government expenditure multiplier than in the case of the export multiplier. If this is the case, an increase in government expenditure will have a more expansionary effect on domestic output than an equivalent increase in exports.

Numerical example: Assume that the marginal propensity to save is 0.25 and the marginal propensity to import is 0.15. The effect of an increase in exports of £100 million on national income is given by:

$$dY = \frac{1}{s+m} dX = \frac{1}{0.25+0.15} £100m = 2.5 \times £100m = £250m$$

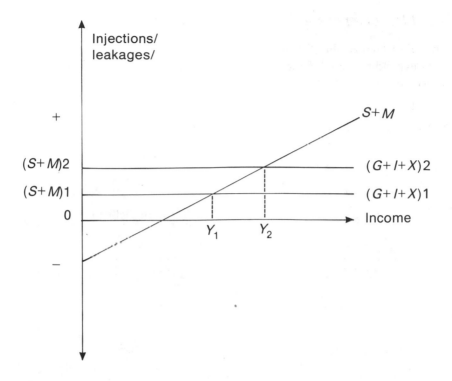

Figure 3.1 *The Government expenditure/foreign trade multiplier*

The effects of either an increase in government expenditure or increase in exports is illustrated in **Figure 3.1**.

In Figure 3.1, on the vertical axis we have injections/leakages and on the horizontal axis we have national income. The savings plus import expenditures are assumed to increase as income rises reflected by the upward slope of the injections schedule. Because the sum of the marginal propensity to import and save is less than unity this schedule has a slope less than unity. Injections are assumed to be exogenous of the level of income and consequently this schedule is a horizontal line. The equilibrium level of national income is determined where injections into the economy (government expenditure, investment plus exports) equal leakages (savings and imports), which is initially at income level Y1. An increase of exports or government expenditure or investment results in an upward shift of the injections schedule from $(G+I+X)1$ to $(G+I+X)2$; this rise in income induces more saving and import expenditure but overall the increase in income from Y1 to Y2 is greater than the initial increase in injections. The lower are the marginal propensities to save and invest, the less steep the leakages schedule and the greater the increase in income.

☐ *The current account multipliers*

The other relationships of interest are the effects of an increase in government expenditure and of exports on the current account balance. Rearranging equation (3.5) we have:

$$Y - C - I - G + M - X = 0$$

Substituting in equations (3.6) and (3.7) yields:

$$Y - cY + mY - C_a + M_a - I - G - X = 0$$

Since $Y(1 - c + m) = Y(s + m)$ we have:

$$Y(s + m) - C_a + M_a - I - G - X = 0$$

Dividing by $(s + m)$ and multiplying through by m yields:

$$mY - \frac{m}{s + m}(C_a - Ma + I + G + X) = 0$$

Adding M_a and X to each side, recalling that $M = M_a + mY$ and rearranging yields:

$$CA = X - M = X - M_a - \frac{m}{s + m}(C_a - M_a + I + G + X) \tag{3.11}$$

Equation (3.11) can now be expressed in difference form as:

$$dCA = dX - dM_a - \frac{m}{s + m}(dC_a - dM_a + dI + dG + dX) \tag{3.12}$$

From equation (3.12) we can derive the effects of an increase in government expenditure on the current account balance which is given by:

$$\frac{dCA}{dG} = \frac{-m}{s + m} < 0$$

That is, an increase in government spending leads to a deterioration of the current account balance which is some fraction of the initial increase in government expenditure. This is because economic agents spend part of the increase in income on imports.

Numerical example: Assume that the marginal propensity to save is 0.25 and the marginal propensity to import is 0.15. The effect of an increase in government expenditure of £100 million on the current account is given by:

$$dCA = \frac{-m}{s + m} dG = \frac{-0.15}{0.25 + 0.15} £100m = -0.375 \times £100m = -£37.5m$$

That is, an increase in government expenditure of £100m leads to an eventual deterioration in current account of £37.5m. The reason is that the increased government expenditure of £100m because of the open economy multiplier increases national income by £250m. Since the marginal propensity to import is 0.15, the £250m increase in income leads to a $0.15 \times £250 = £37.5m$

increase in imports which corresponds to the deterioration in the current account.

The other multiplier of interest is the effect of an increase in exports on the current balance. This is given by the expression:

$$\frac{dCA}{dX} = 1 - \frac{m}{s+m} = \frac{s+m}{s+m} - \frac{m}{s+m} = \frac{s}{s+m} > 0$$

Since $s/s+m$ is less than unity, an increase in exports leads to an improvement in the current balance that is less than the original increase in exports. The explanation for this is that part of the increase in income resulting from the additional exports is offset to some extent by increased expenditure on imports.

Numerical example: Assume that the marginal propensity to save is 0.25 and the marginal propensity to import is 0.15. The effect of an increase in exports of £100 million on the current account is given by:

$$dCA = \frac{s}{s+m} dX = \frac{0.25}{0.25+0.15} £100m = 0.625 \times £100m = £62.5m$$

The explanation is that the £100m increase in exports initially improves the current account by a like amount. However, it also generates an eventual increase of national income of £250m which induces an increase in imports of £37.5m, so the net improvement in the current account is limited to £62.5m.

The simple multiplier analysis that we have looked at here shows that Keynesian income effects are an essential part of balance-of-payments analysis and that the current account of the balance of payments is an integral part of macroeconomic equilibrium for an open economy. Another important conclusion is that an analysis of macroeconomic fluctuations for an open economy requires consideration of what is happening in foreign economies; increases in foreign income raise the exports and income of the home economy. The foreign trade multiplier analysis deals with what happens to the balance of payments when income changes, assuming that prices are held constant. In the next section we look at an analysis that considers what happens to the balance of payments when relative prices change due to a devaluation of the currency assuming that income and all other things are held constant.

 ## 3.4 The elasticity approach to the balance of payments

The elasticity approach to the balance of payments provides an analysis of what happens to the current account balance when the country devalues its currency. The analysis was pioneered by Alfred Marshall, Abba Lerner and later extended by Joan Robinson (1937) and Fritz Machlup (1939). At the outset, the model makes some simplifying assumptions; the model focuses on demand conditions and assumes that the supply elasticities for the domestic export good and foreign import good are perfectly elastic, so that changes in demand volumes have no effect on prices. In effect, these assumptions mean that domestic and foreign prices are fixed so that changes in relative prices are caused solely by changes in the nominal exchange rate.

The central message of the elasticity approach is that there are two direct effects of a devaluation on the current balance, one of which works to reduce a deficit, whilst the other actually contributes to making the deficit worse than before. Let us consider these two effects in some detail:

The current account balance when expressed in terms of the domestic currency is given by:

$$CA = PX_v - SP^* M_v \qquad (3.13)$$

where P is the domestic price level, X_v is the volume of domestic exports, S is the exchange rate (domestic currency units per unit of foreign currency), P^* is the foreign price level and M_v is the volume of imports. We shall set the domestic and foreign price levels at unity, the value of domestic exports (PX_v) is given by X, while the foreign currency value of imports $(P^* M_v)$ is given by M. Using these simplifications equation (3.13) becomes:

$$CA = X - SM \qquad (3.14)$$

In difference form (3.14) becomes:

$$dCA = dX - S\, dM - M\, dS \qquad (3.15)$$

Dividing (3.15) by the change in the exchange rate dS, we obtain:

$$\frac{dCA}{dS} = \frac{dX}{dS} - S\frac{dM}{dS} - M\frac{dS}{dS} \qquad (3.16)$$

At this point we introduce two definitions; the price elasticity of demand for exports η_x, is defined as the percentage change in exports over the percentage change in price as represented by the percentage change in the exchange rate; this gives:

$$\eta_x = \frac{dX/X}{dS/S}$$

so that

$$dX = \eta_x \frac{dS\, X}{S} \qquad (3.17)$$

and the price elasticity of demand for imports η_m, is defined as the percentage change in imports over the percentage change in their price as represented by the percentage change in the exchange rate:

$$\eta_m = -\frac{dM/M}{dS/S}$$

so that

$$dM = -\eta_m \frac{dS}{S}M \tag{3.18}$$

Substituting (3.17) and (3.18) into (3.16) we obtain:

$$\frac{dCA}{dS} = \frac{\eta_x X}{S} + \eta_m M - M$$

Dividing by M

$$\frac{dCA}{dS}\frac{1}{M} = \frac{\eta_x X}{SM} + \eta_m - 1 \tag{3.19}$$

Assuming that we initially have balanced trade $X/SM = 1$, and rearranging (3.19) yields.

$$\frac{dCA}{dS} = M(\eta_x + \eta_m - 1) \tag{3.20}$$

Equation (3.20) is known as the Marshall–Lerner condition and says that starting from a position of equilibrium in the current account, a devaluation will improve the current account, that is, $dCA/dS > 0$, only if the sum of the foreign elasticity of demand for exports and the home country elasticity of demand for imports is greater than unity, i.e. $\eta_x + \eta_m > 1$. If the sum of these two elasticities is less than unity then a devaluation will lead to a deterioration of the current account.

This economic explanation of this result is illustrated in **Table 3.2** which shows the pre-devaluation and possible post devaluation scenarios. Before devaluation the sterling dollar exchange rate is £0.50/\$1 (\$2/£1), whereas after the devaluation the sterling dollar exchange rate £0.666/\$1 (\$1.50/£1). The price of one unit of UK exports is £1 and the price of one unit of US exports is \$4.

Table 3.2 illustrates three possible scenarios following a devaluation. There are two effects in play once a currency is devalued:

(1) *The price effect* – exports become cheaper measured in foreign currency – a UK export earns only \$1.50 post-devaluation compared with \$2 prior to devaluation. Imports become more expensive measured in the home currency, each unit of imports cost £2 prior to the devaluation but costs £2.67 post-devaluation. The price effect clearly contributes to a worsening of the UK current account.

(2) *The volume effect* – the fact that exports become cheaper should encourage an increased volume of exports and the fact that imports become more expensive should lead to a decreased volume of imports. The volume effect clearly contributes to improving the current balance.

Table 3.2 *Devaluation and the balance of payments*

Before devaluation the current account is in balance				
Description	*Volume*	*Price*	*Sterling value*	*Dollar value*
UK exports	100	£1	£100	$200
UK imports	50	$4	£100	$200
Current balance			£0	$0
Case 1 Devaluation leads to a current balance deficit				
UK exports	105	£1	£105	$157.5
UK imports	45	$4	£120	$180
Current balance			−£15	−$22.5
Approximate elasticities: $\eta_x = 0.05/0.33 = 0.15$, $\eta_m = 0.1/0.33 = 0.3$				
Case 2 Devaluation leaves the current balance unaffected				
UK exports	120	£1	£120	$180
UK imports	45	$4	£120	$180
Current balance			£0	$0
Approximate elasticities: $\eta_x = 0.20/0.33 = 0.6$ $\eta_m = 0.1/0.33 = 0.3$				
Case 3 Devaluation leads to a current balance surplus				
UK exports	140	£1	£140	$210
UK imports	45	$4	£120	$180
Current balance			+£20	+$30
Approximate elasticities: $\eta_x = 0.40/0.33 = 1.2$, $\eta_m = 0.1/0.33 = 0.3$				

The net effect depends upon whether the price or volume effect dominates. In **Table 3.2**, Case 1, the increase in export volumes and decrease in import volumes are not sufficient to outweigh the fact that less is received for exports and more has to be paid for imports. The result is that the current balance moves from balance into deficit. Approximate elasticities sum to 0.45. In Case 2, the increased export volumes and decreased volume of imports exactly match the decreased earnings per unit of exports and increased expenditure per unit of imports so that the current balance is unchanged. Approximate elasticities sum to 0.9 which is close to unity. In

Case 3, the increased volume of export sales and decreased volume of imports are sufficient to outweigh the price effects so that the current balance improves following a devaluation. Approximate elasticities sum to 1.5 which fulfils the critical Marshall–Lerner condition for a successful devaluation.

A more complicated formula can be derived which allows for supply elasticities of exports and imports of less than infinity, see for example, Gandolfo (1987, pp. 104–8). The effect of less than infinite supply elasticities is to make the required demand elasticities less stringent in the sense that the current account may improve even if the sum of the demand elasticities is less than unity. If the supply elasticities of exports and imports are less than infinite, an increase in demand for exports will lead to a some rise in the domestic price of exports which will give an additional boost to export revenues. Similarly, the fall in the demand for foreign imports will have the effect of reducing the foreign currency price of imports so lowering import expenditure. Both these effects are absent under the infinite supply elasticities that we have assumed.

3.5 Empirical evidence on import and export demand elasticities

The possibility that a devaluation may lead to a worsening rather than improvement in the balance of payments led to much research into empirical estimates of the elasticity of demand for exports and imports. Economists divided up into two camps popularly known as 'elasticity optimists' who believed that the sum of these two elasticities tended to exceed unity and 'elasticity pessimists' who believed that these elasticities tended to less than unity. It was argued that a devaluation may work better for industrialised countries than for developing countries. Many developing countries are heavily dependent upon imports so that their price elasticity of demand for imports was likely to be very low. While for industrialised countries that had to face competitive export markets the price elasticity of demand for their exports may be quite elastic. The implication of the Marshall–Lerner condition was that devaluation may be a cure for some countries' balance-of-payments deficits but not for others.

There are enormous problems involved in estimating the elasticity of demand for imports and exports. A summary by Gylfason (1987) of ten econometric studies undertaken between 1969 and 1981 has shown that the Marshall–Lerner condition is fulfilled for all of the 15 industrial and nine developing countries surveyed and the results are shown in **Table 3.3**. The results are based on estimates of the elasticities over a two-to-three-year time horizon. As such, while the table demonstrates clearly that a devaluation will improve the current account over a two-to-three-year time span, it does not preclude an initial worsening. Indeed, a study by Artus and Knight (1984) has shown that for up to a period of six months estimated price elasticities are invariably so low that the Marshall–Lerner conditions are not fulfilled.

A general consensus accepted by most economists is that elasticities are lower in the short run than in the long run, in which case the Marshall–Lerner conditions may not hold in the short run but may hold in the medium to long run. Goldstein and Kahn (1985) in an excellent survey of the empirical literature conclude that, in general, long-run elasticities (greater than two years) are approximately twice as much as short-run elasticities (0–6 months). Further, the short-run elasticities generally fail to sum to unity while the long-run elasticities almost always sum to greater than unity.

The possibility that in the short run the Marshall–Lerner conditions may not be fulfilled although it generally holds over the longer run, leads to the phenomenon of what is popularly known as the *J*-curve effect which is illustrated in **Figure 3.2**.

The idea underlying the *J*-curve effect is that in the short run export volumes and import volumes do not change much so that the country receives less export revenue and spends more on imports leading to a deterioration in the current account balance. However, after a time lag export volumes start to increase and import volumes start to decline. Consequently the current account deficit starts to improve and eventually moves into surplus. The issue then is whether the initial deterioration in the current account is less than the future improvement so that overall devaluation can be said to work.

There have been numerous reasons advanced to explain the slow responsiveness of export and import volumes in the short run and why the response is far greater in the longer run. Three of the most important are:

A time lag in consumer responses – It takes time for consumers in both the devaluing country and the rest of the world to respond to the changed competitive situation. Switching away from foreign imported goods to domestically produced goods inevitably takes some time because consumers will be worried about issues other than the price change, such as the reliability and reputation of domestic produced goods as compared with the foreign imports, while foreign consumers may be reluctant to switch away from domestically produced goods towards the exports of the devaluing country.

A time lag in producer responses – Even though a devaluation improves the competitive position of exports it will take time for domestic producers to expand production of exportables. In addition, the orders for imports are

Table 3.3 *The elasticity of demand for exports and imports of fifteen industrial and nine developing countries*

	Elasticity of export demand	Elasticity of import demand	Sum
Industrial Countries			
Austria	1.02	1.23	2.25
Belgium	1.12	1.27	2.39
Canada	0.68	1.28	1.96
Denmark	1.04	0.91	1.95
France	1.28	0.93	2.21
Germany	1.02	0.79	1.81
Iceland	0.83	0.87	1.70
Italy	1.26	0.78	2.04
Japan	1.40	0.95	2.35
Netherlands	1.46	0.74	2.20
Norway	0.92	1.19	2.11
Sweden	1.58	0.88	2.46
Switzerland	1.03	1.13	2.16
United Kingdom	0.86	0.65	1.51
United States	1.19	1.24	2.43
Average	1.11	0.99	2.10
Developing Countries			
Argentina	0.6	0.9	1.5
Brazil	0.4	1.7	2.1
India	0.5	2.2	2.7
Kenya	1.0	0.8	1.8
Korea	2.5	0.8	3.3
Morocco	0.7	1.0	1.7
Pakistan	1.8	0.8	2.6
Philippines	0.9	2.7	3.6
Turkey	1.4	2.7	4.1
Average	1.1	1.5	2.6

Notes:
The above estimates refer to elasticities over a 2–3 year period. Estimates are based upon the results of a number of different studies. Individual studies give differing estimates depending on the time periods involved, the econometric methodology employed and the particular data set used.
Source: T. Gylfason, 'Does Exchange Rate Policy Matter?', *European Economic Review*, vol. 30 (1987), p. 377.

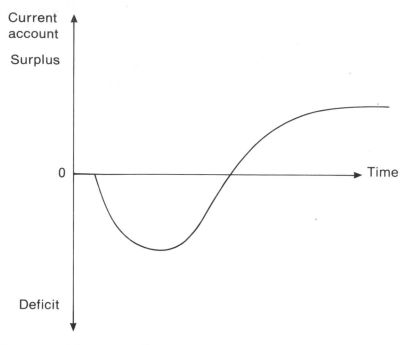

Figure 3.2 *The J-curve effect*

normally made well in advance and such contracts are not readily cancelled in the short run. Factories will be reluctant to cancel orders for vital inputs and raw materials. For example, the waiting list for a Boeing aeroplane can be over five years; it is most unlikely that a British airline will cancel the order just because the pound has been devalued. Also the payments for many imports will have been hedged against exchange risk in the forward market and so will be left unaffected by the devaluation.

Imperfect competition – Building up a share of foreign markets can be a time consuming and costly business. This being the case, foreign exporters may be very reluctant to lose their market share in the devaluing country and might respond to the loss in their competitiveness by reducing their export prices. To the extent that they do this, the rise in the cost of imports caused by the devaluation will be partly offset. Similarly, foreign import competing industries may react to the threat of increased exports by the devaluing country by reducing prices in their home markets, limiting the amount of additional exports of the devaluing country. These effects rely upon some degree of imperfect competition which gives foreign firms some supernormal profit margins enabling them to reduce their prices. If foreign firms were in a highly competitive environment they would only be making normal profits and so would be unable to reduce their prices.

In addition to the above effects it is unlikely that the price of exports as measured in the domestic prices will remain fixed. Many imports used as inputs for exporting industries and the increased price of imports may lead to higher wage costs as workers seek compensation for higher import prices; this will to some extent lead to a rise in export prices reducing the competitive advantage of the devaluation.

■ *3.6* The absorption approach

One of the major defects of the elasticity approach is that it is based upon the assumption that all other things are equal. However, changes in export and import volumes will by definition have implications for national income and consequently income effects need to be incorporated in a more comprehensive analysis of the effects of a devaluation. Alexander (1952) is one of the most important papers evaluating this effect; his paper focuses on the fact that a current account imbalance can be viewed as the difference between domestic output and domestic spending (absorption).

Taking the equation for national income:

$$Y = C + I + G + X - M \tag{3.21}$$

Defining domestic absorption as $A = C + I + G$ equation (3.21), can be rearranged as follows:

$$CA = X - M = Y - A \tag{3.22}$$

Equation (3.22) says that the current balance represents the difference between domestic output and domestic absorption. A current account surplus means that domestic output exceeds domestic spending, while a current account deficit means that domestic output is less than domestic spending. Transforming equation (3.22) into difference form yields.

$$dCA = dY - dA \tag{3.23}$$

What equation (3.23) implies is that the effects of a devaluation on the current balance will depend upon how it affects national income relative to how it affects domestic absorption. If a devaluation raises domestic income relative to domestic spending the current account improves. If, however, devaluation raises domestic spending relative to domestic income the current account deteriorates. Understanding how devaluation affects both income and absorption is therefore central to the absorption approach to balance-of-payments analysis.

Absorption can be divided up into two parts: a rise in income will lead to an increase in absorption which is determined by the marginal propensity to absorb, *a*. There will also be a 'direct effect' on absorption which is all the other effects on absorption resulting from devaluation denoted by *Ad*. Thus the change in total absorption d*A*, is given by:

$$dA = adY + dAd \qquad (3.24)$$

Substituting (3.24) into equation (3.23) yields:

$$dCA = (1 - a)dY - dAd \qquad (3.25)$$

Equation (3.25) reveals that there are three factors that need to be examined when considering the impact of devaluation. A devaluation can affect the current balance only by changing the marginal propensity to absorb (*a*), changing the level of income (d*Y*) and by affecting direct absorption (d*Ad*). The condition for a devaluation to improve the current balance is:

$$(1 - a)dY > dAd$$

that is, any change in income not spent on absorption must exceed any change in direct absorption.

To consider whether the above condition is likely to be fulfilled it is worth distinguishing two possible states of an economy: below full employment so that income may rise and full employment so that national income cannot rise.

 ## 3.7 The effects of a devaluation on national income

Clearly a relevant question if the economy is at less than full employment is whether a devaluation is likely to raise or lower national income. If the marginal propensity to absorb is less than unity then a rise in income will raise the income to absorption ratio and so improve the current account. Whereas, if income were to fall this would raise the absorption to income ratio (as absorption would fall by less than income) which would worsen the current account. There are two important effects on income that need to be examined, the employment effect and the terms of trade effect.

Employment effect – If the economy is at less than full employment, then providing the Marshall–Lerner condition is fulfilled, there will be an increase in net exports following a devaluation which will lead to an increase in national income via the foreign trade multiplier. However, if the Marshall-Lerner condition is not fulfilled then net exports will fall implying that national income falls. Hence, it is not clear whether the employment effect will raise or lower national income.

Terms of trade effect – The terms of trade are the price of exports divided by the price of imports. The terms of trade can be expressed algebraically as:

$$\frac{\text{Price of exports}}{\text{Price of imports}} = \frac{P}{SP^*}$$

where P is the domestic price of exports, P^* is the price of imports, and S is the exchange rate (domestic currency units per unit of foreign currency).

A devaluation (a rise in S) tends to make imports more expensive in domestic currency terms which is not matched by a corresponding rise in export prices, this means that the terms of trade deteriorate. A deterioration in the terms of trade represents a loss of real national income because more units of exports have to be given to obtain a unit of imports. Hence, the terms of trade effect lowers national income.

Overall, the effects of a devaluation on the income of the devaluing country are ambiguous. Even if there are increased net exports earnings (which relies on the Marshall–Lerner condition being fulfilled) the negative terms of trade effect works to reduce national income.

Even if income rises overall, it is still not clear what the implications of a rise in income are for the current account; this will depend upon the value of the marginal propensity to absorb. If this is less than unity then an increase in income generated by the increase in net exports leads to an improvement in the current balance because income rises by more than absorption. If, however, the marginal propensity to absorb is greater than unity then the increased income would lead to an even bigger rise in absorption resulting in a worsening of the current account. Although one may think that the marginal propensity to absorb will be less than unity, this need not be the case. Alexander speculated that unemployed workers who obtain jobs are likely to have a high propensity to consume and that an increase in income may well stimulate a great deal of investment. Workers who obtain jobs may well decide to spend more than their income by borrowing against future prospective income. Similarly as the economy expands firms, expenditure may exceed their revenues as they undertake significant investment in the expectation of high future profits. Hence, it is conceivable in the short run that the marginal propensity to absorb could be greater than unity, so that a rise in income leads to a deterioration in the current account.

Of course, if the economy is at a position of full employment, an increase in income is not possible. In this instance for a devaluation to improve the current account deficit would require a reduction in direct absorption. Income changes are only one of the factors influencing the current balance. The other effect that we need to consider is the impact on direct absorption.

3.8 The effects of devaluation on direct absorption

For the moment, let us assume that the net effect of a devaluation on income is zero. This being the case, we must consider the effect of the devaluation on direct absorption. If the devaluation reduces direct absorption then a devaluation will lead to an improvement in the current balance. Whereas if direct absorption increases then the effect on the current balance will lead to a deterioration of the current account. Let us now consider possible ways in which a devaluation can be expected to impact upon direct absorption.

Real balance effect – A simple formulation of the demand to hold money is that it is a demand to real money balances. If prices double then agents will demand twice as much money as before. Algebraically a money demand function can be expressed as:

$$M/P_1 = k \tag{3.26}$$

where k is some constant and P_1 is an aggregate price index defined as:

$$P_1 = \alpha P + (1 - \alpha) SP^* \tag{3.27}$$

where α is the percentage of expenditure on domestic goods, P is the price of the domestic good, P^* is the price of the foreign import good, and S is the exchange rate defined as domestic currency units per unit of foreign currency.

For example, assume that the price of the domestic good (P) is £1 while the price of the foreign good (P^*) is \$4 and the pre-devaluation exchange rate is £0.5/\$1. Further, that domestic consumers spend 80 per cent of their money on domestic goods $\alpha = 0.8$ then the average price level is:

$$P_1 = 0.8 \, £1 + 0.2 \, \$4 \, (£0.5/\$1) = £1.20$$

If the pound is devalued to £1/\$1 then the average price level becomes:

$$P_1 = 0.8 \, £1 + 0.2 \, \$4 \, (£1/\$1) = £1.60$$

Hence, a 100 per cent devaluation of the pound will raise the average price index facing UK consumers by approximately 33 per cent.

Given an unchanged money stock and the assumption that economic agents aim to maintain a given amount of real money balances as depicted in equation (3.26) then a devaluation (rise in S) by raising the overall price index in (3.27) means that economic agents have to maintain their real balances by cutting down on direct absorption. Economic agents will attempt to increase their money balances by selling bonds; this pushes down the price of bonds and raises the domestic interest rate. The rise in interest rates will reduce investment and consumption, so reducing direct absorption.

For the real balance effect to come into play, it must be emphasised that the authorities must not accommodate the increased money demand by increasing the money supply. If they raise the money supply in line with the increased money demand, this would leave the ratio M/P_1 constant so that the real balance effect will not come into play.

Income redistribution effect – The rise in the general price index (equation (3.27)) resulting from a devaluation is likely to have a number of effects on the income distribution. To the extent that it redistributes income from those with a low marginal propensity to absorb to those with a high marginal propensity to absorb this will increase direct absorption. While to the extent the reverse is true, it will lower direct absorption. A few possibilities in this respect are:

(a) The rise in the general price index will tend to reduce the real income of those with fixed incomes but if overall income is unchanged then those with variable incomes will have gained. It tends to be the case that the group on fixed incomes are the poor who have a high propensity to absorb while those on variable incomes are better off and have a lower propensity to absorb. To the extent that income is redistributed from those with fixed incomes to those with variable incomes, this income redistribution effect will tend to reduce direct absorption.

(b) A devaluation often leads to an improvement of company profits through increased sales in export and import competing industries while real wages are reduced by the rise in the aggregate price index and take time to catch up. The effect on direct absorption of this redistribution is not clear. While firms may have a lower tendency to absorb than workers this will be very much dependent on their expectations about the future. If these expectations are very favourable then the devaluation and profits rise may stimulate investment and even raise direct absorption.

(c) There may be considerable income adjustments within groups of companies and workers. Some companies' profits will benefit from a devaluation as export sales rise; however, some firms that are reliant on imported inputs may find the cost rises reduce their profit margins. Similarly, some workers will be able to protect themselves against the induced price rise because they are represented by strong trade unions while others with no union representation may not secure compensating pay rises. The overall effect on direct absorption will then depend on whether the companies and workers that gain have a higher propensity to absorb than those that lose.

Overall, it is extremely difficult to say whether the income redistribution effects will raise or lower direct absorption.

Money illusion effect – It is possible that even though prices rise because of the devaluation consumers suffer money illusion and buy exactly the same bundle of goods as before, even though their real spending power has been reduced. If this is the case they are actually spending more on direct absorption than before. However, the money illusion effect may work in reverse and consumers because of the price rises may actually decide to cut back direct absorption in more than proportion to the price rise so that direct absorption falls. Whatever way the money illusion effect works it is unlikely to be that significant and is most probably only a temporary rather than permanent factor.

Expectational effects – It is possible that economic agents regard the price rises induced by devaluation as likely to spark further price rises. This would lead to an increase in direct absorption which would worsen the balance of payments. However, against this it can be argued that inflationary expectations may reduce investment which lowers direct absorption.

Laursen–Metzler effect – Laursen and Metzler (1950) noted that the deterioration in the terms of trade following a devaluation will have two effects on absorption, an income effect and a substitution effect. While the deterioration in the terms of trade lowers national income and thereby income related absorption it also makes domestically produced goods relatively cheaper compared with foreign produced goods, which implies a substitution effect in favour of domestically produced goods. Since domestically produced goods become relatively cheaper this will tend to raise direct absorption. If the positive substitution effect outweighs the negative income effect Laursen and Metzler noted that a deterioration of the terms of trade could lead to a net rise in absorption.

Hence, the effects of a devaluation on direct absorption are ambiguous. While the real money balance effect works to lower direct absorption all the other effects may raise or lower direct absorption.

Since we do not know if the marginal propensity to absorb is greater or less than unity, if income rises or falls, or if direct absorption rises or falls, the effects of a devaluation are indeterminate. Indeed, the picture will become much more complex once it is recognised that all the differing effects take place at different speeds over time and that some effects will be more significant in certain economies than in others. Overall, the approach suggests that a devaluation will have many diverse and often conflicting effects on the current account.

None the less, the absorption approach has some important lessons for policy makers. Its central message is that raising domestic income relative to domestic absorption will improve the current balance. In this respect, a devaluation is more likely to succeed if it is accompanied by economic policy measures that concentrate on raising income while constraining absorption.

3.9 A synthesis of the elasticity and absorption approaches

Initially, it was believed that the absorption approach was an alternative to the elasticities approach, the elasticity approach concentrating on price effects while the absorption approach concentrated on income effects. However, authors such as Tsiang (1961), and Alexander (1959) himself, showed that the two models are not substitutes; rather they are complementary.

To understand this complementarity, consider the effects of a devaluation on income. Exports will increase more than imports, so raising income only if the Marshall–Lerner elasticities condition is fulfilled. If the Marshall–Lerner condition is not fulfilled, then exports will rise by less than imports implying that income will fall. Hence, the Marshall-Lerner condition is clearly relevant to the absorption approach. Similarly, when account is taken of income effects the necessary elasticity conditions for a devaluation to improve the current balance is affected. This is because if the elasticities sum to greater than unity so that there is an initial improvement in the current balance, this improvement leads to an increase in income which induces a larger increase in imports than in the absence of such an income effect. For this reason, the initial improvement in the current balance has to be more pronounced than in the absence of such income effects. This implies that the sum of elasticities has to be somewhat greater than the unity value derived from the elasticity approach. Thus, the absorption approach is relevant to the elasticity approach.

3.10 Conclusions

We have seen that the absorption approach like the elasticity approach does not provide an unambiguous answer to the question of whether a devaluation leads to an improvement in the current balance. At issue is how economic agents respond to the change in relative prices that is implied by a devaluation. The two analyses are not alternative theories but rather complementary insights into the processes at work.

Although the two models are comparatively static in nature, they both point to the importance of dynamic forces and a time dimension to the eventual outcome. Demand elasticities are higher in the long run than in the short leading to a possible *J*-curve effect and the effects of a devaluation on income and absorption will be spread over time. Even in these simple models it is seen that there are likely to be a variety of forces at work. No doubt even greater ambiguity would emerge as a result of including time lags, wealth effects and an explicit treatment of expectations.

Despite their simplistic assumptions, ambiguous·conclusions and deficiencies the two approaches have remained influential because they contain clear and useful messages for policy makers. A devaluation is more likely to succeed when elasticities of demand for imports and exports are high and when it is accompanied by measures such as fiscal and monetary restraint that boost income relative to domestic absorption.

The overwhelming weight of empirical estimates suggests that at two years and above horizon the Marshall–Lerner conditions are fulfilled, suggesting that exchange-rate adjustments are an influential tool in eliminating current account deficits. One should not expect a devaluation to work in the same manner for all countries. It will in part be determined by whether or not the economy is at or below full employment and on the structural parameters of the particular economy under consideration. Finally, it should be remembered that both models assume that foreign countries do not react to the competitive advantage gained by the devaluing country. To the extent that they react by devaluing their currencies this will undermine the effectiveness of a devaluation policy.

■ Selected further readings

Alexander, S. (1952) 'Effects of a Devaluation on a Trade Balance', *IMF Staff Papers*, pp. 263–78. Reprinted in R.E. Caves and H.G. Johnson (1968) (eds), *Readings in International Economics* (Homewood, Illinois: Irwin).

Alexander, S. (1959) 'Effects of a Devaluation: A Simplified Synthesis of Elasticities and Absorption Approaches, *American Economic Review*, vol. 49, pp. 22–42.

Artus, J.R. and Knight, M.D. (1984) Issues in the Assessment of the Exchange Rates of Industrial Countries, *IMF Occasional Paper, No. 29*.

Goldstein, M. and Kahn, M.S. (1985) 'Income and Price Effects in Foreign Trade', in R. W. Jones and P.B. Kenen, *Handbook of International Economics*, vol. II (Amsterdam: Elsevier).

Gandolfo, G. (1987) *International Economics*, vol. 2 (New York: Springer-Verlag).

Gylfason, T. (1987) 'Does Exchange Rate Policy Matter?', *European Economic Review*, vol. 30, pp. 375–81.

Johnson, H.G. (1976) 'Elasticity, Absorption, Keynesian Multiplier, Keynesian Policy and Monetary Approaches to Devaluation Theory: a Simple Geometric Exposition', *American Economic Review*.

Laursen, S. and Metzler, L.A. (1950) 'Flexible Exchange Rates and the Theory of Employment', *Review of Economics and Statistics*.

Lerner, A. (1944) *The Economics of Control* (London: Macmillan).

Machlup, F. (1939) 'The Theory of Foreign Exchanges', *Economica*, vol. 6, pp. 375–97.

Machlup, F. (1943) *International Trade and the National Income Multiplier* (Philadelphia: Blakiston).

Machlup, F. (1955) 'Relative Prices and Aggregate Spending in the Analysis of Devaluation', *American Economic Review*, June 1955.

Marshall, A. (1923) *Credit and Commerce* (London: Macmillan).

Meade, J. (1951) *The Theory of International Economic Policy*, vol. 1, *The Balance of Payments* (London: Oxford University Press).

Robinson, J. (1937) 'The Foreign Exchanges', in J. Robinson, *Essays in the Theory of Employment* (Oxford: Basil Blackwell).

Tsiang, S.C. (1961) 'The Role of Money in Trade Balance Stability: Synthesis of the Elasticity and Absorption Approaches', *American Economic Review*, vol. 51, pp. 912–36.

■ *Chapter 4* ■

Macroeconomic Policy in an Open Economy

■ *4.1* Introduction

In Chapter 3, we looked at some of the fundamental identities for an open economy and considered the possible effect of devaluation on the current account. It was noted that the ultimate impact of a devaluation will in large part be dependent upon the economic policies that accompany the devaluation. In this chapter, we shall be examining how both exchange-rate changes and macroeconomic policies impact upon an open economy. A fundamental difference between an open economy and a closed economy is that over time a country has to ensure that there is an approximate balance in its current account. This is because no country can continuously build up a stock of net liabilities to the rest of the world by running a continuous current account deficit. Conversely, it does not make sense for a surplus country to continuously build up a stock of net claims on the rest of the world. Eventually it will wish to spend those claims.

The need for economic policy makers to pay attention to the implications of changes in monetary and fiscal policy on the balance of payments is an important additional dimension for consideration in the formulation of economic policy in an open economy. Ensuring a sustainable balance-of-payments position over time is an important economic objective to go along with high economic growth, low unemployment and low inflation.

One of the additional policy choices that has to be made by the authorities of an open economy is to decide whether to fix the exchange rate, allow it to float, or, perhaps choose some arrangement between these two extremes. The choice between these two regimes is the focus of analysis of Chapter 10; in this chapter we concentrate upon how fiscal and monetary policy operate under both regimes.

 ## 4.2 The problem of internal and external balance

To appreciate the development of the post war literature on open economies readers need to bear in mind that between 1948 and 1973 the international monetary system was one of fixed exchange rates, with the major currencies being pegged to the US dollar. Only in cases of 'fundamental disequilibrium' were authorities allowed to devalue or revalue their currency. This meant that there was considerable interest in the relative effectiveness of fiscal and monetary policies as a means of influencing the economy. Although economic policy makers generally have many macroeconomic aims the discussion in the 1950s and 1960s was primarily concerned with two objectives. The principal goal was one of achieving full employment for the labour force along with a stable level of prices which may be termed internal balance. Although governments were generally committed to achieving full employment it is widely recognised that expanding output in an open economy will have implications for the balance of payments. For instance, expanding output and employment will result in greater expenditure on imports and consequently lead to a deterioration of the current account. As authorities had agreed to maintain fixed exchange rates, they were interested in running an equilibrium in the balance of payments, that is, balance in the supply and demand for their currency. This latter objective can be termed external balance.

Changes in fiscal and monetary policies which aim to influence the level of aggregate demand in the economy are termed **expenditure changing** policies. Whereas policies such as devaluation/revaluation of the exchange rate which attempt to influence the composition of spending as between domestic and foreign goods are known as **expenditure switching policies**.

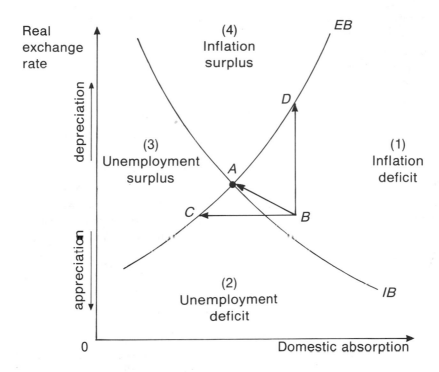

Figure 4.1 *The Swan diagram*

Much of the 1950s and 1960s literature was concerned with how the authorities might simultaneously achieve both internal and external balance. The policy problem of achieving both internal and external balance was conceptualised by Trevor Swan (1955) in what is known as the Swan diagram, which is depicted in **Figure 4.1**.

On the vertical axis we have the real exchange rate. The exchange rate is defined as domestic currency units per unit of foreign currency so that a rise represents a real depreciation which implies improved international competitiveness. On the horizontal axis we have the amount of real domestic absorption which represents the sum of consumption, investment and government expenditure.

The *IB* schedule represents combinations of the real exchange rate and domestic absorption for which the economy is in internal balance, that is, full employment with stable prices. The *IB* schedule is downward sloping from left to right. This is because an appreciation (fall) of the real exchange rate will reduce exports and increase imports, therefore to maintain full employment it is necessary for there to be an increase in domestic expenditure. To the right of the *IB* schedule there are inflationary pressures in the economy because for a given exchange rate domestic expenditure is greater than that required to produce full employment, while to the left there are deflationary pressures because expenditure is short of that required to maintain full employment.

The *EB* schedule shows combinations of the real exchange rate and domestic absorption for which the economy is in external balance, that is, equilibrium in the current account. The *EB* schedule is upward sloping from left to right. This is because a depreciation of the exchange rate will increase exports and reduce imports, so to prevent the current account moving into surplus requires increased domestic expenditure to induce an offsetting increase in imports. To the right of the *EB* schedule domestic expenditure is greater than that required for current account equilibrium so the result is a current account deficit, while to the left there is a current account surplus.

Hence, the Swan diagram is divided into four zones depicting different possible states for an economy:

Zone 1 – a deficit and inflationary pressures.
Zone 2 – a deficit and deflationary pressures.
Zone 3 – a surplus and deflationary pressures.
Zone 4 – a surplus and inflationary pressures.

Only at point A where the *IB* and *EB* schedules intersect is the economy in both internal and external equilibrium. Suppose that the economy for some reason finds itself at point B in zone 1, experiencing both inflationary pressures and a current account deficit. If the authorities maintain a fixed exchange rate and try to reduce the current account deficit by cutting back real domestic expenditure they move the economy towards point C. Achieving external balance by using expenditure reducing policies alone would require such a cut-back in absorption that the economy is pushed into recession with resulting unemployment. Alternatively, the authorities might try to tackle the deficit by devaluing the exchange rate, this has the effect of moving the economy towards point D on the *EB* schedule. While the devaluation has the effect of reducing the current account deficit it does so at the expense of adding further inflationary pressures to the economy. This is shown by the fact that the economy moves further away from the internal balance schedule.

A major lesson of this simple model is that the use of one instrument, be it fiscal expansion or devaluation, to achieve two targets, internal and external balance, is most unlikely to be successful. To move from point B to point A, the authorities need to both deflate the economy and undertake a devaluation by appropriate amounts. The deflation will control inflation and the devaluation improve the current account so that the two objectives can be met. The idea that a country generally requires as many instruments as it has targets was elaborated by the Nobel Prize winning Dutch economist Jan

Tinbergen (1952) and is popularly known as Tinbergen's instruments-targets rule.

While the Swan diagram provides a useful conceptual framework for economic policy discussion it is rather simplistic in that the underlying economic relationships are not explicitly defined. Furthermore, there is no role for international capital movements that were an increasingly important feature of the post-Second World War international economy. In addition there is no distinction made between monetary and fiscal policies as means of influencing aggregate demand and output in the economy. The so called Mundell–Fleming model to which we now turn attempts to integrate such features into a formal open economy macroeconomic model.

■ *4.3* The Mundell–Fleming Model

This model owes its origins to papers published by James Fleming (1962) and Robert Mundell (1962 and 1963). Their major contribution was to incorporate international capital movements into formal macroeconomic models based on the Keynesian *IS–LM* framework. Their papers led to some dramatic implications concerning the effectiveness of fiscal and monetary policy for the attainment of internal and external balance. We shall now examine the main implications of the Keynesian model and the results of Fleming's and Mundell's papers by using what is known as *IS–LM–BP* analysis. First we derive the *IS*, *LM* and *BP* schedules that provide the framework for the analysis.

4.4 The derivation of the IS schedule for an open economy

The *IS* schedule for an open economy shows various combinations of the level of output (Y) and rate of interest that make leakages, that is, savings and import expenditure ($S + M$) equal to injections, that is, investment, government expenditure and exports ($I + G + X$).

In an open economy we have the identity:

$$Y = C + I + G + X - M \tag{4.1}$$

where Y is national income, C is domestic consumption, I is domestic investment, G is government expenditure, X is export expenditure and M is import expenditure.

This identity can be restated in terms of equality between leakages and injections. Since $Y - C = S$, where S is savings we can rewrite (4.1) as:

$$S + M = I + G + X \tag{4.2}$$

For simplicity the following linear relationships are assumed:

$$S = S_a + sY \qquad (4.3)$$

Equation (4.3) says that savings are equal to autonomous savings (S_a) plus savings which are a positive function of income, where s is the marginal propensity to save.

$$M = M_a + mY \qquad (4.4)$$

Equation (4.4) says that imports are equal to autonomous imports (M_a) plus imports which are a positive function of increases in income, where m is the marginal propensity to import.

$$I = I(r) \qquad dI/dr < 0 \qquad (4.5)$$

Equation (4.5) says that investment is assumed to be an inverse function of the rate of interest. As far as government expenditure and exports are concerned these are assumed to be autonomous with respect to the rate of interest and level of national income.

The preceding relationships are depicted in **Figure 4.2**.

Quadrant [1] depicts the relationship between leakages and income, it is an upward sloping line because increases in income lead to increased savings and imports, the slope of the line is given by $(s + m) < 1$. At income level Y1, the corresponding level of leakages is given by $L1$ and likewise at income level Y2 the corresponding level of leakages is given by $L2$. The resulting volume of leakages is transferred to quadrant [2] which has a 45° line that converts any distance along the vertical axis to an equivalent distance on the horizontal axis which measures injections. Hence, the leakages $L1$ are converted into an equivalent amount of injections In_1.

The injections schedule is depicted in quadrant [3]. This schedule shows that given the price level and state of expectations the rate of interest that leads to a level of injections In_1 is given by $r1$. The injections schedule is downward sloping from left to right because investment is inversely related to the rate of interest while the level of government expenditure and exports are assumed to be independent of the rate of interest.

We now know that the income level Y1 generates leakages $L1$ which will be equal to injections In_1 if the interest rate is $r1$. This means that in quadrant [4] we can depict a point on the *IS* curve for an open economy because at interest rate $r1$ and income level Y1 we know that leakages are equal to injections. We can repeat the same process for the income level Y2 to obtain the rate of interest $r2$ for which leakages are equal to injections. By repeating the process we can obtain a large number of income and interest rate levels for which leakages are equal to injections. By joining up these points we obtain the *IS* schedule for an open economy. As can be seen in quadrant [4] the *IS* schedule is downward sloping from left to right in the interest rate income level space. This is because higher levels of income

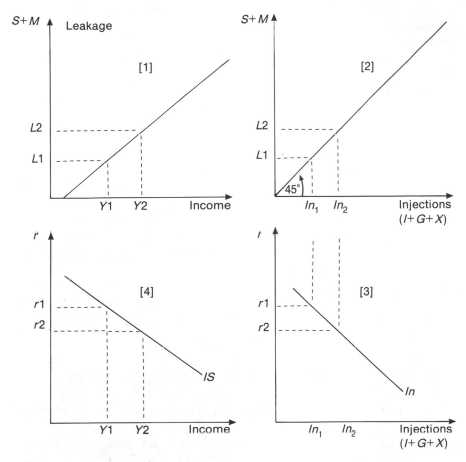

Figure 4.2 *The derivation of the IS schedule*

generate higher levels of leakages requiring a fall in the interest rate to generate increased investment and maintain equality of injections and leakages.

4.5 The derivation of the LM schedule for an open economy

The *LM* schedule shows various combinations of the level of income and rate of interest for which the money market is in equilibrium, that is, for which money demand equals money supply. In the simplified model, we assume that money is demanded for only two reasons; transactions purposes and speculative purposes. With the transactions motive people hold money because there is not normally a synchronisation between their receipt and expenditure of money. In general it is postulated that the higher an individual's income the larger the amount of money that is held for transactions purposes. This is based on the presumption that the higher one's income the greater one's payments and correspondingly the greater the desired holdings of money for transactions purposes. As such, the transactions demand for money is assumed to be a positive function of income. This is expressed algebraically as:

$$M_t = M_t(Y) \tag{4.6}$$

where M_t is the transactions demand for money.

The other reason for holding money is the speculative motive. It is assumed that any money balances held in excess of those required for transactions purposes are speculative balances. If the rate of interest rises then so does the opportunity cost of holding money. For instance, if the rate of interest is 5 per cent per annum the opportunity cost of £100 is £5 per annum but if the interest rate is 10 per cent the opportunity cost is £10 per annum, consequently the demand to hold speculative balances will fall as the rate of interest rises. This inverse relationship between the demand for speculative balances and the rate of interest is expressed algebraically as:

$$M_{sp} = M_{sp}(r) \tag{4.7}$$

where M_{sp} is the speculative demand for money.

In equilibrium, money demand (M_d) made up of transactions and speculative balances is equal to the money supply (M_s). This is expressed algebraically as: $M_d = M_{sp} + M_t = M_s (4.8)$. The derivation of the *LM* schedule is depicted in **Figure 4.3**.

Quadrant [1] depicts the transaction demand for money as a positive function of income. As income rises from Y1 to Y2 the demand for transaction balances rises from M_{t1} to M_{t2}. The transactions balance figure is transferred to quadrant [2] which shows the distribution of the fixed money supply between transaction and speculative balances. The distance $0a$ represents the total money supply so that if M_{t1} is held for transaction purposes then $0a$ minus M_{t1} which is equal to M_{sp1} is held as speculative balances. Quadrant [3] shows the speculative demand for money schedule which is downward sloping from left to right because the demand for speculative balances is inversely related to the rate of interest. The schedule reveals that speculative balances M_{sp1} are only willingly held at the interest rate r1. We now have enough information to plot a point on the *LM* schedule; this is done in quadrant [4] which shows that at interest rate r1 and income level Y1 the demand for speculative and transaction balances is equal to the money supply.

By taking another income level Y2 we can by a similar process find a rate of interest r2 which is compatible with money market equilibrium. Other

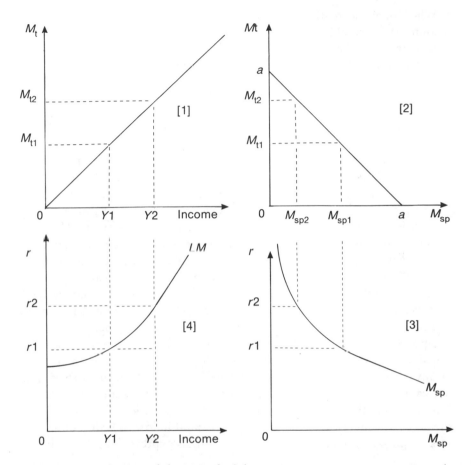

Figure 4.3 *Derivation of the LM schedule*

such derivations can be done and by joining them together we obtain the *LM* schedule. The *LM* schedule is upward sloping from left to right. This is because high income levels require relatively large transaction balances which for a given money supply can only be drawn out of speculative balances by a relatively high interest rate.

4.6 The derivation of the BP schedule for an open economy

The balance-of-payments schedule shows different combinations of rates of interest and income that are compatible with equilibrium in the balance of payments.

When referring to the balance of payments we divide it up into two sections; the current account and the capital account. Exports are assumed to be independent of the level of national income and the rate of interest but imports are assumed to be positively related to income, expressed algebraically as:

$$M = M_a + mY \qquad (4.9)$$

Total imports (M) are a function of autonomous imports (M_a) and the level of income, where m is the marginal propensity to import.

We now need to remind ourselves of the constituent parts of the balance of payments. As we saw in Chapter 2 the overall balance of payments is made up of three major components; the current account (CA), the capital account (K) and the change in the authorities reserves (dR). By maintaining balance in the supply and demand for the currency – that is external balance we mean that there is no need for the authorities to have to change their holdings of foreign exchange reserves. This implies that if there is a current account deficit there needs to be an offsetting surplus in the capital account so that the authorities do not have to change their reserves. Conversely, if there is a current account surplus there needs to be an offsetting deficit in the capital account to have equilibrium in the balance of payments.

Since exports are determined exogenously and imports are a positive function of income, the higher the level of national income the smaller will be any current account surplus or the larger any current account deficit. The net capital flow (K) is a positive function of the domestic interest rate. Assuming that the rate of interest in the rest of the world is fixed, the higher the domestic interest rate the greater the capital inflow into the country or smaller any capital outflow. This relationship is expressed algebraically as:

$$K = K(r) \qquad (4.10)$$

Since the balance of payments schedule shows various combinations of levels of income and the rate of interest for which the balance of payments is in equilibrium then:

$$X - M + K = 0 \qquad (4.11)$$

A positive K indicates a net inflow of funds whereas a negative K indicates a net outflow of funds. The derivation of the BP schedule is depicted in **Figure 4.4**.

Quadrant [1] shows the relationship between the current account and level of national income. The current balance schedule slopes downwards from left to right because increases in income lead to a deterioration of the current account. At income level Y1 there is a current account surplus of $CA1$ whereas at income level Y2 there is a current account deficit of $CA2$. The current account surplus or deficit is transferred to quadrant [2] where the 45° line converts the current account position to an equal capital flow of the

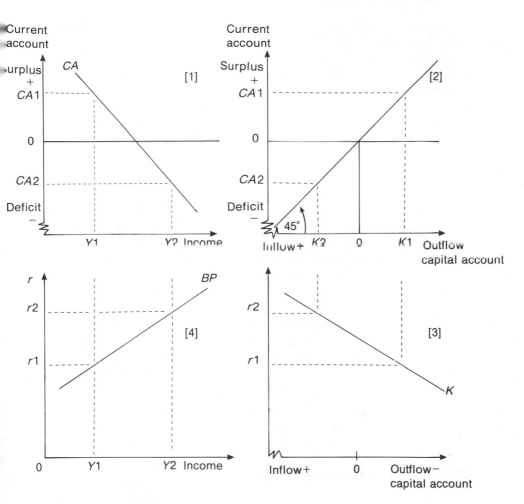

Figure 4.4 *Derivation of the BP schedule*

opposite sign. With a current account surplus CA1 there is a required capital outflow K1 to ensure balance-of-payments equilibrium, while a current account deficit CA2 requires a capital inflow K2. Quadrant [3] shows the rate of interest that is required for a given capital flow. The capital flow schedule is downward sloping from left to right because high interest rates encourage a net capital inflow whereas low interest rates encourage a net capital outflow. To get a capital outflow of K1 requires the interest rate to be r1, while a capital inflow of K2 requires a higher interest rate r2.

Since income level Y1 is associated with a balance-of-payments surplus there has to be an offsetting capital outflow K1 which requires an interest rate r1; these coordinates give a point on the BP schedule that is depicted in quadrant [4]. The BP schedule is upward sloping because higher levels of income cause a deterioration in the current account; this necessitates a reduced capital outflow/higher capital inflow requiring a higher interest rate. Every point on the *BP* schedule shows a combination of domestic income and rate of interest for which the overall balance of payments is in equilibrium. At points to the left of the *BP* schedule the overall balance of payments is in surplus because for a given amount of capital flows the current account is better than that required for equilibrium as the level of income is lower. Conversely, to the right of the *BP* schedule the overall balance of payments is in deficit as the income level is higher than that compatible with overall equilibrium.

At this point, it is worth noting, the slope of the *BP* schedule is determined by the degree of capital mobility internationally. The higher the degree of capital mobility then the flatter the *BP* schedule. This is because for a given increase in income which leads to a deterioration of the current account, the higher the degree of capital mobility, the smaller the required rise in the domestic interest rate to attract sufficient capital inflows to ensure overall equilibrium. When capital is perfectly mobile, the slightest rise in the domestic interest above the world interest rate leads to a massive capital inflow making the *BP* schedule horizontal at the world interest rate. At the other extreme, if capital is perfectly immobile internationally then a rise in the domestic interest will fail to attract capital inflows making the *BP* schedule vertical at the income level that ensures current account balance. Between these two extremes, that is, when we have an upward sloping *BP* schedule we say that capital is imperfectly mobile.

■ *4.7* Equilibrium of the model

In Figure 4.5 the *BP* schedule is steeper than the *LM* schedule. This need not always be the case. As we shall see later, changing the relative slope of the two schedules can lead to somewhat different policy prescriptions. All three schedules pass through a common point A which corresponds to the domestic interest rate $r1$ and income level $Y1$. The income level $Y1$ is seen to be less than that of the full employment level of income Y_f, implying that there is some unemployment in the economy. Although the economy is not in internal equilibrium, the balance of payments is in equilibrium because the *IS* and *LM* schedules intersect at a point on the *BP* schedule.

The explanation as to why the *IS-LM* schedules do not intersect at the full employment level of income Y_f is that at Y_f planned leakages (savings and import expenditure) would exceed planned injections (government expenditure, exports and investment). This would imply a build up of stocks of unsold goods leading producers to reduce output. Only at output

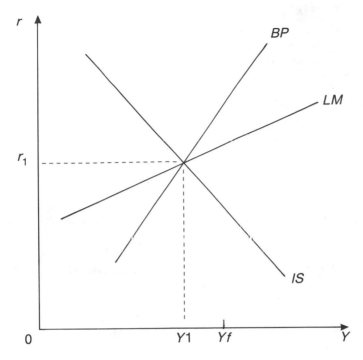

Figure 4.5 *Equilibrium of the model*

level Y1 do planned leakages equal planned injections so that changes in stocks are avoided.

In **Figures 4.6(a)** and **4.6(b)** we depict scenarios where there is a surplus and deficit respectively in the balance of payments.

In **Figure 4.6(a)** because the *IS* and *LM* schedules intersect to the left of the *BP* schedule there is a balance-of-payments surplus. This surplus comes about because the level of income is too low and/or the rate of interest is too high to be compatible with overall equilibrium. In **Figure 4.6(b)** there is a balance-of-payments deficit because the *IS* and *LM* schedules intersect to the right of the *BP* schedule; this means that the income level Y2 is too high and/or interest rate $r2$ too low inducing an overall balance-of-payments deficit.

■ *4.8* Factors shifting the IS–LM–BP schedules

In the analysis of the rest of this chapter we need to consider how changes in the exchange rate and monetary and fiscal policies affect the position of the various schedules.

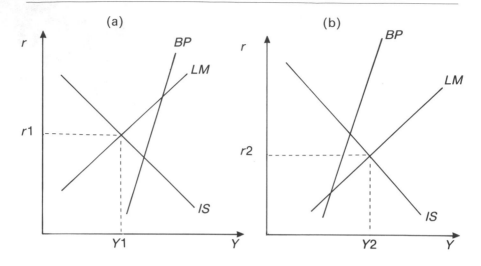

Figure 4.6 *Surplus and deficit in the balance of payments. (a) A surplus. (b) A deficit.*

☐ *Factors shifting the IS schedule*

The *IS* schedule will shift to the right if there is an increase in either investment, government expenditure or exports. This is because an increase in these injections requires a higher level of national income to induce a matching increase in leakages in the form of increased savings and imports. An autonomous fall in savings or imports will also require a rightward shift of the *IS* schedule because a higher level of income is required to induce more savings and import expenditure so as to maintain equality of leakages and injections. Another important factor that causes a rightward shift of the *IS* schedule is a depreciation or devaluation of the exchange rate, providing that the Marshall–Lerner condition holds; this is because a rise in the exchange rate leads to a reduction of import expenditure and an increase in export sales so that injections then exceed leakages requiring an increased level of income to bring them back into equality.

☐ *Factors shifting the LM schedule*

The *LM* schedule will shift to the right if there is an increase in the domestic money supply because for a given rate of interest the increased supply will only be willingly held if there is an increase in income which leads to a rise in transactions demand. A depreciation of the exchange rate will lead to a rise in the aggregate price index, that is, an index made up of a weighted basket of domestic and foreign imported goods (see equation (3.27)) because it implies a rise in the price of imports. This means that real money balances will be reduced and there will be a resulting increase in the demand for money that can only be eliminated by reducing the transactions demand for money implying a lower level of income and leftward shift of the *LM* schedule.

☐ *Factors shifting the BP schedule*

An autonomous increase in exports or autonomous decrease in imports will lead to an improvement in the current account requiring a rightward shift of the *BP* schedule to induce a sufficient increase in imports to maintain balance of payments equilibrium. Another factor that can cause a rightward shift of the *BP* schedule is a depreciation/devaluation of the exchange rate; providing the Marshall–Lerner condition holds, the value of export sales will rise and the value of import expenditure decline. Hence, the only way to ensure overall balance of payments equilibrium is a rise in the level of domestic income.

Bearing in mind these shift factors we proceed to look at how this tool-kit can be usefully applied to some key issues in the realm of open economy macroeconomic policy.

■ *4.9* Internal and external balance

The Swan diagram showed that authorities generally need as many instruments as they have targets and revealed that the use of both expenditure switching and expenditure changing policies can lead to the attainment of internal and external balance. However, it was not possible to distinguish between the fact that fiscal and monetary policies are quite different and independent types of expenditure changing policies. This begs the question as to whether or not it is feasible to achieve the twin objectives of internal and external balance by combining fiscal and monetary policies without the need to adjust the exchange rate?

Before attempting to answer this question we need to consider exactly how monetary and fiscal policy actually work.

☐ *Monetary policy*

When the authorities conduct an expansionary monetary policy they purchase bonds from the public. This pushes up the price of bonds and leads to a fall in the domestic interest rate. The fall in the domestic interest rate will stimulate investment and so lead to a rise in output. As far as the balance of payments is concerned the increased income leads to a deterioration of the current account and the lower interest rate will lead to increased capital outflows so that the balance of payments moves into deficit. Conversely, a contractionary monetary policy involves the authorities selling bonds; this pushes down the price of bonds and leads to a rise in the domestic interest rate. The rise in the interest rate leads to less investment and a fall in output. The balance-of-payments position will improve as imports fall and the higher interest rate attracts capital inflows.

☐ Fiscal policy

With an expansionary fiscal policy, the government increases its expenditure and with pure fiscal policy finances this increased expenditure by selling bonds. The increased expenditure shifts the *IS* schedule to the right having the government expenditure multiplier effect examined in Chapter 3. However, the bond sales will depress the price of bonds and thereby raise the domestic interest rate which will partially offset the expansion in output. The precise effect of the fiscal expansion on the balance of payments is indeterminate because while the expansion of output will worsen the current account the rise in interest rates will improve the capital account. The converse reasoning holds for a contractionary fiscal policy. Note that fiscal policy leaves the money supply in the hands of the private sector unchanged. The money raised from bond sales is re-injected into the economy via increased government expenditure.

☐ Sterilised and non-sterilised intervention

One other policy which we need to clarify is the distinction between sterilised and non sterilised intervention in the foreign exchange market. With sterilised intervention the authorities offset the money base implications of their exchange market interventions to ensure that the reserve changes due to intervention do not affect the domestic money base, whereas with a policy of non-sterilised intervention the authorities allow the reserve changes resulting from their interventions to affect the monetary base.

   Let us illustrate the distinction between sterilised and non-sterilised intervention by way of an example of what happens if there is a monetary expansion under fixed exchange rates. This is depicted in **Figure 4.7**.

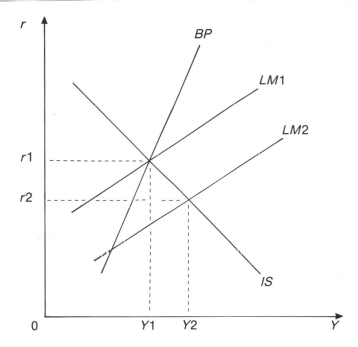

Figure 4.7 *A monetary expansion under fixed exchange rates*

A monetary expansion shifts the *LM* schedule to the right from *LM*1 to *LM*2. This causes a fall in interest rates to *r*2 and a rise in domestic income to Y2. The result is a balance of payments deficit as both the current and capital account deteriorate. The deficit means that there is an excess supply of the currency on the foreign exchange market and to maintain a fixed exchange the authorities have to purchase the home currency with reserves.

Ordinarily, the purchases of the home currency by the authorities would start to shift the *LM* schedule back to the left from *LM*2 back towards *LM*1. This is an example of non-sterilised intervention, that is, the authorities allow their interventions in the foreign exchange market to influence the money supply. However, if the authorities pursue a policy of sterilisation of reserve changes, the reserve falls which reduce the money supply are exactly offset by a further expansion of the money supply so that the *LM* schedule remains at point *LM*2. A clear problem with a sterilisation policy is that by remaining at *LM*2 with interest rate *r*2 and income level Y2 the authorities will suffer continuous balance-of-payments deficits and a continuous fall in reserves. Such a sterilisation policy is only feasible in the short run because over the longer run reserves would eventually run out making a devaluation inevitable.

We can are now in a position to examine how fiscal and monetary policy and exchange-rate policy can be combined in various combinations to simultaneously achieve internal and external balance.

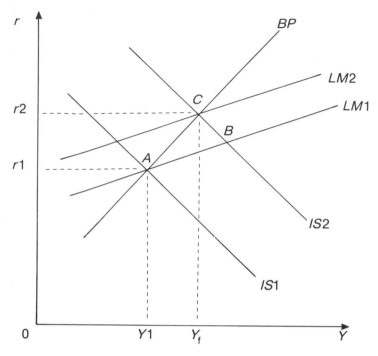

Figure 4.8 *Internal and external balance under a fixed exchange rate*

4.10 Internal and external balance under fixed exchange rates

A situation of fixed exchange rates and unemployment is depicted in **Figure 4.8**. The economy is assumed to be at point A with interest rate $r1$ and income level $Y1$ which means that while the economy is in external balance the income level is below the full employment level of income Y_f.

The government attempts to eradicate the unemployment via a bond financed fiscal expansion; this shifts the IS schedule to the right from $IS1$ to $IS2$. Domestic output expands from $Y1$ to Y_f and the economy would be at point B with excess output $r2$. In raising the level of output beyond the full employment level we find that the induced increase in imports moves the current account into deficit and although the rise in the interest rate attracts some capital inflow the balance of payments is in overall deficit since the economy is to the right of the BP schedule. The authorities are forced to purchase the home currency in the foreign exchange market but because they pursue a sterilisation policy the LM schedule remains at $LM1$. Hence, using only a single policy instrument, in this case fiscal policy, the government can temporarily achieve its internal objective at the expense of a sacrifice in the objective of external balance.

Ideally, however, the authorities would like to achieve both internal and external balance. This is possible if they combine the expansionary fiscal policy – IS1 to IS2 with a contractionary monetary policy which shifts the LM schedule from LM1 to LM2 where it passes through point C on the BP schedule. The restrictive monetary policy raises interest rates further than in the case of a solely fiscal expansion and in so doing attracts additional capital inflows so as to restore the balance of payments back to equilibrium. Hence, by combining an expansionary fiscal policy with a contractionary monetary policy the authorities can achieve both internal and external balance. An important lesson from this example is that the authorities can achieve both internal and external balance without the need to change the exchange rate; this is because they have two independent instruments, monetary and fiscal policy and two targets.

4.11 Internal and external balance under floating exchange rates

According to our analysis of the Swan diagram, by combining an exchange rate change with an expenditure changing policy, it is possible to achieve both internal and external balance. An interesting issue that we can explore within the framework of our model is what are the likely differences of achieving internal and external balance by combining exchange-rate changes with monetary policy as opposed to doing so by combining exchange-rate changes with fiscal policy. To examine this issue we firstly consider the case of combining exchange rate adjustments with monetary policy and then examine the implications of combining exchange rate adjustment with fiscal policy. **Figure 4.9** considers the case of monetary expansion under floating exchange rates.

In **Figure 4.9** initial equilibrium is at point A with interest rate r1 and output level Y1. The authorities adopt an expansionary monetary policy and this shifts the LM schedule from LM1 to LM2. The combination of a fall in the interest rate and increase in income leads to a balance-of-payments deficit at point B. However, the exchange rate is allowed to depreciate and this leads to a rightward shift of the IS schedule from IS1 to IS2 and a rightward shift of the BP schedule from BP1 to BP2. However, it also leads to a leftward shift of the LM schedule from LM2 to LM3 because of the rise in the prices index until all three schedules intersect at a common point like C with new income level Y2 and interest rate r2. Hence, by using monetary policy in conjunction with exchange-rate changes, it is possible to

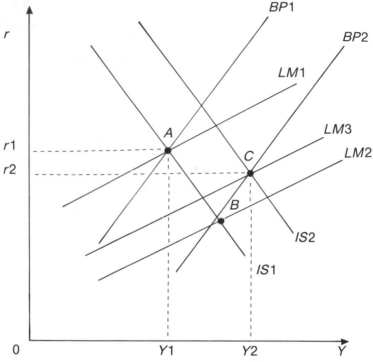

Figure 4.9   *A monetary expansion under floating exchange rates*

raise real output to the full employment level and achieve external balance simultaneously.

Overall, the money supply expansion results in an exchange-rate deprecia-tion, a fall in the domestic interest rate and an increase in income. The lower interest rate implies a lower capital inflow/higher capital outflow than before the money supply expansion, while the increase in income worsens the current account. This implies that the depreciation improves the current account to exactly offset the preceding effects.

Fiscal expansion under floating exchange rates

The effects of a fiscal expansion on the exchange rate under floating rates depend crucially upon the slope of the BP schedule relative to the LM schedule. We shall consider two cases: in case 1 the BP schedule is steeper than the LM schedule while in case 2 the reverse is true.

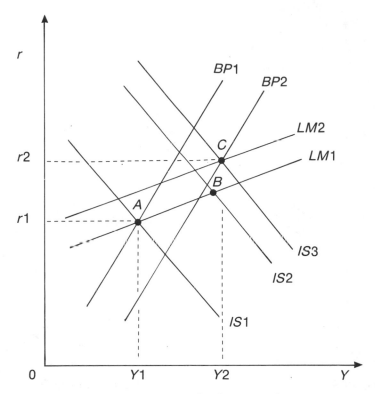

Figure 4.10   *Case 1: fiscal expansion under floating exchange rates*

In **Figure 4.10** the *BP* schedule is steeper than the *LM* schedule, which means that capital flows are relatively insensitive to interest-rate changes, while money demand is fairly elastic with respect to the interest rate.

In **Figure 4.10** an expansionary fiscal policy shifts the *IS* schedule from *IS*1 to *IS*2. The induced rise of the domestic interest rate and domestic income has opposing effects on the balance of payments; the expansion in real output leads to a deterioration of the current account but the rise in interest rate improves the capital account. However, because capital flows are relatively immobile the former effect outweighs the latter so the balance of payments moves into deficit. In turn, the deficit leads to a depreciation of the exchange rates; this has the effect of shifting the *BP* schedule to the right from *BP*1 to *BP*2 and the *LM* schedule to the left from *LM*1 to *LM*2 and the *IS* schedule even further to the right from *IS*2 to *IS*3. Final equilibrium is obtained at point C, with interest rate *r*2 and income level *Y*2. Hence, the deterioration in the balance of payments resulting from the rise in real income is offset by a combination of a higher interest rate and an exchange-rate depreciation.

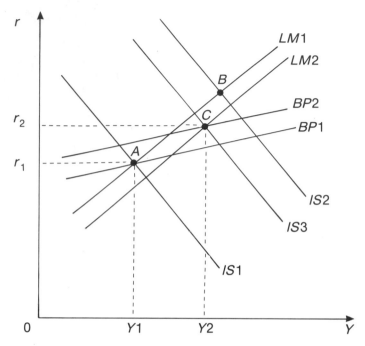

Figure 4.11   *Case 2: fiscal expansion under floating exchange rates*

In **Figure 4.11** an expansionary fiscal policy shifts the *IS* schedule from *IS1* to *IS2*. In this case because capital flows are much more responsive to changes in interest rates the *BP* schedule is less steep than the *LM* schedule. The increased capital inflow more than offsets the deterioration in the current account due to the increase in income and the balance of payments moves into surplus. The surplus induces an appreciation of the exchange rate, which moves the *LM* schedule to the right from *LM1* to *LM2* because of the fall in the price index, the *BP* schedule to the left from *BP1* to *BP2*, and the *IS* schedule to the left from *IS2* to *IS3*. Equilibrium is obtained at a higher level of output, higher interest rate and an exchange rate appreciation.

Hence a fiscal expansion can, according to the degree of international capital mobility, lead to either an exchange-rate depreciation or an exchange-rate appreciation.

 ## *4.12* A small open economy with perfect capital mobility

One prominent feature of the post Second World War international monetary system has been the increasing integration of international capital markets. There has been a great deal of discussion about the desirability of

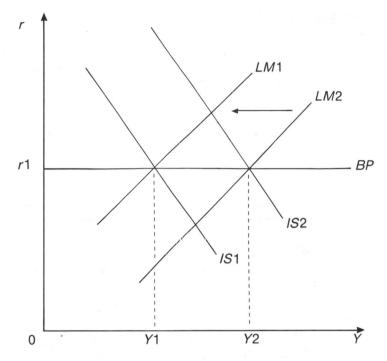

Figure 4.12 *Fixed exchange rates and perfect capital mobility*

these capital flows and how they might threaten the ability of authorities to conduct effective economic policies. In classic papers, Mundell (1962) and Fleming (1962) sought to examine the implications of high capital mobility for a small country that had no ability to influence world interest rates. Their papers showed that for such a country, the choice of exchange rate regime would have radical implications concerning the effectiveness of monetary and fiscal policy in influencing the level of economic activity.

The model assumes a small country facing perfect capital mobility. Any attempt to raise the domestic interest rate leads to a massive capital inflow to purchase domestic bonds pushing up the price of bonds until the interest rate returns to the world interest rate. Conversely, any attempt to lower the domestic interest rate leads to a massive capital outflow as international investors seek higher world interest rates. Such massive bonds sales mean that the domestic interest rate immediately returns to the world interest rate so as to stop the capital outflow. The implication of perfect capital mobility is that the *BP* schedule for a small open economy becomes a horizontal straight line at a domestic interest rate that is the same as the world interest rate.

Figure 4.12 depicts a small open economy with a fixed exchange rate. The initial level of income is where the *IS–LM* curves intersect at the income level

Y1 which is below the full employment level of income Y2. If the authorities attempt to raise output by a monetary expansion the *LM* schedule shifts right from *LM*1 to *LM*2. There is downward pressure on the domestic interest rate and this results in a massive capital outflow. This capital outflow means that there is pressure for a devaluation of the currency, and the authorities have to intervene in the foreign exchange market to purchase the home currency with reserves. Such purchases result in a reduction of the money supply in the hands of private agents. The purchases have to continue until the *LM* curve shifts back to its original position at *LM*1 where the domestic interest rate is restored to the world interest rate. With perfect capital mobility, any attempt to pursue a sterilisation policy leads to such large reserve losses that it cannot be pursued. Hence, with perfect capital mobility and fixed exchange rates, monetary policy is ineffective at influencing output.

By contrast if there is a fiscal expansion this shifts the *IS* schedule to the right from *IS*1 to *IS*2, which puts upward pressure on the domestic interest rate and leads to a capital inflow. To prevent an appreciation the authorities have to purchase the foreign currency with the domestic currency. This means that the amount of domestic currency held by private agents increases and the *LM*1 schedule shifts to the right. The increase in the money stock continues until the *LM* schedule passes through the *IS*2 schedule at the initial interest rate. Hence, under fixed exchange rates and perfect capital mobility an active fiscal policy alone has the ability to achieve both internal and external balance. This is an exception to the instruments-targets rule, although monetary policy does have to passively adjust to maintain the fixed exchange rate.

Floating exchange rates and perfect capital mobility

In **Figure 4.13** initial equilibrium is at the income level Y1 where the *IS*1 schedule intersects the *LM*1 schedule. In this case, we have a floating exchange rate. Suppose, the authorities attempt to expand output by an expansionary fiscal policy. The increased government expenditure shifts the *IS* schedule to the right from *IS*1 to *IS*2 but the bond sales that finance the expansion lead to upward pressure on the domestic interest rate resulting in a massive capital inflow and an appreciation of the exchange rate. The appreciation of the exchange rate results in a reduction of exports and increase in imports. This forces the *IS* schedule back to its original position. Hence, with a floating exchange rate and perfect capital mobility fiscal policy is ineffective at influencing real output.

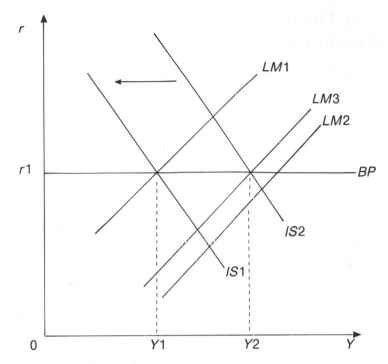

Figure 4.13   *Floating exchange rates and perfect capital mobility*

By contrast, a monetary expansion that shifts the *LM* schedule from *LM1* to *LM2* leads to a fall in the domestic interest rate and a depreciation of the exchange rate. This depreciation then leads to an increase in exports and reduction in imports that shifts the *IS* schedule to the right from *IS1* to *IS2* and some reduction of the real money stock shifting *LM2* to the left to, say, *LM3* so that overall income rises to *Y2*. In this instance, it is monetary policy alone which can achieve both internal and external balance although the exchange rate adjusts passively to the change in the money stock.

The contrast between the effectiveness of fiscal and monetary policy with perfect capital mobility under different exchange-rate regimes is one of the most famous results in international economics. Monetary policy is ineffective at influencing output under fixed exchange rates while it alone can influence output under floating exchange rates. By contrast, fiscal policy alone is effective at influencing output under a fixed exchange rate while it is ineffective under floating exchange rates.

4.13 The principle of effective market classification

While Tinbergen's instruments-targets rule shows us that we generally need two instruments to achieve both internal and external balance, it does not tell us which instrument should be assigned to which target. We have seen that we can use combinations of fiscal and monetary policy to achieve internal and external balance under fixed exchange rates or we can use combinations of monetary or fiscal policy under floating exchange rates.

Mundell (1968) suggested that what he called the principle of effective market classification should be used by economic policy makers in conjunction with Tinbergen's 'instruments-targets' rule. By the principle of effective market classification, Mundell stated that 'Policies should be paired with the objectives on which they have the most influence' (1962, p. 79). For instance, if monetary policy is the most effective instrument at controlling external balance and fiscal policy best at influencing output, then this is also the appropriate pairing of instruments to targets. The principle of effective market classification seems eminently sensible – by analogy a conductor should be assigned to conducting an orchestra and a doctor assigned to a hospital and not vice versa! What makes the Mundell principle of effective market classification interesting, is the suggestion that if this principle is not adopted economies may suffer from cyclical instability.

The problem for economic policy makers to determine which instruments to assign to which targets, is termed the 'assignment problem'. Mundell suggested that under fixed exchange rates monetary policy should be assigned to external balance and fiscal policy to internal balance. An illustration of the assignment problem is shown in **Figure 4.14**.

Figure 4.14 illustrates internal and external balance schedules for various fiscal and monetary policy stances under a fixed exchange rate regime. On the vertical axis we have monetary policy which is neutral at point N_m but expansionary above this while it is contractionary below. Similarly, the fiscal policy stance is neutral at point N_f and expansionary to the right and contractionary to the left. The internal balance schedule has a negative slope; this is because if we start at full employment a contractionary monetary policy has to be accompanied by an expansionary fiscal policy to maintain full employment. To the right of the *IB* schedule the fiscal/monetary policy mix is so expansionary as to cause inflation, whereas, to the left the fiscal/monetary policy mix is deflationary.

The external balance schedule may have a positive or negative slope; this is because an expansionary fiscal policy has two conflicting effects on the balance of payments as we saw in **Figures 4.10** and **4.11**. On the one hand, the increase in income leads to a deterioration in the current account which

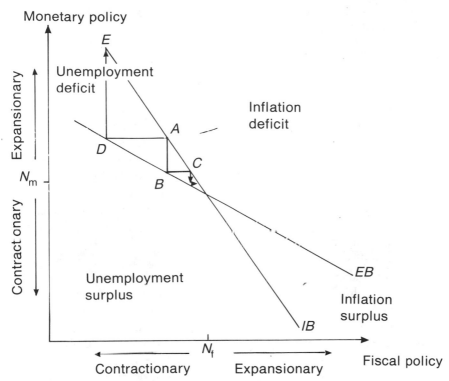

Figure 4.14   *The assignment problem*

worsens the balance of payments but on the other the rise in interest rates leads to an inflow of capital which improves the balance of payments. In **Figure 4.14** we have drawn the *EB* schedule with a negative slope meaning that an expansionary fiscal policy causes a net deterioration in the balance of payments (the current account effect dominates the capital account effect). This being the case, when fiscal policy is expansionary monetary policy has to be contractionary which by raising the domestic interest rate increases capital inflows to ensure equilibrium in the balance of payments.

The *IB* schedule is drawn steeper than the *EB* schedule. This must be the case because a fiscal expansion which causes a rise in income of x per cent will cause less of a deterioration in the balance of payments than a monetary policy that increases income by x per cent. This is because a fiscal expansion will lead to a rise in interest rates which leads to partially offsetting capital inflows while a money expansion leads to a fall in interest rates leading to an additional deterioration in the balance of payments above the income effect. Hence, monetary policy has more effect on external balance than fiscal policy. As monetary policy is relatively more effective at influencing external balance then fiscal policy is relatively more effective with respect to internal balance.

According to Mundell's classification if we are at point A with internal balance but a balance-of-payments deficit a contractionary monetary policy moves the economy to say point B on the external balance curve, but this leads to unemployment which is then tackled by an expansionary fiscal policy moving to point C on the internal balance curve. This pushes the economy back into deficit and is then accompanied by a monetary contraction to achieve external balance. Each time we need less and less adjustment of monetary and fiscal policy. We have a stable assignment as we are clearly converging to the intersection of the internal and external balance schedules.

Suppose policy makers get the assignment wrong and use fiscal policy to eradicate the balance-of-payments deficit and monetary policy for internal balance. In such circumstances, the fiscal contraction moves the economy from point A to point D, external balance is achieved but at the cost of high unemployment. If the authorities then use an expansionary monetary policy to achieve internal balance the economy moves from point D to point E. Clearly, such a policy assignment proves to be unstable moving the economy away from the simultaneous achievement of internal and external balance. The danger exists that the authorities could get the assignment wrong and cause considerable damage to the economy before they eventually reverse their assignment to the correct one. Given this, it may be wise to try to achieve targets gradually by adjusting policy instruments slowly to make sure they are having the intended effect.

Unfortunately, there is no unambiguous answer to the assignment problem. Consider, for example, our analysis of a small open economy under conditions of perfect capital mobility. We have seen that the effectiveness of fiscal and monetary policy at influencing output depends upon whether or not there is a fixed or floating exchange rate. If the exchange rate is fixed then fiscal policy should be paired with the objective of full employment, whereas if the exchange rate is floating then one should assign monetary policy. The assignment problem has no simple solution and is considerably more complicated once we have three targets and three instruments; the appropriate pairing of instruments and targets depending upon the structural parameters governing the behaviour of an economy. This includes amongst others, the degree of capital mobility; marginal propensity to save and import; income and interest elasticity of demand for money; the price elasticity of demand for imports and exports and responsiveness of investment to interest rate variations.

4.14 Limitations of the Mundell–Fleming model

The *IS–LM–BP* model has been one of the major policy models underlying economic policy formulation for open economies in the last three decades. Given this, we need to look at some of the limitations of the model, not least because these criticisms were one of the reasons motivating the formulation of the monetary approach to the balance of payments and economic policy, which is the subject matter of Chapter 5. A number of the criticisms relate to the short run nature of the model.

The Marshall–Lerner condition – the model assumes that the Marshall–Lerner condition holds even though it is essentially of a short-term model which is the time scale when the Marshall–Lerner conditions are least likely to be met.

Interaction of stocks and flows – the model ignores the problem of the interaction of stocks and flows. According to the model a current account deficit can be financed by a capital inflow. While such a policy is feasible in the short run, a capital inflow over time increases the stock of foreign liabilities owed by the country to the rest of the world and this factor means a worsening of the future current account as interest is paid abroad. Clearly, a country cannot go on financing a current account deficit indefinitely as the country becomes an ever increasing debtor to the rest of the world.

Neglect of long run budget constraints – in an excellent review of the Mundell–Fleming model Frenkel and Razin (1987) highlight the fact that one of the major deficiencies of the model is that it fails to take account of long run constraints that govern both the private and public sector. In the long run, private sector spending has to equal its disposable income, while in the absence of money creation government expenditure (inclusive of its debt service repayments) has to equal its revenue from taxation. This means that in the long run the current account has to be in balance. One implication of these budget constraints is that a forward looking private sector would realise that increased government expenditure will imply higher taxation for them in the future and this will induce increased private sector savings today that will undermine the effectiveness of fiscal policy.

Wealth effects – the model does not allow for wealth effects that may help in the process of restoring long-run equilibrium. A decrease in wealth resulting from a fall in foreign assets will ordinarily lead to a reduction in import expenditure which should help to reduce the current account deficit. While such an omission of wealth effects on the import expenditure function may be justified as being of small significance in the short run, the omission nevertheless again emphasises the essentially short term nature of the model.

Neglect of supply-side factors – One of the obvious limitations of the model is that it concentrates on the demand side of the economy and neglects the supply side. There is an implicit assumption that supply adjusts in accordance with changes in demand. In addition, because the aggregate supply curve is horizontal up to full employment, increases in aggregate demand do not lead to changes in the domestic price level, rather they are reflected solely by increases in real output.

Treatment of capital flows – One of the biggest problems of the model concerns the modelling of capital flows. It is assumed that a rise in the domestic interest rate leads to a continuous capital inflow from abroad. However, to expect such flows to continue indefinitely is unrealistic because after a point international investors will have rearranged the stocks of their international portfolios to their desired state and once this happens the net capital inflows into the country will cease. The only way that the country could then continue to attract capital inflows would be a further rise in its interest rate until once again international portfolios are restored to desired state. Hence, a country that needs a continuous capital inflow to finance its current account deficit has to continuously raise its interest rate. In other words, capital inflows are a function of the change in the interest differential rather than the differential itself.

Exchange-rate expectations – A major problem with the model is the treatment of exchange-rate expectations. The model does not explicitly model exchange-rate expectations and implicitly presumes that the expected change is zero which is known as static exchange-rate expectations. While this might not seem to be an unreasonable assumption under fixed exchange rates it is less tenable under floating exchange rates. According to the model a monetary expansion leads to a depreciation of the currency under floating exchange rates – in such circumstances it seems unreasonable to assume that economic agents do not expect a depreciation as well. If agents expect a depreciation this may require a rise in the domestic interest rate to encourage them to continue to hold the currency which will have an adverse effect on domestic investment – implying a weaker expansionary effect of monetary policy than is suggested by the model.

Flexibility of policy instruments – Another criticism is that the analysis is of a comparatively static nature and it assumes that adjusting monetary and fiscal policy is a fairly simple matter. In the real world, the political process means that the degree of flexibility to adjust economic policy, especially fiscal policy presumed in the model, is hard to achieve.

■ *4.15* Conclusions

In this chapter we have illustrated some important aspects concerning the conduct of economic policy in an open economy. While fiscal and/or monetary policy may be useful in achieving full employment, they will also have important implications for the balance of payments and exchange rate which will in turn have feedback effects on the domestic economy. Economic policy formulation in an open economy has to take into account many important additional considerations compared with a simple closed economy.

Among the most important lessons for economic policy makers is that they generally need as many independent policy instruments as they have targets. This result is important because the idea that the authorities can use a single policy instrument such as monetary policy alone to achieve all the targets of economic policy is highly questionable. Nevertheless, policy makers still have a major policy problem in deciding which instrument to assign to which target. Since the structures of economies differ, no general rules exist to solve this problem. Theory warns that an incorrect assignment may provoke rather than limit instability in the economy.

We have seen that the relative effectiveness of fiscal and monetary policy is very much dependent upon the choice of exchange-rate regime. In particular, with perfect capital mobility monetary policy is more effective under a floating exchange-rate regime while fiscal policy is more effective under a fixed exchange rate. One of the crucial parameters determining the effectiveness of both fiscal and monetary policy in an open economy is the degree of financial integration of an economy with the rest of the world as reflected by the mobility of capital internationally.

Although the Mundell–Fleming model has many limitations it none the less focuses attention on the difficulties and dilemmas facing policy makers in an open economy. Perhaps its most significant contribution to international economics is that it focuses on the important role that international capital flows can play in determining the effectiveness of macroeconomic policies under alternative exchange-rate regimes.

■ Selected further readings

De Grauwe, P. (1983) *Macroeconomic Theory for the Open Economy* (London: Gower).

Fleming, J.M. (1962) 'Domestic Financial Policies Under Fixed and Floating Exchange Rates', *IMF Staff Papers*, vol. 9, pp. 369–80.

Frenkel, J.A. and Razin, A. (1987) 'The Mundell–Fleming Model a Quarter Century Later: a Unified Exposition', *IMF Staff Papers*, vol. 34, pp. 567–620.

Kenen, P.B. (1985) 'Macroeconomic Theory and Policy: How the Closed Economy was Opened', in R.W. Jones and P.B. Kenen, *Handbook of International Economics*, vol. II (Amsterdam: Elsevier).

Mundell, R.A. (1962) 'The Appropriate Use of Monetary and Fiscal Policy for Internal and External Stability', *IMF Staff Papers*, vol. 9, pp. 70–9.

Mundell, R.A. (1963) 'Capital Mobility and Stabilization Policy Under Fixed and Flexible Exchange Rates', *Canadian Journal of Economic and Political Science*, vol. 29, pp. 475–85.

Mundell, R.A. (1968) *International Economics* (London: Macmillan).

Swan, T. (1955) 'Longer Run Problems of the Balance of Payments', reprinted in R.E. Caves and H.G. Johnson (eds), *Readings in International Economics* (London: Allen & Unwin, 1968).

Tinbergen, J. (1952) *On the Theory of Economic Policy* (Amsterdam: North Holland).

■ *Chapter 5* ■

The Monetary Approach to the Balance of Payments

■ 5.1 Introduction

In this chapter, we shall look at one of the most influential policy analyses of the balance of payments known as the monetary approach. This approach to balance-of-payments analysis was pioneered by Marina Whitman (1975), Jacob Frenkel and Harry Johnson (1976). The fundamental basis of the monetary approach is that the balance of payments is essentially a monetary phenomenon. Not only is the balance of payments a measurement of monetary flows but such flows can only be explained by a disequilibrium in the stock, demand for and supply of money.

There are several variants of the monetary approach to the balance of payments and not all advocates of the application of monetary concepts to balance-of-payments analysis necessarily accept all the assumptions used. We shall outline a simple model that captures the essential message of the monetary approach. That message is that disequilibrium in the balance of payments reflect disequilibrium in the money market. Consequently, balance of payments analysis needs to focus on the both the supply of and demand for money.

Within the context of the monetary model, we shall examine how a devaluation will impinge upon the balance of payments. We then proceed to examine how the model can be used to highlight some fundamentally different implications of fixed and floating exchange rates. We compare and contrast the effects of a money supply shock, rise in domestic income and foreign price shock under fixed and floating rates. We then summarise the policy implications of the monetary approach and review some of the empirical evidence on the model. Finally we consider how the model differs from the Keynesian model examined in Chapter 4.

■ *5.2* A simple monetary model

There are three key assumptions that underlie the monetary model. These are a stable money demand function, a vertical aggregate supply schedule and purchasing power parity (PPP).

□ *Stable money demand function*

The most basic postulate of the monetary approach to the balance of payments is that there is a stable demand for money function that is made up of only a few variables. The monetarists use the quantity theory of money as the basis of the money demand function. The demand for money function is written as:

$$Md = kPy \qquad \text{where } k > 0 \tag{5.1}$$

where Md is the demand for nominal money balances, P is the domestic price level, y is real domestic income, and k is a parameter that measures the sensitivity of money demand to changes in nominal income.

The demand for money is a positive function of the domestic price level, this is because the demand for money is a demand for real money balances. A rise in the domestic price level will reduce real money balances (M/P) and accordingly lead to an equiproportionate increase in the demand for money. The demand for money is positively related to real domestic income; a rise in real income will *ceteris paribus* lead to an increase in the transactions demand for money. The money demand function forms the basis of the aggregate demand schedule which is depicted in the **Figure 5.1**.

Figure 5.1 depicts the aggregate demand schedule in a simple monetary model. From equation (5.1) if we hold the money supply/money demand fixed and assume that k is a fixed parameter this means that an increase in y

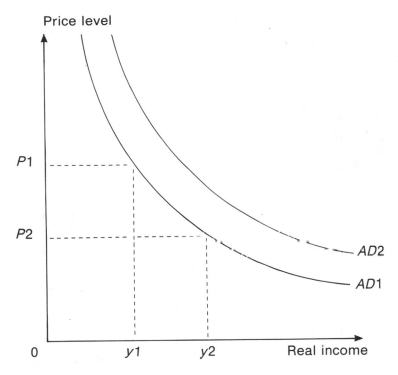

Figure 5.1   *The aggregate demand schedule*

from $y1$ to $y2$ requires an equiproportionate fall in the price level from $P1$ to $P2$. Since $P1y1 = P2y2$ the aggregate demand schedule is a rectangular hyperbola given by $AD1$. A fall in the price level from $P1$ to $P2$ given a fixed money supply will create excess real money balances (M/P) and this leads to increased aggregate demand from $y1$ to $y2$. An increase in the money supply has the effect of shifting the aggregate demand schedule to the right from $AD1$ to $AD2$. This is because at any given price level, there is a rise in real money balances which leads to increased aggregate demand.

☐ *Vertical aggregate supply schedule*

The simple monetary model assumes that the labour market is sufficiently flexible and that the economy is continuously at the full employment level of output. In other words, wages are constantly at the level that equates the supply and demand for labour. For example, a rise in the domestic price level does not lead to an increase in domestic output because wages adjust immediately to the higher price level so that there is no advantage for domestic producers to take on more labour. This means that the aggregate

Figure 5.2 *The aggregate supply schedule*

supply schedule is vertical at the full employment level of output as depicted in **Figure 5.2**.

Although the aggregate supply schedule $AS1$ in figure 5.2 is vertical at the full employment level of output $y1$, this does not mean that output is always constrained to be fixed at $y1$; the aggregate supply schedule may shift to the right to say $AS2$ if there is an improvement in productivity due to technological progress which means that full employment is associated with a higher level of real output.

☐ *Purchasing power parity*

The final assumption that underpins the monetary model is the assumption of purchasing power parity (PPP). PPP theory is examined in much more detail in Chapter 6. However, for the time being we can state that in its simplified version the theory says that the exchange rate adjusts so as to keep the following equation in equilibrium:

$$S = \frac{P}{P^*} \qquad \text{i.e. } P = SP^*$$

$$(5.2)$$

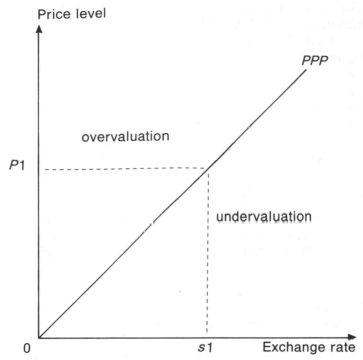

Figure 5.3 *The PPP schedule*

where S is the exchange rate defined as domestic currency per unit of foreign currency so that a rise is a depreciation while a fall is an appreciation of the domestic currency. P is the domestic price level in the domestic currency and P^* is the foreign price in the foreign currency.

Equation (5.2) says that if a basket of goods costs £100 in the UK and the same basket costs $200 in the US then the £/$ exchange rate should be £0.50/$1. This means that the basket of goods has the same price in both countries. If the exchange rate were above £0.50/$1, say £0.60/$1, then the US bundle would cost a UK citizen $200 \times 0.60 = £120$, while the UK bundle would cost a US citizen $100/0.6 = \$166.66$. According to the theory the UK economy would be very competitive. There would be a rush to buy UK goods leading the pound to appreciate to £0.50/$1. Conversely, an exchange rate below PPP say at £0.40/$1 means the US bundle of goods costs a UK citizen $200 \times 0.4 = £80$, while the UK bundle would cost a US citizen $100/0.40 = \$250$. According to the theory this would lead to a rush to buy US goods and a depreciation of the pound until it was restored to £0.50/$1 (PPP theory is examined more fully in Chapter 6).

In **Figure 5.3** we depict the PPP relationship between the domestic price and the exchange rate. The PPP schedule which shows combinations of the domestic price level and exchange rate which are compatible with PPP given the foreign price level P^*. It has a slope given by P^* and implies that an x per cent rise in the domestic price level requires an x per cent depreciation (rise) of the home currency to maintain PPP. Points to the left of the PPP schedule depict an overvaluation of the domestic currency in relation to PPP whereas points to the right depict overvaluation in relation to PPP.

The simple monetary model invokes the three assumptions set out above and then proceeds with the use of some accounting identities and behavioural assumptions to develop a theory of the balance of payments.

The domestic monetary supply in the economy is made up of two components:

$$Ms = D + R \qquad (5.3)$$

where Ms is the domestic money base, D is domestic bond holdings of the monetary authorities, and R is the reserves of foreign currencies.

Equation (5.3) says that the domestic money base is made up of two components. The monetary base can come into circulation in one of two ways:

(i)   The authorities may conduct an open market operation (OMO), which is a central bank purchase of treasury bonds held by private agents. This increases the central bank's monetary liabilities but increases its assets of domestic bond holdings which is the domestic component of the monetary base as represented by D.

(ii)   The authorities may conduct a foreign exchange operation (FXO) which is a purchase of foreign currency assets (money or foreign treasury bonds) held by private agents by the central bank. This again increases the central bank's liabilities but increases its assets of foreign currency and foreign bonds which are represented by R.

We can now rewrite equation (5.3) in difference form as:

$$dMs = dD + dR \qquad (5.4)$$

Equation (5.4) says that any increase (decrease) in the domestic money supply can come about through either an OMO as represented by dD or an FXO as represented by dR. The relationship between the money supply and reserves is depicted in **Figure 5.4**.

In **Figure 5.4** at point $D1$ all the domestic money supply is made up entirely of the domestic component since reserves are zero. For convenience we set the exchange rate of domestic to foreign currency equal to unity; this being the case an increase of 1 unit of foreign currency leads to an increase in the domestic money supply of 1 unit, so that when reserves are $R1$ the money supply is $M1$, that is, $D1 + R1$.

An OMO will have the effect of shifting the Ms schedule by the amount of the increase in the central bank's domestic bond holdings. An OMO

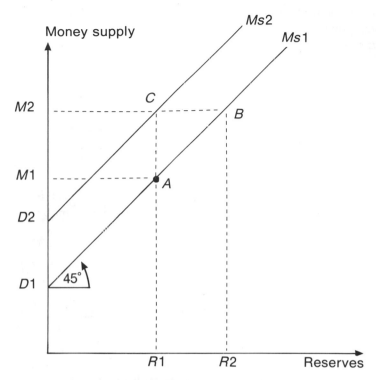

Figure 5.4 *The money supply and reserves*

which increases the domestic component of the monetary base from *D*1 to *D*2 shifts the money supply schedule from *Ms*1 to *Ms*2 and the total money supply rises from *M*1 to *M*2. By contrast, an expansion of the money supply due to a purchase of foreign currencies, that is an FXO, increases the country's foreign exchange reserves from *R*1 to *R*2. This too has the effect of raising the money stock from *M*1 to *M*2 and is represented by a movement along the money supply schedule *Ms*1 from point A to point B.

5.3 The monetarist concept of a balance of payments disequilibrium

The monetarists view balance-of-payments surpluses and deficits as monetary flow due to stock disequilibrium in the money market. A deficit in the balance of payments is due to an excess of the stock of money in relation to money demand, while a surplus in the balance of payments is a monetary flow resulting from an excess demand for money in relation to the stock money supply. Thus a balance of payments disequilibrium is merely a reflection of a disequilibrium in the money market. In this sense the monetary flows are the 'autonomous' items in the balance of payments while the purchases and sales of goods/services and investments (long, medium and short-term) are viewed as the accommodating items. This is completely the reverse of the Keynesian approach. This views the current account items as the autonomous and capital account and reserve changes as the accommodating items. This different way of looking at the balance of payments statistics is sometimes contrasted by saying that Keynesians look at the balance of payments statistics from the 'top down' (i.e. the current account) while the monetarists look from the 'bottom up' (i.e. the change in reserves).

Monetarists observe that the overall balance of payments can be thought of as consisting of the current account balance, capital account balance and change in the authorities' reserves. That is:

$$BP = CA + K + dR = 0$$

So that:

$$CA + K = -dR \tag{5.5}$$

where CA is the current account balance, K is the capital account balance and dR is the change in the authorities' reserves.

If the recorded dR in the balance of payments account is positive, this means that the combined current account and capital account are in deficit. This implies that reserves have fallen as the authorities have purchased the home currency with foreign currency reserves (see Chapter 1).

Equation (5.5) is a distinct way of viewing the balance of payments; increases in reserves due to purchases of foreign currencies constitute a surplus in the balance-of-payments surplus while falls in reserves resulting from purchases of the domestic currency represent a deficit in the balance of payments. If the authorities do not intervene in the foreign exchange market, that is, the currency is left to float, then reserves do not change and as far as monetary view of the balance of payments is concerned the balance of payments is in equilibrium. Under a floating exchange rate regime a current account deficit must be financed by an equivalent capital inflow so the balance of payments is in equilibrium.

With this concept of a balance-of-payments surplus/deficit in mind we can proceed to an analysis of the effects of various shocks under both fixed and floating exchange rates.

The model is in equilibrium when aggregate demand is equal to aggregate supply so that there is no excess demand for goods which is given by the intersection of the aggregate demand and supply schedules at price level $P1$ and output level $y1$ in **Figure 5.5(b)**. Also, PPP holds in the foreign exchange market so that at price level $P1$ and the exogenous foreign price level $P*$ the exchange rate compatible with PPP is given by $S1$ in **Figure 5.5(a)**. Finally,

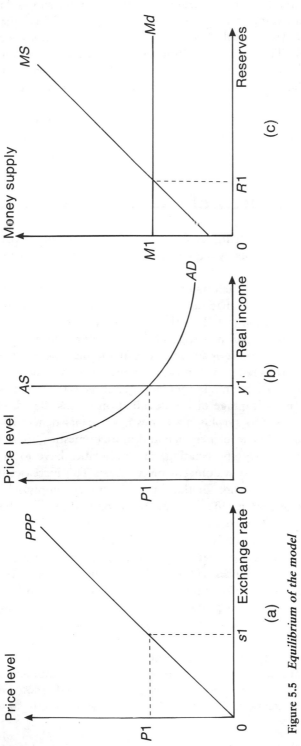

Figure 5.5 *Equilibrium of the model*

the money market is in equilibrium, so with the money supply M1 made up of the domestic component D1 and reserve component R1 is equal to money demand. The *Ms* schedule *Ms*1 cuts the money demand schedule *Md*1 in **Figure 5.5(c)**. The precise position of the money demand schedule is determined by the domestic price level and domestic income level. Equilibrium in the money market also implies equilibrium in the balance of payments.

We are now in a position to examine the effects of various shocks within the context of the monetary approach to the balance of payments.

■ *5.4* The effects of a devaluation

The monetary approach argues that a devaluation can only have an effect on the balance of payments by influencing the demand for money in relation to the supply of money.

Figure 5.6 depicts the effects of a devaluation. The immediate effect of a devaluation of the exchange rate from S1 to S2 is to make domestic goods competitive in relation to PPP as the economy is at point A below the *PPP* line in **Figure 5.6(a)**. As domestic goods become more competitive compared with foreign goods there is an increase in the demand for the domestic currency as represented by a shift of the money demand schedule from *Md*1 to *Md*2. This means that money demand M2 exceeds the money supply M1. The competitive advantage of the devaluation means that the balance of payments moves into surplus as domestic residents demand less foreign goods/services, while foreigners demand more domestic goods. To prevent the domestic currency appreciating, the authorities have to purchase the foreign currency with new domestic money base. This increases the reserves and leads to an expansion of the domestic money supply which in turn raises aggregate demand for domestically produced goods. The aggregate demand schedule shifts to the right from AD1 to AD2 and starts pushing up domestic prices until PPP is restored at price P2.

Once the domestic price level is at P2 and the money supply has increased to M2, real money balances will be at their equilibrium level ($M1/P1 = M2/P2$) and the competitive advantage of the devaluation has been offset. The balance of payments will be back in equilibrium as money supply is once again equal to money demand. In the long run, the effect of an x per cent devaluation is to lead to an x per cent rise in the domestic price level and x per cent increase in the domestic money stock. In other words, the surplus resulting from a devaluation is merely a transitory phenomenon.

The monetary approach emphasises that a devaluation will have a transitory beneficial effect on the balance of payments only so long as the

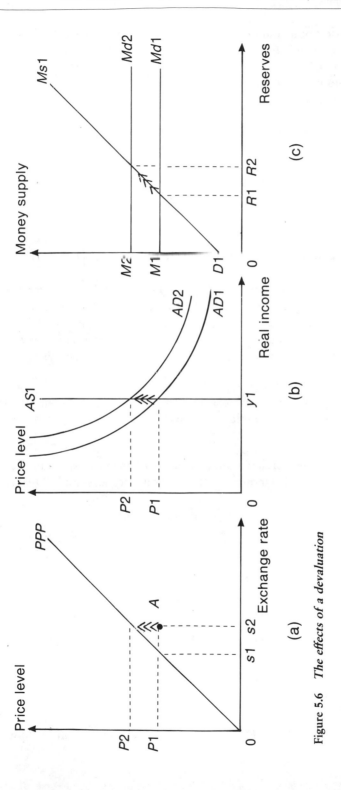

Figure 5.6 *The effects of a devaluation*

authorities do not simultaneously engage in an expansionary OMO. If the authorities immediately increase the money stock to $M2$ via an OMO, there would be an immediate rise in aggregate demand and domestic prices to $P2$ so that the competitive advantage conferred by a devaluation is eliminated.

The important point derived from the monetary model concerning the effect of a devaluation is that exchange rate changes are viewed as incapable of bringing about a lasting change in the balance of payments. A devaluation or revaluation operates strictly by causing a disequilibrium in the money market, causing a deficit or surplus in the balance of payments which continues only until equilibrium is restored in the money market via reserve changes.

■ 5.5 A monetary exchange-rate equation

Before we compare and contrast the effects of various shocks under fixed and floating exchange rates we need to consider how the exchange rate is determined in the context of our simple monetary model.

As we have seen in equation (5.1) which is repeated below as equation (5.6), the demand for money in the home country is given by:

$$Md = kPy \tag{5.6}$$

This being the case, we can postulate that the demand for money in the foreign economy is of a similar type given below as:

$$Md^* = k^*P^*y^* \tag{5.7}$$

Where Md^* denotes foreign money demand, k^* the foreign nominal income elasticity of demand for money, P^* the foreign price level and y^* real foreign income.

The exchange rate is determined by PPP so that

$$S = \frac{P}{P^*} \tag{5.8}$$

In equilibrium money demand is equal to the money supply in each country, so that:

$$Ms = Md \quad \text{and} \quad Ms^* = Md^* \tag{5.9}$$

This being the case, we can denote the relative money supply functions as equation (5.6) divided by (5.7) replacing Md and Md^* with Ms and Ms^* from equation (5.9):

$$\frac{Ms}{Ms^*} = \frac{kPy}{k^*P^*y^*} \tag{5.10}$$

Since $P/P^* = S$ because of PPP then we can rewrite equation (5.10) as:

$$\frac{Ms}{Ms^*} = \frac{kSy}{k^*y^*} \qquad (5.11)$$

Solving the above equation for the exchange rate yields:

$$S = \frac{Ms/Ms^*}{ky/k^*y^*} \qquad (5.12)$$

Equation (5.12) says that the exchange rate is determined by the relative supply and demand for the different national money stocks. An increase in the domestic money stock relative to the foreign money stock will lead to a depreciation (rise) of the home currency, while an increase in domestic income relative to foreign income leads to an appreciation (fall) in the exchange rate. The reason being that an increase in income leads to an increased transactions demand for the home currency leading to an appreciation. With this simple model of exchange rate determination in mind we can proceed to analyse in more detail the effects of money supply, income changes and changes in the foreign price level.

5.6 A money supply expansion under fixed exchange rates

If the exchange rate of a currency is fixed, this means that the authorities have to buy the currency when it is in excess supply and sell the currency when it is in excess demand in the private market to avoid a currency depreciation or appreciation. When the authorities sell the currency this leads to a rise in their reserves of foreign currency. If the authorities buy the domestic currency they do so with foreign currency and so their reserves fall.

Let us now consider what happens if there is a monetary expansion under a fixed exchange rate which raises the money supply by a central bank purchase of treasury bonds.

Figure 5.7 depicts the effects of an expansionary open market operation. A monetary expansion shifts the money supply schedule from $Ms1$ to $Ms2$ and increases the domestic money supply from $M1$ to $M2$, the domestic component of the monetary base rising from $D1$ to $D2$. The immediate effect is that domestic residents have excess real money balances ($M2/P1 > M1/P1$), that is, the money supply $M2$ exceeds money demand $M1$. To reduce their excess real balances residents increase aggregate demand for goods as represented by a shift of the aggregate demand schedule from $AD1$ to $AD2$; this puts upward pressure on domestic goods prices whose price rises from $P1$ to $P2$. At price $P2$ and fixed exchange rate $S1$ the domestic economy is uncompetitive in relation to PPP as it finds itself to the left of the PPP schedule.

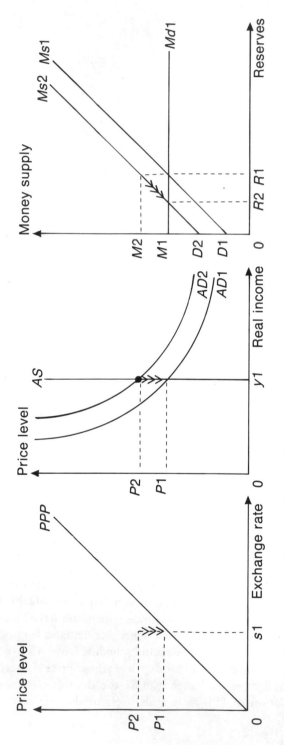

Figure 5.7   *A monetary expansion under fixed exchange rates*

The uncompetitive nature of the economy moves the balance of payments into deficit. To prevent a devaluation of the currency, the authorities have to intervene to purchase the domestic currency and the authorities' reserves start to decline below R1. The purchase back of the domestic money supply starts to reduce the excess money supply and at the same time aggregate demand starts to shift back from AD2 towards AD1. As the excess money balances are reduced this puts downward pressure on the domestic price level which falls back to its original level P1 so as to arrive back at PPP. Once the money supply returns to M1 along the Ms2 schedule the excess supply of money is eliminated and the economy is restored to equilibrium.

In the long run, the price level, output level and money stock return to their initial levels. Thus, an increase in the domestic component of the monetary base from D1 to D2 will, because of the foreign exchange intervention it necessitates to maintain a fixed exchange rate, lead to an equivalent fall in the reserves from R1 to R2. This fall in the reserves due to purchases of the home currency leads to a return of the money stock to its original level. The fact that the money supply has to return to its original level can be explained by reference to equation (5.12). As the parameters S, Ms^*, ky and k^*y^* are all fixed any rise in Ms must eventually be reversed for the equation to hold.

The monetary approach regards the balance-of-payments deficits resulting from the expansion in the money stock to be merely a temporary and self-correcting phenomenon. An expansion of the money supply causes a temporary excess of money and a current and capital account deficit which to maintain the fixed exchange rate necessitates intervention in the foreign exchange market that eventually eliminates the excess supply of the currency.

There are two circumstances under which a balance-of-payments deficit or surplus can become more than a transitory feature. One case is when the authorities practise sterilisation of their foreign exchange operations. When the authorities intervene to purchase their currency to prevent it being devalued there is a reduction of the monetary base, and the authorities could try to offset these money base implications by conducting a further open market purchase of bonds from the public. However, as we have seen, such an open market operation causes a balance-of-payments deficit requiring a further foreign exchange intervention. Hence, sterilisation policies can cause prolonged balance-of-payments deficits. The pursuit of such sterilisation operations will be limited by the extent of a country's reserves.

Another factor that can lead to a continuous deficit would be if the surplus countries were prepared to purchase the deficit country's currency and hold it in their reserves. In such circumstances, the deficit country will have its exchange rate fixed by foreign central bank intervention and such a process can continue so long as foreign central banks are prepared to accumulate the home country's currency in their reserves. Although in this case reserve changes are zero the deficit is reflected as an increase in liabilities to foreign authorities.

 ## 5.7 A money supply expansion under floating exchange rates

Under floating exchange rates the monetary approach maintains that there is no such thing as a balance-of-payments deficit or surplus as the authorities do not intervene to purchase or sell the domestic currency. Since there are no changes in international reserves, there is no balance-of-payments surplus or deficit. Referring to equation (5.5) as the change in reserves is zero any current account deficit (surplus) has to be offset by a net capital inflow (outflow) of a like amount. **Figure 5.8** depicts the effects of a monetary expansion under floating exchange rates.

An expansionary OMO leads to a rise in the money stock from $M1$ to $M2$ and creates excess money balances. The result is that the aggregate demand shifts from $AD1$ to $AD2$ with demand $y2$ exceeding domestic output $y1$. The excess demand for goods translates into increased expenditure on foreign goods/services and investments, leading to a depreciation of the exchange rate. As a result of the excess demand for goods the domestic price level begins to rise and this leads to an increase in money demand as reflected by an upward shift of the money demand function from $Md1$ towards $Md2$. As the domestic price level rises this increases the demand for money leading to a contraction of aggregate demand along the $AD2$ schedule until equilibrium price level $P2$ is reached.

In the long run, the effect of an x per cent increase in the money stock is an x per cent depreciation of the exchange rate and x per cent increase in the domestic price level. The rise in the price level induces a rise in the demand for money so that the excess money balances created by the OMO are eliminated. With reference to equation (5.12) we can see that with the parameters Ms^*, ky and k^*y^* all fixed any rise in Ms leads to a rise in the exchange rate S for the equation to hold.

The case of floating exchange rates provides a clear contrast with the fixed exchange rate case. Under fixed exchange rates an expansionary OMO leads to a disequilibrium in the money market which is resolved by adjustment in the balance of payments and reserves held by the authorities. Under floating exchange rates an expansion in the monetary base leads to a depreciation of the exchange rate and rise in domestic prices. Under fixed exchange rates the authorities can no longer retain independent control of the money supply, and the money supply returns to its original level due to the fall in the

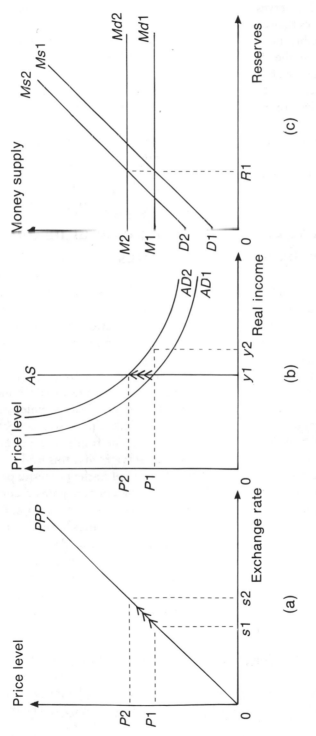

Figure 5.8   *A monetary expansion under floating exchange rates*

international reserves held by the authorities. Whereas under floating exchange rates they can determine the amount of the money supply, money market equilibrium is restored by changes in money demand brought about by changes in the domestic price level and exchange rate. One of the arguments against fixed exchange rates is that the authorities can no longer conduct independent monetary policies, while with floating exchange rates the authorities are free to expand and contract the money supply to their desired levels.

Having contrasted the effects of a money supply expansion under both exchange-rate regimes, we now consider the contrasting effects of changes in domestic income and the foreign price level.

5.8 The effects of an increase in income under fixed exchange rates

Within the context of the monetary approach to the balance of payments an increase in domestic income can only have an effect on the balance of payments by influencing money demand in relation to the money supply. **Figure 5.9** depicts the effects of an increase in domestic income under fixed exchange rates.

The increase in real domestic income is represented by a rightward shift of the aggregate supply schedule from $AS1$ to $AS2$. As a result of the increase in domestic income the demand to hold money increases which shifts the money demand function from $Md1$ to $Md2$. The result is that money demand $M2$ exceeds the money supply $M1$. The result is reduced expenditure on both domestic and foreign goods/services and this leads to a fall in the domestic price level from $P1$ to $P2$. The fall in the domestic price level, means that at the fixed exchange rate $S1$ the country gains a competitive advantage and the current and capital accounts move into surplus. To prevent an appreciation of the currency the authorities have to purchase the foreign currency with newly created money base. As a result of the intervention in the foreign exchange market there is a rise in the reserves and in the domestic money supply. The increase in the money supply shifts the aggregate demand schedule from $AD1$ to $AD2$, which leads to a rise in the domestic price level back towards its purchasing power parity value $P1$. Once the money stock has risen to $M2$ the excess money balances are eliminated.

Notice that in the long run, while the price level has returned to its original level $P1$, the money stock has risen from $M1$ to $M2$ because of the transitory balance-of-payments surplus. This means that real money balances are greater than before, that is, $M2/P1$ is greater than $M1/P1$. The reason why

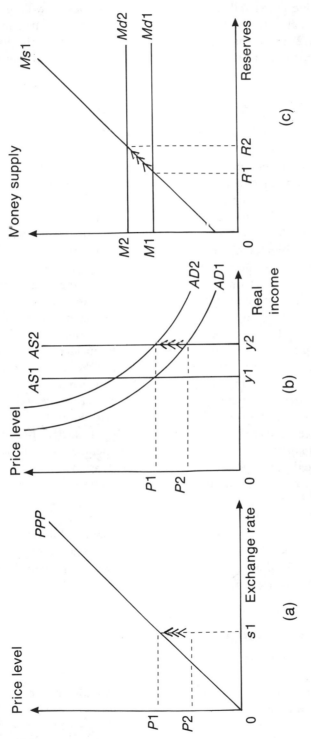

Figure 5.9 *An increase in income under fixed exchange rates*

this is possible is that all the increased money stock is willingly held as transactions balances due to the increase in domestic income. In terms of equation (5.12) given that S, Ms^* and k^*y^* are all fixed, the increase in domestic income is offset by the rise in the domestic money supply.

5.9 The effects of an increase in income under floating exchange rates

An increase in income under floating exchange rates has its impact on the exchange rate by influencing the demand for money in relation to the supply of money as depicted in **Figure 5.10**.

An increase in income represented by a shift of the aggregate supply schedule from $AS1$ to $AS2$ leads to an increase in the transactions demand for money and implies an excess supply of goods ($y2 > y1$) at the existing price level $P1$. This means that there is a downward pressure on the domestic price level which falls from $P1$ to $P2$ so as to equate aggregate demand and supply. As the price level falls, the exchange rate appreciates so as to maintain PPP. Eventually, new equilibrium is obtained at a lower domestic price level $P2$ and an exchange-rate appreciation from $S1$ to $S2$.

In the long run, we note that there has been an increase in real money balances as $M1/P2$ is greater than $M1/P1$. Again, the reason for this is that the increase in real domestic income raises the demand for transaction balances, so that the increased real money balances are willingly held. Overall, the money demand schedule did not shift because while the fall in domestic prices leads to less money demand this is exactly offset by the rise in money demand owing to the increase in real income. In terms of equation (5.12) the fixed parameters are Ms, Ms^* and k^*y^*; a rise in ky due to an increase in income therefore implies an appreciation (fall) in S.

Under fixed exchange rates with an increase in domestic income, eventual adjustment was obtained via an increase in the domestic money supply and reserves so as to satisfy the increased money demand, while under a floating exchange-rate equilibrium is obtained by an appreciation of the exchange rate and fall in the domestic price level (to maintain PPP) with the domestic money supply unchanged.

5.10 A rise in the foreign price level under fixed exchange rates

The effects of an increase in the foreign price level under fixed exchange rates are depicted in **Figure 5.11**.

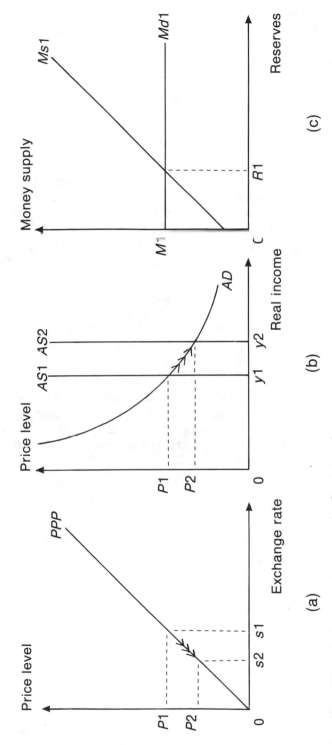

Figure 5.10 *An increse in income under floating exchange rates*

An increase in the foreign price level means that the PPP line swivels upwards from PPP1 to PPP2. This is because at the exchange rate $S1$, a rise in the foreign price level means that at price level $P1$ the domestic economy is now more competitive than PPP. Accordingly, to maintain PPP at the exchange rate $S1$ requires a rise in the domestic price level to say, $P2$.

The initial effect of the rise in foreign prices is to make domestic goods at price $P1$ more competitive as compared with foreign goods. This results in reduced consumption of foreign goods creating a balance-of-payments surplus and an increase in the demand for the domestic currency which is shown by a shift of the money demand schedule from $Md1$ to $Md2$. To prevent an appreciation of the currency the authorities have to purchase foreign currencies with newly created domestic money base. The reserves rise from $R1$ to $R2$ and the money supply rises from $M1$ to $M2$. The increased money supply and undervaluation of the currency in relation to PPP lead to a shift to the right of the aggregate demand schedule from $AD1$ to $AD2$ which pushes up domestic prices from $P1$ towards $P2$, where PPP is restored. Once, PPP is restored the balance-of-payments surplus ceases.

An important point that emerges from this analysis is that by choosing to peg its exchange rate the country also has to eventually accept that movements in its domestic price level will be determined by changes in the world price level. A country that decides to peg its exchange rate therefore runs the risk of imported inflation/deflation. If foreign inflation is determined by changes in the foreign money supply, the monetary approach suggests that a country that opts to fix its exchange rate must change its money supply in line with changes in the foreign money supply. Hence, countries that opt to fix their exchange rates give up their monetary autonomy. As we shall see in section 5.11, this is not the case with floating exchange rates.

5.11 A rise in the foreign price level under floating exchange rates

The effects of a rise in the foreign price level when the exchange rate is left to float freely are depicted in **Figure 5.12**.

A rise in the foreign price level leads to a swivel of the PPP line from $PPP1$ to $PPP2$. With a floating exchange rate the competitive advantage to the domestic economy is offset by an appreciation of the currency from $S1$ to $S2$ to maintain PPP at the existing domestic price level $P1$. Hence, with a floating exchange rate, the domestic price level and aggregate demand and output are left unaffected by the foreign price shock.

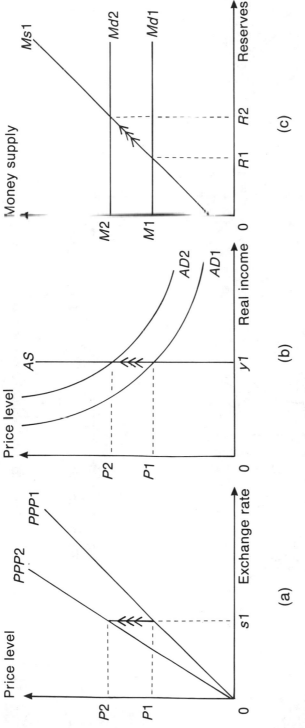

Figure 5.11 *A rise in the foreign price level under fixed exchange rates*

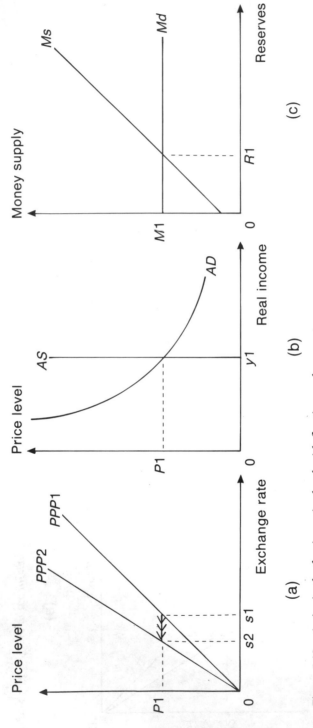

Figure 5.12   *A rise in the foreign price level with floating exchange rates*

The insulation of the domestic economy from the foreign price shock under floating exchange rates with the authorities able to operate an independent monetary policy stands in contrast to the imported inflation experienced under fixed exchange rates. One of the most powerful arguments made by the proponents of floating exchange rates is that it gives the authorities the ability to avoid imported inflation/deflation. In effect a floating exchange rate enables the authorities to pursue an independent monetary policy. The exchange rate will adjust to offset an inflation differential and maintain PPP. Under fixed exchange rates the need to maintain PPP means that an economy has to accept an inflation rate determined by the rate of growth of the foreign money supply, and monetary independence is lost. However, this independence of monetary policy depends crucially upon the exchange rate adjusting in line with PPP.

■ *5.12* Implications of the monetary approach

The distinctive feature of the monetary approach to the balance of payments is that money market disequilibrium is seen as a crucial factor in provoking balance-of-payments disequilibrium. It is maintained that the crucial decision of private agents concerns the level of their real money balances. With real output fixed, aggregate expenditure is viewed as a function of real money balances rather than income. In the monetary model agents decide firstly upon the amount of real balances they wish to hold and then spend accordingly and not the other way round. In this sense, it is money decisions that matter and not the expenditure ones.

The core of the monetary approach is that the demand for money function is a stable and predictable function of a relatively few variables. Variables such as the price elasticities of demand for exports and imports are not considered to be important.

A major implication of the monetary approach is that in a fixed exchange-rate regime the authorities have to accept a loss of control over their domestic monetary policy as the price of fixing the exchange rate. As we have seen, any attempt to expand the domestic money supply under fixed exchange rates leads to a balance-of-payments deficit and the need to purchase back the currency on the foreign exchange market. If foreign prices rise then so does the domestic money supply and domestic price level. Under fixed exchange rates the authorities lose the ability to pursue an independent monetary policy. The only thing that the authorities can do is to control the composition of the monetary base between its domestic and foreign components. With a fixed exchange rate, an increase in the domestic component of the monetary base leads to an equivalent fall in the foreign component.

A further implication of the monetarist approach is that from the viewpoint of the balance of payments it is irrelevant whether the change in the money supply results from an OMO or an FXO. As far as monetarists are concerned both operations bring about disequilibrium in the money market. An expansion of the domestic monetary base under fixed exchange rates whether arising from a purchase of domestic bonds or a purchase of foreign currencies causes an excess of real money balances. The result is a balance-of-payments deficit which requires the authorities to intervene to support their currency, the reserves decline until the money supply is brought back to its original level and excess balances are eliminated.

The contrast between fixed and floating exchange rates in the monetary model is pronounced. Under fixed exchange rates monetary policy is endogenously determined by the need to peg the exchange rate, while with a floating exchange rate the country can exogenously determine its money supply because it is the exchange rate and not monetary changes that restore equilibrium.

There is a split in the monetarist camp over the desirability of fixed as opposed to floating exchange rates. Some monetarists argue that because balance-of-payments deficits and surpluses are necessarily transitory and self-correcting then countries should agree to permanently fix their exchange rates and enjoy the benefits of stable exchange rates. On the other hand, Milton Friedman has long advocated that authorities should allow their exchange rate to float so that countries are left free to determine their own rates of inflation and monetary policies independently of other countries. Many other arguments are brought into play in the fixed versus floating exchange rate debate and these are examined in more detail in Chapter 10.

5.13 Empirical evidence on the monetary approach

Much of the empirical evidence on the monetary approach attempts to measure the so-called 'offset coefficient'. The offset coefficient measures the extent to which an increase in the domestic component of the money base leads to a fall in reserves of a like amount in a fixed exchange-rate regime as postulated by the monetary approach. To validate the monetary model empirical estimates of the offset coefficient under fixed exchange rates require that it be equal to minus one, that is, an increase in domestic component of the monetary base leads to an exactly offsetting fall in the reserves. Some of the better known estimates of the offset coefficient covering various countries and periods of the fixed exchange-rate system that prevailed prior to 1973 are presented in **Table 5.1**.

Table 5.1   *Empirical estimates of the offset coefficient*

Study	Country	Estimation Period	Offset Coefficient
Bean (1976)	Japan	1959–70	−0.67
			(−8.32)
Genberg (1976)	Sweden	1959–70	−1.11*
			(−3.00)
Kouri and Porter (1974)	Australia	1961–72	−0.47
			(−5.29)
	Germany	1960–70	−0.77
			(−18.40)
	Italy	1964–70	−0.43
			(−4.36)
	Netherlands	1960–70	−0.59
			(−7.58)
Obstfeld (1982)	Germany	1961–67	0.003
			(0.001)

Notes:
The hypothesis is that the offset coefficient is equal to −1. An asterisk by the reported estimate indicates that it is statistically in line with the hypothesis.
The t-statistics are in parentheses.

As we can see the empirical evidence on the monetary approach is somewhat mixed. In Bean (1976) and Kouri and Porter (1974) the offset coefficient is of the correct sign but it is statistically below minus unity. One explanation that may help to explain the lower than expected offset coefficient was put forward by Magee (1976) who points out that exchange rates were not rigidly fixed under the Bretton Woods system. This being the case, part of a increase in the domestic component of the monetary base may be absorbed by a depreciation of the exchange rate rather than a fall in the reserves.

None the less, Obstfeld (1982) pointed out that the estimates of Kouri and Porter (1974) and Bean (1976) were likely to have been over estimates of the offset coefficient because of the frequent practice of sterilisation of foreign exchange interventions by central banks. Suppose a country expands the domestic component of the monetary base. There would be pressure for the currency to depreciate and the authorities would then have to buy the domestic currency with a fall in their reserves. To prevent a fall in the money supply, authorities typically tried to sterilise the fall by further purchases of domestic bonds. To the extent that purchasing domestic bonds (which will tend to lower domestic interest rates) does not induce further outflows, the offset coefficient will be greater than minus unity, that is, the expansion of the domestic component of the money base is greater than the fall in reserves. Since the Kouri and Porter and Bean studies estimation procedures did not take into account sterilisation practices they require reestimation using more sophisticated econometric procedures. In his study, Obstfeld (1982) finds that the offset coefficient for Germany changes from -0.55 to an insignificant 0.003 when sterilisation practices have been accounted for. Obstfeld's result therefore casts grave doubt on the monetary approach.

All the empirical estimates need to be treated with caution even if the simultaneous equation bias problem has been accounted for by using appropriate econometric estimation techniques. This is because all the studies assume that the price level, real output and interest rates are exogenous and unaffected by changes in the money supply. Such assumptions have no grounding in economic theory and are most unlikely to be fulfilled in the real world.

■ *5.14* Criticisms of the monetary approach

We need to emphasise that the monetary model presented in this chapter is not necessarily a model which all advocates of the monetary approach to the balance of payments would be in full agreement with. There is a wide spectrum of views that can be categorised within the monetarist camp. Some monetarists argue that an increase in the domestic money supply might not be reflected exclusively in an equivalent fall in the reserves under fixed exchange rates. For instance, if there is unemployment an expansionary monetary policy may lead to some increase in output (reflected in a positive sloping aggregate supply function) which by raising money demand will reduce the devaluation pressures on the home currency. In this instance, reserves would not need to fall in exact proportion as the initial rise in the money supply as some of the expansion would be willingly held as transactions balances.

Some critics have argued that to regard the balance of payments as a monetary phenomenon is only true in the sense that the balance of payments measures monetary flows between domestic and foreign residents. They argue that it is quite wrong to regard the balance-of-payments deficits and surpluses as exclusively due to monetary decisions because the question of causation is an open issue. If suddenly economic agents decide to spend more on foreign goods/services and foreign investments under a fixed exchange-rate system there will be a transitory deficit in the balance of payments. The deficit, then forces the authorities to buy the domestic money base in the foreign exchange market. The cause of the deficit is the expenditure decisions not a decrease in money demand which then leads to excess real money balances and a balance-of-payments deficit. In other words, causation can easily lead from expenditure decisions to changes in money demand rather than changes in money demand inducing changes in expenditure behaviour.

A recent survey of the monetary approach by Boughton (1988) has argued that nearly every assumption made by the proponents is empirically open to question. There is ample evidence that money demand functions can be highly unstable, economies are rarely at full employment and purchasing power parity is useless as a guide to exchange-rate movements (see Chapter 6). Although these assumptions hold reasonably well in the longer run they are very rarely fulfilled in the short run. The empirical violation of these key assumptions must bring into question the policy relevance of the monetary approach.

The proponents of the monetary approach argue that it provides an insight into the short-run disequilibrium in the balance of payments. Yet its assumptions of full employment and purchasing power parity and a stable money demand function are highly questionable in the short run. There is clearly something wrong with using assumptions that may be valid in the long run to explain what is happening in the short run. In this sense, the monetary model's conclusions about the long-run consequences of changes in economic policy are probably more insightful than its postulates about the short-run consequences.

Another criticism of the monetary approach is that no attention is paid to the composition of a deficit and surplus. If there is a large deficit in the current account which is financed by an offsetting surplus in the capital account the monetarists argue that this means that there is no need for any policy concern with regard to the balance of payments. Indeed, because any surplus or deficit is necessarily a transitory feature representing a stock disequilibrium in the money market which is necessarily self correcting, a policy with regard to the balance of payments is unnecessary. Such an approach ignores the dangers of increasing indebtedness due to current account deficits being financed by capital inflows. In the real world it is the increase in such indebtedness, such as the Third World debt crisis, that causes much concern for policy makers of the countries concerned.

■ *5.15* Conclusions

The monetary approach provides a distinctive and clear analysis of the effects of a devaluation and monetary expansion on the balance of payments. Its emphasis on disequilibrium in the balance of payments being a flow response to stock disequilibrium in the money market represents an important contribution to the research on international economics.

Another significant contribution of the monetary approach is that it provides a rich set of policy recommendations. A country that opts to fix its exchange rate will lose its monetary autonomy and a monetary expansion can lead to temporary balance-of-payments deficits, whereas a country that allows its currency to float will have monetary autonomy but a monetary expansion then leads to a depreciation of its currency. Hence, it provides a warning to policy makers that reckless monetary expansion can lead to balance-of-payments problems under fixed exchange rates or a currency problem under floating exchange rates.

With regard to the effects of a devaluation of a currency, starting from a position of equilibrium, the monetary approach suggests that there will be an unambiguous transitory surplus in the balance of payments. This stands in contrast to the elasticity and absorption approaches which suggest the effects are ambiguous. It must be borne in mind, however, that the monetary model is referring to both the current and capital account whereas the latter two are concerned exclusively with the current account. Finally, it needs to be remembered that the monetary approach does not specify precisely how temporary the resulting surplus is; presumably this varies on a country-by-country basis.

■ Selected further readings

Bean, D. (1976) 'International Reserve Flows and Money Market Equilibrium, the Japanese Case', in J.A. Frenkel and H.G. Johnson, *The Monetary Approach to the Balance of Payments* (London: Allen and Unwin).

Boughton, J.M. (1988) 'The Monetary Approach to Exchange Rates: What Now Remains?', *Princeton Essays in International Finance*, Princeton, No. 171.

Copeland, L.S. (1989) *Exchange Rates and International Finance* (Kent: Addison-Wesley).

Frankel, J.A. (1979) 'On the Mark: a Theory of Floating Exchange Rates Based on Real Interest Rate Differentials', *American Economic Review*, vol. 69, pp. 610–22.

Frenkel, J.A. and Johnson, H.G. (eds) (1976) *The Monetary Approach to the Balance of Payments* (London: Allen & Unwin).

Genberg, H. (1976) 'Aspects of the Monetary Approach to Balance of Payments Theory: an Empirical Study of Sweden', in J.A. Frenkel and H.G. Johnson, *The Monetary Approach to the Balance of Payments* (London: Allen & Unwin).

Johnson, H.G. (1976) 'The Monetary Theory of Balance of Payments Policies', in J.A. Frenkel and H.G. Johnson, *The Monetary Approach to the Balance of Payments* (London: Allen & Unwin).

Johnson, H.G. (1977) 'The Monetary Approach to the Balance of Payments: A Nontechnical Guide', *Journal of International Economics*, vol. 7, pp. 251–68

Kouri, P.J.K. and Porter, M.G. (1974) 'International Capital Flows and Portfolio Equilibrium', *Journal of Political Economy*, vol. 82, pp. 443–67.

Kreinin, M.E. and Officer, L.H. (1978) 'The Monetary Approach to the Balance of Payments: A Survey', *Princeton Studies in International Finance*, No. 43.

Magee, S.P. (1976) 'The Empirical Evidence on the Monetary Approach to the Balance of Payments and Exchange Rates', *American Economic Review, Papers and Proceedings*, vol. 66, pp. 163–70.

Obstfeld, M. (1982) 'Can We Sterilize? Theory and Evidence', *American Economic Review, Papers and Proceedings*, vol. 72, pp. 45–50.

Rabin, A. and Yeager, L. (1982) 'Monetary Approaches to the Balance of Payments and Exchange Rates', *Princeton Essays in International Finance*, No. 148.

Whitman, M.V.N. (1975) 'Global Monetarism and the Monetary Approach to the Balance of Payments', *Brookings Papers on Economic Activity*, vol. 2, pp. 491–536.

PART II

Exchange-rate Determination: Theory, Evidence and Policy

■ *Chapter 6* ■

Purchasing Power Parity and Floating Exchange-rate Experience

■ *6.1* Introduction

In Chapter 1, we looked at what exactly the foreign exchange market is, introduced a number of differing exchange rate concepts and examined a simple current account model of exchange-rate determination. In this chapter, we look at one of the earliest and simplest models of exchange-rate determination known as purchasing power parity (PPP) theory. An understanding of PPP is essential to the study of international finance. PPP theory has been advocated as a satisfactory model of exchange-rate determination in its own right and also provides a point of reference for the long run exchange rate in many of the modern exchange-rate theories which we examine in later chapters.

Having looked at PPP theory, we proceed to examine how well suited this theory is to explaining actual exchange-rate behaviour since the adoption of generalised floating in 1973. As we shall see, PPP theory does not provide an adequate explanation of much of the observed features of floating exchange rates. Some of the possible explanations for the failure of PPP to hold are then discussed.

6.2 Purchasing power parity theory and the law of one price

PPP is generally attributed to Gustav Cassell's writings in the 1920s, although its intellectual origins date back to the writings of the nineteenth-century British economist David Ricardo. The basic concept underlying PPP theory is that arbitrage forces will lead to the equalisation of goods prices internationally once the prices of goods are measured in the same currency. As such the theory represents an application of the 'law of one price'.

☐ *The law of one price*

The law of one price simply says that in the presence of a competitive market structure and the absence of transport costs and other barriers to trade, identical products which are sold in different markets will sell at the same price when expressed in terms of a common currency.

The law of one price is based upon on the idea of perfect goods arbitrage. Arbitrage occurs where economic agents exploit price differences so as to provide a riskless profit. For example, if a car costs £5000 in the UK and the identical model costs $10 000 in the US then according to the law of one price the exchange rate should be £5000/$10 000, which is £0.50/$1. Say the exchange rate were higher than this, at £0.60/$1, then it would pay a US resident to purchase a car in the UK because with $8333.33 he would obtain £5000 which can then be used to purchase a car in the UK saving $1666.67 compared with purchasing in the US. According to law of one price, US residents will exploit this arbitrage possibility and start purchasing pounds and selling dollars. Such a process will continue until the pound appreciates to £0.50/$1 at which point arbitrage profit opportunities are eliminated. Conversely, if the exchange rate is £0.4/$1 then a UK car would cost a US resident 5000/0.4 = $12 500 while a US car would cost UK residents 10 000 × 0.4 = £4000, the pound is overvalued. Hence, US residents will not buy UK cars and UK residents will buy US cars so the pound will depreciate on the foreign exchange market to its PPP value of £0.50/$1.

The proponents of PPP argue that the exchange rate must adjust to ensure that the 'law of one price' which applies only to individual goods, also holds internationally for identical **bundles** of goods.

■ *6.3 Absolute and relative PPP*

Purchasing power parity theory comes in two forms. One is a based on a strict interpretation of the law of one price and is termed absolute purchasing power parity. The other is a 'weaker' variation known as relative purchasing power parity. We shall first examine the absolute version of the theory and then consider the relative version.

☐ *Absolute PPP*

The absolute version of PPP holds that if one takes a bundle of goods in one country and compares the price of that bundle with an identical bundle of goods sold in a foreign country converted by the exchange rate into a common currency of measurement, then the prices will be equal. For example, if a bundle of goods costs £100 in the UK and the same bundle costs $200 in the US, then the exchange rate defined as pounds per dollar will be £100/$200 = £0.50/$1. Algebraically, the absolute version of PPP can be stated as:

$$S = \frac{P}{P^*}$$

(6.1)

where S is the exchange rate defined as domestic currency units per unit of foreign currency, P is the price of a bundle of goods expressed in the domestic currency, and P^* is the price of an identical bundle of goods in the foreign country expressed in terms of the foreign currency.

According to absolute PPP a rise in the home price level relative to the foreign price level will lead to a proportional depreciation of the home currency against the foreign currency. In our example, if the price of the UK bundle rises to £160 while the price of the US bundle remains at $200, then the pound will depreciate to £0.80/$1.

☐ *Relative PPP*

The absolute version of PPP is, even proponents of the theory generally acknowledge, unlikely to hold precisely because of the existence of transport costs, imperfect information and the distorting effects of tariffs and protection. None the less, it is argued that a weaker form of PPP known as relative purchasing power parity can be expected to hold even in the presence of such distortions. Put simply, the relative version of PPP theory argues that the exchange rate will adjust by the amount of the inflation differential between two economies. Algebraically this is expressed as:

$$\% \Delta S = \% \Delta P - \% \Delta P^*$$

(6.2)

where $\% \Delta S$ is the percentage change in the exchange rate, $\% \Delta P$ is the domestic inflation rate, and $\% \Delta P^*$ is the foreign inflation rate.

According to the relative version of PPP, if the inflation rate in the UK is 10 per cent whilst that in the United States is 4 per cent, the pounds per dollar exchange rate should be expected to depreciate by approximately 6 per cent. The absolute version of PPP does not have to hold for this to be the case. For example, the exchange rate may be £0.5/$1 while the UK bundle of goods costs £120 and the US bundle of identical goods costs $200 so that absolute PPP is not holding (this requires a rate of £0.60/$1). But if UK prices go up 10 per cent to £132 and the US bundle goes up 4 per cent to $212 the relative version of PPP predicts the pound will depreciate 6 per cent to £0.53/$1 (even though absolute PPP requires £0.622/$1 = £132/$212).

■ *6.4* A generalised version of PPP

One of the major problems with PPP theory as we have so far examined it, is that it suggests that PPP holds for all types of goods. However, a more generalised version of PPP that provides some useful insights makes a distinction between traded and non-traded goods. Traded goods are goods that are susceptible to the rigours of international competition be they exports or import competing industries, such as most manufactured goods. Non-traded goods are ones that cannot be traded internationally at a profit, examples of a non-traded good include houses and certain services such as a haircut and restaurant food.

The point of the traded/non-traded goods distinction is that on a priori grounds PPP is more likely to hold for traded goods than non-traded ones. This is because the price of traded goods will tend to be kept in line by international competition, while the price of non-traded goods will be determined predominately by domestic supply and demand considerations. For example, if a car costs £5000 in the UK and $10 000 in the US arbitrage will tend to keep the pound–dollar rate at £0.50/$1. However, if the price of a house is £150 000 in the UK and $80 000 in the US and the exchange rate is £0.50/$1 arbitrage forces do not easily come into play (unless fed-up UK citizens emigrate to America pushing up US house prices and lowering UK prices). Similarly, if a haircut costs £10 in the UK but $10 in the US and the exchange rate is £0.50/$1 only insane people in the UK will travel to the US for a haircut knowing that they can save £5 because of the time and transport costs involved.

We now consider the importance of the tradables/non-tradables distinction for PPP when aggregate price indices made up of both tradables and non-tradables are considered. In the first instance, we assume that PPP holds for tradable goods, this means:

$$P_T = SP_T. \tag{6.3}$$

where S is the exchange rate defined as domestic currency units per unit of foreign currency, P_T is the price of traded goods in the domestic country measured in terms of the domestic currency, and P_{T^*} is the price of traded goods in the foreign country measured in terms of the foreign currency.

The aggregate price index (P_I) for the domestic economy is made up of a weighted average of the price of both tradable (P_T) and non-tradable goods (P_N) priced in the domestic currency. Likewise, the foreign aggregate price index (P_{I^*}) is made up of a weighted average of the price on tradables (P_{T^*}) and non-tradables (P_{N^*}) priced in the foreign currency. This gives:

$$P_I = \alpha P_N + (1-\alpha)P_T \tag{6.4}$$

where α is the proportion of non-traded goods in the domestic price index.

$$P_{I^*} = \beta P_{N^*} + (1-\beta)P_{T^*} \tag{6.5}$$

where β is the proportion of non-traded goods in the foreign price index.

Dividing equation (6.4) by (6.5) we obtain:

$$\frac{P_I}{P_{I^*}} = \frac{\alpha P_N + (1-\alpha)P_T}{\beta P_{N^*} + (1-\beta)P_{T^*}} \tag{6.6}$$

If we divide the numerator by P_T and the denominator by SP_{T^*} which because of the assumption of PPP for tradable goods are equivalent expressions (see equation (6.3)) we obtain:

$$\frac{P_I}{P_{I^*}} = \left[\frac{\alpha(P_N/P_T) + (1-\alpha)}{\beta(P_{N^*}/P_{T^*}) + (1-\beta)} \right] S \tag{6.7}$$

This can be rearranged to give the solution for the exchange rate as:

$$S = \frac{P_I}{P_{I^*}} \left[\frac{\beta(P_{N^*}/P_{T^*}) + (1-\beta)}{\alpha(P_N/P_T) + (1-\alpha)} \right] \tag{6.8}$$

Equation (6.8) is an important modification to our simple PPP equation because PPP no longer necessarily holds in terms of aggregate price indices due to the multiplicative term on the right-hand side. Furthermore, the equation suggests that the relative price of non-tradables relative to tradables will influence the exchange rate. If the domestic price of non-tradables rises in relative to tradables this will lead to an appreciation (fall) of the home currency. The reason is that PPP holds only in terms of tradable goods. A rise in the relative price of non-tradables while keeping the aggregate price index constant implies that the price of tradables must have fallen which will then induce an appreciation of the exchange rate (to maintain PPP for tradable goods) even though the aggregate price index has remained unchanged. Conversely, a rise in the price of tradables while holding the aggregate price index constant leads to a depreciation of the exchange rate to maintain PPP for tradable goods.

The tradable/non-tradables distinction serves as a warning when testing for PPP. Testing for PPP using price indices based on tradable goods prices is likely to lead to better results than when using aggregate price indices made up of both types of goods. Exchange-rate movements induced by changes in relative prices between tradable and non-tradable goods represent real exchange-rate changes. Among the factors that can lead to such relative price changes are differing rates of productivity in the traded and non-traded sectors of the economy and changing consumer demand patterns.

■ *6.5* Measurement problems in testing for PPP

Many of the proponents of PPP argued prior to the adoption of floating exchange rates that exchange-rate changes would be in line with that predicted by purchasing power parity theory. Before examining some of the empirical evidence on PPP theory, it is worth considering some of the practical problems involved in testing for PPP.

One of the major problems involved in testing for PPP is to decide whether or not the theory is supposed to be applicable to both traded goods and non-traded goods or applicable to only one of these categories. At first sight PPP theory seems more readily applicable to traded goods. However, some authors have argued that the distinction between the two categories is fuzzy and there are mechanisms linking both traded and non-traded goods prices. For example, some non-traded goods are used as inputs into the production of traded goods and vice versa (e.g. shop rents differ in price from the US compared with say Mexico).

The argument over whether or not PPP should be applied to traded or a more general price index made up of both traded and non-traded goods is important for the empirical testing of PPP theory. If the theory is supposed to be applicable to traded goods only, then the price index used for testing the theory needs to be made up only of traded goods. Conversely, if the theory is applicable to both traded and non-traded goods then a more general price index should be employed. In practice, researchers who test PPP theory for traded goods typically use wholesale or manufacturing price indices which are normally dominated by traded goods. If the test involves both traded and non-traded goods then consumer price indices which weight both classes of goods are generally used. An overall problem facing researchers whichever price index they decide to employ is that PPP is only expected to hold for similar baskets of goods but national price indices typically attach different weights to different classes of goods. For instance, consumer price indices in underdeveloped economies typically have a high weighting for food, while those in developed countries have a lower weighting for food and a higher weighting for consumer goods.

Another statistical problem in testing for PPP is that the base period for the test should ideally be one where PPP held approximately. In addition there are divergences of view over the time span during which PPP can be expected to assert itself, a strong version of PPP would suggest it holds on a monthly basis whereas progressively weaker versions would argue that it can be expected to hold only a quarterly, six-monthly or yearly and beyond basis. Bearing in mind some of these practical problems we proceed to look at some of the empirical evidence on PPP theory.

■ 6.6 Empirical evidence on PPP

There are a variety of methods of testing for PPP; these include graphical evidence, simplistic data analysis and more sophisticated econometric evidence. We first look at the graphical evidence.

☐ *Graphical evidence on PPP*

Figures 6.1(a)–(g) which plot the actual exchange rate and the exchange rate that would have maintained PPP illustrate that the exchange rate has diverged considerably from that suggested by purchasing power parity.

In **Figure 6.1(a)** it can be seen that PPP does not do at all well in tracking the dollar–pound rate – it does all right up to 1977 but between mid-1976 and mid-1981 there is a dramatic appreciation of the pound while PPP would have predicted a depreciation. A massive dollar appreciation after 1981 leads to the restoration of PPP in early 1984. Thereafter the pound has a brief period of undervaluation in relation to PPP and from late 1985 to 1991 the pound becomes rather overvalued in relation to PPP. Neither is the deutschmark–dollar rate explained by PPP with the dollar generally undervalued in relation to PPP up to early 1981. Thereafter the dollar becomes substantially overvalued in relation to PPP up until mid-1986 when it once again becomes undervalued in relation to PPP. Again with the yen–dollar and yen–deutschmark rates there are sustained and marked departures from PPP though somewhat less pronounced.

When it comes to tracking the lira, French franc and pound against the deutschmark the plots reveal that although there are deviations from PPP, the order of magnitude is much smaller than against the dollar and that PPP does a reasonable job. This is not that surprising, the lira and French franc have since the adoption of floating spent much of the time linked to the deutschmark in the Snake and European monetary system which has restricted their movements against the deutschmark. More importantly, transport costs and trade barriers between France Italy and Germany are small because of their geographical proximity and membership of the European Economic Community which prohibits the use of trade barriers

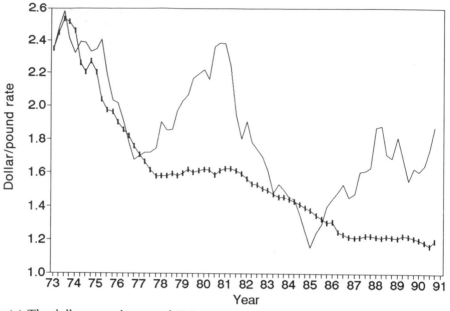

(a) The dollar–pound rate and PPP

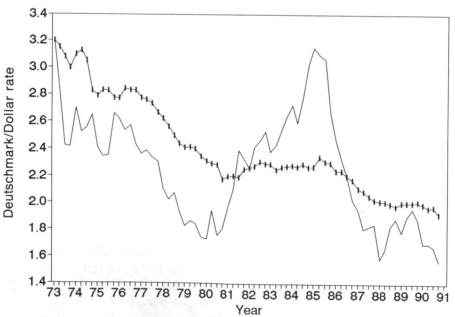

(b) The deutschmark–dollar rate and PPP

Figures 6.1 (a)–(g)   *The actual(——)exchange rate and the PPP(+++)exchange rate*

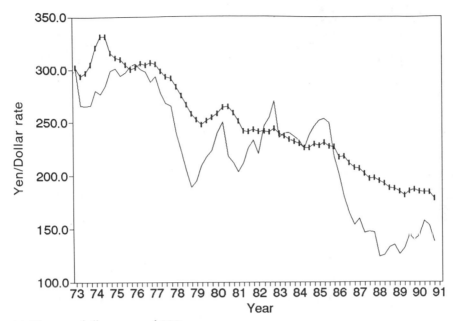

(c) The yen–dollar rate and PPP

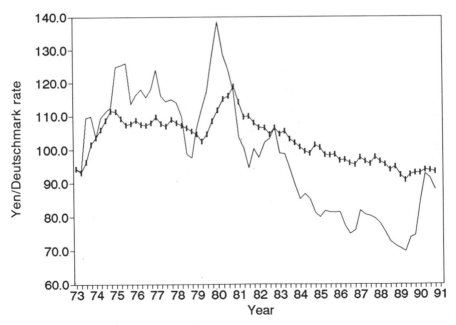

(d) The yen–deutschmark rate and PPP

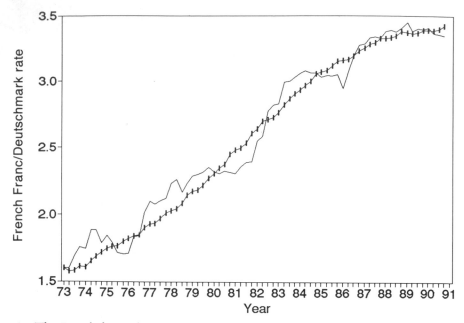

(e) The French franc–deutschmark rate and PPP

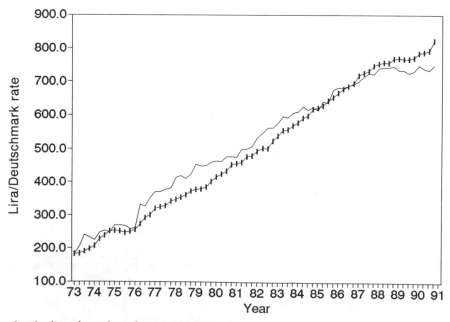

(f) The lira–deutschmark rate and PPP

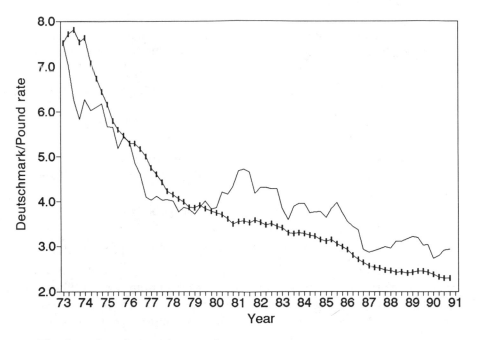

(g) The deutschmark–pound rate and PPP

between its members. These conditions facilitate the goods market arbitrage that PPP is so heavily dependent on.

It is noticeable in all the plots that although the exchange rate is frequently far from PPP it does have a tendency to go back to the PPP rate over the longer run. This provides some evidence that PPP may be a useful guide for the determination of the long-run exchange rate.

☐ *Econometric evidence on PPP*

Apart from comparing the exchange rate that would have maintained PPP with the actual exchange rate, we can test for PPP by use of regression analysis.

In log form the two simple hypotheses may be expressed as follows:

Absolute PPP: $\ln s_t = a_1 + a_2(\ln P_t - \ln P_{t^*}) + u_t$

Relative PPP: $\Delta \ln s_t = a_1 + a_2(\Delta \ln P_t - \Delta \ln P_{t^*}) + u_{t^*}$

where Δ = the one period change in the variable.

$\ln s_t$ = the log of the exchange rate, domestic per unit of foreign currency.

$\ln P_t$ = the log of domestic tradable goods prices.

$\ln P_{t^*}$ = the log of foreign tradable goods prices.

u_t = random error with zero mean and normal distribution.

In both cases, for PPP to hold the regression estimates would yield $a_1 = 0$ and $a_2 = 1$. The price and exchange rate variables are put into log form because the change in the log of a variable approximates to the percentage change in the variable. **Tables 6.1** and **6.2** contain some empirical estimates of the absolute and relative versions of PPP using quarterly data.

The regression estimates provide additional support for the graphical analysis. For the absolute version of PPP the constant term proves to be significantly different from zero both for the overall regression and the various sub-periods, while the evidence on the parameter a_2 is very mixed. For the pound–dollar rate a_2 is not significantly different from zero and is far from the hypothesised value of unity. For the lira–dollar rate while the coefficient a_2 is not significantly different from unity in the first sub-period, it is not significantly different from zero in the second sub-period. For the deutschmark–dollar while a_2 is not significantly different from unity for the first sub-period, the point estimate for the second sub-period is 2.49, well above the unity hypothesis. A similar result holds between the yen and the dollar with the point estimate for the parameter a_2 being 2.13 in the second

Table 6.1 *Absolute purchasing power parity tests* (author's estimates)

Absolute PPP: $\ln s_t = a_1 + a_2(\ln P_t - \ln P_{t^*}) + u_t$

Rate	Period	a_1	a_2	SE	DW
Pound/dollar	72Q4–81Q4	−0.78	0.18	0.049	1.78
		(−10.78)	(0.78)		
	81Q4–90Q3	−0.43	−0.11	0.058	1.92
		(−1.39)	(−0.21)		
	72Q4–90Q3	−0.72	0.24	0.053	1.89
		(−6.20)	(1.08)		
Deutschmark/dollar	72Q4–81Q4	1.01	0.89*	0.068	2.00
		(15.25)	(3.24)		
	81Q4–90Q3	1.76	2.49	0.061	1.98
		(9.12)	(5.31)		
	72Q4 90Q3	1.03	0.80*	0.064	1.98
		(9.32)	(2.66)		
Yen/dollar	72Q4–81Q4	5.63	1.29*	0.046	2.11
		(210.65)	(6.08)		
	81Q4–90Q3	5.97	2.13	0.062	2.01
		(44.02)	(6.05)		
	72Q4–90Q3	5.66	1.35*	0.056	1.98
		(89.78)	(6.71)		
Lira/dollar	72Q4–81Q4	6.33	0.99*	0.051	1.96
		(110.94)	(7.34)		
	81Q4–90Q3	7.17	0.05*	0.055	1.99
		(15.21)	(0.09)		
	72Q4–90Q3	6.42	0.81*	0.054	1.96
		(46.88)	(4.56)		
French Franc/ deutschmark	72Q4–81Q4	0.52	0.85	0.032	1.96
		(17.26)	(17.27)		
	81Q4–90Q3	0.49	0.97*	0.019	1.97
		(6.28)	(8.32)		
	72Q4–90Q3	0.51	0.94*	0.026	2.03
		(21.66)	(20.44)		
Lira/deutschmark	72Q4–81Q4	5.30	1.01*	0.052	1.99
		(162.26)	(19.53)		
	81Q4–90Q3	5.63	0.67	0.015	1.90
		(142.18)	(22.13)		
	72Q4–90Q3	5.34	0.90	0.040	2.06
		(137.70)	(23.75)		

sub-period. The results between the various currencies against the deutsch-mark (except the dollar) are much more favourable to the absolute PPP, in that the point estimate for a_2 is not significantly different from unity.

Table 6.1   *contd*

| Absolute PPP: $\ln s_t = a_1 + a_2(\ln P_t - \ln P_{t^*}) + u_t$ | | | | | |
Rate	Period	a_1	a_2	SE	DW
Pound/deutschmark	72Q4–81Q4	−1.87 (−22.48)	0.64 (4.20)	0.055	2.04
	81Q4–90Q3	−2.10 (−26.03)	0.89* (10.92)	0.040	1.98
	72Q4–90Q3	−1.88 (−35.00)	0.67 (10.05)	0.049	2.04
Yen/deutschmark	72Q4–81Q4	4.59 (77.44)	0.92* (2.19)	0.056	1.97
	81Q4–90Q3	4.39 (125.66)	1.08* (2.97)	0.037	1.91
	72Q4–90Q3	4.49 (75.55)	1.04* (3.24)	0.049	1.96

Notes:
Hypothesis is: $a_1 = 0$ and $a_2 = 1$.
An asterisk by a variable indicates that it is both of the correct sign and not statistically different from its hypothesised value.
The t-statistics are in parentheses.
All estimates have been corrected for autocorrelation using Beach-Mackinnon procedure.

In the case of the relative PPP version, placing the system in first difference form makes the validity of the test somewhat superior as it has the effect of detrending the data. For the pound-dollar rate the coefficient a_2 is wrong signed and statistically insignificant leading to a clear rejection of PPP. PPP does not help much with the deutschmark–dollar rate either, the coefficient a_2 is not significantly different from zero. For the yen–dollar rate in the second sub-period the point estimate is 2.79. PPP does somewhat better for the lira–dollar rate. All currencies (except the dollar) perform better in PPP tests against the German deutschmark than they do against the dollar. However, the results are very mixed, while the coefficient a_2 is not statistically different from unity it is also sometimes not statistically different from zero either. The PPP hypothesis performs much better for the yen–deutschmark rate than any other rate.

The overall evidence on the PPP hypothesis is not very supportive; the graphical evidence and econometric results show that for some rates the deviations from PPP are both substantial and prolonged. This is especially the case for the major currencies against the US dollar where PPP performs abysmally. While PPP has a better explanatory power for a number of currencies against the German deutschmark, the results are still not that

Table 6.2   *Relative purchasing power parity tests* (author's estimates)

Relative PPP: $\Delta \ln s_t = a_1 + a_2(\Delta \ln P_t - \Delta \ln P_{t^*}) + u_t$

Rate	Period	a_1	a_2	SE	DW
Pound/dollar	73Q1–81Q4	0.01 (0.56)	−0.17 (−0.46)	0.050	1.83
	81Q4–90Q3	0.00 (0.03)	−0.21 (−0.26)	0.059	1.85
	73Q1–90Q3	0.00 (0.41)	−0.01 (−0.04)	0.054	1.87
Deutschmark/dollar	73Q1–81Q4	0.00 (−0.25)	0.53 (0.89)	0.069	1.79
	81Q4–90Q3	−0.01 (−0.76)	0.48 (0.59)	0.062	1.96
	73Q1 90Q3	0.01 (−0.80)	0.48 (1.00)	0.064	1.88
Yen/dollar	73Q1–81Q4	0.00 (−0.43)	0.82 (1.82)	0.051	1.94
	81Q4–90Q3	0.01 (0.93)	2.79 (3.67)	0.063	2.01
	73Q1–90Q3	0.00 (−0.26)	1.22* (3.15)	0.058	1.95
Lira/dollar	73Q1–81Q4	0.01 (0.74)	0.68* (2.25)	0.053	1.99
	81Q4–90Q3	−0.01 (−0.70)	0.78* (1.07)	0.055	1.90
	73Q1–90Q3	0.00 (−0.05)	0.73* (2.36)	0.055	1.98
French Franc/ deutschmark	73Q1–81Q4	0.00 (0.21)	0.77* (1.29)	0.034	1.89
	81Q4–90Q3	0.00 (0.59)	0.76* (1.35)	0.021	1.91
	73Q1–90Q3	0.00 (0.53)	0.71* (1.90)	0.027	2.00
Lira/deutschmark	73Q1–81Q4	0.01 (1.32)	0.51* (1.64)	0.054	1.80
	81Q4–90Q3	0.00 (0.56)	0.55* (2.39)	0.017	1.88
	73Q1–90Q3	0.00 (0.87)	0.68* (3.51)	0.040	1.79

supportive as the estimates for the coefficient a_2 can differ substantially in sub-periods and are often not significantly different from zero. In sum, there is much more to exchange rate determination than PPP.

Table 6.2   *contd*

Relative PPP: $\Delta \ln s_t = a_1 + a_2(\Delta \ln P_t - \Delta \ln P_{t^*}) + u_t$

Rate	Period	a_1	a_2	SE	DW
Pound/deutschmark	73Q1–81Q4	0.01 (0.91)	0.16 (0.39)	0.057	1.95
	81Q4–90Q3	−0.01 (−0.71)	1.32* (2.63)	0.045	1.97
	73Q1–90Q3	0.01 (0.83)	0.40 (1.32)	0.051	1.96
Yen/deutschmark	73Q1–81Q4	0.00 (−0.25)	0.90* (1.84)	0.061	1.99
	81Q4–90Q3	0.00 (0.10)	1.18* (2.81)	0.039	1.97
	73Q1–90Q3	0.00 (−0.15)	0.93* (2.78)	0.050	1.99

Notes:

Hypothesis is $a_2 = 1$.

An asterisk by a variable indicates that it is both of the correct sign and not statistically different from its hypothesised value.

The *t*-statistics are in parentheses.

All estimates have been corrected for autocorrelation using the Beach–Mackinnon procedure.

6.7 Summary of the empirical evidence on PPP

1. Our results are very much in line with those presented by Frenkel (1981) that shows PPP performs better for countries that are geographically close to one another and where trade linkages are high. This is also borne out in the graphical plots – the biggest divergences between the actual and PPP exchange rates are between the pound, deutschmark and yen against the dollar, while the lira and French franc rates against the deutschmark are quite accurately tracked by PPP. Not only are France, Italy and Germany in close proximity to one another minimising transport costs but they are also members of the European Community so that there exist no tariff impediments to restrict trade among them.
2. The plots of the exchange rates and PPP rates show that there have been both substantial and prolonged deviations from PPP which have frequently been reversed.
3. Exchange rates have been much more volatile than the corresponding national price levels, see Frenkel and Mussa (1980) and MacDonald (1988). This again is contrary to the PPP hypothesis in which exchange rates are only supposed to be as volatile as prices.

4. Empirically PPP holds better in long run than short run. An important study by Manzur (1990) taking a multi-currency approach, rather than traditional bilateral tests, has shown that PPP cannot be rejected over the long run, although it is convincingly rejected in the short run. Manzur argues that PPP based on testing a currency against a weighted basket of currencies can generally be expected to hold over a period of about five years.

5. The currencies of countries that have very high inflation rates relative to their trading partners such as Israel, Brazil, and Argentina in the 1980s experienced rapid depreciations of their currencies reflecting their relatively high inflation rates. This suggests that PPP is the dominant force in determining their exchange rates.

6. Overall, PPP holds better for traded goods than non-traded goods and this is confirmed in a study by Officer (1986). In addition, a striking and major empirical regularity is that the price of non-traded goods tends to be more expensive in rich countries than in poor countries once they are converted into a common currency. We investigate this phenomenon further in section 6.10.

6.8 Explaining the poor performance of purchasing power parity theory

There have been many explanations put forward to explain the general failure of exchange rates to adjust in line with that suggested by PPP theory. We proceed to look at some of the most important.

☐ *Statistical problems*

We have seen that PPP theory is based upon the concept of comparing identical baskets of goods in two economies. A important problem facing researchers in this respect is that different countries usually attach different weightings to various categories of goods and services when constructing their price indices. This means that it is difficult to compare 'like with like' when testing for PPP. This factor is probably very significant when testing for PPP between developed and developing economies which have vastly different consumption patterns. People in developing countries usually spend a high proportion of their income on basics such as food and clothing while these take up a much smaller proportion of people's expenditure in developed economies.

Box 6.1   The Hamburger Standard

In 1986 *The Economist* magazine launched a Big Mac index. The 'McDonald standard' is based upon the concept of PPP, the price index for measuring PPP being simply the price of a Big Mac hamburger. At the end of April 1990 the average price of a Big Mac in the US was $2.20, in Tokyo the price was yen 370, dividing the yen price by the dollar price yields an implied PPP for the dollar of yen 168 compared with an actual exchange rate of yen 159 – implying a 5 per cent undervaluation for the dollar. Table 6.3 presents the measurements of over/undervaluation of the dollar in terms of PPP against various other currencies using hamburger prices. In Hong Kong a US citizen can.get two big Macs for his $2.20 – once the airfare has been paid!

Table 6.3   *Hamburgers and purchasing power parity*

Country	Price in local currency		Implied PPP of the dollar*	Actual exchange rate 30 April 1990	% over(+) under(−) valuation of the dollar
Australia	A$	2.30	1.05	1.32	+26
Belgium	BFr	97	44.00	34.65	−21
Britain	£	1.40	0.64	0.61	−5
Canada	C$	2.19	1.00	1.16	+16
Denmark	DKr	25.5	11.60	6.39	−45
France	FFr	17.70	8.05	5.63	−30
Holland	FL	5.25	2.39	1.88	−21
Hong Kong	HK$	8.60	3.90	7.79	+100
Ireland	IR£	1.30	0.59	0.63	+7
Italy	Lire	3900	1773	1230	−31
Japan	Yen	370	168	159	−5
Singapore	S$	2.60	1.18	1.88	+59
South Korea	Won	2100	955	707	−26
Russia	Rouble	3.75	1.70	0.60	−65
Spain	Ptas	295	134	106	−21
Sweden	SKr	24	10.90	6.10	−44
USA	$	2.20	—	—	—
West Germany	DM	4.30	1.95	1.68	−14
Yugoslavia	Dinar	16	7.27	11.72	+61

*PPP – foreign price divided by dollar price.
Source: The Economist, 5 May 1990, p. 128.

Differing consumption baskets are not of such significance when comparing most industrialised economies since consumers have fairly similar

consumption baskets in these economies. Even between developed economies, however, there is a problem posed by the differing quality of goods
consumed. Although British and German consumers both spend roughly the
same proportion of their incomes on cars, the Germans tend to drive German
makes like BMW while the British tend to drive Fords and Japanese cars. We
do not necessarily expect PPP to hold in terms of cars between the two
countries because once again we are not comparing like with like.

☐ *Transport costs and trade impediments*

Studies such as Frenkel (1981) which note that PPP holds better when the
countries concerned are geographically close and trade linkages are high can
partly be explained by transport costs and the existence of other trade
impediments such as tariffs. If a bundle of goods costs £100 in the UK and
$200 in the US, PPP would suggest an exchange rate of £0.50/$1. If transport
costs are £20 then the exchange rate could lie anywhere between £0.40 and
£0.60 per dollar without bringing arbitrage forces into play. None the less,
since transport costs and trade barriers do not change dramatically over time
they are not sufficient explanations for the failure of the relative version of
PPP.

☐ *Imperfect competition*

One of the notions underlying purchasing power parity is that there is
sufficient international competition to prevent major departures of the price
a good in one country exceeding that in another. However, it is clear that
there are considerable variations in the degree of competition internationally.
These differences mean that multinational corporations can often get away
with charging different prices in different countries. In fact, the conditions
necessary for successful price discrimination; namely, differences in the
willingness to pay of different sets of consumers, the ability to prevent resale
from the low cost to high cost market and some degree of monopoly power
are for the most part more likely to hold between rather than within
countries.

☐ *Differences between capital and goods markets*

Purchasing power parity is based upon the concept of goods arbitrage and
has nothing to say about the role of capital movements. In a classic paper

which we shall be looking at in more detail in Chapter 7, Rudiger Dornbusch (1976) hypothesised that in a world where capital markets are highly integrated and goods markets exhibit slow price adjustment, there can be substantial prolonged deviations of the exchange rate from PPP. The basic idea is that in the short run goods prices in both the home and foreign economies can be considered as fixed, while the exchange rate adjusts quickly to new information and changes in economic policy. This being the case, exchange-rate changes represent deviations from PPP which can be quite substantial and prolonged.

☐ *Productivity differentials*

As mentioned, one striking empirical observation that is well documented is that when prices of similar baskets of both traded and non-traded goods are converted into a common currency, the aggregate price indices tend to be higher in rich countries than in poor countries. In other words, a dollar buys more goods in say Mexico than in the United States. Further, evidence shows that tradable goods prices are nowhere as dissimilar internationally as those of non-traded goods. Consequently the overall higher price index in rich countries is mainly due to the fact that non-tradable goods prices are higher in developed than developing countries.

An explanation for the lower relative price of non-tradables in poor countries has been put forward separately by Bela Balassa (1964) and Paul Samuelson (1964) and is worth considering in detail.

■ *6.9* The Balassa–Samuelson model

Balassa and Samuelson argue that labour productivity in rich countries is higher than labour productivity in poor countries. Furthermore, this productivity differential occurs predominately in the tradables rather than the non-tradables sector. A Mexican barber tends to be as efficient as his American counterpart (as measured by haircuts per hour) but a Mexican car worker is less efficient than his American counterpart (as measured by cars per hour). Wages are assumed to be the same in the tradables and non-tradables sectors within each economy but positively related to productivity. Prices are determined positively by wages and inversely by productivity. These assumptions lead to the following set of relationships:

In the poor country:

$$P_N = W_N/Q_N \quad \text{and} \quad P_T = W_T/Q_T \tag{6.9}$$

In the rich economy

$$P_{N^*} = W_{N^*}/Q_{N^*} \quad P_{T^*} = W_{T^*}/Q_{T^*} \tag{6.10}$$

where P_N is non-tradables prices, P_T represents traded goods prices, Q_N is output per worker in the non-tradables sector, Q_T is output per worker in the tradables sector and an asterisk denotes high income (high productivity) economy.

Wage rates are the same in both the industries in each of the two economies.

$$W_N = W_T \quad \text{and} \quad W_{N^*} = W_{T^*} \tag{6.11}$$

Productivity is higher in the rich economy's tradables sector than in the poor country's. But in the non-tradables sector productivity in the rich and poor country are the same. This means that:

$$Q_{T^*} > Q_T \quad \text{and} \quad Q_{N^*} = Q_N \tag{6.12}$$

Finally, PPP is assumed to hold only for traded goods

$$S = P_T/P_{T^*} \tag{6.13}$$

The price ratio of traded to non-traded goods in each country is given by:

$$\frac{P_N}{P_T} = \pi \tag{6.14}$$

and

$$\frac{P_{N^*}}{P_{T^*}} = \pi^* \tag{6.15}$$

Since there is higher productivity in the rich economy's tradables sector then the relative price of non-tradables to tradables will be higher in the rich country making $\pi^* > \pi$.

Rewriting equations (6.14) and (6.15) as:

$$\frac{P_N}{P_T} = \pi \tag{6.16}$$

and

$$\frac{SP_{N^*}}{SP_{T^*}} = \pi^* \tag{6.17}$$

However, PPP holds for the tradables sector making $P_T = SP_{T^*}$. This being the case, then with $\pi^* > \pi$, the price of non-tradables in the rich economy must exceed the price of non-tradables in the developing country, i.e. $SP_{N^*} > P_N$. The reason is that low wages in the developing country due to low productivity in its traded sector also lead to a relatively low price for its non-traded goods even though its productivity in this sector is the same as in developed countries, while high productivity in the rich country's tradables sector leads to high wages in its non-tradables sector even though it is no more efficient than the poor country in that sector. Consequently, when we use the exchange rate to examine non-tradable goods prices we find that they are higher in developed countries than in developing countries.

The Balassa–Samuelson model is helpful in explaining why it is that rich countries tend to have overall high price indices and poor countries low price indices when aggregate baskets of traded and non-traded goods are converted into a common currency such as the US dollar. Furthermore, it helps explain why the ratio of non-traded to traded prices tends to be higher in developed economies than developing countries.

It is clear that PPP based on tradable goods alone will undervalue the purchasing power of people in poor countries because they can purchase more non-traded goods per dollar than can people in rich countries even if PPP holds for traded goods. This means that when comparing *per capita* income levels between countries such as Mexico and the United States in dollar terms this should not be done at the PPP rate for tradable goods. Rather, the proportion of Mexican expenditure on non-tradables should be valued at US non-tradable prices thereby raising the value of Mexican incomes in US dollar terms.

The productivity differential theory may also have some application in explaining divergences from PPP in terms of aggregate price indices between developed countries. For instance, Japan has since the Second World War consistently had higher productivity in their tradables sector than the United States. This means that real value of the yen should appreciate against the dollar as the higher productivity of Japanese tradables workers leads to a fall in Japanese traded goods prices relative to US traded goods prices and therefore an appreciation of the Yen to maintain PPP for tradable goods. Richard Marston (1986) found evidence that between the period 1973–83 Japanese productivity growth in its tradables sector outstripped US tradables productivity. During that period the yen appreciated by some 9 per cent in real terms against the dollar.

Although the Balassa–Samuelson model helps explain why PPP does not necessarily hold in terms of aggregate price indices, it is only a partial explanation. By assumption the theory cannot explain the failure of PPP to hold for traded goods.

■ *6.10* Conclusions

At the time of the adoption of floating exchange rates it was widely believed that they would adjust in line with changes in national price level as predicted by PPP theory. However, the experience with floating rates has shown that there can be substantial and prolonged deviations of exchange rates from PPP. A clear conclusion is that in the short to medium term, international goods arbitrage is nowhere near as powerful as proponents of PPP had presupposed.

There are many possible explanations for these deviations from PPP. Among the strongest candidates is that the theory relies too heavily on goods arbitrage and has no role for the international capital movements which have grown enormously in scale since the end of the Second World War. Such capital movements are heavily influenced by prospective returns and therefore agents' expectations about the future. As expectations change then so will exchange rates regardless of whether goods prices are changing. In the following chapters, we shall be looking at some of the most recent theories that attempt to take into account the implications of such capital movements.

None the less, the fact that PPP does not hold very well in the short to medium term does not mean that it has no role to play in exchange-rate determination. Over or undervaluation of currencies in relation to PPP induces changes in current account positions which will eventually lead to exchange-rate changes. It is the case that deviations from PPP do have a habit of reversing themselves over the longer run. Furthermore, although exchange rates may diverge substantially from PPP if the break in this link becomes too large the forces of goods arbitrage do start to come into play and move the exchange rate towards its PPP value.

■ Selected further readings

Balassa, B. (1964) 'The Purchasing Power Parity Doctrine: a Reappraisal', *Journal of Political Economy*, vol. 72, pp. 584–96.

Cassell, G. (1928) *Post-war Monetary Stabilization* (New York: Columbia University Press).

Dornbusch, R. (1976) 'Expectations and Exchange Rate Dynamics', *Journal of Political Economy*, vol. 84, pp. 1161–76.

Dornbusch, R. (1987) 'Purchasing Power Parity', in the *New Palgrave Dictionary of Economics* (London: Macmillan).

Frenkel, J.A. and Mussa, M. (1980) 'The Efficiency of Foreign Exchange Markets and Measures of Turbulence', *American Economic Review*, vol 70, pp. 374–81.

Frenkel, J.A. (1981) 'The Collapse of Purchasing Power Parities during the 1970's', *European Economic Review*, vol. 16, pp. 145-65.

Genberg, H. (1978) 'Purchasing Power Parity under Fixed and Flexible Exchange Rates', *Journal of International Economics*, vol. 8, pp. 247–76.

Hakkio, C.S. (1984) 'A Re-examination of Purchasing Power Parity', *Journal of International Economics*, vol. 17, pp. 265–77.

Isard, P. (1977) 'How Far Can We Push the Law of One Price?', *American Economic Review*, vol. 67, 942–8.

Katseli, L. and Papaefstratiou, L.T. (1979) 'The Re-emergence of the Purchasing Power Parity Doctrine in the 1970s', *Princeton Special Papers in International Economics*, No. 13.

MacDonald, R. (1988) Floating Exchange Rates: Theories and Evidence (London: Unwin Hyman).

Manzur, M. (1990) 'An International Comparison of Prices and Exchange Rates: a New Test of Purchasing Power Parity', *Journal of International Money and Finance*, vol. 9, pp. 75–91.

Marston, R.C. (1986) 'Real Exchange Rates and Productivity Growth in the United States and Japan'. Working Paper No. 1922, National Bureau of Economic Research.

Officer, L. (1976) 'The Purchasing Power Parity Theory of Exchange Rates: a Review Article', *IMF Staff Papers*, vol. 23, pp. 1–61.

Officer, L. (1986) 'The Law of One Price Cannot be Rejected: Two Tests Based on the Tradeable/Non-Tradeable Goods Dichotomy', *Journal of Macroeconomics*, vol. 8, pp. 159–82.

Samuelson, P. (1964) 'Theoretical Notes on Trade Problems', *Review of Economics and Statistics*, vol. 46, pp. 145–54.

■ *Chapter 7* ■

The Monetary Approach to Exchange-rate Determination

■ *7.1* Introduction

The purchasing power parity theory outlined in Chapter 6 is far from a satisfactory explanation of observed exchange-rate behaviour. In particular, it is very much concerned with goods arbitrage and has nothing to say about capital movements internationally. During the post-Second World War era there has been an enormous growth of capital markets meaning that it is possible for international investors to switch huge amounts of money out of one currency into another very speedily. This being the case, speculators will tend to move their money between currencies based on the expected rate of return being greater in one currency compared with another. What people expect to happen to the exchange rate will play a crucial part in determining which currencies to buy and sell – if a currency is expected to depreciate then agents will tend to switch out of that currency into currencies that they expect to appreciate. In this chapter, we look at some more recent and sophisticated exchange rate models that have been developed in an attempt to model exchange rate behaviour more successfully.

The common thread to the models that we analyse in this chapter is that they all emphasise the important role of relative money supplies in explaining the exchange rate. The monetary models start from the observation that the exchange rate is the price of one money in terms of another. However, the monetary models go beyond this simple observation to argue that exchange rate movements can be explained by changes in the supply and demand for national money stocks. There are a variety of models put forward by monetarists to explain exchange rate behaviour and we deal with three of the most important versions in this chapter. The 'flexible price' monetary model, the 'sticky price' monetary model and the 'real interest rate differential' model.

■ 7.2 Asset prices

Since international investors can quickly and easily switch out of domestic assets into foreign assets and vice versa the exchange rate can be viewed as a relative asset price. The fundamental characteristic of an asset price is that its present value will be largely influenced by its expected rate of return. To illustrate this, imagine an investor has money to invest and two alternative investment possibilities, asset A or asset B. If the price of asset A is £100 and he expects that one year later he can sell asset A for £120 the expected rate of return on asset A is given by the formula:

$$\text{Expected rate of return on asset A} = \frac{\text{Expected sale price} - \text{Purchase price}}{\text{Purchase price}} \times 100$$

$$= \frac{120 - 100}{100} \times 100 = 20\%$$

Note that the rate of return refers to a specific time period; if asset A is expected to increase in price by 20 per cent over two years then the rate of return per year is slightly less than 10 per cent per annum. Similarly, if the price of asset B is £200 and he expects that in one year's time he can sell asset B for £240 then the expected rate of return on asset B is given by:

$$\text{Expected rate of return on asset B} = \frac{\text{Expected sale price} - \text{Purchase price}}{\text{Purchase price}} \times 100$$

$$= \frac{240 - 200}{200} \times 100 = 20\%$$

In other words, although they differ in price, assets A and B offer identical expected returns to the investor. If the investor regards both assets A and B as equally risky investments then he will be indifferent between investing in asset A or asset B so long as their expected returns are equal. Suppose the investor changes his view about what he expects to sell asset A at; instead of £120 he expects to sell it at £132. The new expected rate of return on asset A is:

$$\text{Expected rate of return on asset A} = \frac{\text{Expected sale price} - \text{Purchase price}}{\text{Purchase price}} \times 100$$

$$= \frac{132 - 100}{100} \times 100 = 32\%$$

Since asset A is equally as risky as asset B, it no longer makes sense for investors to invest their money in B; instead there will be an increased demand for asset A which will push up the price of A. The price of A will be bid up until the rate of return on A is the same as the return on B, which occurs at a price of £110.

$$\text{Expected rate of return on asset A} = \frac{\text{Expected sale price} - \text{Purchase price}}{\text{Purchase price}} \times 100$$

$$= \frac{132 - 110}{110} \times 100 = 20\%$$

Hence, a change in expectations concerning the future price of asset A from £120 to £132 will lead to a change in the current price from £100 to £110 so as to equalise the expected return in relation to another equally risky asset B. Clearly what people expect to happen to future prices of assets will be crucial in determining their current prices.

▉ 7.3 Uncovered interest rate parity

Imagine the case of an international investor who has the option of investing his money in UK bonds or US bonds of similar risk and maturity. If he regards the bonds as equally risky and can switch between the two assets instantaneously, the only difference between the bonds is their currency of denomination and possibly the interest rate attached to them. There will be two factors that international investors will bear in mind when considering whether to purchase, say, UK bonds or US bonds. These are the rates of interest on UK bonds and US bonds and what they expect to happen to the pound–dollar exchange rate.

$$E\dot{s} = r_{uk} - r_{us} \tag{7.1}$$

where $E\dot{s}$ is the expected rate of depreciation of the exchange rate of the pound, defined as pounds per dollar, r_{uk} is the UK interest rate, and r_{us} is the US interest rate.

Equation (7.1) is known as the uncovered interest parity condition (UIP). UIP says that the expected rate of depreciation of the pound–dollar exchange rate is equal to the interest rate differential between UK and US bonds. For example, if the interest rate in the UK is 10 per cent per annum, while the interest rate in the US is 4 per cent per annum, then on average international investors expect the pound to depreciate by 6 per cent per annum.

With an initial pound per dollar exchange rate of £0.50/$1, investing £1000 in UK bonds will yield the investor £100 return (10 per cent) at the end of the year. If he expects the pound to depreciate by 6 per cent during the year he expects the pound–dollar exchange rate to be £0.53/$1. Hence, he could purchase £1000 worth of dollars today at £0.50/$1 which gives him $2000 that will earn the US interest rate of 4 per cent meaning he will then have $2080 which he expects to convert back into pounds at £0.53 giving him £1102.4. This implies an expected return of £102.4 (approximately 10 per cent) from investing in US bonds which is approximately equal to the expected return on UK bonds. Hence, the UIP condition implies that the expected rates of return on domestic and foreign bonds are equal.

If the expected rate of depreciation of the pound was 10 per cent then according to UIP the UK interest rate will have to be 10 per cent higher than the US interest rate to ensure the equalisation of expected yields on UK and US bonds. Crucially for the uncovered interest rate parity condition to hold continuously requires that capital is **perfectly mobile** so that investors can instantly alter the composition of their international investments. In addition, they have to regard UK and US bonds as equally risky – were this not the case then investors who are risk averse would require a higher expected return on the riskier asset. For example, if risk averse UK investors viewed the risk on UK bonds as being greater than the risk on US bonds they would require a higher expected rate of return on UK bonds than US bonds so that the uncovered interest parity condition no longer holds.

When there is both perfect capital mobility and equal riskiness of domestic and foreign bonds, UK and US bonds are said to be **perfect substitutes**. Perfect substitutability of domestic and foreign bonds implies that the uncovered interest rate parity condition will hold on a continuous basis. The monetarist models that we examine in this chapter make a crucial assumption that domestic and foreign bonds are perfect substitutes.

■ 7.4 Modelling exchange-rate expectations

The uncovered interest rate parity condition emphasises the importance of exchange-rate expectations. Assuming that the exchange rate is

£0.50/$1, while UK and US interest rates are given at 10 per cent and 4 per cent per annum respectively, the uncovered interest rate parity condition implies that expected rate of depreciation of the pound is approximately 6 per cent per annum.

Suppose all of a sudden investors become much more pessimistic about the pound and expect it to depreciate by 10 per cent during the year even though the UK and US authorities peg interest rates at 10 and 4 per cent respectively. Investors will immediately sell pounds and purchase dollars since US bonds offer higher expected yields (4 per cent interest plus a 10 per cent dollar appreciation). The sales of pounds would lead to an immediate depreciation of the pound by approximately 4 per cent to £0.5189 (0.55/1.06) per dollar so that the pound is only expected to depreciate by 6 per cent during the rest of the year in line with the uncovered interest rate parity condition. Hence, changes in the future expected exchange rate can exert powerful effects on the current exchange rate.

Given the importance of future expected exchange rates for the current exchange rate, any satisfactory model of exchange rates must model exchange-rate expectations. The problem is, that modelling economic agents' expectations is an area of considerable controversy in economics. There are a variety of alternative but plausible methods of modelling expectations. We now briefly look at some of the popular hypotheses for modelling exchange-rate expectations.

☐ *Static expectations*

$$Es_{t+1/t} = s_t$$

The expected exchange rate in one period's time ($Es_{t+1/t}$) is equal to the current exchange rate (s_t). In other words, the average expectation is that the exchange rate will not change. Such an average exchange-rate expectation could be rationalised by assuming that economic agents consider that there is an equal probability of the exchange rate appreciating or depreciating by a given percentage. In other words, if the current exchange rate is £0.50/$1 the exchange rate expected one year hence is also £0.50/$1.

☐ *Adaptive expectations*

$$Es_{t+1/t} = \alpha s_t + (1-\alpha)Es_{t/t-1} \qquad 0 \leqslant \alpha \leqslant 1$$

The expected exchange rate in one period's time is equal to a weighted function of the current exchange rate and the exchange rate that was expected to be the current exchange rate one period before $(Es_{t/t-1})$. Thus, if the current exchange rate exceeds the previously anticipated current exchange rate then agents will revise upwards their forecasts as compared with previous period's forecast. For instance, if the current pound–dollar rate is £0.50/$1 but agents had one year previously thought it would be £0.40/$1, their forecast for the pound in one year's time will be above £0.40/$1 but below £0.50/$1. How close it is to the current rate will depend on the weight attached to the current exchange rates (the larger is α).

☐ *Extrapolative expectations*

$$Es_{t+1/t} = s_t + m(s_t - s_{t-1}) \qquad m > 0$$

The expected exchange rate in one period's time is equal to the current exchange rate plus some multiple (m) of the change in the exchange rate during the preceding period. If the current exchange rate is £0.50/$1 and one year previously the pound stood at £0.40/$1 (i.e. it depreciated by £0.10/$1 over the previous year), the expected exchange rate one year hence will be somewhere above £0.50/$1. If m is less than 1 it will be between £0.50/$1 and £0.60/$1, while if m is greater than 1 it will be above £0.60/$1. In other words, if the pound depreciated the previous year it is expected to depreciate in the forthcoming year.

☐ *Regressive expectations*

$$Es_{t+1/t} = \alpha s_t + (1 - \alpha)\bar{s} \qquad 0 \leqslant \alpha \leqslant 1$$

The expected exchange rate in one period's time is a weighted function of the current exchange rate and agents' estimate of the long-run equilibrium exchange rate ($\bar{s}$). If the current exchange rate is different from the long-run equilibrium exchange rate the expected exchange rate in the next period exchange rate will lie closer to the equilibrium rate than the current exchange rate. For example, if the current exchange rate is £0.50/$1 but the underlying long-term equilibrium rate is believed to be £0.60/$1 then the expected exchange rate in one year will lie between £0.50/$1 and £0.60/$1. In other words, the exchange rate is expected to converge towards its long-run equilibrium exchange rate.

☐ *Rational expectations*

$$Es_{t+1/t} = s_{t+1} + u_{t+1}$$

The expected exchange rate in the next period will on the average equal the actual exchange rate (s_{t+1}), although it may deviate by a random error of u_{t+1}, the average of u_{t+1} is zero. On average the exchange rate that is expected to materialise is the exchange rate that materialises. The rational expectations hypothesis is that on the average, over a number of time periods economic agents do not systematically over or under predict the exchange rate. They may make forecast errors but these mistakes consist of sometimes over-predicting the future exchange rate and sometimes under-predicting the exchange rate.

☐ Perfect foresight

$$Es_{t+1/t} = s_{t+1}$$

The expected exchange rate in the next period is equal to the actual exchange rate that materialises in the next period. This suggests that economic agents have a complete knowledge of the model underlying exchange rate determination so that they do not make any errors concerning the future exchange rate.

■ 7.5 Which expectations hypothesis is best?

The static expectation, adaptive expectation and extrapolative expectation mechanisms are all somewhat arbitrary because they say that the future exchange rate can be predicted entirely on the basis of current and past values of the exchange rate. As such, no attention is paid to other information that may be relevant to the future exchange rate such as domestic and foreign inflation rates, interest rates, fiscal and monetary policy stance etc.

The regressive expectations mechanism, rational expectations and perfect foresight models are much better suited to dealing with exchange rates because they all allow for economic agents using a far wider set of information. The regressive expectations mechanism requires that economic agents form a view concerning the appropriate long-run equilibrium exchange rate, while the rational expectations hypothesis suggests that although agents do not always get the exact exchange rate right, they nevertheless do not systematically get things wrong. Finally, the perfect foresight model implies that economic agents actually have the correct model of exchange rate determination and thereby they do not make errors with regard to the future exchange rate. While this latter case may seem unrealistic, it does have the major advantage that the exchange-rate implications from models that employ perfect foresight are purely due to the structure of the model itself and not because of an arbitrary specification of exchange-rate expectations.

 ## 7.6 The monetary models of exchange-rate determination

Having provided the basic background to the monetary models of exchange-rate determination we now proceed to examine the specific characteristics and predictions of three of the major monetarist models of exchange-rate determination. These are commonly termed the 'flexible price,' 'sticky price' and 'real interest rate differential' monetary models. A common characteristic of these models is that the supply and demand for money are the key determinants of exchange-rate determination. Another common starting point is that all the models employ the UIP condition, that is, they assume that domestic and foreign bonds are equally risky so that their expected rates of return are equalised.

Beyond this similarity there are some significant differences between the models. The 'flexible price' monetary model argues that all prices in the economy be they wages, prices or exchange rates are perfectly flexible both upwards and downwards in both the short and the long run. It also incorporates a role for the effect of inflationary expectations. The 'sticky price' model which was first elaborated by Rudiger Dornbusch (1976a) argues that in the short run wages and prices tend to be sticky and only the exchange rate changes in response to changes in economic policy. Only in the medium to long run do wages and prices adjust to changes in economic policy and economic shocks. In the Dornbusch model, inflationary expectations are not explicitly dealt with. The 'real interest rate differential' model combines the role of inflationary expectations of the flexible price monetary model with the sticky prices of the Dornbusch model.

7.7 The flexible price monetary model

The flexible price monetary model was developed by Frenkel (1976), Mussa (1976) and Bilson (1978a) and assumes that purchasing power parity holds continuously, but it represents a valuable addition to exchange-rate theory because it explicitly introduces relative money stocks into the picture as determinants of the relative prices which in turn determine the exchange rate.

We start by assuming that there is a conventional money demand function, given by:

$$m - p = \eta y - \sigma r \tag{7.2}$$

where m is the log of the domestic money stock, p is the log of the domestic price level, y is the log of domestic real income, and r is the nominal domestic interest rate.

Equation (7.2) says that the demand to hold real money balances is positively related to real domestic income due to increased transactions demand, and inversely related to the domestic interest rate.

A similar relationship holds for the foreign money demand function which is given by:

$$m^* = p^* - \eta y^* - \sigma r^* \tag{7.3}$$

where m^* is the log of the foreign nominal money stock, p^* is the log of the foreign price level, y^* is the log of foreign real income, and r^* is the foreign interest rate.

It is assumed that purchasing power parity holds continuously. This is expressed as:

$$s = p - p^* \tag{7.4}$$

where s is the log of the exchange rate defined as domestic currency units per unit of foreign currency

The monetarist models make a crucial assumption that domestic and foreign bonds are perfect substitutes. This being the case, the uncovered interest parity condition holds:

$$E\dot{s} = r - r^* \tag{7.5}$$

where $E\dot{s}$ is the expected rate of depreciation of the home currency.

Equation (7.5) says that the expected rate of depreciation of the home currency is equal to the interest rate differential between domestic and foreign bonds.

We can rearrange equations (7.2) and (7.3) to give solutions for the domestic and foreign price levels:

$$p = m - \eta y + \sigma r \tag{7.6}$$

$$p^* = m^* - \eta y^* + \sigma r^* \tag{7.7}$$

We then substitute equations (7.6) and (7.7) into equation (7.4) to obtain:

$$s = (m - m^*) - \eta(y - y^*) + \sigma(r - r^*) \tag{7.8}$$

Equation (7.8) is what is known as a 'reduced form' exchange rate equation. The spot exchange rate (the dependent variable) on the left-hand side is determined by the variables (explanatory variables) listed on the right hand side of the equation.

What does equation (7.8) predict about the effect of a change in one of the right hand variables on the exchange rate?

Relative money supplies affect exchange rates

A given percentage increase in the home money supply leads to an exactly equivalent depreciation of the currency, while a given percentage increase in the foreign money supply leads to an exactly equivalent percentage appreciation of the currency. The rationale behind this is that a 10 per cent increase in the home money supply leads to an immediate 10 per cent increase in prices and because PPP holds continuously this also implies a 10 per cent depreciation of the currency. Conversely, a 10 per cent increase in the foreign money supply leads to a 10 per cent rise in foreign prices and for PPP to hold this means the home currency appreciates 10 per cent.

Relative levels of national income influence exchange rates

If the domestic income were to rise, this increases the transactions demand money, and the increased demand for money means that if the money stock and interest rates are held constant, the increased demand for real balances can only come about through a fall in domestic prices (see equation (7.2)). The fall in domestic prices then requires an appreciation of the currency to maintain purchasing power parity. On the other hand, an increase in foreign income leads to a fall in the foreign price level and therefore a depreciation of the home currency to maintain PPP.

Relative interest rates affect exchange rates

An increase in the domestic interest rate leads to a depreciation of the domestic currency. The rationale behind this assumption is that the nominal interest rate is made up of two components, the real interest rate and the expected inflation rate, that is:

$$r = i + P\grave{e}$$

where i is the real rate of interest and $P\grave{e}$ is the expected rate of price inflation.

Similarly the foreign nominal interest rate is given by:

$$r^* = i^* + P\dot{e}^*$$

where i* is the foreign real rate of interest and $P\dot{e}^*$ is the expected rate of foreign price inflation. Assuming that the real rate of interest is constant and identical in both countries $(i = i^*)$, an increase in the domestic nominal interest rate is due to an increase in domestic price inflation expectations. Such increased inflation expectations lead to a decreased demand for money and increased expenditure on goods, and this in turn leads to a rise in domestic prices. The rise in domestic prices then requires a depreciation of the currency to maintain PPP. Conversely, a rise in the foreign price level reduces foreigners' money demand leading to increased expenditure on foreign goods and a rise in the foreign price level, requiring an appreciation of the home currency to maintain PPP.

Equation (7.8) can be rewritten using price inflation expectations differential instead of interest rate differentials as:

$$s = (m - m^*) - \eta(y - y^*) + \sigma(P\dot{e} - P\dot{e}^*) \tag{7.9}$$

The flexible price monetary model is based upon the premise that all prices in an economy are fully flexible, bonds are perfect substitutes and what matters for exchange-rate determination is the demand for money in relation to the supply of money. In such circumstances, countries with high monetary growth rates will have high inflationary expectations which leads to reduction in the demand to hold real money balances, increased expenditure on goods, a rise in the domestic price level and a depreciating currency in order to maintain PPP. There have been many tests of the monetarist models but given that the theory is based upon PPP, it is not surprising that it has not performed well empirically (empirical tests of this and other exchange rate models are contained in Chapter 9).

Despite its shortcomings and reliance on PPP, the flexible price monetarist model is an important addition to exchange rate theory because it introduces the role of money supplies and inflationary expectations and economic growth as determinants of exchange-rate changes.

7.8 The Dornbusch sticky price monetarist model

One of the major deficiencies of the flexible price monetarist model is that it assumes that purchasing power parity holds continuously and that prices are as flexible upwards and downwards as exchange rates. Indeed, it is price changes that are supposed to induce exchange-rate changes via the PPP condition. As such, the model is of no use in explaining the observed prolonged departures from PPP since the adoption of floating exchange rates. In a classic article, Rudiger Dornbusch (1976a) proposed a monetary exchange-rate model that could explain large and prolonged departures of the exchange rate from PPP.

The model outlined by Dornbusch is termed the 'sticky price' monetarist model and introduces the concept of exchange-rate 'overshooting'. The basis underlying the model is that the prices in the goods market and wages in the labour market are determined in 'sticky price' markets and they only tend to change slowly over time in response to various shocks such as changes in the money supply. Prices and wages are especially resistant to downward pressure. However, the exchange rate is determined in a 'flex price' market; it can immediately appreciate or depreciate in response to new developments and shocks. In such circumstances, exchange-rate changes are not matched by corresponding price movements and there can be persistent and prolonged departures from PPP.

As the Dornbusch overshooting model represents such an important contribution to exchange rate theory and understanding exchange-rate behaviour we shall first consider a simple explanation of the model without recourse to the use of mathematics to grasp the essential ideas. Only then shall we proceed to a more formal presentation of the model.

7.9 A simple explanation of the Dornbusch model

In the Dornbusch model the UIP condition is assumed to hold continuously, that is, if the domestic interest rate is lower than the foreign interest rate then there needs to be an equivalent expected rate of appreciation of the domestic currency to compensate for the lower domestic interest rate. This is because there is perfect arbitrage of expected returns in capital markets. By contrast, goods prices adjust only slowly over time to changes in economic policy partly because wages are only adjusted periodically and partly because firms are slow to adjust their prices upwards or downwards, so we have 'sticky' domestic prices.

In such an environment, imagine that everyone believes that the long-run exchange rate is determined by PPP. Also, that the economy is initially in full equilibrium with a domestic interest rate $r1$ equal to the world interest rate, so that there is no expected appreciation or depreciation of the currency. Such a situation is depicted in **Figure 7.1**. The domestic money stock is given by $M1$ which gives a domestic price level of $P1$ and an exchange rate $S1$ which given the foreign price level corresponds to PPP. Let us now suppose that at time $t1$, the authorities unexpectedly expand the domestic money supply by 20 per cent from $M1$ to $M2$.

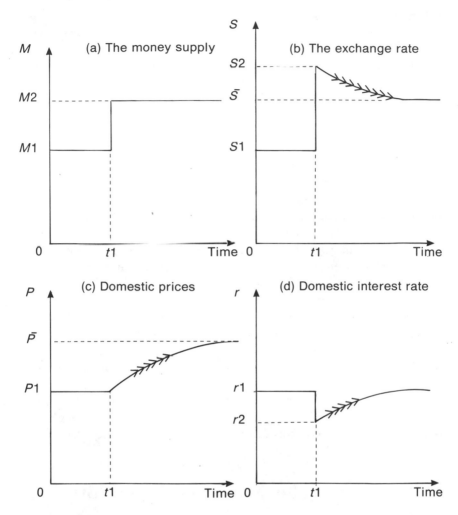

Figure 7.1 *The dynamics of the Dornbusch overshooting model*

In the long run everyone knows that a 20 per cent rise in the domestic money supply will lead to a 20 per cent rise in domestic prices from $P1$ to $\bar{P}$ and therefore a 20 per cent depreciation of the domestic currency from $S1$ to $\bar{S}$ to maintain long run PPP. However, in the short run the Dornbusch model shows that things will be very different.

In the short run because domestic prices are sticky they remain at $P1$. The unexpected increase in the domestic money supply will mean that at price level $P1$ there is now an excess supply of money that will only willingly be held if the domestic interest rate falls from $r1$ to $r2$. As the domestic interest rate is now lower than the world interest rate this means that speculators will require an expected appreciation of the domestic currency to compensate.

For this reason, the domestic currency jump depreciates at time $t1$ from $S1$ to $S2$ overshooting its long run equilibrium value $\bar{S}$. The exchange rate has to 'overshoot' its long run equilibrium value because it is only by depreciating by more than 20 per cent that there can be an expected appreciation of the domestic currency to compensate for the lower rate of interest on domestic bonds.

After the initial response of the exchange rate and interest rate to the increase in the money stock, there are a number of forces that come into play to move the economy to its long run equilibrium. As a result of the fall in the domestic interest rate and the depreciation of the domestic currency, there is an increase in the demand for domestic goods. As output is assumed to be fixed this excess demand for domestic goods starts to drive up domestic prices from $P1$. The increased demand for domestic goods by foreigners leads to an exchange rate appreciation from $S2$ towards $\bar{S}$ (thus the expected appreciation is matched by an actual appreciation). At the same time, the rise in the domestic price level leads to an increase in domestic money demand and a rise in the domestic interest rate to maintain money market equilibrium. Over time the domestic price level rises from $P1$ to $\bar{P}$ by the same percentage as the increase in the money supply, and the exchange rate appreciates from $S2$ to $\bar{S}$ which corresponds to a restoration of PPP. Meanwhile, the domestic interest rate rises from $r2$ to its original level $r1$, so that once again there is neither an expected appreciation nor depreciation of the domestic currency.

Having outlined the principal idea we now proceed to a more formal exposition of the Dornbusch model of exchange-rate 'overshooting'. Those readers that wish to skip this can proceed straight to section 7.14.

7.10 A formal explanation of the Dornbusch model

In the model outlined, we focus upon a 'small country' in the sense that it faces a fixed world interest r^* which it cannot influence. The demand to hold money in the home country is given by a conventional money demand function:

$$m - p = \eta y - \sigma r \qquad (7.10)$$

where m is the log of the domestic money stock, p is the log of the domestic price level, y is the log of domestic real income, and r is the nominal domestic interest rate.

We again assume that domestic and foreign bonds are perfect substitutes so that the UIP condition holds, that is:

$$E\dot{s} = r - r^* \tag{7.11}$$

where $E\dot{s}$ is the expected rate of depreciation of the home currency.

The major difference between the sticky price and flexible price monetary model is that the sticky price model assumes that PPP holds only in the long run, not continuously as assumed in the flexible price monetary model. The hypothesis that the long-run exchange rate is determined by PPP yields:

$$\bar{s} = \bar{p} - \bar{p}^* \tag{7.12}$$

where $\bar{s}$ is the log of the long-run equilibrium exchange rate, $\bar{p}$ is the log of the long run domestic price level, and $\bar{p}^*$ is the log of the long run foreign price level.

Since the model allows for departures from PPP, it is necessary to specify an equation for the expected rate of change of the exchange rate. The Dornbusch model specifies regressive exchange expectations given by:

$$E\dot{s} = -\theta(s - \bar{s}) \quad \text{where } \theta > 0 \tag{7.13}$$

Equation (7.13) says that the expected rate of depreciation of a currency is determined by the speed of adjustment parameter θ, and the gap between the current exchange rate s and its long-run equilibrium value $\bar{s}$.

We now proceed to derive the two schedules vital to the Dornbusch model, the goods market equilibrium schedule which shows equality of aggregate demand and supply for goods and the money market equilibrium schedule which shows equality between the demand and supply of money.

 # 7.11 Derivation of the goods market equilibrium schedule

The goods market equilibrium schedule shows the equality of demand and supply for goods in the price–exchange rate plane. The model postulates that the rate of price inflation in the model is determined by the gap between aggregate demand and aggregate supply. That is:

$$\dot{p} = \pi(d - y) \tag{7.14}$$

where $\dot{p}$ is the rate of domestic price inflation, π is the speed of adjustment of prices, and d is the log of aggregate demand.

Aggregate demand is assumed to be a function of exogenous expenditure β, a positive function of the real exchange rate expressed in log form as $(s - p + p^*)$, a positive function of domestic income and a negative function of the domestic nominal interest rate. This yields:

$$d = \beta + \alpha(s - p + p^*) + \varphi y - \lambda r \tag{7.15}$$

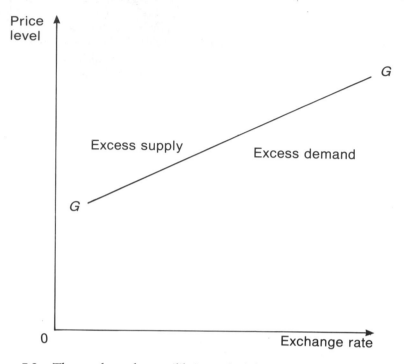

Figure 7.2   *The goods market equilibrium schedule*

Substituting equation (7.15) into equation (7.14) we obtain:

$$\dot{p} = \pi[\beta + \alpha(s - p + p^*) + (\varphi - 1)y - \lambda r] \tag{7.16}$$

Along the goods market equilibrium schedule (GG) the equality of supply and demand for goods means that there is zero inflation, that is $\dot{p} = 0$. To find the slope of the goods market schedule we must substitute solution for r from equation (7.10), into equation (7.16) to obtain:

$$\dot{p} = \pi[\beta + \alpha(s - p + p^*) + (\varphi - 1) - \lambda/\sigma(p - m + \eta y)] \tag{7.17}$$

Then by setting equation (7.17) to zero we find that the slope of the GG schedule in the price-level–exchange-rate plane. Along the GG schedule aggregate demand equals aggregate supply implying zero price inflation. The slope of the GG schedule is given by:

$$\frac{dp}{ds}(\dot{p} = 0) = \frac{\alpha}{\alpha + \lambda/\sigma} \tag{7.18}$$

From equation (7.18) we can see that the GG schedule is upward sloping from left to right and has a slope of less than unity as depicted in **Figure 7.2**.

The rationale behind the GG schedule is that a depreciation (rise) of the exchange rate leads to an increased demand for exports and this increase in demand can only be offset by a rise in the domestic price level which negates the competitive advantage of the depreciation. However, because the rise in the price level increases money demand it is accompanied by a rise in interest rates which further reduces demand. This means that the percentage depreciation of the exchange rate has to exceed the percentage rise in the price level to keep aggregate demand in line with aggregate supply.

To the left of the GG schedule there is an excess supply of goods owing to the fact that, assuming output to be fixed for any given price level, an exchange rate appreciation (fall) reduces aggregate demand. The excess supply of goods will put downward pressure on prices. Conversely, to the right of the GG schedule for any given price level, the exchange-rate depreciation (rise) leads to an excess demand for domestic goods causing an upward pressure on prices.

7.12 Derivation of the money market equilibrium schedule

The money market schedule shows different combinations of the price level and exchange rate that are consistent with equilibrium in the money market, that is, equilibrium of the supply and demand for money. To derive the money market schedule we first of all invert the money demand function (7.10) to solve for the domestic interest rate. This yields:

$$r = \frac{p - m + \eta y}{\sigma} \tag{7.19}$$

We then substitute the solution for $E\dot{s}$ in equation (7.11) into equation (7.13) and replace the solution for r in equation (7.19) to obtain:

$$s = \bar{s} - \frac{1}{\sigma\theta}[p - m + \eta y - \sigma r^*] \tag{7.20}$$

This means that the slope of the money market schedule is given by:

$$\frac{dp}{ds} = -\sigma\theta \tag{7.21}$$

Hence the MM schedule is shown to have a negative slope in the price-level–exchange-rate plane as depicted in **Figure 7.3**.

The explanation is that for a given money stock a fall in the price level implies a relatively high real money stock, and high real money balances will only be willingly held if the domestic interest rate falls. A fall in the domestic interest rate requires an expected appreciation of the currency to compensate

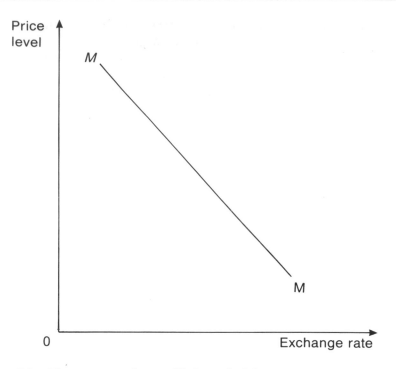

Figure 7.3   *The money market equilibrium schedule*

holders of the domestic currency. Given that exchange-rate expectations are regressive, such an expected appreciation can only occur if the exchange rate depreciates.

Equilibrium of the model occurs when both the goods and money markets are in equilibrium and the exchange rate is at its PPP value as depicted in **Figure 7.4**.

The PPP line is depicted as a ray from the origin indicating that if the domestic price level increases by x per cent then the exchange rate must also depreciate by x per cent to maintain PPP. The GG schedule as we have seen is less steep than the PPP line because an x per cent rise in the price level needs to be accompanied by a greater than x per cent depreciation of the exchange rate. The money market schedule is given by MM; it is assumed that the money market is in continuous equilibrium so that the economy is always somewhere on the MM schedule. The economy is in full equilibrium when the exchange rate corresponds to PPP, aggregate supply equals aggregate demand and there is money market equilibrium. This occurs where all three schedules intersect at point A.

We are now in a position to consider the effects of an economic shock such as an increase in the domestic money supply in the Dornbusch model.

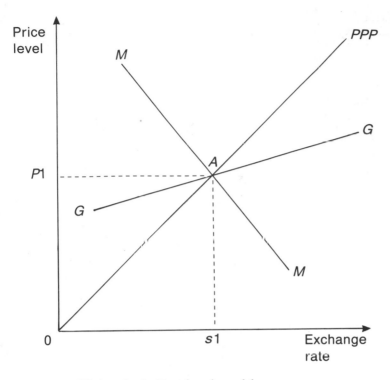

Figure 7.4   *Equilibrium in the Dornbusch model*

7.13 A money supply expansion and exchange-rate 'overshooting'

The effects of an x per cent increase in the money supply in the context of the Dornbusch model are illustrated in **Figure 7.5**.

Initially the economy is in full equilibrium at point A where the G1G1 schedule intersects the M1M1 schedule. Let us now suppose that the authorities unexpectedly expand the money supply by x per cent. Before examining the short-run effects of the money expansion it is worth considering what will be the long-run effects. In the long run, we know that domestic prices will rise by the same percentage as the rise in the money stock, this gives a long-run price of $\bar{p}$ which is x per cent above $p1$. As PPP holds in the long run, a rise in the domestic price level of x per cent requires a depreciation of the exchange rate by x per cent, this gives a long-run exchange rate $\bar{s}$. Bearing this in mind we can now consider the short run effects of the monetary expansion.

In the short run, the x per cent increase in the money supply results in a rightward shift of the M1M1 schedule to M2M2. We know that the M2M2

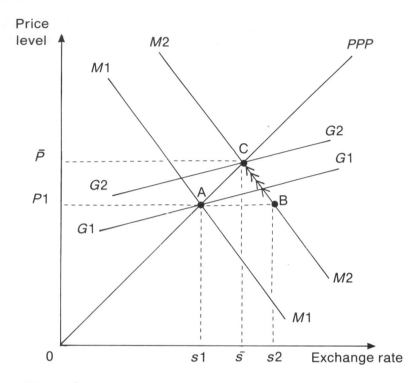

Figure 7.5   *Exchange-rate overshooting*

schedule must pass through the long-run equilibrium price $\bar{p}$ and long-run exchange rate $\bar{s}$ at point C. The major feature of the Dornbusch model is that in the short run domestic prices are sticky, while money markets are in continuous equilibrium as indicated by the UIP condition. In the context of **Figure 7.5** this means the economy is always on the new money market equilibrium schedule M2M2. As domestic prices do not initially change the price level remains at $p1$ and this is consistent with a jump in the exchange rate from $s1$ to $s2$ on the money market equilibrium schedule M2M2. The fact that the short-run equilibrium exchange rate $s2$ exceeds the long run equilibrium rate $\bar{s}$ is known as the phenomenon of exchange-rate 'overshooting'.

The reason why in the short run the exchange rate overshoots its long-run equilibrium value is as follows: given that domestic prices are fixed in the short run the money supply expansion creates an excess of real money balances which (given a fixed output level) are only willingly held at a lower domestic interest rate. According to the UIP condition, a fall in the domestic interest rate means that international investors will require an expected appreciation of the domestic currency to compensate for the lower domestic interest rate. An expected appreciation of the domestic currency is only possible if the exchange rate depreciation in the short run exceeds the required long run depreciation. This is shown in **Figure 7.5** by the fact that the exchange rate jump depreciates from $s1$ to $s2$ overshooting the long run equilibrium exchange rate $\bar{s}$. The exchange rate is then expected to appreciate from $s2$ to $\bar{s}$.

Having had a short-run jump in the exchange rate to point B on the M2M2 schedule forces come into play to move the economy along the M2M2 schedule over time from point B to the long-run point C. There are two factors at work in the movement from B to C during which time the currency appreciates from $s2$ to its long-run equilibrium value $\bar{s}$ and the price level rises from $p1$ to its long-run value $\bar{p}$. First, the reduced domestic interest rate will encourage increased expenditure. Second, the undervaluation of the currency in relation to its PPP value will mean that domestic goods become relatively cheap as compared with foreign goods and this leads to a substitution of world demand in favour of domestic goods which Dornbusch (1976b) identifies as the 'arbitrage effect'. These two factors shift up the goods market expenditure schedule from G1G1 to G2G2 and drive up the domestic price level and appreciate the exchange rate until the long-run equilibrium is established at point C. During the transition, the rise in the price level reduces real money balances requiring a rise in the domestic interest rate until at $\bar{p}$ the original interest rate is restored and there is no expected change in the exchange rate.

7.14 Importance of the sticky price monetary model

The sticky price monetary model represented a major advance in the exchange rate literature and it has had lasting appeal. The major innovation of the model is its emphasis on capital market rather than goods market arbitrage being the major determinant of exchange rates in the short run. Goods market arbitrage is viewed as relevant to exchange-rate determination only in the medium to long run, while the desire of investors to equalise expected yields on their international portfolios is viewed as the major determinant of the short-run exchange rate.

The model provides an intuitively appealing explanation of why exchange-rate movements have been largely relative to movements in international prices and changes in international money stocks. Furthermore, it explains such movements as the outcome of a rational foreign exchange market, that produces an exchange rate that deviates from PPP based on economic fundamentals not in isolation from them. Most economists find it hard to accept the notion that observed divergences of exchange rates from

PPP have been due to irrational speculation. The existence of models such as Dornbusch's that explain such deviations as the result of rational speculation provide considerable comfort.

Another important point that comes from the Dornbusch model is that it helps explain why observed exchange rates are usually even more volatile than supposed determinants such as the money supply. Since the exchange rate initially depreciates by more than x per cent in the short run in response to an x per cent increase in the money supply, it follows that the exchange rate will be more volatile than domestic monetary policy.

 # 7.15 The Frankel real interest rate differential model

The sticky price monetary model of Dornbusch represents a major advance on the flexible price monetary exchange-rate model but unlike the former, the Dornbusch model does not explicitly take into account inflationary expectations. However, the 1970s period of floating exchange rates was dominated by inflation. In a bid to combine the inflationary expectations element of the flexible price monetary model with the insights of the sticky price model, Frankel (1979) developed a general monetary exchange-rate model that accommodates the 'flexible price' and 'sticky price' monetarist models as special cases.

As in the other monetarist models, there is a conventional money demand function:

$$m - p = \eta y - \sigma r \tag{7.22}$$

where m is the log of the domestic money stock, p is the log of the domestic price level, y is the log of domestic real income, and r is the nominal domestic interest rate.

Similar relationships are postulated for the rest of the world as represented by the foreign country:

$$m^* - p^* = \eta y^* - \sigma r^* \tag{7.23}$$

where an asterisk represents a foreign variable.

For simplicity it is also assumed that elasticities (η and σ) are identical across countries. Combining (7.22) and (7.23) yields:

$$(m - m^*) = (p - p^*) + \eta(y - y^*) - \sigma(r - r^*) \tag{7.24}$$

Like the other monetarist models the theory assumes that domestic and foreign bonds are perfect substitutes so that the uncovered interest parity condition holds:

$$E\dot{s} = r - r^* \tag{7.25}$$

where $E\dot{s}$ is the expected rate of depreciation of the home currency.

As in the Dornbusch model, it is assumed that the expected rate of depreciation of the exchange rate is a positive function of the gap between the current (spot) rate s and the long-run equilibrium rate $\bar{s}$. In addition it is also a function of the expected long-run inflation differential between the domestic and foreign economies. This yields:

$$E\dot{s} = -\theta(s - \bar{s}) + P\dot{e} - P\dot{e}^* \tag{7.26}$$

where θ is the speed of adjustment to equilibrium, $P\dot{e}$ is the expected long run domestic inflation rate, $P\dot{e}^*$ is the expected long run foreign inflation rate.

Equation (7.26) states that in the short run, the spot exchange rate as given by s is expected to return to its long-run equilibrium value $\bar{s}$ at a rate θ. In the long run since $s = \bar{s}$, the expected rate of depreciation of the currency is equal to the difference of the domestic to foreign inflation via the relative PPP condition.

Combining equations (7.25) and (7.26) yields:

$$s - \bar{s} = \frac{-1}{\theta}[(r - P\dot{e}) - (r^* - P\dot{e}^*)] \tag{7.27}$$

Equation (7.27) states that the gap between the current real exchange rate and its long run equilibrium value is proportional to the real interest rate differential as given by the term in brackets. Thus, if the expected real rate of interest on foreign bonds is greater than the expected real rate of interest on domestic bonds there will be a real depreciation of the domestic currency as capital flows from domestic to foreign bonds until the real interest rates are equalised in the long run steady state.

By invoking long-run PPP the long run equilibrium exchange rate $\bar{s}$ can be expressed in log form as the difference between the long-run price levels:

$$\bar{s} = \bar{p} - \bar{p}^* \tag{7.28}$$

In the long run the expected real rates of interest are equalised so that any long run nominal interest rate differentials are explained by differences in the steady-state inflation rates:

$$r - r^* = P\dot{e} - P\dot{e}^* \tag{7.29}$$

By combining (7.29) and (7.28) with equation (7.24) we can obtain an expression for the long-run steady-state equilibrium exchange rate given by:

$$\bar{s} = (m - m^*) - \eta(y - y^*) + \sigma(P\dot{e} - P\dot{e}^*) \tag{7.30}$$

Equation (7.30) states that the long-run equilibrium exchange rate is determined by the relative supply $(m - m^*)$ and relative demands as given by $\eta(y - y^*) + \sigma(P\dot{e} - P\dot{e}^*)$ of the two national money stocks. The reader will note that equation(7.30) which refers to the long-run exchange rate is identical to equation (7.9) of the flexible price monetarist model for the short-run exchange rate. However, the solution for the short-run exchange rate in the Frankel model differs because of sticky goods prices in the short run. We now proceed to find the solution for the short-run exchange rate in the Frankel model.

In the Frankel generalisation of the Dornbusch model, the speed of adjustment of the goods market is relevant to the determination of the short-run exchange rate, so that equation (7.27) has to be taken into account when solving for the short-run exchange rate. Combining equation (7.30) with (7.27) and rearranging terms yields the following solution for the short-run exchange rate:

$$s = (m - m^*) - \eta(y - y^*) + \sigma(P\dot{e} - P\dot{e}^*) \frac{-1}{\theta} [(r - P\dot{e}) - (r^* - P\dot{e}^*)]$$

(7.31)

The Frankel formulation makes clear that if there is a disequilibrium set of real interest rates, then the real exchange rate will deviate from its long-run equilibrium value. If the real domestic interest rate is below the real foreign interest rate then the real exchange rate of the domestic currency will be undervalued in relation to its long run equilibrium value, so that there is an expected appreciation of the real exchange rate of the domestic currency to compensate.

The fully flexible price monetarist school argues that all markets clear instantaneously so that the speed of adjustment parameter θ, in equation (7.31) is infinite, so that the solution for the short-run exchange rate is given by equation (7.9). In the real interest model as portrayed by equation (7.31), the goods and labour market prices are assumed to be slow to adjust to shocks so the speed of adjustment parameter θ is finite. Thus, rational expectations holds for the foreign exchange market but not for domestic markets. In such circumstances, an unanticipated monetary expansion leads to a fall in the real domestic interest rate relative to the real foreign interest rate while domestic price level is initially unchanged but expected to rise. The result according to equation (7.31) is that the short-run exchange rate overshoots its long-run equilibrium value, depreciating proportionately more than the increase in the money stock so that there are expectations of a future real appreciation of the currency to compensate for the lower real rate of return on domestic bonds.

 ## 7.16 Implications of the monetary views of exchange-rate determination

Whichever monetarist model one adopts, a clear implication is that monetary policy is the only predictable and effective means of influencing the exchange rate. Furthermore, because domestic and foreign bonds are assumed to be perfect substitutes there is no distinction to be made between the effects of an open market operation (OMO) and a foreign exchange market operation (FXO). An expansionary OMO is a purchase of domestic treasury bills, while an expansionary FXO is a purchase of foreign bonds. As far as the monetary model is concerned if they increase the money supply by a like amount they have identical exchange-rate effects. What matters for the exchange rate is the supply of money in relation to the demand for it. The source of creation of the money stock is irrelevant.

From the above, it follows that there is no scope for the authorities to pursue a sterilised foreign exchange operation (SFXO) that will have exchange-rate effects. An SFXO is an exchange of domestic for foreign bonds that leaves the supply of money in relation to the demand for it unaffected. Within the context of the monetary approach to exchange-rate determination, because the two assets are perfect substitutes and the money supply is left unchanged, an SFXO cannot exert exchange rate effects.

In the flexible price monetarist model, while the authorities can influence the nominal exchange in a predictable fashion by monetary policy, they cannot do likewise with the real exchange rate. If there is a once and for all x per cent increase in the money supply this will lead to a once and for all x per cent depreciation of the home currency and simultaneous x per cent increase in both the domestic price level and wages. This is a case of complete neutrality of monetary policy with respect to the real economy. Monetary policy influences only nominal not real variables.

Within the context of the 'sticky price' monetarist approach the authorities can exploit the finite speed of adjustment of domestic markets to influence the real exchange rate in the short run, provided that real output is fixed. For example, if there is an unexpected increase in the domestic money stock, we have seen that with domestic prices sticky in the short run there will be a depreciation of the real exchange rate. The Frankel model makes clear that the overshooting of the exchange rate is proportional to the deviation of the real domestic interest rate from its equilibrium value.

The possibility of real exchange-rate overshooting due to the adoption of an expansionary or contractionary monetary policy has strengthened the arguments of those that call for 'gradualism' in the implementation of monetary policy. The basis of their claim is that economic agents in the goods and labour markets take time to adjust to a new monetary policy regime because they need convincing that the authorities mean what they say. For this reason, domestic wage restraint is unlikely to follow immediately following the adoption of a tighter monetary policy. If this is the case, then the real exchange rate will appreciate in the short run and thereby place pressure on the tradables sector of the economy. Gradualists argue that if the authorities implement their policy of restraint gradually then economic agents will have time to observe that the authorities are implementing their stated policy and wage behaviour will then adjust without the high cost imposed upon the economy of overshooting.

Whichever monetarist view one adheres to, the clear implication is that monetary policy is the most effective means of managing the exchange rate. Furthermore, in the long run the authorities should abandon any attempt to influence the real exchange rate because it is determined by real and not monetary factors. Thus, in the long run (short run in the flexible price version) the authorities should direct exchange rate policy at stabilising the domestic price level. Whether stabilising the domestic price level will stabilise the nominal exchange rate depends upon the stability of the foreign price level and therefore upon the monetary policies of foreign countries. The authorities should not seek to stabilise the nominal exchange rate by monetary policy because this may involve destabilising the domestic price level if the foreign authorities are not pursuing stable monetary policies.

■ *7.17* Conclusions

A common characteristic of the three monetary models of exchange rate determination examined in this chapter is that what matters for the exchange rate is the money supply in relation to money demand in both the home and foreign countries. The exchange rate is the relative price of two national monies and is consequently a monetary phenomenon.

All the monetary models build upon PPP. The flexible price monetary model assumes that PPP holds continuously and maintains that the price level adjusts instantaneously to changes in the supply and demand for money. This then leads to an immediate exchange-rate adjustment to maintain PPP. Changes in real income and inflation expectations induce changes in the exchange rate because they affect the demand for money. In the sticky price monetary models, the asymmetric speeds of adjustment in goods and asset markets can lead to divergences from PPP in the short run, although PPP reasserts itself in the long run.

The sticky price monetary models provide an explanation of both exchange rate volatility and misalignment. Exchange rates can become misaligned in relation to PPP because of the phenomenon of exchange rate 'overshooting', while instability in monetary policies can result in even greater instability in exchange rates. An important point made by the sticky price models is that both divergences from PPP and highly volatile exchange rates can be explained by rational speculation and are not necessarily the result of 'irrational' foreign exchange speculation.

Perhaps the most noticeable omission of the monetary models of exchange-rate determination is an explicit role for the current account to influence the exchange rate. Furthermore, domestic and foreign bonds are regarded as perfect substitutes – that is, they are regarded as equally risky so there is no role for risk perceptions to play a part in the determination of exchange rates. The portfolio balance model of exchange-rate determination that we examine in the next chapter has an explicit and important role for both of these factors to influence exchange rates.

■ Selected further readings

Bilson, J.F.O. (1978a) 'Rational Expectations and the Exchange Rate', in J.A. Frenkel and H.G. Johnson, *The Economics of Exchange Rates* (Reading, Mass.: Addison-Wesley).

Bilson, J.F.O. (1978b) 'The Monetary Approach to the Exchange Rate: Some Empirical Evidence', *IMF Staff Papers*, vol. 25, pp. 48–75.

Bilson, J.F.O. (1979) 'Recent Developments in Monetary Models of Exchange Rate Determination', *IMF Staff Papers*, vol. 26, pp. 201–23.

Dornbusch, R. (1976a) 'Expectations and Exchange Rate Dynamics', *Journal of Political Economy*, vol. 84, pp. 1161–76.

Dornbusch, R. (1976b) 'The Theory of Flexible Exchange Rate Regimes and Macroeconomic Policy', *Scandinavian Journal of Economics*, vol. 84, pp. 255–75.

Dornbusch, R. (1983) 'Flexible Exchange Rates and Interdependence', *IMF Staff Papers*, vol. 30, pp. 3–30.

Frankel, J.A. (1979) 'On the Mark: A Theory of Floating Exchange Rates Based on Real Interest Rate Differentials', *American Economic Review*, vol. 69, pp. 610–22.

Frenkel, J.A. (1976) 'A Monetary Approach to the Exchange Rate: Doctrinal Aspects and Empirical Evidence', *Scandinavian Journal of Economics*, vol. 78, pp. 169–91.

Isard, P. (1978) 'Exchange Rate Determination: a Survey of Popular Views and Recent Models', *Princeton Studies in International Finance*, No 42.

MacDonald, R. and Taylor, M.P. (1989) 'Economic Analysis of Foreign Exchange Markets: An Expository Survey', in R. MacDonald and M.P. Taylor, *Innovations in Open Economy Macroeconomics* (Oxford: Basil Blackwell).

Mussa, M. (1976) 'The Exchange Rate, the Balance of Payments, and Monetary and Fiscal Policy Under a Regime of Controlled Floating', *Scandinavian Journal of Economics*, vol. 78, pp. 229–48.

■ *Chapter 8* ■

The Portfolio Balance Model

■ *8.1* Introduction

The monetary models of exchange rate determination examined in Chapter 7 made the crucial assumption that domestic and foreign bonds are perfect substitutes. This implied that the expected yields on domestic and foreign bonds are equalised. In effect, apart from their currency of denomination domestic and foreign bonds are regarded by international investors as the same. In this chapter, we examine the portfolio balance model which is distinguished from the monetary models because it allows for the possibility that international investors may regard domestic and foreign bonds as having different characteristics other than their currency of denomination. In particular, they might for various reasons regard one of the bonds as being more risky than the other. This being the case they will generally require a higher expected return on the bond that is considered more risky to compensate for the additional risk it entails.

Allowing for domestic and foreign bonds to have different characteristics is potentially very important because operations that influence the exchange rate affect the composition of domestic and foreign bonds in agents' portfolios in different ways. In this chapter we shall be examining three operations that are commonly used to influence the exchange rate:

1. An open market operation (OMO) which is defined as an exchange of domestic money base for domestic bonds or vice-versa.

2. A foreign exchange operation (FXO) which is an exchange of domestic money for foreign bonds or vice-versa. Such foreign exchange market intervention affects the domestic money supply and is termed a non-sterilised intervention in the foreign exchange market.
3. A sterilised foreign exchange operation (SFXO) which is an exchange of domestic bonds for foreign bonds or vice-versa leaving the domestic money base unchanged.

The interesting thing about an SFXO is that it represents the difference between an OMO and FXO. An expansionary FXO means that the authorities purchase foreign bonds with domestic money; this means that the public holds more money and less foreign bonds. If the authorities decide they wish to keep the money supply at its original level they can conduct a contractionary monetary policy by selling domestic bonds to the public so that the money held by the public returns to its original level. If they conduct such a sterilisation operation, the net effect is that the public holds less foreign bonds and more domestic bonds with the money supply unchanged.

In the monetary models examined in Chapter 7, the only thing that matters for the exchange rate is money supply in relation to money demand the source of money creation being unimportant. This meant that there was no difference in the exchange rate and interest rate effects of an FXO or OMO that change the money supply by a like amount. The reason being, that in the monetary models there is no distinction between domestic and foreign bonds. Within the context of the monetary models an SFXO will have no exchange rate or interest rate effect because it leaves money supply unchanged and is merely the exchange of domestic for foreign bonds which are perfect substitutes.

To understand the differences between the portfolio balance model and the monetary models section 8.2 introduces the concept of a risk premium. We then proceed to examine different types of risks that may make domestic and foreign bonds imperfect substitutes which is the basis for the portfolio balance model. Next we outline a simple version of the portfolio balance model and use this to examine the differing effects of OMOs, FXOs, and SFXOs. We then look at the results in the light of their effects on the risk premium. Finally, we consider some of the dynamic features of the portfolio balance model.

■ *8.2* The concept of a risk premium

The distinguishing feature of the portfolio balance model is that investors no longer regard domestic and foreign bonds as perfect substitutes. This being the case the expected returns on the two assets no longer have to be equal. In other words, the uncovered interest parity condition which was a key condition in the monetary models generally no longer holds. For example, if investors are risk averse and regard domestic bonds as being relatively risky as compared to foreign bonds, they will require a higher expected return on domestic bonds than foreign bonds. This additional expected return on the relatively risky as compared to the less risky bond is known as the 'risk premium'. For a risk premium to exist, all of the following three conditions must be fulfilled (see Isard, 1983):

1. There must be perceived differences in risks between domestic and foreign bonds – the essence of a risky asset being that its expected real rate of return is uncertain. Either domestic bonds are viewed as relatively risky compared with foreign bonds or vice versa. If the two bonds were equally risky then with perfect capital mobility they must be perfect substitutes.

2. There has to be risk aversion on the part of economic agents to the perceived differences in risk – the principle of risk aversion is that investors will only be prepared to take on increased risk if there is a sufficient increase in expected real returns to compensate. If investors were not risk averse then they would not expect a higher return on relatively risky bonds.

3. There must be a difference between the risk minimising portfolio and the actual portfolio forced at market clearing prices into investors' portfolios. Given the different risks on domestic and foreign bonds there is a theoretical portfolio known as the risk minimising portfolio which would minimise the risks facing private agents. However, the amount of domestic and foreign bonds held by private agents is determined by the respective authorities that issue them. If the risk minimising portfolio is not held then agents will demand a risk premium to compensate.

If all three of the above conditions are fulfilled, then the uncovered interest parity condition will not hold due to the existence of a risk premium which represents the compensation required by private agents for accepting risk exposure above the minimum possible.

$$r - r^* = E\dot{s} + RP \qquad (8.1)$$

where r is the domestic interest rate, r^* is the foreign interest rate, $E\dot{s}$ is the expected rate of depreciation of domestic currency defined as domestic currency units per unit of foreign currency, and RP is the risk premium required on domestic bonds which may be either positive or negative.

The difference between the equation (8.1) and the uncovered interest parity condition (equation (7.1) is the risk premium expression. The expected rate of return on domestic bonds may be higher (a positive risk premium) or lower (a negative risk premium) when compared with foreign bonds. For example, if domestic bonds are regarded as more risky than foreign bonds, if the domestic interest rate is 10 per cent, foreign interest rate 6 per cent and the expected rate of depreciation of the domestic currency is only 3 per cent, then there is a 1 per cent risk premium on the domestic currency. Foreign assets have an expected yield of 9 per cent, the 6 per cent interest and 3 per cent expected appreciation of the foreign currency. This is lower than the 10 per cent yield on domestic bonds. The 1 per cent positive risk premium on the domestic currency is a negative 1 per cent risk premium on the foreign currency.

An issue that we need to briefly examine concerns what types of risk may cause the emergence of a risk premium?

■ *8.3* Different types of risk

When analysing risk, economists make some postulates about economic agents. Investors are assumed to be rational in that they wish to maximise their expected utility which is a positive function of expected real returns and a negative function of the perceived level of risk. The basis of investors' portfolio decisions is choosing an optimum combination of expected rate of return and risk given their risk-return preferences (degree of risk aversion). The less risk averse investors are, the more they will be prepared to take on risk. Conversely, the more risk averse they are the less risk they will be prepared to take on.

In the first instance we need to define a risky asset. The definition of a risky asset is that its expected real rate of return is uncertain. In other words, economic agents for various reasons cannot be sure what the value of the return in terms of purchasing power will be. Typically risks fall into one of two main categories (see Wihlborg, 1978), 'currency risks' and 'country risks'. Currency risks arise because domestic and foreign bonds are denominated in different currencies, while country risks arise because they are issued by countries with different legal jurisdictions and different political regimes.

☐ *Currency risks*

There are two types of currency risk that we shall consider. One is called 'inflation risk' and the other is termed 'exchange risk'.

Inflation risk – this type of risk occurs because the inflation rates in the domestic and foreign economies are uncertain. If PPP were to hold continuously, the real rate of return on the domestic bond is given by the nominal interest rate less the expected domestic inflation rate ($P\dot{e}$). If the latter is uncertain then so will be the real return on the asset considered. Similarly, the expected real rate of return on foreign bonds is given by the nominal foreign interest rate less the expected foreign inflation rate ($P\dot{e}^*$). If the latter is also subject to uncertainty then so will be the real return on foreign bonds.

If PPP holds continuously and the expected domestic price inflation rate rises this reduces the expected real rate of return on domestic bonds but does not increase the expected real rate on foreign bonds because the currency will depreciate by the same amount as the expected inflation rate. The risk of holding a domestic bond can therefore be represented as a positive function of the variance in the domestic inflation rate while the risk of holding a foreign bond can be represented as a positive function of the variance of the foreign inflation rate. A greater variance of the expected domestic inflation rate raises the relative riskiness of domestic as compared with foreign bonds and vice versa.

Exchange risk – If PPP holds continuously, then inflation risk would be the sole currency risk facing international investors. However, we saw in Chapter 6 that the overwhelming weight of empirical evidence since the advent of floating exchange rates rejects the use of PPP as a valid approximation of short-run exchange rate determination. This being the case, then one has to take into account deviations from PPP when calculating the expected real rate of return on domestic and foreign bonds during the holding period. While the expected real rate of return on domestic bonds is given by the nominal interest rate minus the expected rate of inflation, the expected rate of return from holding foreign bonds is now given as the foreign interest rate less the expected foreign inflation rate plus the expected deviation of the exchange rate from PPP. For simplicity, let us assume that inflation and domestic and foreign interest rates are equal and exchange rates are initially at PPP. In this case an expected real depreciation of the currency in terms of PPP means that there is an expected appreciation of the foreign currency implying an increased expected return from holding foreign bonds. The expected real rate of return on domestic bonds is, however, unaffected by such deviations from PPP.

The expected deviation of the exchange rate from PPP causes a risk specific to foreign bonds given by the variance of the expected deviation from PPP. That is, fluctuations in the exchange rate that cause deviations from PPP constitute a risk specific to foreign investments which is called 'exchange risk'. Exchange-rate changes only cause exchange risk to the extent that they represent deviations from PPP. If exchange-rate changes ensure that PPP holds then they do not constitute exchange risk. Theoretically, therefore, exchange rate fluctuations are an incorrect measure of exchange risk. It is fluctuations of the exchange rate around PPP that constitute exchange risk.

☐ *Country risks*

Country risks are somewhat less amenable to economic analysis than currency risks. Nevertheless, since the definition of a risky asset is that its expected real rate of return is uncertain, it is not difficult to conceptualise country risks. Country risks can be divided into three types; exchange control risk, political risk and default risk.

Exchange control risk – one type of country risk whereby investors face uncertain real rates of return is exchange rate control risk. The real rate of return on domestic and foreign bonds may be uncertain due to the risk of the imposition of a tax on the interest element during the holding period. This risk may be greater or less for domestic as compared with foreign bonds.

Default risk – Another, more serious country risk is 'default risk' whereby a government refuses to pay the interest and sometimes the principal on bonds issued by them and denominated in a foreign currency. Note that the bonds need to be denominated in foreign currency because a government will not default on bonds issued in its own currency because it can always print the money to redeem the bonds if they are issued in its own currency.

Political risk – this risk covers an extremely broad range of scenarios. Basically, political risk refers to the danger that investors, because of the political environment in the country, may lose part or all of their investment including returns due, or find costly restrictions imposed on how they may manipulate their investment.

From the above discussion we can see that there are a variety of reasons as to why domestic and foreign bonds may have different relative riskiness which is a necessary precondition for making them imperfect substitutes. What matters, to produce imperfect asset substitutability and a risk premium, is perceived differences in risks between domestic and foreign bonds. If assets are regarded as equally risky then with perfect capital mobility they must be perfect substitutes.

■ *8.4* A portfolio balance model

The portfolio balance model of exchange rates was pioneered by William Branson (1976, 1977, 1984) and Pennti Kouri (1976) and has been subsequently modified and extended in various directions by Maurice Obstfeld (1980), Girton and Henderson (1977), Allen and Kenen (1980), Kenen

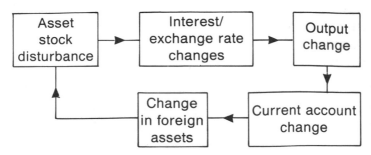

Figure 8.1   *The operation of the portfolio balance model*

(1982). The model we shall look at is based upon Branson (1976) and Kouri (1976). This model is a simple version of many portfolio balance models because it utilises the assumption of static exchange-rate expectations, that is, the exchange rate is not expected to change. The *Es* expression in equation (8.1) is assumed to be zero.

In the model outlined we assume that domestic prices and output are fixed following a policy disturbance. This means the focus of the analysis is on the accumulation or decumulation of foreign assets resulting from imbalances in the current account following an operation to influence the exchange rate. A current account surplus means that the country is building up a stock of claims on the rest of the world as represented by an increased holding of foreign bonds, while a deficit in the balance of payments corresponds to a decline in foreign bond holdings. The operation of the portfolio balance model is depicted in **Figure 8.1**.

In the portfolio balance model an OMO, FXO or SFXO creates a disturbance in asset holders' portfolios requiring a change in the exchange rate and domestic interest rate. These changes then lead to effects on the current account. A current account surplus/deficit leads to an accumulation/decumulation of foreign assets. This leads to further changes in asset holders' portfolios with implications for the exchange rate and domestic interest rate and so on until the model is restored to long-run equilibrium.

■ 8.5 The model

In the model that follows, we can distinguish between OMOs and FXOs because domestic and foreign bonds are assumed to be imperfect substitutes. This means that an SFXO which represents the difference of an FXO and OMO becomes feasible. The model outlined follows the portfolio balance framework as developed by William Branson (1976, 1977, 1984). The analysis focuses on a 'small country' in the sense that it can influence its real exchange rate without provoking a reaction from the rest of the world. This assumption enables the derivation of some concrete results; the point that the foreign country's reaction may reinforce or offset the policy pursued by the home country is self-evident. In addition, because the domestic economy is small, its assets are assumed not to be of any interest to the rest of the world and hence they are held only by domestic residents.

There are a number of simplifying assumptions that we shall make at the outset; these are that both the domestic and foreign price levels are fixed and that real domestic output is also fixed. We do, however, discuss the possible implications of OMOs, FXOs and SFXOs on real output in **Section 8.11.**

☐ *The model*

There are assumed to be three assets that are held in the portfolios of the private agents and the authorities:

1.   Domestic monetary base, M.
2.   Domestic bonds denominated only in the domestic currency, B.
3.   Foreign bonds denominated only in the foreign currency, F.

Domestic bonds may be held by either domestic private agents or the authorities. Thus, we may denote the net supply of domestic bonds which is assumed to be fixed as:

$$B = Bp + Ba \qquad (8.2)$$

where B is the fixed net supply of domestic bonds, Bp is the domestic bond holdings of private agents, Ba is the domestic bond holdings of the authorities.

Similarly, the country's net holding of foreign bonds is held by private agents and the authorities, which we assume in our analysis to be positive in both cases and equal to the summation of previous current account surpluses. Unlike the stock of domestic bonds the holdings of foreign assets may be increased or decreased over time via a current account surplus or deficit. Thus we have:

$$F = Fp + Fa \qquad (8.3)$$

where F is the net foreign bond holdings of the country, Fp is the foreign bond holdings of private agents, and Fa is the stock of foreign bonds held by the authorities.

The domestic monetary base liability of the authorities is equivalent to the assets of the authorities so that:

$$M = Ba + SFa \qquad (8.4)$$

where S is the exchange rate defined as domestic currency units per unit of foreign currency.

For simplicity it is assumed that capital gains or losses to the authorities as a result of exchange rate changes do not affect the monetary base.

Total private financial wealth (W) at any point in time is given by the identity:

$$W = M + Bp + SFp \tag{8.5}$$

An important point concerning equation (8.5) is that the domestic currency value of foreign bonds is given by the value of foreign bonds times the exchange rate defined as domestic currency units per unit of foreign currency, that is, SFp. This means that an excess demand for foreign bonds can be partly met by a depreciation (rise) of the domestic currency which raises the domestic currency value of foreign bond holdings.

The demand to hold money by the private sector is inversely related to the domestic interest rate, inversely related to the expected rate of return on foreign bonds and positively to domestic income and wealth. This yields:

$$M = m(r, E\dot{s}, Y, W) \qquad m_r < 0, m_{\dot{s}} < 0, m_y > 0 \quad \text{and} \quad m_w > 0 \tag{8.6}$$

where r is the domestic nominal interest rate, $E\dot{s}$ is the expected rate of depreciation of the domestic currency, Y is the domestic nominal income, and m_r, $m_{\dot{s}}$, m_y and m_w are partial derivatives.

The demand to hold domestic bonds as a proportion of private wealth is positively related to the domestic interest rate, inversely related to the expected rate of return on foreign assets and inversely related to domestic nominal income and positively to wealth. This yields:

$$Bp = b(r, E\dot{s}, Y, W) \qquad b_r > 0, b_{\dot{s}} < 0, b_y < 0 \quad \text{and} \quad b_w > 0 \tag{8.7}$$

where b_r, $b_{\dot{s}}$, b_y and b_w are partial derivatives.

The demand to hold foreign bonds as a proportion of total wealth is inversely related to the domestic interest rate, positively related to the expected rate of return from holding foreign bonds and inversely related to domestic nominal income and positively to wealth. This yields:

$$SFp = f(r, E\dot{s}, Y, W) \qquad f_r < 0, f_{\dot{s}} > 0, f_y < 0 \text{ and } f_w > 0 \tag{8.8}$$

where f_r, $f_{\dot{s}}$, f_y and f_w are partial derivatives.

Since any increase in wealth is held as either money, bonds or foreign bonds then the sum of the partial elasticities with respect to wealth must sum to unity. This is known as the balance sheet constraint and is given by the identity:

$$m_w + b_w + f_w = 1 \tag{8.9}$$

The balance sheet identity is coupled with the assumption that assets are gross substitutes implying the following constraints on the partial derivatives:

$$m_r + b_r + f_r = 0 \tag{8.10}$$

$$m_{\dot{s}} + b_{\dot{s}} + f_{\dot{s}} = 0 \tag{8.11}$$

From equation (8.10) it can be inferred that the demand for domestic bonds is more responsive to the domestic interest rate than foreign bond demand. The demand for domestic bonds is less responsive to the foreign interest rate than foreign bond demand. Also, from equation (8.11) it can be inferred that the demand for domestic bonds is less responsive to the expected rate of return on foreign bonds than foreign bond demand.

The current account balance is crucial to the dynamics of the system because the current account surplus gives the rate of accumulation of foreign assets. That is:

$$C = \frac{dFp}{dt} = \dot{F}p = T + r^*(Fp + Fa) \tag{8.12}$$

where C is the current account surplus measured in foreign currency, T is the trade balance measured in foreign currency, and r^* is the foreign interest rate.

The current account is made up of two components; the revenue from net exports (the trade balance) and interest rate receipts from net holdings of foreign assets.

Net exports are assumed to be a positive function of the real exchange rate, inversely related to domestic income via the marginal propensity. This yields:

$$T = T(S/P, Y) \qquad T_s > 0 \quad \text{and} \quad T_y < 0 \tag{8.13}$$

where P is the domestic price level, and T_s and T_y are partial derivatives.

The assumption that net exports are a positive function of the real exchange rate is quite strong because it rules out the possibility that there may be an initial *J*-curve effect on the trade balance (see Chapter 3); the assumption implies that the Marshall–Lerner condition always holds.

■ *8.6 Derivation of the asset demand functions*

We now proceed to analyse the effects of OMOs, FXOs and SFXOs on the exchange rate and domestic interest rate using a comparative static framework. To make things easier we set the initial value of the exchange rate S and level of wealth equal to unity. Taking the total differential of equation (8.5) we obtain:

$$dW = dM + dB + Fp\,dS + S\,dFp \tag{8.14}$$

Taking the total differentials of the asset market functions given by equations (8.6) to (8.8) we obtain:

$$dM = m_r\, dr + m_\dot{s}\, dE\dot{s} + m_w\, (dM + dBp + Fp\, dS + S\, dFp) \tag{8.15}$$

$$dBp = b_r\, dr + b_\dot{s}\, dE\dot{s} + b_w\, (dM + dBp + Fp\, dS + S\, dFp) \tag{8.16}$$

$$dFp = f_r\, dr + f_\dot{s}\, dE\dot{s} + f_w\, (dM + dBp + Fp\, dS + S\, dFp) \tag{8.17}$$

Setting the left-hand side of the above equations to zero and noting that because of static exchange rate expectations $dE\dot{s} = 0$, we can obtain the slope of the various asset market schedules in the interest-rate–exchange-rate plane.

☐ The money market schedule

The money market (MM) schedule depicted in **Figure 8.2** shows various combinations of the domestic interest rate for which money supply is equal to money demand. Keeping the money supply fixed ($dM = 0$) and since $dE\dot{s} = 0$ from equation (8.15) we find that the money market schedule has a positive slope given by:

$$\frac{dr}{dS} = \frac{-m_w\, Fp}{m_r} > 0 \tag{8.18}$$

☐ The bond market schedule

The bond market schedule (BB) schedule depicted in **Figure 8.2** shows various combinations of the domestic interest rate and exchange rate for which the private bond supply is equal to private bond demand. Keeping the private bond supply fixed($dBp = 0$) and since $dE\dot{s} = 0$ from equation (8.16) we find that the bond market schedule has a negative slope given by:

$$\frac{dr}{dS} = \frac{-b_w\, Fp}{b_r} < 0 \tag{8.19}$$

☐ The foreign bond schedule

The foreign bond market schedule (FF) schedule depicted in **Figure 8.2** shows various combinations of the domestic interest rate and exchange rate for which the domestic holding of foreign bond supply is equal to private foreign bond demand. Keeping the private foreign bond supply fixed ($dFp = 0$) and since $dE\dot{s} = 0$ from equation (8.17) we find that the foreign bond market schedule has a negative slope given by:

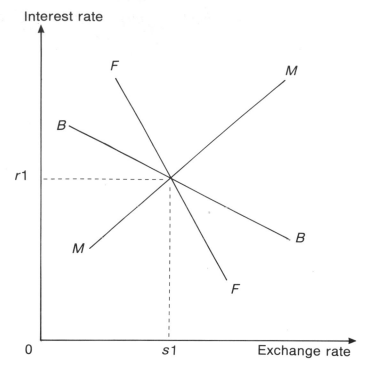

Figure 8.2 *Equilibrium of the model*

$$\frac{\mathrm{d}r}{\mathrm{d}S} = \frac{(1-f_\mathrm{w})\,Fp}{f_\mathrm{r}} < 0 \tag{8.20}$$

■ *8.7* Equilibrium of the model

The asset market of the model is in equilibrium when all three asset markets, that is, the money markets and the domestic and foreign bond markets clear at the appropriate domestic interest rate and exchange rate. This is depicted in **Figure 8.2**.

The *MM* schedule depicts equilibrium in the domestic money market; this is upward sloping from left to right in the interest-rate–exchange-rate plane. The reason for this is that a depreciation (rise) of the exchange rate leads to an increase in the value of domestic residents' wealth as it raises the domestic currency value of their holdings of foreign bonds. This being the case, they will wish to hold more domestic money; however, given the existing money stock, the increased money demand can only be offset by a rise in the domestic interest rate. An increase in the money supply for a given exchange rate requires a fall in domestic interest rate to be willingly held, implying a rightward shift of the *MM* schedule.

The *BB* schedule depicts equilibrium in the domestic bond market; this is downward sloping from left to right. A depreciation by raising domestic wealth also leads to an increased demand for domestic bonds which given the existing stock of domestic bonds can only be offset by a fall in the domestic interest rate that will reduce their attractiveness to investors. An increase in the domestic bond supply for a given exchange rate requires a rise in the domestic interest rate to be willingly held, implying a rightward shift of the *BB* schedule.

Finally, the *FF* schedule depicts equilibrium in the foreign bonds market; this slopes downward from left to right. A rise in the interest rate on domestic bonds makes them relatively more attractive as compared with foreign bonds, inducing agents to sell foreign bonds to purchase domestic bonds leading to an appreciation of the domestic currency. An increase in the supply of foreign bonds given the assumption of a fixed foreign interest rate and a given exchange rate requires a fall in the domestic interest rate to be willingly held, implying a leftward shift of the *FF* schedule.

The *FF* schedule is steeper than the *BB* schedule on the assumption that changes in the domestic rate of interest affect the demand for domestic bonds more than they influence the demand for foreign bonds. The different slopes of the *BB* and *FF* schedules shows that the two assets are regarded by private agents as different.

□ *The short-run behaviour of the model*

We now proceed to examine the short-run effects of an FXO, OMO and SFXO respectively. In each case, we shall assume that the operation is designed to produce a depreciation of the exchange rate to improve the international competitiveness of the country.

 ## 8.8 The effects of a foreign exchange operation

With an expansionary FXO, the authorities purchase foreign bonds from the private sector with newly created monetary base. This means that there is an increase in the private sector's holdings of money and an equivalent fall in their holdings of foreign bonds ($dM = -s\,dFp = s\,dFa$). The short-run effects of an FXO are depicted in **Figure 8.3**.

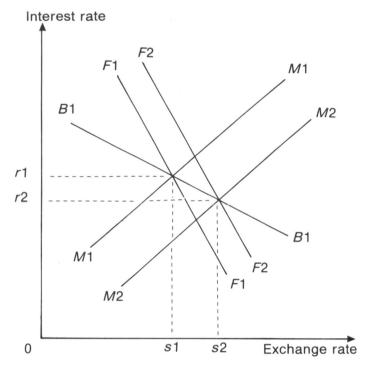

Figure 8.3   *The effects of a foreign exchange operation*

An FXO is an exchange of domestic money for foreign assets; this will lead to a rightward shift of the *MM* and a rightward shift of the *FF* schedule. Since agents hold less foreign assets than before the operation we know that the exchange rate will have depreciated to *S2* and the domestic interest rate must have fallen to *r2* at point B on the unchanged *B1B1* schedule. The exchange rate depreciation is required because the FXO creates a shortage of foreign assets in agents' portfolios which can only be satisfied in the short run by a depreciation which raises the domestic currency value of agents' remaining holdings of foreign assets, while the fall in interest rates is required to encourage agents to hold the increased money stock.

■ *8.9* The effects of an open market operation

With an expansionary OMO, the authorities increase the private sector's holdings of money and decrease its holdings of domestic bonds by an equivalent amount, that is, $dM = -dBp = dBa$. The effects of an OMO are depicted in **Figure 8.4**.

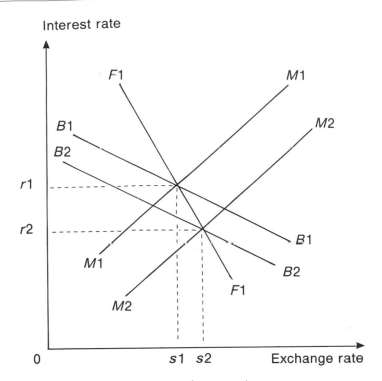

Figure 8.4 *The effects of an open market operation*

In contrast to an FXO an OMO leaves the *FF* schedule unchanged while leading to a rightward shift of the money supply schedule from *M*1 to *M*2 and a leftward shift of the *BB* schedule from *B*1 to *B*2. This means that there is a depreciation of the exchange rate and fall in the domestic interest rate. This is because the OMO creates an excess supply of money in agents' portfolios which leads to an increased demand for both domestic and foreign bonds, and this results in a fall in the domestic interest rate and a depreciation of the currency which raises the value of foreign bond holdings.

8.10 The effects of a sterilised foreign exchange operation

One means of comparing the relative effects of an OMO and an FXO in the model is to combine the two operations by having an expansionary FXO and a contractionary OMO of an equivalent amount: that is the authorities first purchase foreign assets with domestic money base then offset the increase in the monetary base by selling domestic bonds. Such an operation represents a sterilised intervention in the foreign exchange market since it

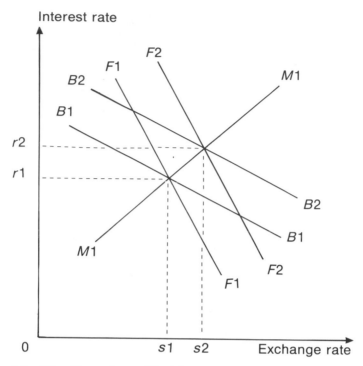

Figure 8.5 *The effects of a sterilised foreign exchange operation*

leaves the domestic monetary base unchanged ($dM = -s\,dFp$ and $-dM = dBp$ so that $-sdFp = dBp$). It is tantamount to the authorities altering the currency composition of bonds held in private portfolios. The effects of an SFXO are illustrated in **Figure 8.5**.

The SFXO has the effect of increasing the supply of domestic bonds shifting the *BB* schedule to the right from *B1* to *B2* whilst decreasing agents' holdings of foreign assets shifting the *FF* schedule to the right from *F1* to *F2*. The *MM* schedule remains unchanged because the domestic money base is left unaffected. The net effect of the operation is a depreciation of the exchange rate and a rise in the rate of interest. The exchange rate depreciates because the SFXO causes a shortage of foreign assets in agents' portfolios requiring an exchange rate depreciation to achieve the desired holdings. The interest rate rises because the excess supply of domestic bonds in agents' portfolios depresses the domestic bond prices.

The fact that an SFXO can have exchange rate and interest rate effects in the portfolio balance model stands in marked contrast to the monetary models (examined in Chapter 7). In the monetary models, domestic and foreign bonds are perfect substitutes, so a swap of domestic for foreign bonds by the authorities is an exchange of identical assets as far as private agents are concerned; Hence there is no need for interest or exchange-rate changes, while in the context of the portfolio balance model domestic and foreign bonds are regarded by economic agents as different assets. This being the case, an SFXO that increases agents' holdings of domestic bonds while decreasing agents' holdings of foreign bonds causing a disequilibrium in agents' portfolios. Agents find themselves with more domestic bonds than they want and less foreign bonds, and this means that their portfolio is more exposed to domestic risks. Equilibrium is restored to agents' portfolios by a higher domestic interest rate which compensates for the increased risk owing to increased domestic bond holdings and a depreciation of the exchange rate which reduces risk exposure by revaluing the remaining holdings of foreign assets.

 ## 8.11 A comparison of an FXO, OMO and SFXO

Having analysed all three operations separately we can compare and contrast the short-run effects of the three operations on a single figure as depicted in **Figure 8.6**.

In **Figure 8.6** we can see the contrasting effects of the three operations. The effects of an OMO and an FXO on the domestic interest rate and exchange rate are qualitatively similar; however, an FXO leads to a larger depreciation of the exchange rate while an OMO leads to a larger fall in the domestic interest rate. The rationale for this result is that an FXO leads to a fall in agents' holdings of foreign bonds while an OMO does not, consequently an FXO creates a greater excess demand for foreign bonds which is satisfied only by a stronger depreciation of the exchange rate. By contrast, an OMO creates a greater shortage of domestic bonds creating a greater excess demand for domestic bonds which is offset only by a larger fall in the domestic interest rate.

In the model real, output has been assumed to be fixed and this has the advantage of yielding some clear and useful insights. It is also worth briefly considering the effects of an OMO and FXO on real output. Dan Lee (1983) has analysed the dynamics of an FXO and OMO in a model where the level of output in the short run is endogenously determined. The question he attempted to answer was whether an OMO or FXO would have a more expansionary effect on domestic output. Using a portfolio balance framework he too finds that an expansionary OMO lowers the domestic interest rate more than an FXO, while the latter leads to a larger depreciation of the exchange rate than the former. He assumes that domestic investment is

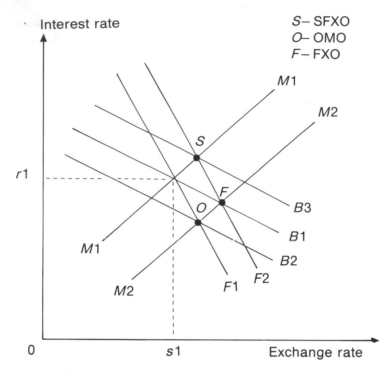

Figure 8.6 *Differing effects of an FXO, OMO and SFXO*

inversely related to the real domestic interest rate and net exports are positively related to the real exchange rate.

Lee finds that because an OMO has more effect on the domestic interest rate its expansionary effect on output depends relatively more than an FXO on the responsiveness of investment to the fall in the real interest rate that follows the operation, while the effect of an FXO on real output depends relatively more than an OMO on the effect of the real exchange rate depreciation on the trade account balance. Overall, an expansionary OMO may or may not have a greater effect on output than an expansionary FXO. If the response of the trade balance to changes in the real exchange rate is relatively weak and slower than that of investment to interest rate changes it will be the case that an OMO has a stronger effect on output. If, however, the foreign sector is large and highly responsive to the real exchange rate we may be able to say the opposite. Thus, Lee concludes that at the theoretical level one cannot say whether an FXO or OMO will have a more expansionary effect on output without imposing restrictions on the relevant parameters.

When comparing an FXO with an SFXO we find that an SFXO has a relatively weaker effect on the exchange rate than in the case of an FXO and

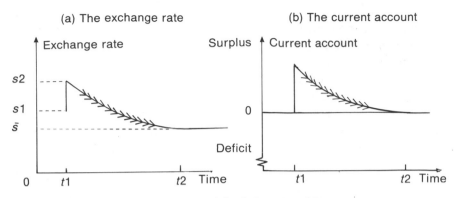

Figure 8.7 *The dynamics of the portfolio balance model*

the interest rate effects are opposite in sign. The reason for these differing effects is that an FXO increases the money stock, by lowering the domestic interest rate and encourages a greater excess demand for foreign assets leading to a greater depreciation. By contrast, an SFXO increases the stock of domestic bonds requiring a higher domestic interest rate which by reducing the attractiveness of holding foreign bonds limits the exchange rate depreciation.

In contrast to an FXO, the effects of an SFXO on real output will be ambiguous. This is because while the exchange rate depreciation will encourage net exports, the rise in the domestic interest rate will discourage domestic investment. Even if the former outweighs the latter effect, so that there is a net increase in domestic output, the expansion will be less than in the case of an FXO because the exchange rate effect is weaker.

■ *8.12* The dynamics of the model

To distinguish between short-run and long-run equilibrium in the model we should note that in the long run the current account should be in balance and the rate of change of the exchange rate should also be zero. This means that the country is neither increasing nor decreasing its foreign bond holdings and the exchange rate is at its equilibrium value. **Figure 8.7** depicts the dynamics of the exchange rate and current account in the model following an OMO, FXO or SFXO that cause an exchange rate depreciation assuming that real output remains fixed.

At time $t1$ there is an OMO, FXO or SFXO that causes a depreciation of the exchange rate from $s1$ to $s2$; with prices fixed this means that there has been a real exchange-rate depreciation. The resulting improvement in the country's international competitiveness moves its current account into surplus. A counterpart to the current account surplus is that the country starts to accumulate more foreign bonds. This increases the proportion of foreign assets in investors' portfolios and to reduce this risk exposure they start to purchase domestic assets(most probably domestic bonds rather than money) leading to appreciating exchange rate. In turn, the exchange rate appreciation erodes the country's competitive advantage and so reduces the current account surplus. The dynamics come to an end when the exchange rate has appreciated sufficiently that the current account is brought back into balance.

One of the features of the model is that it is long-run non-neutral with respect to the real exchange rate since the long-run exchange rate $\bar{S}$ lies below the initial exchange rate $S1$. This is because the current account surplus that follows an operation results in an accumulation of foreign assets and an accompanying increase in the contribution of interest rate receipts from the holding of foreign assets on the service component of the current account. As such, it is necessary for the real exchange rate to have appreciated in the long-run equilibrium so that there is a deterioration of the trade account to offset the improvement in the service account and so ensure that the current account is restored to balance in the long run.

During the transition from the short run to the long run the economy experiences an appreciating currency and a current account surplus, Kouri (1983) labels this link the 'acceleration hypothesis'. It is worth noting that the stable transition to equilibrium we have described depends crucially upon certain stability conditions being fulfilled. Following an operation that causes an exchange-rate depreciation which moves the current account into surplus, there are two conflicting effects at work on the current account. The surplus will induce an exchange-rate appreciation which will work to eliminate the surplus. However, the current account surplus also implies an accumulation of foreign assets and with it increased interest rate receipts which improves the surplus. Consequently, for the appreciation of the exchange rate to reduce the surplus it is necessary that the fall in net exports exceed the increased interest receipts.

 ## 8.13 The effects of a change in risk perceptions

A key feature of the portfolio balance model is that it provides a role for risk factors to influence exchange rates which may account for some of the

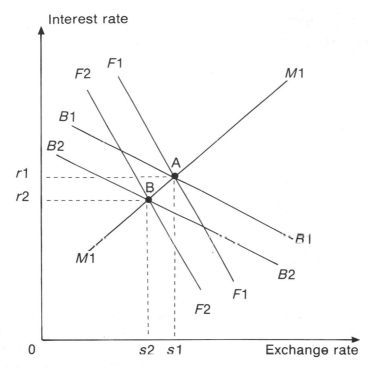

Figure 8.8   *Foreign bonds become more risky*

exchange-rate changes experienced under floating exchange rates. Consider the case where for some reason investors perceive that foreign bonds have become more risky as compared with domestic bonds. The effects of such a change in perceptions is illustrated in **Figure 8.8**.

As a result of the perceived increase in risks attached to holding foreign bonds there is a decreased demand for foreign bonds and increased demand for domestic bonds. Both the foreign bond schedule $F1$ and domestic bonds schedule $B1$ shift to the left and the new schedules $F2$ and $B2$ intersect at point B. The increased demand for domestic bonds is reflected in an appreciation of the exchange rate from $s1$ to $s2$ and fall in the domestic interest rate from $r1$ to $r2$.

The exchange-rate appreciation leads to a current account deficit. This in turn leads to a decline in foreign asset holdings which creates a shortage of foreign bonds in agents' portfolios; consequently agents try to purchase foreign bonds leading to a depreciation of the exchange rate. Over time, the depreciation improves the country's international competitiveness so reducing the current account deficit.

8.14 Money versus bond financed fiscal expansion

There are two ways that authorities may try to finance increased government expenditure. One is by simply printing extra money and using the money to directly finance its expenditure. The other is to finance expenditure by borrowing, that is, by selling bonds to economic agents. We now proceed to examine short-run implications of these two alternative methods of financing increased government expenditure, within the context of the portfolio balance model. In the analysis we shall ignore the possible expansionary effects of the increased expenditure on national income since this considerably complicates the picture.

☐ *Money financed expenditure*

An increase in public expenditure financed by printing money means that investors will find that their wealth has risen because they will hold more money and the same amounts of domestic and foreign bonds. The problem is that they will find that they have a larger proportion of money in their portfolios, and for this reason they will demand more domestic bonds and more foreign bonds. The results of this portfolio adjustment are depicted in **Figure 8.9**.

The increased money supply is reflected in a rightward shift of the money market schedule from M1 to M2. It is worth noting that this shift is less than in the case of an OMO which increases the money by a like amount because the money supply increases wealth and part of this is reflected in an increase in the demand for money. In addition, the increase in wealth leads to an increase in the demand for both domestic and foreign bonds, the bond market schedule shifts to the left from B1 to B2, while the foreign bond schedule shifts to the right. The net effect of the money based expansion is a depreciation of the exchange rate and a fall in the domestic interest rate.

☐ *Bond financed expenditure*

An increase in public expenditure financed by borrowing will again increase investors' wealth because they will hold more bonds and the same amounts of domestic money and foreign bonds. While the bond sales reduce the public's holdings of money, the money is then put back in private agents' hands by increased government expenditure. In this instance, agents will find that they have a larger proportion of domestic bonds in their portfolios

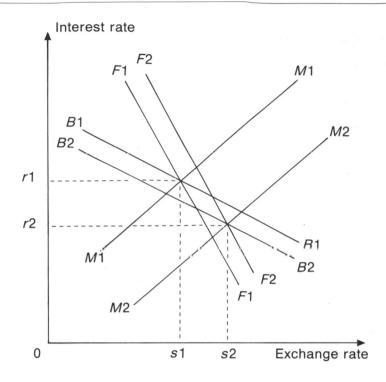

Figure 8.9   *Money financed expenditure*

than desired. This will lead investors to demand more money and foreign bonds. The results of this portfolio adjustment are depicted in **Figure 8.10**.

The increase in the supply of bonds will shift the *BB* schedule to the right from *B*1 to *B*2. Since investors are holding more bonds and the same amount of money and foreign bonds their wealth must have increased. This increase in wealth will lead to an increase in the demand for bonds so reducing the extent of the rightward shift of the bond schedule and an increase in the demand for money represented by a leftward shift of the *MM* schedule. The net effect on the demand for foreign bonds is uncertain. While the rise in wealth will lead to increased foreign bond demand tending to shift the foreign bond schedule to the right, the rise in the domestic interest rate will lead to a substitution of demand away from foreign bonds towards domestic bonds which will shift the foreign bond schedule to the left.

If the wealth effect dominates the *FF* schedule moves to the right as is depicted in **Figure 8.10(a)** and equilibrium is obtained at a higher interest rate and an exchange-rate depreciation. Conversely, if the interest rate effect dominates, the *FF* schedule moves to the left as depicted in **Figure 8.10(b)** and equilibrium is obtained at a higher interest rate and an exchange-rate

(a) Exchange rate depreciation

(b) Exchange rate appreciation

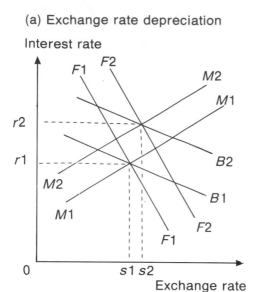
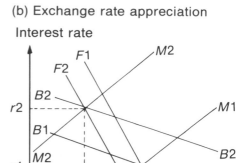

Figure 8.10   *Bond financed expenditure*

appreciation. Thus, fiscal policy will have an ambiguous effect on the exchange rate.

In this section we have seen that the impact of fiscal expansion on interest rates and the exchange rate depends not only on the size of the expansion but on how the policy is financed. If it is financed by printing money this leads to a short-run depreciation and a fall in interest rates, while if it is financed by borrowing the effect is a rise in interest rates and the exchange rate may depreciate or appreciate. It is important to remember that these are only the short-run results. The money financed fiscal expansion is likely to translate quickly into inflation as the expansionary fiscal policy will be further boosted by the exchange-rate depreciation and fall in the domestic interest rate, while bond financed fiscal expansion effects on prices and output are likely to be less inflationary because in the case where the exchange rate depreciates the expansion of demand will be reined back to some extent by the rise in interest rates. Demand will be even further restrained if the fiscal expansion leads to an exchange-rate appreciation. In sum, a bond financed fiscal expansion will be less inflationary than a money financed expansion.

Before concluding this section, it is worth remembering that the rising US budget deficit in the early 1980s was primarily financed by US government bond sales, a rising US interest rate and an appreciating dollar. In the context of the portfolio balance model this would suggest that the substitution effect of rising US interest rates dominated the wealth effect.

8.15 The risk premium, imperfect and perfect substitutability

The portfolio balance model that we have examined in this chapter has been based upon the assumption that domestic and foreign bonds are imperfect substitutes. This is shown by the fact that although the foreign interest rate is fixed and exchange-rate expectations are static the domestic interest rate could diverge from the foreign interest rate. The reason being that the differing operations influence the risk premium, allowing the domestic interest rate to diverge from the foreign rate. This point is illustrated below.

In the portfolio balance model the domestic interest rate can diverge from the foreign interest rate not only because of exchange rate expectations but also because of the risk premium in accordance with equation (8.1) which is repeated below as (8.21).

$$r - r^* = E\dot{s} + RP \tag{8.21}$$

This can be expressed in difference form as:

$$dr - dr^* = dE\dot{s} + dRP \tag{8.22}$$

Throughout we have been assuming static exchange-rate expectations ($dE\dot{s} = 0$) and a fixed foreign interest rate so that $dr^* = 0$. Substituting in these values into (8.22) we find:

$$dr = dRP \tag{8.23}$$

Hence, all changes in the domestic interest rate can be interpreted as due to changes in the risk premium. A rise in the domestic interest rate reflects a rise in the risk premium on domestic assets, while a fall in the interest rate reflects a fall in the risk premium. In the case of perfect substitutability there is no risk premium so that the uncovered interest parity condition is the relevant equation, that is:

$$r - r^* = E\dot{s} \tag{8.24}$$

In difference form:

$$dr - dr^* = dE\dot{s} \tag{8.25}$$

With static expectations and a fixed foreign interest rate this means:

$$dr = 0 \tag{8.26}$$

For this to be the case both the *BB* and *FF* schedules must coincide and be horizontal at the world interest rate r^*, as illustrated in **Figure 8.11**.

In **Figure 8.11**, the *BB* and *FF* schedules are horizontal and coincide as represented by the schedule *BF*; only changes in monetary policy as reflected by shifts in the *MM* schedule can influence the exchange rate. There is no

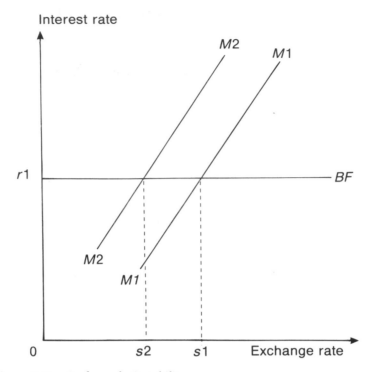

Figure 8.11   *Perfect substitutability*

distinction to be made between an OMO or FXO on the exchange rate. An SFXO leaves the *MM* schedule unchanged and the *BF* remains in the same position so it has no exchange rate or interest rate effects. A bond financed fiscal expansion in this special case will have an unambiguous effect. Although the *BF* schedule remains at *BF*, the increased wealth resulting from the increased supply of bonds will raise money demand causing a leftward shift of the *MM* schedule and an exchange rate appreciation.

■ *8.16* Conclusions

The portfolio balance model represents an important contribution to the exchange-rate literature because it allows changes in perceived risk and/or risk aversion to play a role in the determination of the exchange rate. An increase in the perceived riskiness of domestic bonds compared with foreign bonds can lead to both a rise in the domestic interest rate and a depreciation of the currency, while an increase in the perceived riskiness of foreign bonds can lead to an appreciation of the domestic currency and fall in the domestic interest rate. These effects accord with intuition and are frequently invoked to explain observed exchange rate changes. Such effects are, however, absent from the monetary models which assume that domestic and foreign bonds are perfect substitutes.

Another important contribution of the portfolio balance model is that there is a significant role for the current account to play in the determination of the exchange rate over time. A current account surplus implies an accumulation of foreign assets and an increase in wealth, and the result is a larger proportion of foreign bonds in investors' portfolios than they desire. In turn, this leads to purchases of domestic bonds and money and a resulting appreciation of the exchange rate which works to reduce the current account surplus.

Another contribution of the portfolio balance model is that it permits a relatively easy discussion of the role of fiscal policy in determining the exchange rate. A bond financed fiscal expansion has an ambiguous effect on the exchange rate. This is because while a higher proportion of domestic bonds and an increase in asset holders' wealth will lead to an increase in the demand for foreign bonds, the higher domestic interest rate will lead to a fall in the demand for foreign bonds. If the former effect is greater than the latter, the exchange rate depreciates but if the reverse is true the exchange rate appreciates.

A significant policy implication that emerges from the portfolio balance model is that a given change in the money stock has a more powerful effect on the exchange rate when carried out by a purchase of foreign assets (an FXO) than when achieved via a purchase of domestic assets (an OMO). It is only in the limiting case when domestic and foreign bonds are perfect substitutes that the effects become identical. This is an important result because it at least provides a rationale for the observed interventions of authorities in foreign exchange markets. Another result that emerges is that it is only by assuming that domestic and foreign bonds are imperfect substitutes that an SFXO can exert exchange-rate effects. However, even if a SFXO can affect the exchange rate it will have a relatively weaker effect on the exchange rate than an FXO. The lesson for policy makers is that non-sterilised intervention has a more powerful effect on the exchange rate than sterilised intervention.

One issue that is not explicitly dealt with by the portfolio balance model is the precise reason for the perceived differences in risks between domestic and foreign bonds. This can be caused amongst other things by unstable economic policies and differing perceived political risks. In the circumstance where unstable economic policies create the risks, it may be best that the authorities stabilise their economic policies. In the case where political risks are concerned the authorities might consider ways of reducing the perceived risks. In sum, reducing perceived risks may be an important mechanism for reducing exchange-rate fluctuations.

■ Selected further readings

Allen, P.R. and Keren, P.B. (1980) *Asset Markets, Exchange Rates and Economic Integration* (Cambridge: Cambridge University Press).

Branson, W.H. (1976) 'Asset Markets and Relative Prices in Exchange Rate Determination'. *Institute for International Economic Studies, Seminar Paper No 66*, Stockholm.

Branson, W.H., Huttunen, H. and Masson, P. (1977) 'Exchange Rates in the Short Run: Some Further Results', *European Economic Review*, vol. 12, pp. 395–402.

Branson, W.H. and Henderson, D.W. (1985) 'The Specification and Influence of Asset Markets', in P.B. Kenen and R.W. Jones (eds), *Handbook of International Economics* (Amsterdam: North-Holland).

Branson, W.H. (1984) 'A Model of Exchange Rate Determination with Policy Reaction: Evidence from Monthly Data', in P. Malgrange and P.A. Muet, *Contemporary Macroeconomic Modelling* (Oxford: Basil Blackwell).

Frankel, J.A. (1982) 'A Test of Perfect Substitutability in the Foreign Exchange Market', *Southern Economic Journal*, vol. 49, pp. 406–16.

Frankel, J.A. (1983) 'Monetary and Portfolio Balance Models of Exchange Rate Determination', in J.S. Bhandari and B.H. Putnam, *Economic Interdependence and Flexible Exchange Rates* (Cambridge Mass.: MIT).

Girton, L. and Henderson, D.W. (1977) 'Central Bank Operations in Foreign and Domestic Assets Under Fixed and Flexible Exchange Rates', in P.B. Clark, D.E. Logue, and R.J. Sweeny, *The Effects of Exchange Rate Adjustment* (Washington: Government Printing Office).

Isard, P. (1983) 'An Accounting Framework and Some Issues for Modeling How Exchange Rates Respond to the News', in J.A. Frenkel, *Exchange Rates and International Macroeconomics* (Chicago: University of Chicago Press).

Kenen, P.B. (1982) 'Effects of Intervention and Sterilization in the Short Run and the Long Run', in R.N. Cooper, P.B. Kenen, J.B. Machedo and J.V. Ypersele, *The International Monetary System Under Flexible Exchange Rates*. (Cambridge Mass: Ballinger)

Kouri, P.J.K. (1976) 'The Exchange Rate and the Balance of Payments in the Short Run and the Long Run: A Monetary Approach', *Scandinavian Journal of Economics*, vol. 78, pp. 280–304.

Kouri, P.J.K. (1983) 'Balance of Payments and the Foreign Exchange Market: A Dynamic Partial Equilibrium Model', in J.S. Bhandari and B.H. Putnam, *Economic Interdependence and Flexible Exchange Rates* (Amsterdam: North-Holland).

Lee, D. (1983) 'Effects of Open Market Operations and Foreign Exchange Market Operations Under Flexible Exchange Rates', in M. Darby and J.R. Lothian, *The International Transmission of Inflation* (Chicago: University of Chicago Press).

Obstfeld, M. (1980) 'Imperfect Asset Substitutability and Monetary Policy Under Fixed Exchange Rates.' *Journal of International Economics*, vol 10, pp. 177–200.

Wihlborg, C. (1978) 'Currency Risks in International Finance Markets', *Princeton Studies in International Finance*, no. 44.

■ *Chapter 9* ■

Empirical Evidence on Exchange Rates

■ *9.1* Introduction

We have so far considered the exchange-rate literature from a predominately theoretical viewpoint. The exchange-rate field has been rich in empirical research. Apart from empirical investigation into the validity of the PPP theory which we examined in Chapter 6, two other key questions that empirical research on exchange rates has addressed are:

1. Is the foreign exchange market efficient?
2. What model best predicts exchange rate movements?

The answer to both of these questions is of enormous importance from a policy viewpoint. If it can be shown that the foreign exchange market is 'efficient' then the case for government intervention in the foreign exchange market would be considerably undermined, while if we can identify a model that successfully explains exchange-rate determination, it would be possible for the authorities to determine the best way to influence exchange rates and limit exchange-rate volatility. Furthermore, the consequences of alternative economic policy measures could be better evaluated as their implications for the exchange rate would be understood.

■ *9.2* What is an efficient market?

Following Eugene Fama, an efficient market is conventionally defined as one 'in which prices always "fully reflect" available information'. (1970, p.383). In the specific application to the foreign exchange market this implies that market participants use all relevant available information bearing on the appropriate value of the exchange rate, to produce a set of exchange rates – spot and forward—that does not provide an opportunity for unusual *ex-ante* profit opportunities. In other words, unusual profits cannot be made by speculators who make exchange rate forecasts on a similar information set.

There are a number of tests that have been proposed to determine whether or not the foreign exchange market is efficient. One of the most popular has been to see if the forward exchange rate systematically over or under predicts the future spot exchange rate. If it were to do so then this would be indicative of foreign exchange market inefficiency.

For example, suppose that the forward exchange rate were to systematically under predict the value of the future spot rate of a currency. There would be a simple rule which could yield a speculator abnormal profits, the rule being to buy the currency forward today knowing that he can sell it when the contract is due at a higher value. A numerical example will illustrate the point. Suppose the three-month forward rate of the pound against the dollar is £0.60/$1 but speculators know that the forward rate systematically under predicts the future rate by 5 per cent. This means that the future spot exchange rate in three months time will be above £0.60/$1 at £0.63/$1. Hence, by buying dollars forward today for £0.60/$1 a speculator will know that in three months time when he is due to pay the £0.60/$1 for each dollar purchased he can immediately expect £0.63/$1 for each dollar sold.

According to the **efficient market hypothesis** (EMH) the scenario depicted above would not persist because the opportunity for abnormal profits would lead to massive purchases of dollars forward. This would lead to a rise in the forward rate above £0.60/$1 towards £0.63/$1 until any abnormal profits are eliminated.

However, there is a major problem with exchange market efficiency tests. Even if one were to discover that the forward rate systematically over or under predicted the future spot rate this discrepancy is not necessarily a sign of foreign exchange market inefficiency; it may be indicative of the existence of a risk premium in the foreign exchange market. If the forward exchange rate of a foreign currency were to systematically undervalue its future spot exchange rate as in our numerical example, this may be due to the existence of a positive risk premium attached to the foreign currency. In our numerical example the difference between the forward rate of £0.60/$1 and the actual/ expected future spot rate of £0.63/$1 may be viewed as a £0.03 risk premium on the dollar, that is, speculators will only buy dollars forward if they expect to be able to sell them in the future and make £0.03 profit. This profit represents the compensation required by speculators to buy dollars forward which are regarded as more risky than pounds.

Hence, any expected excess profits to be earned on buying the foreign currency forward might be merely the compensation required by an efficient foreign exchange market to compensate for the risks associated with holding the foreign currency forward. Conversely, if the forward exchange rate of the foreign currency is systematically overvalued in relation to the future spot exchange rate, this may be evidence of the existence of a negative risk premium attached to the foreign currency. That is, international investors are prepared to accept a lower return on the foreign currency as compared with the domestic currency because they regard it as a relatively safe asset to hold compared with the domestic currency. A positive risk premium on the foreign currency corresponds to a negative risk premium on the domestic currency and vice-versa.

■ *9.3* Exchange market efficiency tests

The **rational expectations hypothesis** is particularly useful when examining the concept of exchange market efficiency. This is because like the EMH it presumes that economic agents do not make systematic errors when making their predictions. According to the rational expectations hypothesis (REH) economic agents have a good knowledge of the economic model relevant to predicting a variable so that they do not persistently over or under predict the future value of that variable. Applying rational expectations to the prediction of the future exchange rate we find:

$$s_{t+1} = Es_{t+1} + u_{t+1} \tag{9.1}$$

where s_{t+1} is the log of the actual spot exchange rate in one period's time defined as domestic currency units per unit of foreign currency, Es_{t+1} is the log of the expected exchange rate in one period's time, and u_{t+1} is a random error term with a normal distribution and mean of zero.

Equation (9.1) says that the actual future exchange rate corresponds to that which was anticipated by economic agents plus or minus some random error. The next step is to assume that investors are risk neutral (i.e. there is no risk premium) and consequently they set the forward rate at a level that corresponds to the expected future spot exchange rate. This gives:

$$f_t = Es_{t+1} \tag{9.2}$$

where f_t is the log of the forward exchange rate at time t defined as domestic currency units per unit of foreign currency.

Substituting equation (9.2) into equation (9.1) we obtain:

$$s_{t+1} = f_t + u_{t+1} \tag{9.3}$$

Equation (9.3) says that providing economic agents have rational expectations and there is no risk premium in the foreign exchange market, then the future spot rate should be equal to today's quoted forward rate plus a random error. In other words, on the average the forward rate should neither over nor under predict the actual exchange rate one period ahead.

Equation (9.3) constitutes a joint test of both exchange market efficiency and no risk premium. The forward rate may systematically over or under predict the future actual exchange rate not because of exchange market inefficiency but because there is a positive or negative risk premium on the domestic currency. If a risk premium is present we have to modify equation (9.3) to yield:

$$s_{t+1} = f_t + RP_t \tag{9.4}$$

where RP_t is the risk premium on the foreign currency.

For regression purposes equation (9.4) becomes:

$$s_{t+1} = f_t + RP_t + u_{t+1} \tag{9.5}$$

Equation (9.5) says that the forward rate may systematically over or under predict the future spot rate because of the presence of a risk premium. If there is a positive risk premium on the foreign currency (negative risk premium on the domestic currency) the one period ahead forward rate of the domestic currency will systematically overvalue the currency as compared with its actual rate one period ahead. Whereas, if there is a negative risk premium on the foreign currency (positive risk premium on the domestic currency) then the one period ahead forward rate of the domestic currency will systematically undervalue the currency compared with its actual rate one period ahead.

The exchange market efficiency test that has been most commonly employed is based on equation (9.3) and is set out as follows, e.g. Levich (1978) and Frenkel (1982).

$$s_{t+1} = a_1 + a_2 f_t + u_{t+1} \tag{9.6}$$

According to this test, if the foreign exchange market is efficient in the sense that the exchange rate (spot and forward) incorporates all currently available information and there is no risk premium in the foreign exchange market, then the forward rate will be an unbiased predictor of the future spot exchange rate. Hence, the expected sign of a_1 is zero; if it were non zero then the forward exchange rate would systematically over or under predict the

Table 9.1   *Risk premium/market efficiency test*
Estimated equation $s_{t+1} = a_1 + a_2 f_t + u_{t+1}$

Study	Rate	Period	a_1	a_2	DW	$\bar{R}^2$
Levich (1978)	Pound	73M3–78M5	0.02*	0.98*	1.51	0.81
			(0.17)	(9.33)		
	French franc	73M3–78M5	0.00*	0.86*	1.79	0.59
			(1.00)	(5.05)		
	Deutschmark	73M3–78M5	0.00*	1.00*	1.40	0.99
			(1.00)	(110.78)		
Frenkel (1982)	Pound	73M6–79M7	0.03*	0.96*	1.74	0.95
			(1.67)	(38.44)		
	French franc	73M6–79M7	−0.24	0.84	2.24	0.78
			(−2.95)	(15.92)		
	Deutschmark	73M6–79M7	−0.02*	0.97*	2.10	0.93
			(−0.78)	(30.41)		

Notes:
Hypothesis is $a_1 = 0$ and $a_2 = 1$.
An asterisk by a variable indicates that it is both of the correct sign and not statistically different from its hypothesised value.
All rates are against the US dollar.
The *t*-statistics are in parentheses.

future spot exchange rate and rational economic agents could use this information to make systematic profits. The coefficient a_2 will be equal to unity showing that the forward exchange rate on average correctly predicts the future spot exchange rate. Finally, the error term (u_{t+1}) will possess the classical ordinary least squares (OLSQ) properties. In particular, errors will be serially uncorrelated. By no serial correlation we mean that there is no statistically significant relationship between the errors of one period and errors made in other periods. One cannot forecast future errors on the basis of past errors. If agents could predict future errors on the basis of past errors this would be a sign of foreign exchange market inefficiency, that is, there would be unexploited profit opportunities. The results of some of the studies of Levich and Frenkel for equation (9.6) are reported in **Table 9.1**.

The results presented in **Table 9.1** were interpreted by the two authors as highly supportive of the joint hypothesis of foreign exchange market efficiency and no risk premium. The coefficient a_1 does not differ significantly from zero, while the coefficient a_2 does not differ significantly from unity. In addition, the Durbin–Watson statistic reveals that there is no first order serial correlation in the residuals. The adjusted $\bar{R}^2$ for the entire sample period is generally high, suggesting that most information is incorporated in the forward rate. The implication of these results is that the foreign exchange market is efficient and there is no risk premium.

Nevertheless, it has been pointed out by authors such as Hansen and Hodrick (1980), Meese and Singleton (1982) and Cumby and Obstfeld (1984) that the Levich/Frenkel regression is inappropriate if exchange rates follow a non-stationary process – that is, there is some trend exchange-rate appreciation or depreciation in the exchange rate. In this case, it is necessary to detrend the data and Cumby and Obstfeld argue that we should re-estimate the previous equation by running the following regression.

$$(s_{t+1} - s_t) = a_1 + a_2(f_t - s_t) + u_{t+1} \tag{9.7}$$

where s_t = the log of the spot exchange rate.

Equation (9.7) detrends equation (9.3) and constitutes a more powerful statistical test of the EMH. It says that a currency that is at a forward discount $(f_t - s_t)$ of x per cent should on the average depreciate $(s_{t+1} - s_t)$ by x per cent, whereas a currency that is at a forward premium of x per cent should on the average appreciate by x per cent.

If the foreign exchange market is efficient and characterised by rational expectations so that we can substitute the actual exchange rate for the expected exchange rate, along with the assumption that there is no risk premium, then one would again expect a_1 to be zero and the coefficient a_2 to not differ significantly from unity, indicating that on the average the realised change in the exchange rate is correctly forecasted by the forward premium/discount. **Table 9.2** reports the results of Boothe and Longworth (1986) on equation (9.7) for a variety of currencies against the US dollar.

The results of Boothe and Longworth (which confirm the findings of Cumby and Obstfeld) show that one can decisively reject the null hypothesis of exchange market efficiency. Similar findings have been found for the period March 1976–July 1986 by Taylor (1988). These results reveal that once we take account of the trend in the exchange rate, market participants have on the average mispredicted the direction of movement of the exchange rate. As Taylor and MacDonald (1989) note in a survey of these tests, the coefficient a_2 is usually closer to minus one than the hypothesised value of unity!

The tests of equation (9.7) suggest that on the average currencies that were at a forward discount actually appreciated, while those at a forward premium actually depreciated! This is a clear rejection of the joint market efficiency test because it suggests that there exists a fairly simple rule for investors to make excessive profits: simply put your money in a currency that is at a forward discount (because of the relatively high interest rate in that country), and you will not only benefit from the higher interest rate but also from an exchange-rate appreciation of that currency. This is a clear violation of uncovered interest parity.

A major problem with these decisive rejections is that because they are a joint test of exchange-market efficiency (rational expectations) and the non-existence of a risk premium, there is no clear-cut interpretation. It may be evidence of exchange-market inefficiency (that is REH does not hold) or be indicative of the existence of a risk premium (possibly time varying) in the foreign exchange market.

■ 9.4 Alternative tests of the efficient market hypothesis

According to the EMH, the forward rate is supposed to embody all the relevant information concerning the future expected spot exchange rate. This implies that it should not be possible to add a further variable available at time t to regression (9.3) which proves to be statistically significant. Were we to do so, this can be taken as evidence that the forward exchange rate does not contain all relevant information concerning the future spot exchange rate. An example of a regression that tests to see if another variable can improve the fit of regression (9.3) is:

$$s_{t+1} = a_1 + a_2 f_t + a_3 f_{t-1} + u_{t+1} \tag{9.8}$$

where f_{t-1} is the log of the forward rate in the previous period.

According to the EMH a variable such as the previous period's forward exchange rate should not contain any additional information relevant to the future exchange rate (i.e. a_3 should not be statistically different from zero). Using monthly data (July 1973 to September 1979) for the pound–dollar, French franc–dollar, lira–dollar and deutschmark–dollar, Edwards (1983b) finds that the coefficient a_3 is not statistically different from zero, implying that f_{t-1} contains no useful additional information. Edwards's study is very supportive of exchange-market efficiency.

Another test of the efficient market hypothesis concerns an examination of the errors between the expected future exchange rate and the actual future exchange rate. If the foreign exchange market is efficient then it should not be possible to predict these errors on the basis of information available at the time the forecast is made. That is:

$$u_{t+1} = a_1 + a_2 I_t + v_{t+1} \tag{9.9}$$

Where u_{t+1} is the forecast error, i.e. $s_{t+1} - f_t$, I_t is a subset of information available at time t, and v_{t+1} is a random error term with a normal distribution and mean of zero.

If the foreign exchange market is efficient then the coefficient a_2 should be equal to zero. That is, we can not put in any relevant economic variables at time t, such as the current spot exchange rate s_t, the previous period's spot s_{t-1} or lagged forward rate f_{t-1} or any other known variable at time t and use this to predict the error. This efficiency test is known as the orthogonality property and it implies that agents use all relevant information in making their forecasts so as to avoid predictable forecast errors. The EMH holds that the forecast error u_{t+1} is due to unpredictable shocks and will be unrelated to

Table 9.2   *Risk premium/exchange market efficiency test with detrended data*
Estimated equation: $(s_{t+1} - s_t) = a_1 + a_2(f_t - s_t) + u_{t+1}$

Exchange rate	Period	a_1	a_2
Canadian dollar	70M7–81M12	0.0005*	−0.389
		(0.55)	(−0.71)
French franc	73M8–81M12	−0.0066*	−1.838
		(−1.74)	(−2.10)
German mark	73M6–81M12	0.0021*	−0.533*
		(0.41)	(−0.38)
Italian lira	73M6–81M12	−0.0106	−0.4786
		(2.41)	(−1.01)
Japanese yen	73M6–81M12	0.0008*	−0.480
		(0.26)	(−1.01)
UK pound	73M6–81M12	−0.006*	−1.533
		(−1.62)	(−1.82)

Notes:
Hypothesis is: $a_1 = 0$ and $a_2 = 1$.
An asterisk by a variable indicates that it is both of the correct sign and not statistically different from its hypothesised value.
All currencies are against the US dollar.
t-statistics are in brackets.
Source: P. Boothe and D. Longworth, 'Foreign Exchange Market Efficiency Tests: Implications of Recent Empirical Findings', *Journal of International Money and Finance*, vol. 5 (1986) pp. 135–52

Box 9.1   *Exchange market efficiency and the distinction between anticipated and unanticipated economic policy*

The efficient market hypothesis has some important implications for exchange rate dynamics in response to changes in economic policy. Let us consider the case of monetary policy. When the foreign exchange market is efficient it is only unanticipated monetary expansion that can cause discrete jumps in the exchange rate. If, a monetary expansion is expected to occur, market efficiency implies that there would be no discrete jump in the exchange rate when the money supply expansion takes place because it has already been appropriately discounted in advance. **Figures 9.1(a)** and **9.1(b)** contrast the effects of unanticipated and anticipated money expansions in the context of

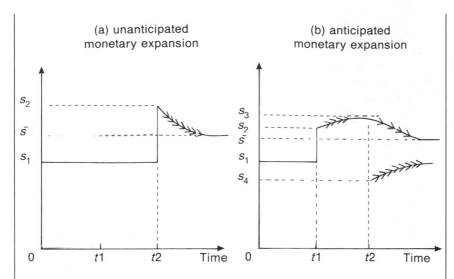

Figure 9.1 *The dynamics of unanticipated and anticipated money expansions*

the 'overshooting' exchange rate model. **Figure 9.1(a)** depicts what happens if a money supply expansion takes place unannounced at time t_2, this leads to a sudden discrete jump of the exchange rate from s_1 to s_2 which represents an 'overshoot' from its long-run equilibrium rate $\bar{s}$, thereafter, the exchange rate heads towards its long-run value $\bar{s}$. This contrasts to the dynamics of the exchange rate when the authorities announce at time t_1 that they will expand the money supply at time t_2, which is depicted in **Figure 9.1(b)**. In this case, there would be an immediate initial depreciation at the time of the announcement t_1 to s_2. This depreciation raises the average level of prices and since the money stock has not yet expanded raises money demand and the domestic interest rate. The higher domestic interest rate means that between time t_1 and t_2 when the money stock is expanded there needs to be a depreciation of the domestic currency to maintain uncovered interest parity. At time t_2 when the money supply is expanded, the domestic interest rate falls and there follows a subsequent exchange rate appreciation to its long run equilibrium rate $\bar{s}$.

The lack of a discrete exchange-rate jump when the money supply expansion is anticipated (because of the prior announcement), follows from the EMH. If the exchange rate did not depreciate until the expansion actually took place at time t_2 this would imply a large discrete depreciation of the exchange rate at that time. However, since the money expansion was expected, such a discrete jump would imply a missed abnormal *ex-ante* profit opportunity as speculators could easily have sold the currency in advance of the depreciation. As the foreign exchange market is efficient the expectation of a money supply expansion leads to a smaller discrete depreciation of the rate (reflecting the news of future monetary expansion) at the time of the announcement, with a smooth depreciation thereafter. In this way, all anticipated disturbances are fully discounted and therefore unusual *ex-ante* profit opportunities eliminated.

An interesting issue concerns what would happen if we arrive at time t_2 and the authorities fail to carry out the announced money expansion? This itself represents a further piece of news to the foreign exchange market. The exchange rate will appreciate to the exchange rate s_4 so that there is a period of an overvalued exchange rate to correct for the unjustified previous undervaluation. Thereon the exchange rate appreciates back to s_1. Hence, it is possible that much of the exchange-rate volatility witnessed under floating is due to the failure of authorities to carry out their stated policy intentions.

This EMH has implications for exchange-rate movements generally. The announcement of bad economic news like a large deficit in the current account will only cause an exchange rate depreciation to the extent that it is worse than what the market was anticipating prior to the announcement. If a large current account deficit is not as bad as the market was expecting it could lead to an exchange rate appreciation!

any information available at the time expectations are formed. Among the other information available at time t is the previous period's forecast errors u_t. As such, a test of the orthogonality assumption would be to see if the forecast error $s_{t+1} - f_t = u_{t+1}$ is independent of the previous period's forecast error, $s_t - f_{t-1} = u_t$. That is:

$$s_{t+1} - f_t = a_1 + a_2(s_t - f_{t-1}) + v_{t+1} \tag{9.10}$$

where v_{t+1} is a random normally distributed error.

Equation (9.10) can be rearranged to yield:

$$s_{t+1} = a_1 + a_2(s_t - f_{t-1}) + a_3 f_t + v_{t+1} \tag{9.11}$$

According to the efficient market hypothesis if there is no risk premium and the foreign exchange market uses all information efficiently then $a_1 = 0$, $a_2 = 0$ and $a_3 = 1$. Frankel (1979b) produces results for the French franc–dollar, pound–dollar and Italian lira–dollar for the period July 1974–April 1978 using weekly data that lead to a rejection of the efficient market hypothesis.

Other tests of the efficient market hypothesis have been variations on the traditional tests. Most notably they have involved using alternative proxies for the future expected exchange rate Es_{t+1} other than the actual exchange rate at time $t+1$. In addition, more sophisticated estimation techniques have been used. Finally, in tests of the orthogonality property authors have used a wider range of variables in the information set.

9.5 Summary of findings on exchange market efficiency

There has been a great deal of testing of the joint hypothesis of foreign exchange market efficiency and the non-existence of a risk premium. The problem with all these tests is that even when the joint hypothesis is rejected there is no means of knowing whether this is due to the existence of a risk premium or due to foreign exchange market inefficiency.

Overall, the results of the various exchange-market efficiency tests are fairly mixed depending upon the exchange rate used and the particular test considered. None the less, there is an accumulation of evidence suggesting that for certain periods and certain rates the joint hypothesis does not hold. Specifically, tests of EMH using the forward premium/discount as a prediction for the future appreciation/depreciation of the currency convincingly reject the joint hypothesis.

Accepting that the joint hypothesis does not hold, then the big issue left to resolve is whether or not the rejection is due to the existence of a risk premium or the existence of inefficiency/non-rational expectations in the foreign exchange market. At the theoretical level Frankel (1986) has argued that the risk premium if it does exist it is likely to be too small to account for the failure of exchange market efficiency tests. In addition, Frankel (1986) and Rogoff (1984) test to see if the risk premium behaves as predicted by the portfolio balance model, that is, if it increases with the supply of domestic bonds and decreases with the supply of foreign bonds. In both studies the relevant coefficients prove statistically insignificant.

A tentative suggestion is that the more likely candidate for the failure is not the existence of a risk premium but rather non-rational expectations in the foreign exchange market. Indeed, Frankel and Froot (1987) suggest that neither the rational expectations hypothesis nor alternative expectations hypotheses correctly specify exchange market expectations. While preliminary research into this question by MacDonald and Torrance (1989) suggests that both the existence of a risk premium and non rational expectations are to blame.

9.6 Empirical test of exchange-rate models

As we saw in Chapters 7 and 8, there are a variety of models of exchange-rate determination for the authorities to choose from with radically different implications for the conduct of exchange-rate policy. In particular, the monetary and portfolio balance models have very different implications concerning the effectiveness of sterilised intervention.

Predictably, some authors have conducted empirical tests of their exchange-rate model and found evidence to support it, while others using either different time periods or different bilateral exchange rates have found evidence against a given model. Another problem is that some authors have taken the empirical evidence to support their exchange-rate model when the same predictions are also made by rival theories. In an attempt to overcome this latter problem, Jeffrey Frankel (1983, 1984) has extended his monetary synthesis equation (1979a—see chapter 7) to incorporate a portfolio balance effect. The basic derivation of his synthesis exchange rate equation is as follows (see Frankel, 1983):

One begins with a conventional domestic money demand function given by:

$$m = p + \eta y - \sigma r \tag{9.12}$$

where m is the log of domestic money supply, p is the log of domestic price level, y is the log of domestic real income, η is the money demand elasticity with respect to income, and σ is the money demand semi-elasticity with respect to the interest rate.

A similar money demand function is postulated for the foreign country and assuming identical elasticities for the foreign economy, we have:

$$m^* = p^* + \eta y^* - \sigma r^* \tag{9.13}$$

where an asterisk represents a foreign variable.

Taking the difference of the two equations yields the relative money demand function:

$$(m - m^*) = (p - p^*) + \eta(y - y^*) - \sigma(r - r^*) \tag{9.14}$$

By invoking long-run PPP the long-run equilibrium exchange rate $\bar{s}$ can be expressed in log form as the difference between the long run price levels:

$$\bar{s} = \bar{p} - \bar{p}^* \tag{9.15}$$

where $\bar{p}$ is the log of the long-run domestic price level and $\bar{p}^*$ is the log of the long-run foreign price level.

Substituting (9.15) into (9.14) and rearranging gives the following expression for the long-run equilibrium exchange rate:

$$\bar{s} = (m - m^*) - \eta(y - y^*) + \sigma(r - r^*) \tag{9.16}$$

Rather than assume uncovered interest rate parity which is inconsistent with a portfolio balance framework, we have to allow for the possible existence of a risk premium. The most simple formulation of the risk premium on the domestic currency is to say that it is positively related to the supply of domestic bonds and negatively related to the supply of foreign bonds. One means of expressing such a function in log form is given by:

$$b - s - f = \alpha + \beta(r - r^* - E\dot{s}) \tag{9.17}$$

where b is the log of domestic bonds in the hands of private agents, f is the log of foreign currency denominated bonds in the hands of private agents and $E\dot{s}$ is the expected rate of depreciation of the domestic currency.

That is, in order to hold more domestic currency denominated bonds domestic investors would require either a rise in the interest rate differential in favour of domestic bonds or an expected appreciation of the domestic currency (expected fall in the exchange rate). The parameter β measures the degree of substitutability; if β is equal to infinity then moving it and α to the left-hand side would leave the UIP condition.

The expected change in the exchange rate is given by the following expression:

$$E\dot{s} = -\theta(s - \bar{s}) + P\dot{e} - P\dot{e}^* \tag{9.18}$$

where θ is the speed of adjustment to equilibrium, $P\dot{e}$ is the expected long-run domestic inflation rate, and $P\dot{e}^*$ is the expected long-run foreign inflation rate.

That is, the expected rate of change in the exchange rate is determined by the speed of adjustment to the long-run equilibrium rate θ, the gap between the current and long-run exchange rate and the expected inflation differential.

Solving for $E\dot{s}$ in equation (9.17) we find that:

$$E\dot{s} = \frac{-b + s + f + \alpha}{\beta} + r - r^* \tag{9.19}$$

Thus, substituting (9.19) into (9.18) and rearranging we find that:

$$s - \bar{s} = \frac{b - s - f - \alpha}{\theta\beta} + \frac{1}{\theta}[(r^* - P\dot{e}^*) - (r - P\dot{e})] \tag{9.20}$$

Finally, substituting our expression for the long-run equilibrium exchange rate given by equation (9.16) into equation (9.20) and after some algebraic manipulation we obtain an exchange-rate equation that synthesises both the monetary and portfolio balance approaches to exchange-rate determination given by:

$$s = \frac{-\alpha}{\theta\beta + 1} + \frac{\theta\beta}{\theta\beta + 1}(m - m^*) - \frac{\eta\theta\beta}{\theta\beta + 1}(y - y^*)$$

$$+ \frac{\beta(\sigma\theta + 1)}{\theta\beta + 1}(P\dot{e} - P\dot{e}^*) \frac{-\beta}{\theta\beta + 1}(r - r^*) + \frac{1}{\theta\beta + 1}(b - f) \tag{9.21}$$

Table 9.3   *Predictions of exchange rate models*

Model	a_2 $(m-m^*)$	a_3 $(y-y^*)$	a_4 $(r-r^*)$	a_5 $(P\dot{e}-P\dot{e}^*)$	a_6 $(b-f)$
Flexible price monetary model	+	−	0	+	0
Sticky price Dornbusch monetary model	+	−	−	0	0
Real interest differential monetary model	+	−	−	+	0
Sticky price portfolio model	+	−	−	+	+

Notes:
$m-m^*$, log of relative money supply; $y-y^*$, log of relative income; $r-r^*$, nominal interest rate differential; $P\dot{e}-P\dot{e}^*$, expected inflation differential, $b-f$, log of relative bond supplies.

Equation (9.21) can be rewritten as:

$$s = \frac{-\alpha}{\theta\beta+1} + \frac{1}{1+1/\theta\beta}(m-m^*)\frac{-\eta}{1+1/\theta\beta}(y-y^*)$$

$$+ \frac{\sigma+1/\theta}{1+1/\theta\beta}(P\dot{e}-P\dot{e}^*)\frac{-1}{\theta+1/\beta}(r-r^*) + \frac{1}{\theta\beta+1}(b-f) \tag{9.22}$$

The fully flexible price monetarist version postulates that both the parameters θ and β approach infinity; this reduces equation (9.22) to the flexible price monetary equation (7.8) of Chapter 7. The sticky price monetarist school holds that θ is less than infinite while β is infinite so we end up with the real interest differential equation (7.31), whereas the sticky price portfolio balance model holds that both the parameters β and θ are less than infinite, so that relative bond supplies have an impact on the exchange rate and the relevant equation is therefore (9.22).

Equation (9.22) yields the following reduced form regression for the exchange rate:

$$s = a_1 + a_2(m-m^*) + a_3(y-y^*) + a_4(r-r^*) + a_5(P\dot{e}-P\dot{e}^*) + a_6(b-f) + ut \tag{9.23}$$

Table 9.3 reveals the conflicting predictions of the four main models of exchange rate determination derived from equation (9.22). The Frankel formulation shows that the theoretical predictions of the main models of exchange-rate determination are sufficiently different that a resort to empirical testing should allow us to discriminate between the various theories. Frankel tests his synthesis equation for the US dollar against the deutschmark using monthly data for the period January 1974–October 1978. In a similar vein, Pilbeam (1991) tests the Frankel equation for the US dollar

Table 9.4 *Test of exchange-rate models*

Frankel (1983), Estimation: for dollar–deutschmark

Estimated equation:

$$s = a_1 + a_2(mus - mg) + a_3(yus - yg) + a_4(rus - rg) + a_5(\dot{P}eus - \dot{P}eg) + a_6(bus - bg) + ut$$

Sample period	a_1	a_2	a_3	a_4	a_5	a_6	$\bar{R}^2$
1974M1 1978M9	−0.26	−0.01	−0.13	−0.40	0.85	−0.40	0.93
	(−1.13)	(−0.03)	(−0.06)	(−0.79)	(0.21)	(−4.37)	

Source: J.A. Frankel, 'Monetary and Portfolio Balance Models of Exchange Rate Determination', in J.S. Bhandari and B.H. Putnam, *Economic Interdependence and Flexible Exchange Rates* (Cambridge, Mass.: MIT Press, 1983), p. 104.

Pilbeam (1991), Estimation: for dollar–pound

Estimated equation:

$$s = a_1 + a_2(mus - muk) + a_3(yus - yuk) + a_4(rus - ruk) + a_5(\dot{P}eus - \dot{P}euk)$$
$$+ a_6(bus - buk) + ut$$

Sample period	a_1	a_2	a_3	a_4	a_5	a_6	$\bar{R}^2$
1973Q1 1984Q4	3.85	0.64*	−0.50	0.16	0.02	−0.28	0.93
	(3.67)	(2.79)	(−1.01)	(0.40)	(0.21)	(−1.56)	

Source: K.S. Pilbeam, *Exchange Rate Management: Theory and Evidence* (London: Macmillan, 1991)

Notes:

Hypothesis is: $a_2 > 0$; $a_3 < 0$; $a_4 \lesssim 0$; $a_5 \geqslant 0$; $a_6 \geqslant 0$.

An asterisk by a variable indicates that it is both of the correct sign and not statistically different from its hypothesised value.

t-statistics are in parentheses.

against the pound for the period January 1973 to December 1984. Results from these two studies are reported in **Table 9.4**.

The results reported in Table 9.4 are typical examples of most exchange-rate tests. As we can see from the reported regressions, the results rather than favouring any particular model of exchange-rate determination are not favourable to any. In the Frankel study the only variable to be significant is the equation for relative bond supplies but this is of the wrong sign! In the Pilbeam study, the only variable to be significant is the money stock but this is a prediction common to all three models. The coefficient for real output is correctly signed in the Pilbeam study but incorrectly signed in the Frankel study and statistically insignificant in both. As for the nominal interest-rate differential and expected inflation differential the actual estimated coefficients were not significantly different from zero, revealing that there is no clear-cut empirical relation between interest rates and price expectations for either the dollar–deutschmark or the dollar–pound exchange rate. The regression coefficient for the portfolio balance parameter is incorrectly signed in both studies.

 ## *9.7* Exchange-rate models: a forecasting analysis

From the regression coefficients reported in Table 9.4, it is not possible to rank any of the alternative theories derived from the Frankel synthesis equation. Although the regression coefficients provide very little support for any of the theories, this does not rule out the possibility that one of the exchange-rate models may prove useful for forecasting purposes. In two important papers Meese and Rogoff (1983a) and (1983b) have tested the forecasting accuracy of popular exchange-rate models. Their test procedures and results have been replicated by Pilbeam (1991) for the dollar–pound exchange rate and it is the results of that study which are reported here.

Three models are tested, the flexible price monetary model, the real interest rate model and the sticky price portfolio balance model. For the purposes of forecasting the exchange rate, the three models are tested by using the variables which are deemed to be of interest from the Frankel synthesis equation regardless of whether the coefficients proved statistically significant or not. Pilbeam tests the forecasting accuracy of the models for the period 1979:1 to 1988:3 using a quarterly data set.

In order to forecast the one period ahead exchange rate a rolling regression technique was used, this meant reestimating the regression coefficients for each period t to forecast the exchange rate in time $t+1$. For example, to forecast the 1979:1 exchange rate, a regression for the period 1973:1 to 1978:4 was undertaken using the coefficients deemed to be relevant by a given theory, and these estimated coefficients were then used to forecast the 1979:1 exchange rate. Next, to forecast the 1979:2 exchange rate the regression was redone using data from 1973:1 to 1979:1 to reestimate the coefficients and these new estimates were then used to forecast the 1979:2 period exchange rate and so on. For the purposes of forecasting the exchange rate in time $t+1$, the actual values of the exogenous (right-hand side) variables in time $t+1$ were used. This latter point is important because it means that forecasts for one period ahead will not be based on the wrong money supplies, interest rates etc. so that any forecasting error is due to the weakness of the models rather than inaccurate forecasting of the fundamentals.

It is important to emphasise that for the purposes of forecasting it was the regression estimates of coefficients that were employed and that these rarely corresponded to the theoretical values. For instance, the fully flexible prices monetarist model predicts that the coefficient a_2 for the money stock will be unity but in the regressions it hovered between 0.2 and 0.55, while for the portfolio balance model the coefficient for relative bond supplies was persistently wrong signed. The purpose of the exercise was to see if any of the three models could be empirically useful devices to forecast the exchange rate. Meese and Rogoff (1983b) have used plausible theoretical coefficient values as opposed to the estimated coefficients for forecasting purposes but their results were largely the same as using the above procedure which is the basis of their (1983a) study. **Table 9.5** shows the forecast values of the exchange rate of the three alternative models tested in the Pilbeam study and the actual exchange rate.

For the purposes of ranking the forecasting accuracy of the three models a commonly used statistical measure known as the root mean squared error (RMSE) criterion was used. The RMSE criterion compares the predicted exchange rate with the actual exchange rate using the following formula:

$$\text{Mean Squared Error (MSE)} = \frac{1}{n} \sum_{i=1}^{n} \frac{(s_{t^*} - s_t)^2}{s_{t-1}}$$

where n is the number of forecasts, s_{t^*} is the predicted exchange rate for period t, s_t is the actual exchange rate in period t, and s_{t-1} is the actual exchange rate in period $t-1$.

Root Mean Squared Error (RMSE) $= \sqrt{\text{MSE}}$.

The lower the RMSE the better the forecasting capability of the model. The results of the RMSE test for the three alternative exchange-rate models are printed on p 239:

These results are compared with the RMSE of a simple random walk model of the exchange rate whereby the current exchange rate at time t is used as the forecast for the exchange rate in period $t+1$. In other words, a random walk forecast involves a speculator saying that the exchange rate forecast for one period's time (in this case three months) will be the same as it is today. Anyone without any knowledge of economics can make a random walk forecast simply by opening his/her daily newspaper!

The reported results are in line with those of Meese and Rogoff (1983a and 1983b) in showing that a simple random walk model has a superior forecasting power to any of the popular models of exchange-rate determination. Such a result is quite devastating for professional forecasters who use sophisticated econometric models because it suggests that anyone by opening a newspaper can on the average outperform a sophisticated exchange-rate model designed by a group of professional forecasters (this leaves us with the puzzle of explaining these forecasters' high salaries!). In addition to the poor root mean squared errors, **Table 9.5** shows that none of the models does very well at forecasting the exchange rate at the three-month horizon. In fact, in the Meese and Rogoff studies, it is shown that it is only at the twelve-month plus horizon that exchange-rate models start (in

Table 9.5   *Exchange-rate forecasts of different exchange-rate models*

Period	Flexible price monetary model	Real interest differential model	Sticky price portfolio model	Actual
1979Q1	1.998 1	1.988 8	2.007 0	2.068 8
1979Q2	2.112 0	2.095 4	2.127 4	2.168 4
1979Q3	2.101 9	2.088 4	2.105 5	2.197 6
1979Q4	2.186 6	2.178 9	2.181 7	2.224 0
1980Q1	2.206 5	2.257 7	2.256 1	2.166 8
1980Q2	2.148 1	1.996 5	2.043 9	2.362 0
1980Q3	2.358 8	2.389 7	2.376 2	2.388 3
1980Q4	2.319 2	2.330 7	2.328 6	2.385 0
1981Q1	2.357 8	2.354 7	2.315 8	2.244 2
1981Q2	2.210 5	2.213 6	2.284 9	1.942 8
1981Q3	1.928 7	1.914 7	1.912 2	1.800 5
1981Q4	1.794 0	1.791 1	1.762 8	1.908 0
1982Q1	1.941 2	1.965 4	1.953 4	1.781 7
1982Q2	1.774 9	1.774 6	1.776 2	1.738 3
1982Q3	1.747 4	1.740 9	1.724 5	1.692 7
1982Q4	1.730 6	1.734 0	1.714 1	1.614 5
1983Q1	1.649 2	1.650 9	1.657 6	1.479 0
1983Q2	1.464 1	1.463 8	1.456 5	1.530 4
1983Q3	1.560 9	1.561 0	1.554 3	1.495 7
1983Q4	1.494 9	1.494 6	1.488 8	1.450 6
1984Q1	1.449 0	1.449 7	1.429 3	1.442 6
1984Q2	1.429 8	1.428 4	1.427 3	1.352 7
1984Q3	1.363 1	1.362 2	1.353 8	1.248 0
1984Q4	1.244 0	1.241 6	1.231 0	1.156 5
1985Q1	1.163 0	1.163 0	1.185 1	1.243 0
1985Q2	1.217 7	1.216 3	1.230 0	1.295 1
1985Q3	1.346 5	1.352 3	1.340 8	1.401 0
1985Q4	1.410 8	1.415 9	1.382 2	1.444 5
1986Q1	1.448 3	1.450 9	1.469 3	1.485 3
1986Q2	1.514 8	1.512 4	1.503 1	1.530 3
1986Q3	1.523 9	1.530 5	1.514 4	1.450 0
1986Q4	1.486 5	1.486 2	1.466 4	1.474 5
1987Q1	1.427 8	1.425 0	1.444 3	1.605 0
1987Q2	1.647 6	1.648 2	1.637 4	1.610 0
1987Q3	1.615 9	1.616 1	1.581 5	1.629 7
1987Q4	1.613 0	1.613 1	1.616 2	1.871 5
1988Q1	1.946 4	1.948 2	—	1.879 8
1988Q2	1.868 1	1.868 1	—	1.709 3
1988Q3	1.639 0	1.640 0	—	1.685 5

Notes:

The above is dollar–pound rate.

Source: K.S. Pilbeam, *Exchange Rate Management: Theory and Evidence* (London: Macmillan, 1991) p. 158.

Root Mean Squared Error

Flexible price monetary model	0.0806
Real interest differential model	0.0882
Sticky price portfolio model	0.0870
Random walk model	0.0769

Note: the above results are based on the values of the exchange rate listed in Table 9.5.

some instances) to outperform the random walk model. The abysmal performance of the theories requires some explanation which is attempted in the next section.

9.8 Explaining the poor results of exchange-rate models

In addition to the Meese and Rogoff studies and the Pilbeam study, other researchers comparing existing exchange-rate models with varying degrees of econometric technicality have shown that exchange-rate models perform poorly empirically, such as Frankel (1984) who tests his synthesis equation for the deutschmark, yen, pound sterling, French franc and Canadian dollar against the US dollar, Bakus (1984) who concentrates on the Canadian–US dollar rate, Leventakis (1987) who concentrates on the deutschmark–US dollar and Hacche and Townend (1981) who failed in their attempt to model sterling's effective exchange rate. These diverse studies reveal that the failure of existing exchange-rate models is quite general.

No doubt, one could engage in a data mining exercise looking at particular sub periods, a variety of bilateral exchange rates using different estimation techniques and present evidence (by excluding results that do not support your model!) favouring a given theory. However, it is surely better to recognise that there is no clear-cut empirical support for any given theory. This failure to satisfactorily account for exchange-rate behaviour does not mean that the exchange-rate models are necessarily wrong; rather it probably reflects the enormous econometric problem of modelling exchange-rate behaviour. In fact, the exchange-rate theories provide many reasons as to why exchange rates will be difficult to model empirically. Among the more important are:

- Exchange rates are determined not simply by the stance of monetary policy but depend in a complex and as yet little understood manner upon the monetary/fiscal policy mix and the interactions of these macroeconomic policies between countries.
- The theoretical literature on exchange-rate determination since the advent of floating exchange rates has made it abundantly clear that the

current exchange rate depends not only upon the present fundamentals but also upon the expected future course of those fundamentals. For this reason, new information which alters perceptions about the future course of these fundamental factors will have an impact upon the current exchange rate. It is extremely difficult to identify and model changes in new information and how they are discounted into the current exchange rate.

- Another related problem has become known in the literature as the 'Finance Minister Problem' or 'Peso Problem'. Even if we have a correct model of exchange-rate determination and an event relevant to the exchange rate is widely expected to occur at some time in the future (the appointment of a new finance minister or increase in the money supply) this will affect the current exchange rate. However, if the expected event does not materialise (the finance minister is not appointed or the money supply is not increased) then the movements in the exchange rate will appear unrelated to the supposed underlying determinants. The model itself would not be wrong but the empirical test would not verify it.

- Another, closely related problem to the above, is seen in **Box 9.1**. The dynamic path of the exchange rate will be completely different depending upon whether a given shock or policy disturbance has been anticipated or unanticipated. As we shall see in section 9.9, while some empirical progress has been made in identifying anticipated and unanticipated exchange-rate movements, it has so far not been possible to accurately integrate such effects into an empirically testable exchange-rate model.

- All modern asset market models of exchange-rate determination are in agreement that expectations are crucial to the determination of the current exchange rate. However, both in theory and when it comes to the empirical test of a theory the econometrics requires that we adopt some major simplifications. In the first instance, most theories assume that expectations are homogeneous when in the real world they are clearly heterogeneous as taking the predictions for the future spot exchange rate from professional forecasters will testify (see **Box 9.2**). Also, when it comes to empirical implementation it becomes necessary to adopt further radical simplifications. Some models assume perfect foresight on the part of foreign exchange market participants, so that expectations are fully consistent with the underlying theoretical model, while other models assume that exchange-rate expectations are static or follow a regressive expectations scheme. It is unlikely that any of these expectation mechanisms properly specifies expectations formation in an uncertain world. Frankel and Froot (1987) use survey data on exchange-rate forecasts of market participants and find little evidence to favour any of the previously mentioned expectations hypotheses. Until we are able more realistically to model exchange-rate expectations and their relation to expectations formation in other markets we shall remain unable to satisfactorily model exchange-rate behaviour.

- Another problem that may be particularly acute is that it has not only been changes in the supply of money that have been important in explaining the exchange rate but also instability in the demand for money schedules. Theoretically such shifts are as important in determining the exchange rate as changes in the money stock.
- A particularly acute problem in attempts to model exchange-rate behaviour since the advent of floating rates is to incorporate into the empirical model the role of real shocks on exchange-rate movements.
- A final problem worth mentioning and probably of considerable importance during the 1970s and 1980s has been the enormous changes in the financial and real structure of economies. These have had important implications for the performance of the economies and thereby on the exchange rate.

This list of reasons as to why it may prove empirically difficult to verify existing exchange-rate models is rather formidable. The implication is that a given theory may be correct but it may not pass an empirical test.

 ## 9.9 The 'news' approach to modelling exchange rates

Although models of exchange-rate determination measured in terms of levels have not proved particularly successful some success has been achieved with modelling exchange-rate behaviour in a 'news' context. An attractive feature of the 'news' approach is that it combines the concept of exchange-market efficiency with modern models of exchange-rate determination. For this reason it is worth considering this approach in some detail.

Authors such as Dornbusch (1980) and Frenkel (1982) have suggested that the correct way to model exchange-rate movements is to presume that the foreign exchange market is efficient, in the sense that all *ex-ante* profit opportunities are eliminated. This being the case, movements in exchange rates will be due to the arrival of new information. As we shall see, the way that the two authors model news is somewhat different but their results do provide some support for the 'news' approach.

The basic tenet of the news approach is that if the foreign exchange market is efficient then any difference between the forward rate and the corresponding rate that later transpires must (with no risk premium) be due

Box 9.2   *The role of chartists and fundamentalists in exchange-rate determination*

Partly due to the failure of existing exchange-rate models to satisfactorily account for exchange-rate behaviour a number of recent papers, e.g. Goodhart (1987), Allen and Taylor (1989) and De Grauwe and Vansanten (1991), have started to analyse the role played by various groups in the foreign exchange market. Two groups that have attracted an increasing amount of attention are so-called 'Chartists' and 'Fundamentalists'.

Chartists claim to be able to successfully predict the future behaviour of a variable such as the exchange rate merely by examining a variety of recent charts of the exchange rate. Chartists claim that certain patterns of behaviour repeat themselves and that by detecting the relevant pattern in play, considerable success can be had in predicting the future exchange rate. Many of the patterns are given names such as 'head and shoulders', 'a triple bottom', 'ascending triangle', and 'double top'. Feeny (1989) provides an excellent summary of chartist methodology. The important point about chartists is that the only information they require to predict exchange rates is the recent past behaviour of the exchange rate itself, 'economic fundamentals' such as money supplies, interest rates, the balance-of-payments position are not required. Critics of chartists are inclined to accuse them of 'having long rulers and small brains!'

Fundamentalists are economists who argue that the best way to predict the future course of exchange rates is to look at the prospectives for underlying economic fundamentals such as the future interest rates, balance-of-payments prospects, inflation rates and so forth. The important thing about fundamentalists is that they believe that the foreign exchange market is efficient, so past behaviour of the exchange rate will be of little use in predicting the course of the exchange rate. What matters for the exchange rate is the prospective development of the economic fundamentals.

Recent research argues that much exchange-rate behaviour may be explained by the fact that at certain times chartists have the upper hand in determining the exchange rate while at other times the fundamentalists have the upper hand. In periods of high uncertainty over the course of economic fundamentals chartists tend to be the predominant force in the exchange market, while at times when economic fundamentals strongly point to a certain path for the exchange rate, the fundamentalists become the predominant force.

There are a wide range of views within both chartism and fundamentalism. Allen and Taylor (1989) conducted a survey of the influence of chartism on the London foreign exchange market – they found that chartism is widely used as an input for short-term forecasting, while fundamental analysis is mainly used for longer-term forecasting. On each Tuesday during the period June 1988 to March 1989 they asked a sample of chartists for their exchange-rate forecasts for the sterling–dollar, dollar–mark and dollar–yen for both one week and one

---

Box 9.2   *contd*

month ahead. It was noted that there was a tendency for chartists to underpredict a rise in the exchange rate and overpredict in a falling market. This suggests that chartists' 'elasticity of expectations' is less than unity – that is, a 1 per cent rise (fall) in the exchange rate appears to induce a less than 1 per cent expected rise (fall) in the following period. Although one chartist code-named 'Mr M' did manage to consistently outperform the random walk model. They found that there were significant differences in the forecasts between individual chartists and that on average chartist forecasts were worse than a random walk forecast. It seems that chartists are just as bad as economists in forecasting exchange rates.

---

to the arrival of new information. In other words, unanticipated exchange-rate movements are due to unexpected changes in the fundamentals.

A typical specification of a 'news' model of exchange rates is the following:

$$s_t - f_{t/t-1} = a_1 + a_2 uX_t + a_3 uY_t + a_4 uZ_t + u_t \tag{9.24}$$

where s_t is the log of the spot exchange rate at time t, $f_{t/t-1}$ is the log of the forward exchange for time t at time $t-1$, and uX_t, uY_t and uZ_t are the log of unexpected changes in the fundamental variables X, Y and Z.

The left hand side of equation (9.24), i.e. $(s_t - f_{t/t-1})$, represents the unexpected change in the exchange rate. In devising a proxy for the unexpected change in the exchange rate we can invoke the EMH. In other words, the expected spot rate is given by the forward exchange rate in the previous period. Hence, by deducting from the actual exchange rate the previous period's forward rate we have a proxy for the unexpected change in the exchange rate.

As for the unexpected change in the fundamentals (the right-hand side of equation (9.24)), one has to first decide what are the fundamental variables X_t, Y_t and Z_t etc. This choice will obviously be dependent upon the exchange-rate model selected. Having selected the model it is then necessary to devise the proxies for the unexpected change in the variables chosen. While the actual changes in the selected fundamentals are known, the problem rests with devising proxies for what was the expected change. By deducting from the actual change in a variable the proxy for the expected change in that variable we are left with the unexpected change. There are several alternative methods for devising such proxies:

(i)   Use publicly available forecasts – this is the approach taken by Dornbusch (1980); he takes the six-monthly forecasts made by the OECD as broadly representative of informed opinion about expected economic growth rates and current account balances. By deducting these forecasts from what subsequently occurred he obtains a proxy for the unexpected change in these variables.

(ii)   Use regression analysis. We can take a fundamental variable X, make it a dependent variable and make a forecast of what X will be the next period on the basis of the expected values of its supposed determinants. That is:

$$X_{t/t-1} = a_1 + a_2 L_{t/t-1} + a_3 M_{t/t-1} + a_4 N_{t/t-1} + \ldots + ut$$

where $X_{t/t-1}$ is the forecast value for the fundamental variable X_t at time $t-1$, and $L_{t/t-1}$, $M_{t/t-1}$ and $N_{t/t-1}$ are the expected values for variables L, M and N for time t at time $t-1$ that are supposed to be useful for predicting variable X one period ahead.

The above regression would then yield a forecast (expected) value for X_t that could be deducted from the actual value to yield the unexpected change. This method is not very popular because it depends on having a good explanatory model for the variable X. This is very rarely the case in economics!

(iii)   Use a time series methodology known as autoregression. With this method the forecast value of fundamental variable X is determined purely by a regression of past values of X. That is:

$$X_{t/t-1} = a_1 + a_2 X_{t-1} + a_3 X_{t-2} + a_4 X_{t-3} + \ldots + ut$$

where X_{t-1}, X_{t-2}, and X_{t-3} etc are increasingly previous values of the variable X.

This method is a fairly popular way of generating a forecast for the value of X as one is effectively extrapolating from the current and past values of X in order to generate an expected value of X.

In the Dornbusch (1980) and Frenkel (1982) studies that pioneered the 'news' approach, the results were found to be highly supportive. Generally, the unexpected change in the fundamentals (i.e. the news items) were found to be significant determinants of the unexpected change in the exchange rate and the coefficients of the expected sign. However, the choice of fundamental variables in the studies was rather *ad hoc* not involving tests of formal exchange-rate models.

In a test of the news version of the real interest rate differential model, Edwards (1982) runs the following regression:

$$s_t = a_1 f_{t/t-1} + a_2(um - um^*) + a_3(uy - uy^*) + a_4(ui - ui^*) + ut$$

where $f_{t/t-1}$ is the one period ahead forward exchange rate at time $t-1$, um is the log of unexpected change in domestic money supply, uy is the unexpected increase in domestic income, and ui is the unexpected change in the domestic real interest rate. An asterisk denotes the corresponding unexpected change in the foreign variable.

Table 9.6 *Test of the news exchange rate model*

Estimated equation: $s_t = a_1 f_{t/t-1} + a_2(um - um^*)_t + a_3(uy - uy^*)_t + a_4(ui - ui^*)_t + ut$

Rate	a_1	a_2	a_3	a_4	DW
Pound/dollar	0.97*	0.10	0.01	0.01	1.85
	(48.5)	(0.67)	(3.00)	(0.39)	
French franc/dollar	0.95*	0.36*	0.18	−0.01	1.88
	(25.70)	(2.53)	(7.91)	(−0.33)	
Deutschmark/dollar	0.96*	0.37*	0.24	0.01	2.09
	(45.60)	(2.04)	(1.40)	(0.48)	

Notes:

Hypothesis is: $a_1 = 1$; $a_2 > 0$; $a_3 < 0$; $a_4 < 0$.

An asterisk by a variable indicates that it is both of the correct sign and not statistically different from its hypothesised value.

All currencies are against the US dollar.

t-statistics are in parentheses.

Source: S. Edwards (1982) 'Exchange Market Efficiency and New Information', *Economic Letters*, vol. 9, pp. 377–82.

The expected signs in the coefficients are $a_1 = 1$ as the forward rate is an unbiased predictor of the future spot rate (i.e. EMH); a_2 is positive so that a relative unexpected rise in the domestic money supply leads to an unexpected depreciation; a_3 should be negative as an unexpected rise in relative domestic income leads to an unexpected appreciation; a_4 should be negative as an unexpected rise in domestic real interest should lead to an unexpected appreciation. The results of the Edwards study are reported in **Table 9.6**.

The results in **Table 9.6** provide mixed support for the 'news' approach. As can be seen, the unexpected money supply coefficient is right signed and significant for two of the currencies, while the coefficient for expected output is significant but of the wrong sign! However, the unexpected change in the real interest differential is not statistically significant.

Apart from the original Dornbusch and Frenkel studies, MacDonald (1983) tests a news type model for six currencies against the US dollar over the period 1972Q1 to 1979Q4. He finds that unexpected monetary developments are sometimes statistically important but occasionally with the wrong sign!

An interesting finding by both Edwards (1983b) and MacDonald(1983) is that in some regressions past news (i.e. lagged news terms) can have a significant effect on the unexpected exchange-rate change. Such an effect is incompatible with the concept of exchange-market efficiency. Edwards argues that this effect may be due to a lag in the publication of data. MacDonald also finds that lagged news terms can be statistically significant even with a lag of up to four periods. This is something of a mystery because while publication lags may account for significant one period lags it is difficult to rationalise two or three period lags. In sum, although some of the news items move exchange rates in the direction predicted, the results are not particularly robust across different currencies and the news items are sometimes statistically significant but wrong signed! Furthermore, the fact that lagged news items can be significant for more than one period does not tie in with the concept of exchange-market efficiency, although results using lagged news effects are not particularly robust.

Overall, the news approach which combines the concept of exchange-market efficiency with conventional exchange-rate models has proved a relatively fruitful area for exchange-rate research. None the less, given that the empirical evidence on exchange-market efficiency and conventional exchange-rate models both have little empirical support, it is not surprising that the news approach which combines the two concepts has mixed empirical support.

■ *9.10* Conclusions

In contrast to the exciting advances in the theoretical modelling of exchange rates, empirical tests of these theories have been notoriously unrewarding. None of the major theories stands up well to empirical examination. In large part, the empirical failure of the models reflects the enormous econometric problems involved in modelling exchange rates. However, even the use of ever more sophisticated econometric techniques has not led to any significantly better success.

There is, however, mounting empirical evidence that rejects the joint test of exchange-market efficiency and no risk premium, that is, uncovered interest parity. This is especially damaging for the monetarist models which assume both. Although the portfolio balance model allows for departures from uncovered interest parity due to the existence of a risk premium, there is no empirical evidence to support it as an alternative to the monetary models. Attempts to explain the risk premium in terms of its theoretical underlying determinants have failed. In sum, the possibility that the modern theories of exchange rate determination are very incomplete explanations cannot be ruled out.

On the other hand, empirical rejection of the models does not necessarily mean that they are wrong because tests of exchange-rate models do little justice to the complexities of the various theories. Thus, policy makers should not ignore the theories but it may be unwise to base policy on any single theory. In this respect, most theories emphasise the importance of pursuing stable monetary policies in order to avoid disruptive exchange-rate movements.

In all probability many of the major empirical issues concerning exchange rate determination are likely to remain unresolved in the foreseeable future. Recent research focusing on the role played by different groups such as chartists and fundamentalists in the determination of the exchange rate is yielding new and useful insights. However, this approach is most unlikely to yield a significant improvement in the empirical modelling of exchange rates. The core of the problem lies in the fact that all sides accept that expectations are crucial to the modelling of the exchange rate but we have no satisfactory method of modelling and measuring these expectations. Until we can more satisfactorily model expectations we shall be unable to satisfactorily model exchange-rate behaviour.

■ Selected further readings

Allen, H.L. and Taylor M.P. (1989) 'Charts and Fundamentals in the Foreign Exchange Market', *Bank of England Discussion Papers*, No 40.

Bailey, M.J., Tavlas, G.S. and Ulan, M. (1986) 'Exchange Rate Variability and Trade Performance: Evidence for the Big Seven Industrial Countries', *Weltwirtschaftliches Archiv*, vol. 122, pp. 466–77.

Bakus, D. (1984) 'Empirical Models of the Exchange Rate: Separating the Wheat from the Chaff', *Canadian Journal of Economics*, vol. 17, pp. 824–46.

Boothe, P. and Longworth, D. (1986) 'Foreign Exchange Market Efficiency Tests: Implications of Recent Empirical Findings', *Journal of International Money and Finance*, vol. 5, pp. 135–52.

Brooks, S., Cuthbertson, K. and Mayes, D. (1986) *The Exchange Rate Environment* (Kent: Croom Helm).

Caves, D. and Feige, E. (1980) 'Efficient Foreign Exchange Markets and the Monetary Approach to Exchange Rate Determination', *American Economic Review*, vol. 70, 120–34.

Cooper, R.N. (1982) 'Flexible Exchange Rates 1973–80, How Bad Have They Really Been?' in R.N. Cooper, P.B. Kenen, J.B. Macedo and J.V. Ypersele, *The International Monetary System Under Flexible Exchange Rates* (Cambridge, Mass.: Ballinger).

Cumby, R.E. and Obstfeld, M. (1984) 'International Interest Rate and Price Level Linkages Under Flexible Exchange Rates: A Review of Recent Evidence', in J.F.O. Bilson and R.C. Marston (eds), *Exchange Rate Theory and Practice* (Chicago: University of Chicago Press).

De Grauwe, P. (1991) 'Speculative Dyamics and Chaos in the Foreign Exchange Market', in *Finance and the International Economy: 4* (Oxford: Oxford University Press).

Dornbusch, R. (1980) 'Exchange Rate Economics Where Do We Stand?', *The Brookings Papers on Economic Activity*, vol. 1, pp. 143–85.

Dornbusch, R. (1987) 'Exchange Rate Economics: 1986', *The Economic Journal*, vol. 97, pp. 1–18.

Edwards, S. (1982) 'Exchange Market Efficiency and New Information', *Economic Letters*, vol. 9, pp. 377–82.

Edwards, S. (1983a) 'Exchange Rates and "News": a Multi-Currency Approach', *Journal of International Money and Finance*, vol. 3, pp. 211–24.

Edwards, S. (1983b) 'Floating Exchange Rates, Expectations and New Information', *Journal of Monetary Economics*, vol. 11, pp. 321–36.

Evans, G.W. (1986) 'A Test for Speculative Bubbles and the Sterling–Dollar Rate. 1981–84', *American Economic Review*, vol. 76, pp. 621–36.

Fama, E. (1970) 'Efficient Capital Markets: a Review of Theory and Empirical Work', *Journal of Finance*, pp. 383–417.

Feeny, M. (1989) 'Charting the Foreign Exchange Markets', in C. Dunis and M. Feeny, *Exchange Rate Forecasting* (Cambridge: Woodhead-Faulkner).

Frankel, J.A. (1979a) 'On the Mark: a Theory of Floating Exchange Rates Based on Real Interest Differentials', *American Economic Review*, vol. 69, pp. 610–22.

Frankel, J.A. (1979b) 'Tests of Rational Expectations in the Forward Exchange Market', *Southern Economic Journal*, pp. 1083–1101.

Frankel, J.A. (1982a) 'In Search of the Exchange Risk Premium: a Six Currency Test Assuming Mean Variance Optimization', *Journal of International Money and Finance*, vol. 1.

Frankel, J.A. (1982b) 'A Test of Perfect Substitutability in the Forward Exchange Market', *Southern Economic Journal*, pp. 406–16.

Frankel, J.A. (1983) 'Monetary and Portfolio Balance Models of Exchange Rate Determination', in J.S. Bhandari and B.H. Putnam, *Economic Interdependence and Flexible Exchange Rates* (Cambridge, Mass.: MIT).

Frankel, J.A. (1984) 'Tests of Monetary and Portfolio Balance Models of Exchange Rate Determination', in J.F.O. Bilson and R.C. Marston, *Exchange Rate Theory and Practice* (Chicago: University of Chicago Press).

Frankel, J.A. (1986) 'The Implications of Mean-Variance Optimization for Four Questions in International Macroeconomics', *Journal of International Money and Finance*, vol. 5, supplement, pp. 53–75.

Frankel, J.A. and Froot, K.A. (1987) 'Using Survey Data to Test Standard Propositions Regarding Exchange Rate Expectations', *American Economic Review*, vol. 77, pp. 133–53.

Frankel, J.A. and Froot, K.A. (1989) 'Chartists, Fundamentalists, and Trading in the Foreign Exchange Market', *American Economic Review Papers and Proceedings*, vol. 80, pp. 181–5.

Frenkel, J.A. (1982) 'Flexible Exchange Rates, Prices and the Role of "News": Lessons from the 1970s', in R.A. Batchelor and G.E. Wood, *Exchange Rate Policy* (London: Macmillan).

Frenkel, J.A. and Mussa, M. (1980) 'The Efficiency of Foreign Exchange Markets and Measures of Turbulence', *American Economic Review*, vol. 70, pp. 374–81.

Goodhart, C. (1987) 'The foreign exchange market: a random walk with a dragging anchor', *Economica*, vol. 55, pp. 437–60.

Hacche, G. and Townend, J. (1981) 'Exchange Rates and Monetary Policy: Modelling Sterling's Effective Exchange Rate 1972–1980', in W.A. Eltis and P.J.N. Sinclair, *The Money Supply and the Exchange Rate* (Oxford: Clarendon).

Hansen, L.P. and Hodrick, R.J. (1980) 'Forward Exchange Rates as Optimal Predictors of Future Spot Rates. An Econometric Analysis', *Journal of Political Economy*, vol. 88, pp. 829–53.

Isard, P. (1987) 'Lessons from Empirical Models of Exchange Rates', *IMF Staff Papers*, vol. 34, pp. 1–28.

Leventakis, J.A. (1987) 'Exchange Rate Models: Do they Work?', *Weltwirtschaftliches Archiv*, vol. 123, pp. 363–76.

Levich, R.M. (1978) 'Tests of Forecast Models of Market Efficiency in the International Money Market', in J.A. Frenkel and H.G. Johnson, *The Economics of Exchange Rates* (Reading, Mass.: Addison-Wesley).

Levich, R.M. (1985) 'Empirical Studies of Exchange Rates, Price Behavior, Rate Determination and Market Efficiency', in R.W. Jones and P.B. Kenen, *Handbook of International Economics*, vol. II (Amsterdam: Elsevier).

Longworth, D. (1981) 'Testing the Efficiency of the Canadian–US Exchange Market Under the Assumption of No Risk Premium', *Journal of Finance*, vol. 36, pp. 43–9.

MacDonald, R. (1983) 'Some Tests of the Rational Expectations Hypothesis in the Foreign Exchange Market', *Scottish Journal of Political Economy*, vol. 30, pp. 235–50.

MacDonald, R. (1988), *Floating Exchange Rates: Theories and Evidence* (London: Unwin Hyman).

MacDonald, R. and Torrance, T.S. (1989) 'Some Survey Based Tests of Uncovered Interest Parity', in R. MacDonald and M.P. Taylor, *Exchange Rates and Open Economy Macroeconomic Models* (Oxford: Basil Blackwell).

Meese, R. and Singleton, K.J. (1982) 'A Note on Unit Roots and the Empirical Modelling of Exchange Rates', *Journal of Finance*, vol. 37, pp. 1029–35.

Meese, R. and Rogoff, K. (1983a) 'Empirical Exchange Rate Models of the Seventies: Do they Fit Out of Sample?' *Journal of International Economics*, vol. 14, pp. 3–24.

Meese, R. and Rogoff, K. (1983b) 'The Out of Sample Failure of Empirical Exchange Rate Models: Sampling Error or Misspecification', in J.A. Frenkel (ed), *Exchange Rates and International Economics* (Chicago: University of Chicago Press).

Mussa, M. (1979) 'Empirical Regularities in the Behaviour of Exchange Rates and Theories of the Foreign Exchange Market', in K. Brunner and A.H. Meltzer (eds), *Policies for Employment, Prices and Exchange Rates*. Carnegie–Rochester Conference Series on Public Policy. (Amsterdam: North-Holland).

Pilbeam, K.S. (1991) *Exchange Rate Management: Theory and Evidence* (London: Macmillan).

Rogoff, K. (1984) 'On the Effects of Sterilized Intervention. An Analysis of Weekly Data', *Journal of Monetary Economics*, vol. 14, pp. 133–50.

Taylor, M.P. (1988) 'A Dynamic Model of Forward Foreign Exchange Risk, with estimates for Three Major Exchange Rates', *The Manchester School*, vol. 56, pp. 55–68.

Taylor, M.P. and MacDonald, R. (1989) 'Exchange Rate Economics: An Expository Survey', in M.P. Taylor and R. MacDonald, *Exchange Rates and Open Economy Macroeconomic Models* (Oxford: Basil Blackwell).

Wasserfallen, W. and Kyburz, H. (1985) 'The Behaviour of Flexible Exchange Rates in the Short Run – A Systematic Investigation', *Weltwirtschaftliches Archiv*, vol. 121, pp. 646–60.

■ *Chapter 10* ■

Fixed, Floating and Managed Exchange Rates

■ *10.1* Introduction

Prior to the move to generalised floating in 1973, the adoption of floating exchange rates had long been advocated by eminent economists such as Milton Friedman (1953), Egon Sohmen (1961) and Harry Johnson (1969). However, the experience with floating rates has not been the panacea that many advocates had presupposed and this has led many economists to propose schemes designed to limit exchange-rate flexibility.

In this chapter, we examine the traditional and more recent arguments for and against fixed and floating exchange rates. We start by looking at the traditional debate over the two regimes, which is based upon evaluating the arguments for and against each of the regimes. As we shall see, the traditional debate is inconclusive with floating rates having some advantages and disadvantages as compared with fixed exchange rates. The failure of the traditional debate stimulated an alternative method of evaluating these regimes based upon comparing which regime best stabilises an economy in the face of various shocks within the context of a formal macroeconomic model. To give a flavour of the insights gained by this more modern approach we use a simple macroeconomic model to evaluate the two regimes.

Although exchange rates have been allowed to float since 1973, authorities have frequently intervened in the foreign exchange market in a bid to influence the exchange rate at which their currency is traded, hence the term 'managed' floating. The final part of the chapter looks at the rationale behind discretionary intervention in the foreign exchange market.

■ *10.2* The case for fixed exchange rates

The case for fixed exchange rates usually has two sides to it; on the one hand there are some positive arguments in favour of fixed exchange rates and on the other there are arguments against floating exchange rates. One needs to be careful with this approach because arguments against floating exchange rates are not necessarily arguments in favour of fixed rates. They may well constitute arguments for some degree of exchange-rate management rather than for fixed parities. In this spirit, let us consider both the positive arguments in favour of fixed rates and the arguments against floating rates.

Fixed exchange rates promote international trade and investment

The proponents of fixed exchange rates argue that fixed parities provide the best environment for the conduct of international trade and investment. It is argued that just as a single currency is the best means of promoting economic activity at the national level, fixed exchange rates are the best means of promoting international trade and investment at the international level. Exchange rate fluctuations cause additional uncertainty and risk in international economic transactions and inhibit the growth and development of such transactions.

Fixed exchange rates provide discipline for macroeconomic policies

An argument frequently put forward in favour of fixed exchange rates is that the commitment to a fixed exchange-rate regime provides a degree of discipline to domestic macroeconomic policy that is absent if exchange rates are allowed to float. If the authorities are in a fixed rate regime the pursuit of reckless macroeconomic policies (such as excessive monetary growth) will lead to pressure for a devaluation of the currency necessitating intervention by the authorities to defend their currency and a fall in their reserves. If the pressures continue the authorities would eventually have to devalue the currency which would be taken as a sign by economic agents that the authorities have mismanaged the economy. Such an unpleasant scenario should encourage governments to resist adopting unsound expansionary macroeconomic policies which they are invariably tempted to undertake prior to elections and in their attempts to reconcile conflicting demands.

Fixed exchange rates promote international co-operation

Another argument in favour of fixed exchange rates is that they necessitate a degree of international co-operation and co-ordination between countries that is generally absent under floating exchange rates (see Chapter 13 for more on international policy co-ordination). Countries that agree to peg their exchange rates generally have to agree on measures to be undertaken when the agreed exchange-rate parity comes under pressure. At a minimum, fixed exchange rates require an agreement to avoid conflicting exchange-rate targets ruling out the dangers of competitive devaluation scenarios such as occurred in the 1930s. The enhanced degree of international co-operation should bring benefits and lead to a more stable environment for the conduct of international trade and investment.

Speculation under floating rates is likely to be destabilising

The major argument advanced against floating exchange rates is that they are likely to be characterised by destabilising private speculation producing the 'wrong' exchange rate, the wrong exchange rate being an exchange rate that is sub optimal from the viewpoint of resource allocation. There are several ways in which private speculation can bring about the wrong exchange market. Some of the arguments depend on 'irrational' speculation while others depend upon uncertainty.

One example of 'irrational' speculation frequently cited is that the foreign exchange market can be **too risk adverse**. It often attaches too high a probability to the possibility of a depreciation of a 'weak' currency or equivalently too high a probability to the possibility of an appreciation of a 'strong' currency, even when this is not justified by the fundamentals. That is, one currency, say the pound sterling, is regarded as 'too risky' while another, say the US dollar, is regarded as 'safe' – market participants are basing their exchange-rate forecasts not only on currently available information but also past performance. The result is that there may be an unjustified reluctance to move out of dollars and to hold pounds, so that there is a larger depreciation of the pound than is justified by the fundamentals required as a premium by speculators to hold the pound. As a result, the dollar becomes overvalued while the pound becomes undervalued. The argument does not imply that risk aversion is an inefficient feature of the foreign exchange market, but rather that excessive risk aversion unjustified by the fundamentals is. Instability of a country's economic policies may well create uncertainty and therefore risk concerning estimates about the correct value of its currency. Excessive risk aversion, however, implies that part of the risk premium required by the market is unjustified by the fundamentals.

Another case where irrational private speculation can produce the wrong rate is via the **'bandwagon' effect**. The idea is that there is too much self-generating speculation detached from the fundamentals, 'speculation feeding upon speculation' rather than the fundamentals. A possible scenario involving the 'bandwagon effect' is when some news hits the market, say an unexpected increase in the UK money supply; this then sets off unjustified speculation that the eventual rate of monetary growth will be even greater bringing with it an unduly pessimistic inflation forecast. Assuming that the rate of growth of the money supply contained in the news turns out to be the actual rate, the depreciation of the pound will turn out to have been greater than was justified by the news and this will then reverse itself when it becomes evident that a 'bandwagon effect' has been in play.

The excessive risk aversion and bandwagon effect arguments presuppose that the foreign exchange speculators do not use all the information and news available to them efficiently and consequently speculation produces the wrong exchange rate until eventually fundamentals reassert themselves. More recently, authors such as Dornbusch (1983) have emphasised reasons as to why even rational speculators can produce the 'wrong' exchange rate. These explanations are all based upon the concept of exchange rate uncertainty.

One reason why rational speculators may produce the wrong exchange rate is that in a world of uncertainty they do not know the correct exchange rate model and as such they use a **seriously defective model**. Their expectations based on the wrong (irrelevant) exchange rate model will then generally lead to the wrong exchange rate. This point is important because market participants may be impressed by a plausible but relatively unimportant fundamental variable and make their expectations based upon movements in that variable come true. Furthermore, changes in irrelevant variables may lead to significant exchange rates movements. A further danger is that economic agents may shift their attention between many irrelevant pieces of information, causing excessive exchange rate variability and even major exchange rate collapses.

Another reason why rational speculators may produce the wrong exchange rate is known as the **'Peso Problem'**. Exchange rates are determined not only by what is held to be the underlying fundamentals today but by what is expected to happen to those fundamentals in the future. Even if the speculators' model of the underlying fundamentals is correct, their perceptions about the future can prove to be seriously wrong. In such cases, the exchange rate moves immediately in anticipation of events that do not materialise. Such *ex-post* unjustified exchange-rate movements can seriously interfere with the conduct of macroeconomic policy and with it macroeconomic stability.

Another reason for rational speculation producing the wrong rate has been proposed by Blanchard (1979) known as a **'rational bubble'**. An exchange-rate bubble exists when holders of a currency realise that it is overvalued but they are nevertheless willing to hold it, since they believe that the appreciation will continue for a while longer and that there is only a limited risk of a serious depreciation during a given holding period. So speculators expect to be able to sell eventually at an exchange rate that will provide them with a sufficient capital gain to compensate them for running the risk of a sudden collapse. Such speculation both prolongs an exchange overvaluation and aggravates the macroeconomic costs associated with it.

Hence, there are a variety of arguments as to why private speculation may be destabilising. Such destabilising speculation is often used as an argument for a fixed exchange rate and against a floating exchange rate. However, we have to be extremely careful here because a fixed exchange rate can be fixed at the wrong rate just as a floating rate can float to one. Even if a fixed exchange rate is initially fixed at the optimal exchange rate, when the economic fundamentals change the fixed parity then becomes the wrong rate.

■ *10.3* The case for floating exchange rates

The case for floating exchange rates is a mixture of positive arguments in favour of floating and arguments against fixed exchange rates. Again caution is warranted with the arguments against fixed exchange rates because they do not necessarily constitute arguments for completely floating exchange rates.

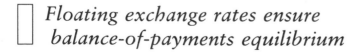

Floating exchange rates ensure balance-of-payments equilibrium

Proponents of floating exchange rates argue that in a floating regime the exchange rate automatically adjusts to ensure continuous equilibrium between the demand for and supply of the currency. If a country is running an unsustainable current account deficit, its exchange rate will depreciate which will reduce imports and increase exports until the balance of payments is restored to a sustainable level. Conversely, a structural surplus in the balance of payments will lead to an exchange-rate appreciation that will reduce the surplus to sustainable levels.

In other words, floating exchange rates ensure a balance between the demand for and supply of a currency; excess demand leads to an appreciation whereas excess supply leads to a depreciation. This contrasts to the scenario under fixed exchange rates where an overvalued rate leads to an excess supply and thereby a fall in the authorities' reserves, while fixing it at an undervalued rate leads to excess demand and increase in the authorities' reserves. Even if by chance the authorities initially peg the exchange rate at the point where supply equals demand, that rate will soon become inappropriate when a change in the economic fundamentals affects the supply or demand for the currency. Exchange rate adjustments by taking care of the balance of payments deficits relieve the authorities of having to adopt unpopular alternatives such as deflation or resort to protectionism.

Floating exchange rates ensure monetary autonomy

One of the major arguments put forward in favour of floating exchange rates is that they enable each country to operate an independent monetary policy, that is, they restore **monetary autonomy** enabling each country to determine its own inflation rate. Countries that prefer low inflation rates are free to adopt tight macroeconomic policies experiencing appreciating currencies. While countries that pursue expansionary macroeconomic policies will suffer higher inflation and depreciating currencies. This contrasts with what happens under fixed exchange rates where the need to have common inflation rates to maintain competitiveness constrains countries to pursue similar monetary policies (see chapter 5).

Floating exchange rates insulate economies

A further argument put forward in favour of floating exchange rates is that they can **insulate** the domestic economy from foreign price shocks. If there is an increase in foreign prices under floating exchange rates provided the exchange rate moves roughly in line with PPP the domestic currency would merely appreciate so preventing the country importing foreign inflation. This contrasts to what happens under fixed exchange rates where a foreign price rise makes the home economy overcompetitive leading to a balance-of-payments surplus which necessitates purchases of the foreign currency with newly created domestic currency to peg the exchange rate. The increase in the domestic money supply leads to an accompanying rise in domestic prices ending the surplus. Hence, fixed exchange rates lead to the importing of foreign price inflation/deflation (see Chapter 5).

Floating exchange rates promote economic stability

A forceful argument put forward by Milton Friedman (1953) in favour of flexible exchange rates is that it is better to let exchange rates adjust in response to shocks to an economy than to fix the exchange rate and force the adjustment on to other economic variables. He argued that floating exchange rates are more conducive to economic stability. The exchange rate is a variable which can easily rise or fall whereas domestic prices tend to be very difficult to reduce. Hence, if there is a loss of international competitiveness it is better to allow the exchange rate (one price) to depreciate rather than maintain a fixed exchange rate and require deflationary policies to restore international competitiveness. Since the domestic price level is resistant to downward pressure, it may require quite severe deflationary policies with associated high unemployment to induce the fall in domestic wages and prices necessary to restore international competitiveness.

Private speculation is stabilising

The advocates of floating exchange rates argue that private speculators are a stabilising rather than destabilising force. It is in the interests of speculators to move the exchange rate to its fundamental economic value. Speculators will attempt to buy the currency at a low value and sell it at a high value and in so doing reduce the gap between the low and high values. Of course, occasionally speculators will make mistakes and buy a currency which they think has depreciated sufficiently and find that it continues to depreciate, but such destabilising speculation will involve losses. This being the case, there is every reason to suppose that private speculators will move the exchange rate towards its fundamental equilibrium value.

Many of the preceding arguments advanced for and against the two regimes are extremely difficult if not impossible to prove. No doubt there are elements of truth on both sides of the argument; speculation can at times be stabilising and at other times may be destabilising. Fixed exchange rates can provide a stable framework for international trade but so too can floating rates by ensuring countries maintain their international competitiveness. Economic policies can be more or less stable under a fixed exchange rate regime as compared with a floating one.

Since the traditional advantages/disadvantages approach leaves plenty of scope for disagreement this has stimulated an alternative more modern approach to evaluating the two regimes. In this approach, the relative merits of the two regimes are evaluated within the context of a formal macro-economic model. We now look at the insights provided by this alternative approach by using a relatively simple macroeconomic model.

10.4 The modern evaluation of fixed and flexible exchange-rate regimes

The modern exchange-rate literature has attempted to evaluate the choice between fixed and flexible exchange rates by seeing which regime best stabilises the domestic economy in the face of various shocks to the economy. The exchange-rate regime that provides the most stability to the domestic economy is deemed to be the preferred regime. As we shall see, although more sophisticated, this literature does not provide an unambiguous answer to the question of which is the best exchange-rate regime. What it shows is that the choice between the two regimes is crucially dependent upon a multiplicity of factors. In our model, we highlight three of these factors; the specification of the objective function of the authorities as between price and output stability, the type of the shock impinging upon the economy and the structural parameters of the economy.

10.5 The specification of the objective function

There are many factors that the authorities have to take into account when designing their policies. Most importantly, they have to decide what are their objectives and the weight to be attached to each of them. For simplicity, we shall deal with an economy where the authorities have two objectives, price and output stability. The aim of the authorities is viewed as being the minimisation of fluctuations of the price level P and output level Y around their target values. The authorities will wish to minimise the value of the following objective function:

$$O(P,Y) = w(Y - Yn)^2 + (1-w)(P - Pn)^2 \qquad 0 \leqslant w \leqslant 1$$

where $O(P,Y)$ is the objective function of the authorities, w is the weight attached to output stability in the overall objective function, Yn is the natural/target value for domestic real income, and Pn is the natural/target value for the domestic price level.

The idea of incorporating a weighted objective function is that there may be a trade off for the authorities as between income and price stability. Some authorities may attach a high weight to price stability whereas others may attach a high priority to income stability and a weighted objective function allows for this possibility. A value of $w = 1$ means that the objective involves only domestic income stability, whereas if $w = 0$ the sole concern is with price stability.

■ *10.6* The model

We now investigate the choice between fixed and flexible exchange rate regimes for an economy that is buffeted by various transitory shocks. The fact that the shocks are assumed to be transitory, that is, self-reversing in the next period is an important assumption because it means that the economy is always expected to return to its natural price (Pn) and output level(Yn). In terms of the model, it means some simple rules can be made concerning expectations. If the exchange rate depreciates today it is expected to appreciate back to its normal level the next period. Similarly, if the price or output levels rise above their normal levels they will be expected to go back to their normal levels the next period. In the model that follows, we shall examine the performance of fixed and floating exchange rate regimes in the face of three types of transitory shocks, money demand, aggregate demand and aggregate supply.

In the following all variables except interest rates are expressed in logarithms.

The demand for the home country's money is a positive function of the aggregate price index, a positive function of real domestic income and inversely related to the domestic nominal interest rate. That is:

$$Md_t = Pi_t + \eta Y_t - \sigma r_t + Ut_1 \tag{10.1}$$

where Md_t is the demand to hold money in current period t, Pi_t is the currently observable aggregate price index made up of a weighted average of the domestic and foreign price levels as set out in equation (10.1a), Y_t is the real domestic income in period t, r_t is the domestic nominal interest rate in current period t which is a currently observable financial variable, and Ut_1 is a transitory money demand shock term with zero mean and normal distribution.

The idea of incorporating the aggregate price index in the demand for money function is derived from the monetarist proposition that the demand to hold money is a demand for real balances related to the purchasing power of money. The aggregate price index is a weighted average of the domestic price level and the domestic price of the imported foreign good, which is equal to the exchange rate times the price of the foreign good. That is:

$$Pi_t = \alpha P_t + (1 - \alpha)(s_t + P_t^*) \qquad 0 \leqslant \alpha \leqslant 1 \tag{10.1a}$$

where α is the weight of the domestic good in the overall consumption basket, st is the exchange rate defined as domestic currency per unit of foreign currency in the current period, P_t is the price of the domestic good in the current period, and P_t^* is the price of the imported foreign good in the foreign currency in the current period.

The demand for domestic output is a positive function of the real exchange rate and inversely related to the domestic real interest rate and a positive function of the natural level of income. That is:

$$Yd_t = \theta(s_t + P_t^* - P_t) - \beta(r_t + P_t - P_{t+1/t}) + \pi Yn + Ut_2 \tag{10.2}$$

where $P_{t+1/t}$ is the the the expected price level in one periods time given the information available in the current period, Yn is the the natural level of output, and Ut_2 is the a transitory aggregate demand shock term with zero mean and normal distribution.

The real exchange rate is given by the first bracketed expression; an appreciation of the exchange rate would reduce the demand for the domestic good. Similarly, the real domestic interest rate is given by the second bracketed expression and is equivalent to the nominal interest rate minus the expected rate of price inflation. A rise in the real interest rate will act to reduce the current demand for the domestic good.

The supply of domestic output depends upon the price at which producers are able to sell their output relative to the wage rate that they must pay per unit of labour. That is:

$$Ys_t = \varphi(P_t - W_t) + Ut_3 \tag{10.3}$$

$$Ys_t = Ys_t(L_t) \qquad \text{where } \delta Ys_t/\delta L_t > 0 \qquad \text{and } \delta^2 Ys_t/\delta^2 L_t < 0 \tag{10.3a}$$

where Ys_t is the supply of domestic good, L_t is the labour input, W_t is the wage rate and Ut_3 is the transitory aggregate supply shock term with zero mean and normal distribution.

Equation (10.3) says that if the price of the domestic good rises relative to the wage rate domestic producers will increase their output and employment levels as the real wage facing them falls. While equation (10.3a) says that output is a positive function of labour input but is subject to the law of diminishing returns. It is assumed that financial capital is perfectly mobile and that domestic and foreign bonds are perfect substitutes. As a result the uncovered interest parity condition is assumed to hold continuously. That is:

$$r_t = r_t^* + (s_{t+1/t} - s_t) \tag{10.4}$$

where r_t^* is the foreign interest rate in current period, and $s_{t+1/t}$ is the expected exchange rate in period $t+1$ given information available at time t.

The expression $(s_{t+1/t} - s_t)$ gives the expected rate of depreciation of the currency.

The contracting arrangement that determines the setting of nominal wages is central to the behaviour of the model. The contracts have a duration of one period and establish a nominal base wage W_t. It is assumed that the base wage W_t is set at the level required to generate an expected level of output at the natural level Yn, which is also the target level of the authorities.

$$W_t = W_t^* \tag{10.5}$$

where W_t^* is the wage rate that will in the absence of any shocks to the economy lead to full employment at the natural rate of output.

In order to close the model we require the simultaneous fulfilment of the following two equations: that money demand in the current period (Md_t) equal the current money supply (Ms_t) and that current aggregate supply equal current aggregate demand. That is:

$$Ms_t = Md_t \tag{10.6}$$

and

$$Ys_t = Yd_t \tag{10.7}$$

Under fixed exchange rates perfect capital mobility means that the domestic interest rate equals the foreign interest rate and the money supply is endogenously determined, while under floating exchange rates the money supply is exogenously determined and the domestic interest rate and exchange rate are endogenously determined but tied together via the uncovered interest rate parity condition. We now set out the model using a diagrammatic exposition.

■ *10.7* Determining equilibrium

We use for exposition purposes aggregate supply and demand schedules defined by equations (10.2) and (10.3) respectively and also make use of the money market curve as set out by equation(10.1). Initial equilibrium is found where all three schedules intersect as depicted in **Figure 10.1**.

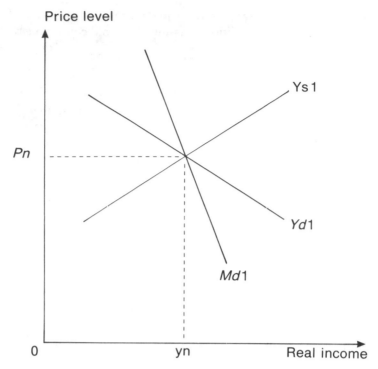

Figure 10.1 *Equilibrium of the model*

The aggregate demand schedule is given by *Yd* and is derived from equation (10.2). It is downward sloping because a rise in the domestic price level leads to a fall in aggregate demand for the domestic good *ceteris paribus* for two reasons: first, by inducing a decline in net exports and secondly since any rise in the domestic price level leads to a future expected return of the price to its target level, the expected rate of price inflation will be negative which raises the real interest rate. The absolute slope of the *Yd* schedule is given by the reciprocal of the summation of the elasticities of aggregate demand with respect to the real exchange rate and real interest rate, i.e. $1/(\theta + \beta)$.

Md depicts the money demand schedule derived from equation (10.1) of the model. It also has a negative slope because a rise in the domestic price level increases the demand for money requiring a fall in real income to maintain money demand equilibrium. The absolute slope of the *Md* schedule is given by the income elasticity of money demand divided by the share of the domestic good in the aggregate price index, i.e. η/α.

The slope of the *Yd* schedule may be flatter or steeper than the *Md* schedule and this proves to be critical when comparing fixed and floating exchange rates in the face of an aggregate supply shock. The condition for

Yd schedule to be flatter than the Md schedule is that $\eta(\theta + \beta) > \alpha$. For most of the analysis we shall assume that this condition is satisfied. Obviously, it is more likely to be satisfied the more open the economy (i.e. the smaller is α) and the greater the elasticity of the demand for the home good with respect to the real exchange rate and real interest rate. However, in order to see the importance of the relative slopes, in the case of an aggregate supply shock both cases are examined.

The aggregate supply curve has a positive slope since a rise in the domestic price level for a fixed nominal wage reduces the real wage facing producers, encouraging them to take on more workers which results in increased output. It has a positive slope given by $1/\varphi$.

Equilibrium of the system is determined by the simultaneous interaction of all three schedules through a common point. In the absence of unanticipated disturbances to the economy, output is at its natural level Yn and the price level at the natural level Pn. In the analysis, we shall also assume that these are the optimal target values of the authorities, so that the economy is initially in full equilibrium.

If the system is initially in full equilibrium only unanticipated disturbances will cause the schedules to shift from their equilibrium levels, inducing corresponding adjustments in price and output. Under fixed exchange rates the money stock adjusts passively to shifts in the Ys and Yd schedules because the money stock is endogenously determined, whereas, under floating exchange rates the exchange rate and interest rate adjust to equilibrate the system causing shifts in both the Md and Yd schedules. For example, an appreciation of the exchange rate shifts the Yd schedule to the left due to a loss of competitiveness with a resulting fall in exports as well as the fact that an appreciation leads to an expected future depreciation as the shocks impinging upon the economy are known to be self-reversing. As a result, the domestic interest rate is forced up further to maintain uncovered interest parity shifting the Yd schedule to the left. The rise in the domestic interest rate to the extent that the demand for money is interest elastic lowers the demand for money which for a given money stock requires a shift to the right of the Md schedule. We now compare the relative performance of fixed and floating exchange rates in the face of various shocks to the economy.

◼ *10.8* Money demand shock

Suppose that there is an unanticipated rise in money demand. This has the effect of shifting the Md schedule to the left. It is assumed that there are no other shocks impinging upon the economy.

An increase in money demand causes a shift to the left of the money demand schedule from $Md1$ to $Md2$. As the $Ys1$ and $Yd1$ schedules intersect

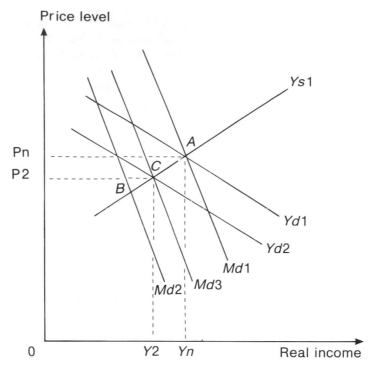

Figure 10.2   *Money demand shock*

to the right of the *Md2* schedule there is an excess demand for money. Under fixed exchange rates the excess demand for money will cause a tendency for the currency to appreciate, and as a result the authorities have to purchase the foreign currency in the foreign exchange market which expands the domestic money stock. The purchases continue until the *Md2* schedule shifts back to *Md1*. Thus, short run equilibrium remains at point A under fixed exchange rates with no disturbance to either domestic prices or domestic output. This means that fixed exchange rates prove optimal. In effect, all the authorities do is increase the money stock in line with the increased demand to hold money so that there are no required adjustments to price and output.

   If we are in a floating exchange-rate regime, the appreciation of the exchange rate shifts *Yd1* to the left to *Yd2* due to the fall off in export demand and rise in the domestic interest rate as there is an expected future depreciation of the currency. The rise in the interest rate leads to a fall off in money demand shifting *Md2* to *Md3*. Temporary equilibrium is attained where all three schedules intersect at point C. Thus, it can be seen that under floating exchange rates a rise in the demand to hold money leads to a fall in both the domestic price and output level. From this, it is obvious that

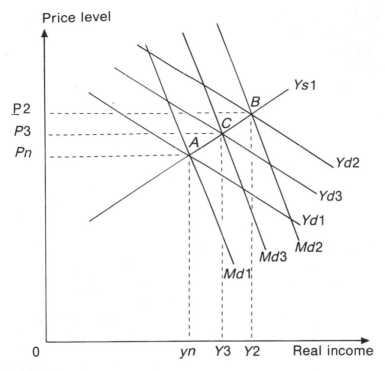

Figure 10.3 *Aggregate demand shock*

whether the principal objective is price or output stabilisation fixed exchange rates are preferable for dealing with monetary shocks and in fact prove optimal.

■ *10.9* Aggregate demand shock

Assume that there is an unanticipated increase in aggregate demand. This has the effect of shifting the Yd schedule to the right.

An increase in aggregate demand shifts $Yd1$ to $Yd2$. As the $Ys1$ and $Yd2$ schedules intersect to the right of the $Md1$ schedule there is an excess demand for money. The excess demand for money will cause the exchange rate to appreciate. As a result, the authorities have to intervene in the foreign exchange market to purchase the foreign money with newly created domestic money so that $Md1$ shifts to $Md2$ and the excess money demand is eliminated. Thus, under fixed exchange rates short-run equilibrium is found at point B with rises in both the domestic price and output level to $P2$ and $Y2$ respectively.

If, however, the authorities allow the exchange rate to float, the excess demand for money will result in an appreciation of the domestic currency which will have two effects: the aggregate demand schedule will shift to the left from $Yd2$ to $Yd3$ due to the fall off in exports and the money demand schedule will shift to the right from $Md1$ to $Md3$ due to the rise in the domestic interest rate. Equilibrium of the system is obtained at point C with price $P3$ and output Y3.

From this, it is evident that in the case of an aggregate demand disturbance, whether the objective of the authorities is price or output stability, floating exchange rates outperform fixed rates. Floating exchange rates keeping the economy closer to Pn and Yn than fixed exchange rates.

■ *10.10* Aggregate supply shock

Assume that there is an unanticipated fall in aggregate supply. This has the effect of shifting the aggregate supply schedule to the left. Here, it is necessary to distinguish two cases; in case 1 the Md schedule is steeper than the Yd schedule while in case 2 the Yd schedule is steeper than the Md schedule.

The economy is initially in equilibrium at point A in **Figure 10.4** with price Pn and output Yn. The economy is then hit by a transitory inflationary supply shock which shifts $Ys1$ to $Ys2$. In this case, point B corresponds to a position of excess supply of money as $Yd1$ and $Ys2$ intersect to the left of the $Md1$ schedule; hence there is a tendency for the currency to depreciate. In order to maintain a fixed exchange rate the authorities have to contract the money supply until the excess supply is eliminated, so the Md schedule shifts from $Md1$ to $Md2$. Thus, under fixed exchange rates the inflationary supply shock leads to a rise in price to $P2$ and a fall in output to Y2.

If, however, the authorities allow the exchange rate to float the excess supply of money resulting from the aggregate supply shock will lead to a depreciation of the currency. The depreciation shifts the aggregate demand schedule to the right from $Yd1$ to $Yd2$ since it results in increased export sales of the domestic good. Furthermore, the depreciation leads to an expected appreciation and therefore a fall in the domestic interest rate which leads to an increased demand to hold money which shifts the money demand schedule from $Md1$ to $Md3$. Equilibrium of the system under floating exchange rates is therefore obtained at point C with a rise in price to $P3$ and a fall in output to Y3.

From this, we notice that our evaluation of the choice between fixed and floating exchange-rate regimes would depend primarily upon the objectives of the authorities. This is because fixed exchange rates favour price stability

Figure 10.4 *Aggregate supply shock*
Case 1: Md schedule is steeper than the Yd schedule, i.e. $\eta(\theta + \beta) > \alpha$

while floating exchange rates favour income stability. Clearly, if the objective function of the authorities is biased towards price stability the authorities would find fixed rates preferable to floating. If, however, the authorities are more concerned with output stability they would find floating rates preferable to fixed. This is a good illustration of the importance of the specification of the objective function. Since depending upon the weighting of the objective function either fixed or floating exchange rates could be deemed superior.

In **Figure 10.5** we again assume that there is a transitory inflationary aggregate supply shock that shifts the aggregate supply function from Ys1 to Ys2. This time, however, the money supply schedule is less steep than the aggregate demand schedule.

In this case, the aggregate supply shock under fixed exchange rates causes there to be an excess demand for money at point B as Yd1 and Ys2 intersect to the right of the Md1 schedule and consequently there is a tendency for the currency to appreciate. In order to avoid an appreciation of the currency the authorities intervene in the foreign exchange market to purchase the foreign currency resulting in an increase in the domestic money stock until the Md

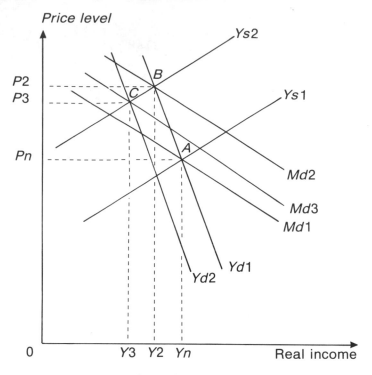

Figure 10.5   *Aggregate supply shock*
Case 2: Yd schedule is steeper than the Md schedule, i.e. $\eta(\theta+\beta)<\alpha$

schedule shifts from $Md1$ to $Md2$. The end result under fixed exchange rates is that the domestic price level rises to $P2$ and output falls to $Y2$.

Under floating exchange rates, the excess demand for money resulting from the shock leads to an appreciation of the exchange rate. This has the effect of shifting the aggregate demand schedule to the left from $Yd1$ to $Yd2$. In addition, the appreciation leads to the expectation of a future deprecia-tion which via the uncovered interest rate parity condition raises the domestic interest rate constituting an additional reason for the leftward shift of the Yd schedule. The rise in the domestic interest rate by reducing the demand for money shifts the Md schedule to the right from $Md1$ to $Md3$. The result is that short-run equilibrium under floating exchange rates is obtained at point C with a rise in the domestic price level to $P3$ and fall in domestic output to $Y3$.

In this case, we again observe a conflict when choosing between fixed and floating exchange rates. The difference is that in this instance fixed exchange rates favour output stability while floating exchange rates favour price stability.

The point of including this second case is that it illustrates the point that the choice between fixed and floating exchange rates is very closely related

Table 10.1 *Summary of the results under fixed and floating rates*

	Floating rates		Fixed rates	
Shock	*Price stability*	*Output stability*	*Price stability*	*Output stability*
Money demand	X	X	√	√
Aggregate demand	√	√	X	X
Aggregate supply				
Md steeper than *Yd*	X	√	√	X
Yd steeper than *Md*	√	X	X	√

√, performs best, X, performs worst.

to the structural parameters of the economy. In the first case, greater output stability could be obtained by floating exchange rates while in the second case fixed exchange rates prove superior. From this, it follows that any policy recommendations should be based on a study of the characteristics of the particular economy. Even if economies have similar objectives and face similar shocks we may be led to make different policy recommendations due to structural differences between economies. The results of the analysis of our model are summarised in **Table 10.1**.

What **Table 10.1** reveals is that the choice between fixed and floating exchange rates is nowhere near as clear-cut as their advocates are prone to argue. The choice between the two regimes is seen to depend crucially upon the type of shock impinging upon the economy, the objectives of the authorities and the structural parameters of the particular economy considered (the steepness of the *Md* schedule relative to the *Yd* schedule).

Before concluding this section it is worth reminding readers that the model set out is extremely simple. In practice, the choice between a fixed or floating exchange rate will be even more complex. We considered only the case of transitory shocks but economies are subjected to both transitory and permanent disturbances. In addition, some economies have wage indexation while others do not, indexation will lead to wage adjustments following movements in the domestic price level or the exchange rate which can alter the ranking of the two regimes (see Pilbeam, 1991). Finally, we have not touched upon the problem of interdependence; while a fixed exchange rate may be the preferred choice for one economy its trading partners may prefer a floating regime. If this is the case, the appropriate exchange-rate regime for the two countries is clearly greatly complicated.

■ *10.11* Managed floating

Since the advent of floating exchange rates in 1973, it has become evident that authorities have not always let their currency float freely but rather they have frequently intervened to influence the exchange rate. A number of rationales have been put forward to justify such intervention and are worth consideration.

Before examining some the most frequently used arguments for intervention it is necessary to assume that the authorities can influence the nominal and or real exchange rate in their desired direction. Without such an assumption no rationale for intervention can exist. Further, when assessing the validity of intervention policy it is necessary to compare exchange market intervention with alternative policies. Only if it can be demonstrated that intervention has a superior benefit to cost impact than other policies or that constraints prevent the use of superior policies can exchange market intervention be justified. Throughout, it should be remembered that exchange rate management by the authorities can vary in degree from occasional intervention to influence the exchange rate to a permanent pegging.

The arguments for some degree of discretionary intervention to some extent overlap but fall into three main categories:

1. The authorities can choose an exchange rate more in line with economic fundamentals than the market.
2. Intervention is required to mitigate the costs of exchange rate 'overshooting'.
3. Intervention is an appropriate instrument for smoothing necessary economic adjustments.

Authorities might be able to produce a more appropriate exchange rate

As we argued in section 10.2, for a variety of reasons the exchange rate produced by the market may be the wrong rate compared with underlying economic fundamentals. The market may use the wrong model, it may have the wrong perception about the future and will have difficulty in interpreting the implications of news relevant to the exchange rate. However, the fact that the market may produce the wrong rate does not justify intervention by the authorities. It is necessary to demonstrate that the authorities can choose a more appropriate rate.

There exists a case for intervention if the news or information available to the market is efficiently used but the news itself is either inadequate – increasing risk, or misleading and the authorities are in possession of superior relevant information. Intervention in such circumstances can prove both stabilising and profitable. However, it could be argued that a superior policy is for the authorities to abstain from intervention and release the relevant information to the market. Nevertheless, there may be circumstances under which such an information release is not considered desirable and even if the authorities were to release the relevant information to the market, there is no guarantee that the market would believe them.

Connected with the above argument is a far more convincing reason for the authorities to intervene. While it may be the case that the authorities do not know any more than the market regarding what is the correct rate, they should know better and sooner what they themselves are about to do (in most cases!). Since the exchange rate is an asset price it incorporates expectations concerning its future price appropriately discounted into the current price so that unusual *ex-ante* speculative profits cannot be made. For example, if the money supply is expected to increase at a given date in the future, this implies a depreciation of the exchange rate, and if the exchange rate did not depreciate until the expected increase in the money supply took place this would imply a large discrete depreciation of the exchange rate at that time. However, since the depreciation was expected such a discrete jump would imply a missed abnormal *ex-ante* profit opportunity. Since the foreign exchange market is efficient the expectation of a depreciation leads to a smaller discrete depreciation of the current rate (reflecting the news of future monetary expansion), with a gradual depreciation thereafter until the actual increase in the money supply takes place. In this way all anticipated disturbances are fully discounted and therefore unusual *ex-ante* profit opportunities eliminated.

The point is that the authorities should be more capable than the market in predicting the future course of their policies and this is of relevance to the correct exchange rate. Given this, intervention in the foreign exchange market may be interpreted by the market as a commitment by the authorities to adopt a given course of action. If this is the case, economic agents may more readily lend their support to the new policy helping to make it more effective and more speedily so than would otherwise be the case. Thus, there exists a case for official intervention on the grounds that the authorities have a better knowledge of their future policy intentions than private market participants. Official intervention in the foreign exchange market may literally 'buy credibility', convincing economic agents that the authorities intend to fulfil their stated domestic policy targets by committing the assets of the Central Bank in support of its declared future policy. A key postulate of the rational expectations literature is that the authorities will only be able to achieve their short-run inflation objectives painlessly if economic agents are convinced that the authorities intend to carry out their stated objectives. The opportunity to purchase some credibility by intervening in the foreign exchange market could prove to be a useful policy tool.

To illustrate the above point, consider the case where there is news of an increase in the rate of growth of the money supply. This may be viewed as affecting speculators' expectations in at least three possible ways: It may be seen as only a transitory development of a counter-cyclical nature that will subsequently be reversed. Or, it may be seen as a once and for all change in the money stock that will not be reversed but which will not affect the underlying rate of growth of the money stock. Alternatively, it may be seen as heralding a more permanent increase in the rate of growth of the money stock. Each of the alternatives has different implications concerning the required depreciation of the currency; the greater the actual growth the greater the required depreciation. There is no a priori reason to believe that the market in the short run at least, will on balance know what is the required depreciation. The authorities, however, should know and could indicate their feeling regarding the appropriate rate via an intervention policy.

☐ *Intervention needed to mitigate costs of exchange rate overshooting*

The Dornbusch (1976) overshooting model examined in Chapter 7 showed that a move to monetary restraint can lead to a short run real exchange-rate appreciation while an expansionary monetary policy can lead to a real depreciation. These real exchange-rate movements (over and undervaluations in relation to PPP) will exert effects on the real economy. In what follows we shall refer to substantial and prolonged deviations from PPP as exchange-rate misalignments.

Misaligned exchange rates distort the allocation of resources between tradables and non-tradables as well as consumption patterns between the two. Undervaluation by raising the domestic price level and placing downward pressure on real wages may spark off inflationary pressures, while overvaluation by squeezing the tradables sector may result in increased unemployment. Misalignment complicates and inhibits investment decisions because uncertainty as to the duration of the over/undervaluation will affect the profitability calculations concerning whether to invest in tradables or non-tradables, particularly inhibiting marginal investment decisions.

Misalignments almost certainly exert a ratchet effect on protectionism. In periods of undervaluation of the currency, resources that would ordinarily not be viable enter into the tradables sector but as the rate corrects itself they will come under increasing pressure and will then seek recourse to protection. Alternatively, if the currency is overvalued this will tend to lead to automatic protectionist cries due to the pressure on the tradables sector. It should also be remembered that undervaluation for one currency involves overvaluation for another and vice versa, so that one could expect protectionism to be a global and persistent phenomenon so long as exchange rates are misaligned. Since an under/overvaluation must necessarily eventually be corrected, this will involve the various adjustment costs arising because of factor immobility occupationally and geographically, retraining of labour will involve cost and time and absorption cannot be painlessly varied at will.

Foreign exchange intervention designed to reduce the costs and extent of exchange rate overshooting could be justified. It is worth noting that the case for intervention in this instance is not in any way due to inefficiency in the foreign exchange market. The rate produced by the market is the correct rate but because of 'sticky' goods prices there are short run real exchange rate changes. If the price level increased (decreased) by x per cent price immediately following an x per cent change in the money supply as in the flexible price monetary model then there would be no overshooting of the exchange rate. This latter observation has led some authors to propose that rather than intervene in the foreign exchange market the authorities should tackle the inefficiencies in the goods and labour markets. If these markets were made more flexible so that the rate of inflation adjusted quickly to changes in monetary policy then this would reduce the amount of over-shooting. The measures proposed would include anti-trust legislation to tackle monopolies, reductions in trade union power and the reduction of social security benefits all of which would make goods and factors prices more flexible and thereby reduce the problem of overshooting. Not surprisingly, by comparison to the likely resistance and turmoil associated with such policies, exchange market intervention can prove a superior policy tool.

Intervention to smooth the economic adjustment process

There may exist a rationale for the authorities to intervene in the foreign exchange market to achieve a preferable exchange rate in the short run to permit a smoothing of the necessary adjustments that the economy must for various reasons undergo. The rationale for smoothing the adjustment process is that it is a painful process for those who have to adjust and is more acceptable at a controlled pace than a market determined one.

Suppose that a country has a persistent balance-of-payments surplus because the traded goods sector is too large relative to the non-traded sector. There will consequently be a tendency for an appreciation of the real exchange rate which will encourage factors to move from the traded goods sector to the non-traded sector. If the authorities are concerned about the possibility of large transitional unemployment resulting from such an appreciation, they may try to moderate the appreciation to allow time for the traded goods sector to contract and the non-tradables sector to expand, so as to avoid what they consider to be excessive transitional unemployment costs. Corden (1982) has coined the phrase 'exchange rate protection' to describe an exchange rate policy whereby a country protects its tradable goods sector relative to the non-tradables sector by either devaluing the real exchange rate, allowing the exchange rate to depreciate by more than it otherwise would or preventing an exchange rate appreciation that would otherwise take place.

The preceding case is only one variant of the need to switch resources in the economy. Another may occur when the tradables sector itself is divided into a 'booming' and 'lagging' sector. The booming sector will cause the real exchange rate to have a tendency to appreciate and in so doing will speed up the demise of the lagging sector. In either of the two cases cited, the case for exchange-rate protection is clearly linked to the speed at which adjustment can take place, be it between the traded and non traded sector or within the tradables sector.

Exchange market intervention can compare favourably to other methods of protection, such as tariff protection, for the purpose of slowing down the necessary adjustment. This is because exchange rate protection which involves influencing the real exchange rate and with it the accumulation of reserves must necessarily be a temporary method of protection whereas tariffs and subsidies have a habit of becoming permanent features and because of their explicit protective nature tend to invite retaliation. Nevertheless, it is difficult to say that either form of protection is to be preferred, for while tariffs distort production patterns within the tradables sector in favour of the lagging (protected) sector, exchange-rate protection protects all tradables whether they require assistance or not and it could be argued that because it is a more widespread means of protection it is more likely to invite retaliation.

Another rationale for intervention may exist if the economy is caught in a 'vicious circle'. Consider a country experiencing for whatever reason a current account deficit that it is trying to eliminate by permitting the depreciation of the currency. If wages adjust fully and instantaneously to the increased domestic price level implied by such a policy and the authorities adopt an accommodating monetary policy to avoid an increase in unemployment, the country will be back where it started. A further depreciation will be necessary and via the same process this will again lead the country back where it started, the country will be caught in a vicious circle of depreciation, price and wage rises and further depreciation. Under such circumstances, intervention in the foreign exchange market to limit the depreciation may serve to slow down or even avoid the spiral, allowing the authorities to adopt a more appropriate policy designed to bring about the necessary reduction in real wages or to await productivity improvements in the economy which means that real wages do not have to fall.

It should be noted, however, that the real issue behind the vicious circle argument for intervention concerns the effectiveness of different policy instruments in bringing about the ultimate reduction in real wages that is essential for adjustment (in the absence of productivity improvements), while minimising the harmful consequences for other macro objectives such as the maintenance of full employment and reasonable price stability. Here one should recall Keynes's argument that price changes may prove a more acceptable method of reducing real wages because they hit the labour force more or less equally and by so doing do not upset to any great extent wage differentials. The alternative policy of deflation may prove a lot more painful process of reducing real wages especially with regard to the employment objective because it may require a large rise in unemployment before the principle of real wage cuts becomes accepted by the labour force. Thus, there may be a case in the vicious circle argument for government intervention to slow down the rate of depreciation so that real wages are reduced only gradually at a more acceptable pace.

Before concluding this section, it is worth emphasising that the adjustment arguments advanced for exchange rate intervention involve smoothing the adjustment process not preventing it. Ideally, the exchange rate should be allowed to adjust towards its equilibrium rate at an optimum pace the determination of which is clearly a policy problem. It is the acceptance of the principle of exchange rate adjustment that ensures that the required changes in the economy do take place.

■ *10.12* Conclusions

The clear result that emerges from this chapter is that neither the traditional advantages/disadvantages approach nor modern literature provide a clear-cut reason to prefer fixed exchange rates to floating or vice-versa. Fixed exchange rates have some advantages and disadvantages as compared with floating exchange rates. Indeed, many of the proposed advantages can under some circumstances be viewed as disadvantages. For example, floating exchange rates restore monetary autonomy but whether this is a good thing or bad thing will depend upon whether the authorities use the autonomy wisely. While fixed exchange rates may promote international trade, a currency can at times become pegged at an overvalued exchange rate which can result in trade frictions and the use of protectionism which curtails trade.

The modern approach to evaluating the two regimes shows that only under very specific conditions can we say that one regime is better than the other. The analysis has focused on three crucial factors that determine the choice of exchange-rate regime, the specification of the objective function, the type of shock impinging upon the economy and the structure of the economy. In particular, the analysis highlighted the importance of the specification of the objective function and demonstrated how a slight modification to this can completely reverse the ranking of the regimes. Different countries, even if they have similar economic structures and face similar shocks, may well require different exchange-rate regimes simply because their objectives differ.

There are a host of other factors that will complicate the choice of exchange-rate regime such as the implications of wages indexation, the possibility of permanent shocks and relationships between various shocks. It should also be remembered that in practice, it is extremely difficult to know if an economy is being afflicted by a supply or demand shock or a shock to money demand. Even if a shock is identified, there is the question as to whether or not it is a permanent or transitory phenomenon.

The lack of decisive arguments in favour of either fixed or floating exchange rates has frequently been taken as a rationale for some degree of exchange-rate management between the two regimes. The argument being that such exchange-rate management has the potential to combine the advantages of both regimes while limiting the disadvantages. However, a demonstration that private speculation may produce the wrong rate, or that exchange rates are prone to 'overshoot' does not by itself justify intervention. It is necessary to demonstrate that the authorities can choose a more appropriate rate and that intervention can influence the exchange rate in the desired direction. In addition, it is necessary to demonstrate that intervention in the foreign exchange market is the best means of tackling the economic problem in hand. Instability of the exchange rate may merely be due to unstable macroeconomic policies by the country concerned and the best means for reducing such fluctuations is to stabilise domestic economic policies, not intervention in the foreign exchange market.

Since there is no unique case for exchange-rate management there can be no unique set of rules expected to deal with the wide variety of circumstances that can arise. An appropriate intervention policy may involve reducing or exacerbating exchange-rate movements, intervention may need to be temporary or prolonged and the amount of intervention required will vary with the circumstances. In other words, even if intervention can be justified the precise direction, duration and volume of intervention required need to be determined.

Finally, it should not be forgotten that we have examined the choice between alternative regimes within the context of a specific model specification of a small open economy. One of the implications of the analysis is that different countries may need to opt for different exchange-rate regimes. It may be the case that the choice of exchange-rate policy by one country may well be a crucial factor in determining the choice of exchange-rate policy for other countries and this is an issue that merits further attention.

■ Selected further readings

Argy, V. (1982) 'Exchange Rate Management in Theory and Practice', *Princeton Studies in International Finance*, No. 50.

Artus, J.R. and Crockett, A. (1978) 'Floating Exchange Rates and the Need for Surveillance', *Princeton Essays in International Finance*, No. 127.

Artus, J.R and Young, J.H. 'Fixed and Flexible Exchange Rates: a Renewal of the Debate', *IMF Staff Papers*, vol. 26, pp. 654–98.

Basevi, G. and De Grauwe, P. (1977) 'Vicious and Virtuous Circles. A Theoretical Analysis and a Policy Proposal for Managing Exchange Rates', *European Economic Review*, vol. 10, pp. 277–301.

Blanchard, O. (1979) 'Speculative Bubbles, Crashes and Rational Expectations', *Economic Letters*, vol. 3, pp. 387–9.

Claassen, E.M. (1976) 'World Inflation Under Flexible Exchange Rates', *Scandinavian Journal of Economics*, vol. 78, pp. 346–65.

Corden, W.M. (1982) 'Exchange Rate Protection', in R.N. Cooper, P.B. Kenen, J.B. Machedo and J.V. Ypersele, *The International Monetary System Under Flexible Exchange Rates* (Cambridge, Mass.: Balinger).

Dooley, M. (1981) 'An Analysis of Exchange Market Intervention of Industrial and Developing Countries', *IMF Staff Papers*, vol. 29, pp. 233–69.

Dornbusch, R. (1976) 'Expectations and Exchange Rate Dynamics', *Journal of Political Economy*, vol. 84, pp. 1161–76.

Dornbusch, R. (1983) 'Flexible Exchange Rates and Interdependence', *IMF Staff Papers*, vol. 30, pp. 3–30.

Friedman, M. (1953) 'The Case for Flexible Exchange Rates', in M. Friedman, *Essays in Positive Economics* (Chicago: University of Chicago Press).

Goodhart, C. (1988) 'The Foreign Exchange Market: a Random Walk with a Dragging Anchor', *Economica*, vol. 55, pp. 437–60.

Johnson, H.G. (1969) 'The Case for Flexible Exchange Rates, 1969', *Federal Reserve Bank of St Louis Review*, vol. 51, pp. 12–24.

Kenen, P.B. (1987) 'Exchange Rate Management: What Role for Intervention', *American Economic Review Papers and Proceedings*, pp. 194–9.

Kenen, P.B. (1988) *Managing Exchange Rates* (London: Routledge).

Mussa, M. (1979) 'Macroeconomic Interdependence and the Exchange Rate Regime', in R. Dornbusch and J.A. Frenkel, *International Economic Policy* (Baltimore: Johns Hopkins University Press).

Mussa, M. (1981) The Role of Official Intervention. *Group of 30 Occasional Papers*, No. 6, New York.

Nurkse, R. (1944) *International Currency Experience* (League of Nations, Columbia University Press).

Pilbeam, K.S. (1991) *Exchange Rate Management: Theory and Evidence* (London: Macmillan).

Sohmen, E. (1961) *Flexible Exchange Rates* (Chicago: University of Chicago Press).

Turnovsky, S.J. (1984) 'Exchange Market Intervention in a Small Open Economy: An Expository Model', in P. Malgrange and P.A. Muet, *Contemporary Macroeconomic Modelling* (Oxford: Basil Blackwell).

PART III

The Post-war International Monetary System

■ *Chapter 11* ■

The Post-War International Monetary System

■ *11.1* Introduction

The international monetary system is broadly defined as the set of conventions, rules, procedures and institutions that govern the conduct of financial relations between nations. In this chapter we look in some detail at the development of the post-Second World War international monetary system. An understanding of the historical, institutional and economic developments that have occurred since the end of the Second World War are an essential background to the study of international finance. Many of the proposals for reform of the international monetary system have been based upon the desire to avoid the problems and mistakes of the past. There are many facets of the post-war system that merit attention and that are studied in this chapter. Among these are the Bretton Woods system and its eventual breakdown, the move to floating exchange rates and economic events of the 1970s, the setting up of the European Monetary System and economic policy divergences of the 1980s. Much of the story of the post-war international monetary order is about the central role of the US dollar which still remains the major international currency.

■ *11.2* The Bretton Woods system

The initial talks on reconstructing a post-war international monetary system started between the United States and United Kingdom as early as 1941. The lead negotiators were Harry Dexter White for the US and John Maynard Keynes for the British. Given the US economic and political dominance at the end of the war, it is not surprising that the eventual system reflected more the US proposals. The system that emerged was ratified at an international monetary conference held at Bretton Woods, New Hampshire in 1944, which was attended by some 44 countries.

The motivation behind creating a new international monetary order was the desire to avoid the breakdown in international monetary relations that had occurred in the 1930s. In the 1920s Germany witnessed hyperinflation and the US stockmarket collapse of 1929 heralded a worldwide recession. The 1930s were marked by major trade imbalances which in turn led to the adoption of widespread protectionism, the adoption of deflationary policies, competitive devaluations and the abandonment of the gold exchange standard. In an influential report for the League of Nations Ragnar Nurkse (1944) argued that experience with floating exchange rates had shown that they discouraged international trade, caused a misallocation of resources and were generally characterised by bouts of destabilising speculation.

■ *11.3* Features of the system

There were several important features to the system; a fixed but adjustable exchange rate and the setting up of two new international organisations. These were the International Monetary Fund (IMF) with the duty of monitoring and supervising the system and the International Bank for Reconstruction and Development (IBRD), commonly known as the World Bank, charged initially with the role of assisting the reconstruction of Europe's devastated economies. In fact, the World Bank is a pair of institutions the IBRD and the International Development Association (IDA) which obtains money from developed nations and lends out the funds to the poorest Less Developed Countries (LDCs) at concessional terms. A third institution, the International Finance Corporation (IFC), is affiliated to the World Bank and provides risk capital direct to the private sector of LDCs.

☐ *Fixed but adjustable exchange rates*

Bretton Woods established a system of fixed but adjustable exchange rates. Under the Articles of Agreement of the IMF, each currency was assigned a central parity against the US dollar and was allowed to fluctuate by plus or minus 1 per cent either side of this parity. The dollar itself was fixed to the price of gold at $35 per ounce.

The idea of fixing the dollar to the price of gold was to provide confidence in the system. In 1945 the US authorities held approximately 70 per cent of the world's gold reserves. It was reasoned that foreign central banks would be more willing to hold dollars in their reserves if they knew that they could be converted into gold. The US authorities made a commitment to keep the dollar convertible into gold at $35 dollars per ounce. This commitment was in effect a pledge on the part of the US to preserve the purchasing power of dollars making the dollar 'as good as gold'.

A country was expected to preserve the par value of its currency *vis-à-vis* the dollar but in the case of 'fundamental disequilibrium' in its balance of payments could devalue or revalue its currency. Providing the proposed change was less than 10 per cent the IMF could not object, but larger realignments required the permission of the Fund. The ability of a country to alter its par rate as a last resort was seen as an essential part of the system. It offered countries an ultimate alternative to deflation or import controls as a means of correcting persistent balance-of-payments imbalances.

Under the Articles of Agreement of the Fund the member governments committed themselves to make their currencies convertible for current account transactions as soon as was feasible. Convertibility for current account transactions meant that while governments could still employ capital controls, they could not prevent their residents or residents of other countries from buying or selling their currency for current account transactions. It is notable, however, that such a commitment to convertibility was not required with respect to capital account transactions. This omission reflected the widespread suspicion that capital movements were potentially highly destabilising.

☐ The IMF and credit facilities

The IMF was set up with its general objective being to oversee and promote international monetary cooperation and the growth of world trade. To these ends, one of the principal tasks of the Fund was to ensure the smooth functioning of the fixed exchange-rate system. In particular, minimising the need for countries to devalue and revalue their currencies by providing them with credit facilities with which to finance temporary balance-of-payments imbalances.

One of the major problems envisaged with the fixed exchange rate system was that countries facing a temporary balance of payments deficit would be forced to deflate their economies if they wished to maintain their exchange rate parity. As most governments had committed themselves to the maintenance of full employment such a scenario was not particularly appealing. To avert this, a credit mechanism was set up to provide support for countries facing transitory balance of payments problems. Avoidance of deflationary policies was viewed as helpful in maintaining the volume of world trade.

Under the credit facility, each member of the IMF was allocated a quota, the size of the quota being related to its economic importance as reflected in the size of its subscription to the Fund. A country had to place a quarter of its quota in reserve assets (mainly gold) and the remaining three quarters in its own currency with the Fund. This gave the IMF a stock of funds which could be lent to countries facing balance-of-payments difficulties. A country facing difficulty could draw upon its quota should it need to do so. A country was entitled to the first 25 per cent of its quota known as its gold tranche automatically and a further four tranches of 25 per cent could be drawn providing the country agreed to conditions set by the IMF which became increasingly austere with each tranche drawn. The conditions attached to the latter tranches are known as IMF **conditionality** and generally constitute a set of measures designed to improve a country's balance of payments. The IMF commenced operations in March 1947 with the total sum of initial quotas available at $8.8 billion.

When drawing upon the IMF resources a member purchases reserve assets (usually dollars) in exchange for further deposits of its currency. The Fund decides what assets and currencies the drawing country receives on the basis of the composition of its own resources. As a rule any borrowing from the Fund has to be repaid over a period of three to five years. When repaying the Fund a country buys back its currency with foreign reserves.

 ## *11.4* A brief history of the Bretton Woods system

When the system of fixed parities commenced operation in March 1947 currencies were not freely convertible, there were many restrictions on the amount of dollars that could be bought on the foreign exchange market as most authorities had insufficient reserves to meet the huge demand for dollars. In the immediate years after the Second World War, the US ran a healthy current account surplus and the European economies large deficits. This was partly because the Europeans did not have strong exporting capabilities and partly because they were importing investment goods for reconstruction purposes and satisfying a pent-up consumer demand.

The setting up of the Bretton Woods system did not *per se* provide the basis for the reconstruction of the European countries. One of the major problems confronting the Europeans was their lack of dollars for purchasing the vital capital goods required to rebuild their war-torn economies. In 1948, partly out of a desire to help the Europeans help themselves, the US Secretary of State George Marshall announced a massive package of aid to the European economies. The 'Marshall aid' package was a very significant contribution to European reconstruction and the development of the post-war world economy. Between mid 1948 and mid 1952 Marshall aid provided some $11.6 billion of grants and $1.8 billion in loans and this greatly relieved the problem of the dollar shortage. The funds enabled the Europeans to purchase the capital and raw materials necessary for reconstruction.

Marshall aid was made partly conditional on greater cooperation between the European economies. One sign of this cooperation was the setting up of the Organisation for European Economic Cooperation (OEEC) which administered the Marshall aid funds. Later this organisation became the Organisation for Economic Cooperation and Development (OECD) with the US and Canada joining in 1961 and Japan in 1964. Another result of US encouragement to greater European cooperation was the European Payments Union (EPU) which commenced operations in 1950. The EPU enabled the European member countries to settle trade credits among themselves with the minimal use of dollars. This further relieved the dollar shortage and contributed to the faster liberalisation and growth of intra-European trade as compared with extra-European trade.

In 1949 the European deficits led to a series of currency devaluations (UK, France, Scandinavian countries) which received the approval of the IMF. The Fund recognised that the parities that were fixed in 1944 overvalued the European currencies and that not to allow the devaluations would require a severe deflation in the European economies which would be undesirable as they sought to reconstruct their economies. Furthermore, the funds that the IMF had available for financing these deficits were considered to be inadequate and should not to be used to finance the reconstruction of the European economies.

From the early 1950s onwards the US basic balance moved from its post-war surplus into deficits of approximately $1.5 billion per year. The counterpart of this was that the Europeans and Japanese started to run surpluses. Initially the US deficits caused no worries because its trading partners notably West Germany and Japan were experiencing export led growth and were happy to build up dollar reserves. So long as the US deficits were of reasonable proportions and US gold reserves exceeded its dollar liabilities the system functioned well. The operation of the EPU, the Marshall aid package and the improved health of the European economies in the 1950s enabled the Europeans to relax their trade and capital controls.

Table 11.1 *The US balance of payments, 1959–73 (US$ billions)*

Year	Trade balance	Current balance	Basic balance
1959	0.91	− 2.14	− 2.00
1960	4.89	1.80	− 3.20
1961	5.57	3.07	− 3.11
1962	4.52	2.46	− 3.69
1963	5.22	3.20	− 5.04
1964	6.80	5.79	− 6.19
1965	4.95	4.29	− 6.19
1966	3.82	1.94	− 4.12
1967	3.80	1.54	− 5.36
1968	0.64	0.96	− 1.08
1969	0.61	− 1.63	− 2.27
1970	2.16	− 0.32	− 3.02
1971	− 2.72	− 3.91	− 6.27
1972	− 6.99	− 9.81	− 1.67
1973	0.62	0.67	− 2.52

Source: US Department of Commerce, *Survey of Current Business.*

In December 1958 the Europeans had acquired sufficient reserves that they were able to make their currencies convertible and abolish the EPU.

During the period 1958–61 there was a more rapid deterioration in the US balance of payments (see **Table 11.1**). Many of the dollars acquired were converted into gold by foreign central banks. This gold drain provoked some concern in the US administration about the US deficit. In March 1961 there was a 5 per cent revaluation of the deutschmark and the Dutch guilder. In addition, to forestall speculation against the dollar, the US and nine other countries set up a General Arrangement to Borrow (GAB). The GAB members who became known as the group of ten (G-10) agreed to lend additional funds to the IMF should one of the members require large scale borrowing. The GAB arrangements were opened in October 1962 with potential lending commitments totalling $6 billion. In the event the US never used the facility which was not activated until the UK used the facility at the end of 1964.

In 1954 the London gold bullion market had reopened for private trading in gold. Around 1961 due to speculation of a US dollar devaluation against gold there was persistent upward pressure on the price of gold. Indeed, in 1962 there was such persistent upward pressure on the gold price that the central banks of the US and seven other industrialised countries set up a 'gold pool'. The purpose of the pool was to increase the supply of gold on the private market when there was an upward pressure on its price so as to keep it in line with the official price of $35 per ounce. In 1965 President De Gaulle made a speech extolling the virtues of gold as compared with the dollar and the French started to convert dollars into gold with the US authorities. By mid 1967 it was becoming apparent that with US dollar liabilities exceeding its gold reserves (see **Table 11.2**) any attempt by central banks to convert their dollar reserves into gold would lead to a breakdown of the system. This led to an agreement by central banks not to convert their dollar reserves into gold. In addition, the authorities decided to give up their sales of gold to the private market. A two-tier market for gold was established with the official rate remaining at $35 per ounce while the private market price was allowed to rise.

During the early 1960s the US balance-of-payments position stabilised but by the mid-1960s with US involvement in the Vietnam war the US balance of payments began to deteriorate more noticeably as depicted in **Table 11.1**. There was a growing feeling that the dollar was overvalued in relation to other currencies. Things started coming to a head in 1967 when after a series of current account deficits the UK authorities decided to devalue the pound by 14 per cent. In 1968 problems with the French balance of payments and concerns about student riots in Paris led to a devaluation of the franc. These devaluations reminded speculators that exchange rates were adjustable and that considerable profits could be made in anticipating and selling currencies which would be devalued.

Little action was taken to reduce the size of the US balance-of-payments deficits which continued to rise. By 1971 it became increasingly apparent to speculators that the dollar was overvalued and the deutschmark and yen were undervalued. In April 1971, the US trade balance went into deficit for the first time this century. This led to a massive capital outflow from the dollar in anticipation of a dollar devaluation. During May the speculation against the dollar was so immense that the Bundesbank had to purchase some $2 billion in just two days. Speculation became so intense that foreign exchange trading was halted for a week. When trading recommenced, the deutschmark was revalued by 7 per cent and the Austrian schilling by 5 per cent.

The revaluations were not considered to be sufficient and with the private market price of gold exceeding the official price speculators felt that a devaluation of the dollar was inevitable. Massive speculation against the dollar continued with speculators buying yen and deutschmark in anticipation of quick short-term profits from a dollar devaluation. With continued massive speculation against the dollar, on the 15 August 1971 President Nixon officially announced that the dollar was no longer convertible into gold. In addition, he announced an emergency 10 per cent tariff on all US imports as an interim measure until US trading partners agreed to revalue their currencies against the dollar. Nixon also announced some domestic polices designed to stabilise the US inflation rate; these included price and wage controls.

The motivation behind the Nixon measures was to prompt other countries to revalue their currencies against the dollar. The US authorities did not feel that devaluing the dollar against gold was a desirable course of action. One reason was that the administration believed it would be a break of faith with foreign central banks that had been persuaded to hold dollars rather than gold. Furthermore, a devaluation of the dollar against gold would not improve US competitiveness if other countries continued to peg against the dollar. The hope was that the Nixon measures would encourage other countries to revalue their currencies against the dollar and so restore US competitiveness.

The immediate response of foreign governments to the Nixon measures was along the lines sought by the US administration. Foreign governments allowed their exchange rates to float and agreed to a further liberalisation of trade barriers. In a bid to restore the pegged exchange-rate system, the G-10 nations met in December at the Smithsonian Institute in Washington. They tried to tackle the problem of the overvalued dollar by devaluing it against gold from $35 to $38 and revaluing currencies against the dollar by an average of 8 per cent. In addition, the margin by which other currencies could fluctuate against the dollar was widened from ±1 to ±2.25 per cent. In return for the revaluations the US agreed to remove its 10 per cent import tariff. Although President Nixon hailed the package as 'the most significant monetary agreement in the history of the world' it was in tatters within 15 months. The devaluation and increased flexibility were really a case of too little too late, especially as inflation rate differentials between the industrialised countries began to diverge (see **Table 11.6**). The devaluation did little to remedy the US balance of payments which reached record proportions in 1972.

By mid-1972 the UK ran into further balance of payments difficulties and in June the UK authorities decided to let the pound float. The worsening US deficit led to further speculation against the dollar and in January 1973 the Swiss authorities announced that the Swiss franc was to float against the dollar, this was soon followed in February by the Japanese decision to allow the yen to float despite a further 10 per cent dollar devaluation on 12 February. With further speculation against the dollar at the beginning of March the foreign exchange markets again had to be closed and when they reopened on 19 March the European currencies began a joint float against the dollar known as the 'Snake in the Tunnel', an arrangement which meant that many European currencies were allowed to fluctuate a maximum of ±2.25 per cent against one another (the Snake) and a maximum of ±4.5 per cent against the dollar (the Tunnel). In June 1973 the Snake in the Tunnel became the plain Snake in which the maximum fluctuation against the dollar was abandoned.

The adoption of floating exchange rates stood in marked contrast to the setting up of the Bretton Woods system. There was no general agreement to adopt floating exchange rates or what rules should govern the conduct of future exchange-rate policies. Rather, the move to floating rates was a somewhat disorderly and haphazard product of the breakdown of the fixed exchange-rate system.

 ## *11.5* Why did the Bretton Woods system break down?

The Bretton Woods System operated with reasonable success and only occasional realignments from 1947 to 1971. Explanations of the breakdown of the Bretton Woods system generally concentrate on the problems of liquidity and the lack of an adequate adjustment mechanism.

☐ *The liquidity problem*

Well before the eventual demise of Bretton Woods, Robert Triffin (1960) had predicted an eventual loss of confidence in the system. Triffin argued that there was an inherent contradiction in the gold–dollar standard. For the Bretton Woods system to function successfully it was essential that confidence was maintained in the US dollar. So long as central banks knew that dollars could be converted into gold at $35 per ounce they would willingly hold dollars in their reserves. Triffin pointed out that as international trade grew so would the demand for international reserves, namely US dollars. To meet the demand for these reserves the Bretton Woods system depended on the US running deficits, with other countries running surpluses and purchasing dollars to prevent their currencies appreciating. Hence over time, the stock of US dollar liabilities to the rest of the world would increase and this rate of increase would be higher than the annual addition to the US gold reserves resulting from gold-mining activities. As a result, the ratio of US dollar liabilities to gold held by the US Federal Reserve would deteriorate until eventually the convertibility of dollars into gold at $35 per ounce would become *de facto* impossible.

As it became apparent that the US authorities would not be able to fulfil their convertibility commitment, Triffin predicted that central banks would begin to anticipate a devaluation of the dollar rate against gold. In anticipation of this central banks would start to convert their reserves into

Table 11.2   *Ratio of US reserves to liquid liabilities*

1950	2.73	1964	0.58
1952	2.38	1966	0.50
1954	1.84	1968	0.41
1956	1.59	1970	0.31
1958	1.34	1972	0.16
1960	0.92	1974	0.14
1962	0.71	1976	0.22

Source: Milner and Greenaway 1979, *An Introduction to International Economics,* Longman, London, p. 271.

gold and stop pegging their currencies against the dollar leading to an inevitable breakdown of the system.

Table 11.2 shows the decline in the ratio of US reserves relative to its liquid liabilities as predicted by Triffin's analysis. The Bretton Woods system worked well in the 1950s but the confidence in the system slowly deteriorated in the 1960s as US liquid liabilities began to outstrip US reserves. The deterioration is particularly marked from 1968 to 1972 corresponding to the collapse of the system.

An alternative interpretation of the demise of Bretton Woods

Although the Triffin Dilemma at first sight seems to fit the facts quite well and is commonly held as the major cause of the breakdown of the Bretton Woods system, more recently, Paul De Grauwe (1989) has suggested a somewhat different interpretation of events. His interpretation is based upon an application of what is known as Gresham's Law. Thomas Gresham (1529–79) argued that when there is a discrepancy between the official rate of exchange between two assets and their private market rate of exchange, the asset that is undervalued at the official rate will disappear from circulation while the asset that is overvalued will continue in circulation. When applied to the monetary field this means that 'bad money drives out good money'.

Gresham's law can equally provide an insight into the collapse of the Bretton Woods system. In this case, the two assets to be considered are gold and the dollar. Under the Bretton Woods System the official rate of exchange of these two assets was set at $35 per troy ounce. The US authorities were committed to buy and sell gold with foreign monetary authorities at this price. With US prices increasing by some 40 per cent between 1959 and 1969, the price of gold should *ceteris paribus* have risen by a similar amount. Indeed, as we have seen in the private market there was a persistent upward

Box 11.1 *The creation of Special Drawing Rights*

Although the international monetary system was under no real strain around the mid-1960s, there was a feeling that the growth of international reserves was inadequate. This led to fears that the growth of world trade and with it economic growth would be unnecessarily constrained. In addition, the mechanism for increasing reserves was regarded as being too dependent upon the US running balance of payments deficits which as Triffin's analysis had shown could eventually undermine the whole system. These factors led to a discussion among IMF members over how to supplement the stock of international reserves.

The result of these deliberations was the First Amendment of the IMF Articles of Agreement in 1967 which empowered the Fund to create a Special Drawing Account to supplement its quota system which operates under its General Account. Under the scheme a new reserve asset was to be created by the Fund called the Special Drawing Right (SDR). Unlike quotas which are backed by the deposits of Fund members, the SDR's value as a reserve asset rests on it being regarded as an acceptable means of exchange between Central Banks and the Fund.

Under the SDR scheme each member of the Fund is allocated a specified annual amount of SDRs in proportion to their quota with the Fund. The cumulative total holdings of SDRs allocated to a country is known as its 'net cumulative allocation'. The value of an SDR was originally set at 1/35th of an ounce of gold which was equivalent to $1. A country can draw upon its SDR allocation whenever it is experiencing balance-of-payments difficulties or needs to supplement its reserves. In contrast to quota drawings, SDR drawings do not require consultation with the Fund, do not have conditionality attached and are not subject to repayment. Since SDR drawings are not subject to repayment they constitute a net addition to global reserves. However, over a five-year period a member had to maintain its SDR balance at an average of 30 per cent of its net cumulative allocation (reduced to 15 per cent in 1979).

A country that draws upon its SDR allocation can exchange the SDRs with foreign authorities for their currencies thereby increasing its reserves. All members of the Fund are obliged to accept SDRs in exchange for their national currency up to three times its net cumulative allocation. Countries drawing SDRs have to pay interest while countries in receipt of SDRs receive interest.

An increase in SDR allocations requires the consent of 80 per cent of IMF votes. The first planned allocation of SDRs for the period 1970–72 was $9.5 billion. In the event, these allocations proved very ill-timed because they coincided with a massive surge in international liquidity resulting from massive purchases of dollars in the final years of the Bretton Woods system.

In July 1976 the value of the SDR was changed from $1 to a weighted basket of 16 currencies and in January 1981 the SDR value was redefined as a weighted basket of five currencies, these currencies being the US dollar, the deutschmark, yen, French franc and pound sterling.

pressure on the price of gold leading to the setting up of the gold pool. However, these gold sales became so significant the loss of gold led central banks to disband the gold pool in 1968. A two-tier market for gold led to the private market price of gold rising above the official rate.

Once the official price of gold became undervalued compared with the private rate, central banks could easily have caused a major run on the dollar by converting their dollar reserves into gold and then sold the gold on the private market at a profit. In a bid to preserve the fixed exchange-rate system in 1967 the US secured an agreement from foreign central banks not to convert their dollar reserves into gold or to sell gold to private markets. In effect, the dollar was *de facto* no longer convertible into gold. In the end, following a further deterioration of the US balance of payments in 1970 and 1971, President Nixon announced the *de jure* suspension of dollar convertibility into gold. Dollars had driven out gold in accordance with Gresham's law.

☐ Lack of an adjustment mechanism

The Bretton Woods system permitted a realignment of exchange-rate parities as a last resort in case of 'fundamental disequilibrium' of a member's balance of payments. In practice, however, countries proved extremely reluctant to either devalue or revalue their currencies or undertake other economic policy measures required to ensure sustainable balance-of-payments positions. The fact that 'fundamental disequilibrium' was not defined did not help.

The US could not devalue the dollar in terms of gold since this would undermine confidence in the whole system. In addition, a dollar devaluation against gold did not improve US competitiveness if other countries maintained their exchange-rate parities against the dollar. As such, the US was expected to pursue appropriate deflationary policies at home to keep the size of its balance-of-payments deficit under control. In practice, the US was extremely reluctant to deflate its economy to regulate its deficit. Indeed, contrary to what was expected of it, US involvement in Vietnam from the mid-1960s led to inflationary US policies and a widening of its balance-of-payments deficits.

Other countries suffering persistent current account deficits could have resorted to devaluation. In practice, deficit countries proved extremely reluctant to devalue their currencies because such action was viewed as a sign of governmental and national weakness. The sense of national crisis that accompanied the Labour government's devaluation of sterling in 1967 is an example of this phenomenon. The deficit countries were equally reluctant to adopt deflationary policies which could cure the deficits since most had committed themselves to the objective of achieving full employment. With the deficit countries reluctant to adjust it was then necessary that surplus countries take action to reduce their surpluses.

The surplus countries included Germany, Japan and Switzerland but they proved as reluctant to revalue their currencies as the deficit countries were to devalue. This was because the undervaluation of their currencies had enabled them to experience strong export growth and biased their economies towards the production of tradable goods. They believed that to revalue their currencies would risk ending export growth and lead to unemployment in their economies as their tradables industries would be forced to contract. In addition, they were not prepared to reflate their economies as a means of reducing their surpluses because they feared the inflationary consequences.

The recognition that in a fixed exchange-rate regime the pressure was normally on debtors to undertake economic adjustment because of the fall in their reserves required to defend the exchange rate had led to the inclusion of a 'scarce currency clause' in the IMF articles. This permitted debtor countries to adopt penal measures against persistent surplus countries but it was never invoked.

With neither deficit nor surpluses countries being prepared to adjust their economies or exchange rates the question of how to maintain fixed exchange-rate parities in the face of persistent balance-of-payment imbalances required an answer. In a bid to prevent exchange-rate realignments, the surplus countries supplied the deficit countries' central banks with reserves on a credit basis to enable them to prevent devaluations of their currencies. Packages were arranged to support the Italian lira in 1964 and sterling in 1965. In retrospect, it is clear that such packages were only delaying the day when exchange-rate parities would have to be realigned, and constituted no more than a papering over the cracks.

☐ *The seigniorage problem*

The US, because of the pivotal role of the dollar, was the major source of international liquidity under the Bretton Woods system. To acquire reserves the rest of the world had to run balance-of-payments surpluses while the US ran deficits. President Charles de Gaulle of France argued that the system conferred an 'exorbitant privilege' on the US, the US being able to gain productive long-term assets from its overseas investments in exchange for short-term dollar liabilities. Dollars treasury bills accumulated by the rest of the world yielded relatively low rates of interest and their purchasing power was eroded by US inflation. In effect, the US was able to borrow at very low real rates of interest. The actual methodology to calculate and the value of such 'seigniorage' benefits has been an area of controversy. The perceived

Table 11.3   *The real price of OPEC crude oil*

1973	1974	1975	1976	1977	1978	1979	1980
100	226	224	241	239	213	280	402

Note: Index of OPEC oil prices, deflated by index of prices of exported manufactured goods of the major industrial countries.
Source: Adapted BEQB, Dec. 1980, p. 404.

Table 11.4   *Current account balances, 1973–80 ($ billions)*

	1973	1974	1975	1976	1977	1978	1979	1980
Industrial countries	11.3	−9.6	19.4	−0.5	−4.6	30.8	−7.8	−44.1
OPEC	6.2	66.7	35.0	40.0	31.1	3.3	68.4	112.2
LDCs	−8.7	−42.9	−51.3	−32.9	−28.6	−37.5	−57.6	−82.1

Sources: IMF, *Annual Reports*, various issues.

seigniorage benefits conferred to the US, while not one of the major reasons for the breakdown of the Bretton Woods scheme, did, however, when the system was under strain weaken the resolve to save the system.

■ *11.6* The post-Bretton Woods era

□ *The first oil shock and its aftermath*

The return to floating exchange rates was initially regarded by central bankers as only a temporary development until a new monetary order could be established. In the event, any hopes of a return to fixed parities were overtaken by events. As a result of the Arab-Israeli conflict at the end of 1973 the Organisation Petroleum Exporting Countries (OPEC) quadrupled the price of oil which had a huge impact on the world economy and effectively ended any hopes of restoring a fixed exchange-rate system. The huge oil price rise meant a significant deterioration of the oil importing countries' terms of trade (average price of imports/average price of exports) with the OPEC countries, depicted in **Table 11.3** and with it significant deficits in their current accounts, depicted in **Table 11.4**.

The Non-Oil Exporting Less Developed Countries were particularly hard hit both by the rise in the price of their oil imports and by the recession in the

Table 11.5   *Current account balances of the major industrialised countries, 1972–80 (percentage of GNP*/GDP)*

Country	1972	1973	1974	1975	1976	1977	1978	1979	1980
United States*	−0.5	0.5	0.1	1.1	0.2	−0.7	−0.7	0	0
Japan*	2.2	0	−1.0	−0.1	0.7	1.6	1.7	−0.9	−1.0
Germany*	0.5	1.5	2.8	1.0	0.8	0.8	1.4	−0.7	−1.7
France	0.1	0.6	−1.4	0.8	−1.0	−0.1	1.4	0.9	−0.6
Italy	1.5	−1.5	−4.3	−0.3	−1.3	1.0	2.1	1.6	−2.2
United Kingdom	0.3	−1.3	−3.8	−1.4	−0.8	−0.1	0.7	−0.2	1.2
Canada	−0.3	0.2	−0.9	−2.7	−2.1	−2.0	−2.0	−1.7	−0.4

Source: OECD, *World Economic Outlook*, December 1990.

Table 11.6   *Inflation rates in the major industrialised countries, 1972–80*

Country	1972	1973	1974	1975	1976	1977	1978	1979	1980
United States	3.9	6.1	10.5	8.1	5.8	6.6	7.2	9.2	10.8
Japan	5.6	10.7	21.2	11.3	9.2	7.2	4.5	3.6	7.1
Germany	5.7	6.3	7.0	6.2	4.2	3.6	2.7	3.9	5.8
France	6.3	7.4	14.8	11.8	9.9	9.4	9.1	10.8	13.3
Italy	6.4	13.8	21.3	16.6	17.7	17.6	13.1	14.5	20.5
United Kingdom	6.5	8.6	16.9	23.7	15.8	14.8	9.1	13.6	16.3
Canada	4.2	6.4	10.5	10.6	7.3	7.4	7.6	8.5	10.0

Note:
The above inflation rates are based on private consumption deflators.
Source: OECD, *World Economic Outlook*, December 1990.

industrialised countries which reduced their export earnings. As a result the LDCs as a group experienced massive current account deficits which rose from $8.7 billion in 1973 to $51.3 billion in 1975. In order to assist them, the IMF set up an 'oil facility' which borrowed funds from the surplus OPEC countries for lending to the LDCs.

The impact of the oil shock was far from uniform as some countries were more dependent than others on oil imports. For example, Japan, a major oil importer, suffered greatly from the shock as its current account surplus of $100m in 1973 became a deficit of $4500 million in 1974; the UK deficit widened from $1200 million in 1973 to $7800 million in 1974.

Due to its differential impact and the different policy responses adopted by governments to deal with the shock there were marked divergences in inflation rates. Italy and Britain, both keen to avoid recessions, adopted expansionary macroeconomic policies which, superimposed upon the inflationary impact of the oil shock, led to rapid inflation and a significant

Table 11.7   *Growth rates of real GDP/GNP* in the major industrialised countries, 1972–80 (percentage change from previous period)*

Country	1972	1973	1974	1975	1976	1977	1978	1979	1980
United States*	5.0	5.2	−0.5	−1.3	4.9	4.7	5.3	2.5	−0.2
Japan*	8.5	7.9	−1.4	2.7	4.8	5.3	5.2	5.3	4.3
Germany*	4.2	4.7	0.2	−1.4	5.6	2.7	3.3	4.0	1.5
France	4.4	5.4	3.1	−0.3	4.2	3.2	3.4	3.2	1.6
Italy	2.7	7.1	5.4	−2.7	6.6	3.4	3.7	6.0	4.2
United Kingdom	3.5	7.1	−1.5	−0.7	2.7	2.3	3.6	2.8	−1.9
Canada	5.7	7.7	4.4	2.6	6.2	3.6	5.6	3.6	1.1

Source: OECD, *World Economic Outlook*, December 1990.

Table 11.8   *Standardised unemployment rates in the major industrialised countries, 1972–80 (per cent of total labour force)*

Country	1972	1973	1974	1975	1976	1977	1978	1979	1980
United States	5.5	4.8	5.5	8.3	7.6	6.9	6.0	5.8	7.0
Japan	1.4	1.3	1.4	1.9	2.0	2.0	2.2	2.1	2.0
Germany	0.8	0.8	1.6	3.6	3.7	3.6	3.5	3.2	2.9
France	2.8	2.7	2.8	4.0	4.4	4.9	5.2	5.9	6.3
Italy	6.3	6.2	5.3	5.8	6.6	7.0	7.1	7.6	7.5
United Kingdom	4.0	3.0	2.9	4.3	5.6	6.0	5.9	5.0	6.4
Canada	6.2	5.5	5.3	6.9	7.1	8.0	8.3	7.4	7.4

Source: OECD, *World Economic Outlook*, December 1990.

worsening in their current accounts (see **Tables 11.5 and 11.6**). Other countries such as Germany and Japan who were much more concerned to control their inflation rates, adopted tight macroeconomic policies. Apart from its effect on current account balances the oil shock plunged the world into recession in 1974–5 with the US, Japan, UK and Germany all experiencing negative real growth rates having previously experienced very high growth rates in 1973 (see **Table 11.7**). There was also a pronounced rise in unemployment levels in many countries (see **Table 11.8**).

■ *11.7* The Jamaica Conference of 1976

In November 1975 a meeting of the major industrial nations at Rambouillet agreed to amend the Articles of Agreement of the IMF to legitimise the floating exchange-rate regime. The details of the Second Amendment were worked out in the IMF annual conference held at Kingston, Jamaica in January 1976. At Kingston the members of the Fund formally legitimised the new floating exchange-rate system. In addition to abolishing the official price of gold, the conference aimed at increasing the importance of SDRs (see **Box 11.1**) in international reserves, and there was a declaration that the SDR should become the 'principal reserve asset'.

☐ *The Second Amendment*

The Second Amendment of the IMF's Articles which came into effect in April 1978 formally gave national authorities a large degree of discretion in selecting their exchange-rate arrangements. It also urged the IMF to adopt a policy of 'firm surveillance' over its members' exchange-rate policies.

Article IV of the Second Amendment defined the obligations and responsibilities of Fund members. Each member was obliged to notify the Fund of its exchange rate arrangement but Fund members were basically free to do as they wished – peg to the SDR or another currency, pursue cooperative arrangements with other members or adopt other exchange-rate arrangements of the members' choice! About the only thing members could not do was to peg their currency to gold.

In addition to defining what members of the Fund could do the amendment also defined the role of the IMF as being to oversee the international monetary system to ensure its effective operation. In particular, the Fund was expected to:

> exercise firm surveillance over the exchange rate policies of members, and shall adopt specific principles for the guidance of all members with respect to those policies.

Member countries are obliged to supply the Fund with information necessary for surveillance and when requested consult with the Fund over its exchange rate policy. The initial guidelines drawn up by the Fund were summarised by three principles:

> A) A member shall avoid manipulating exchange rates or the international monetary system in order to prevent effective balance-of-payments adjustment or to gain an unfair competitive advantage over other members.
> B) A member should intervene in the exchange market if necessary to counter disorderly conditions which may be characterised *inter alia* by disruptive short-term movements in the exchange value of its currency.
> C) Members should take into account in their intervention policies the interests of other members, including those of countries in whose currencies they intervene.

Indications of attempts to maintain unrealistic exchange rates include sustained one-way reserve movements, the introduction of trade and/or capital controls and large scale official borrowing. However, the IMF was not empowered to penalise governments that choose to ignore its guidelines.

■ *11.8* The Snake and the EMS

The member countries of the European Economic Community (EEC) had long been concerned that their large degree of trading links with one another could be threatened by exchange-rate instability. This coupled with the longer term aspiration for a fully-fledged economic and monetary union between the EEC countries led to the setting up of the Snake in 1971 which had a chequered history and was replaced by the EMS which commenced operations in 1979. The operation of the Snake and EMS is dealt with more extensively in Chapter 14. What is important in the scheme of international monetary relations is that both the arrangements involved a zone of exchange-rate stability between the exchange rates of the European currencies reflecting in large part a dissatisfaction with the US dollar and allowing exchange rates to be determined by the free market.

■ *11.9* The second oil shock

Towards the end of 1978 the Iranian revolution disrupted its oil exports and led to a further hike in OPEC oil prices from $13 a barrel in mid-1978 to $32 a barrel in mid-1980. Although this hike was not as great as in the case of the first oil price shock the recession that followed in the industrialised nations was far more pronounced. This was mainly because on the basis of experience from the earlier shock governments were keen to minimise the inflationary consequences. As a result, authorities of the industrialised countries adopted restrictive policy responses. These policies led to a rise of world interest rates and major recessions in the years 1980–81 particularly in the US and UK. None the less, the recessions meant that the adjustment of the balance-of-payments deficits caused by the shock was quicker than that following the first oil shock. The OPEC surplus in 1980 of $112 billion was turned into a deficit by 1982.

■ *11.10* The dazzling dollar, 1980–85

The period January 1980 to May 1985 witnessed a relentless substantial appreciation of the US dollar, the dollar nominal effective exchange rate

Table 11.9 *Inflation rates in the major industrialised countries, 1981–90 (per cent per annum)*

Country	1981	1982	1983	1984	1985	1986	1987	1988	1989	1990
United States	9.2	5.7	4.1	3.8	3.3	2.4	4.6	3.9	4.5	5.4
Japan	4.4	2.6	1.9	2.1	2.2	0.6	−0.2	−0.1	1.7	3.1
Germany	6.2	4.8	3.2	2.5	2.1	−0.5	0.6	1.2	3.2	2.7
France	13.0	11.6	9.7	7.7	5.7	2.7	3.1	2.7	3.3	3.4
Italy	18.1	16.9	15.2	11.8	9.0	5.8	5.0	5.2	6.0	6.1
United Kingdom	11.2	8.8	4.8	5.0	5.4	4.4	4.3	4.9	5.9	9.5
Canada	11.2	10.2	6.3	3.9	3.7	3.8	3.9	4.0	4.7	4.8

Note:
The above inflation rates are based on private consumption deflators.
Source: OECD, *World Economic Outlook*, December 1990.

Table 11.10 *Growth rates of real GDP/GNP* in the major industrialised countries, 1981–90 (percentage change from previous period)*

Country	1981	1982	1983	1984	1985	1986	1987	1988	1989	1990
United States*	1.9	−2.5	3.6	6.8	3.4	2.7	3.4	4.5	2.5	0.9
Japan*	3.7	3.1	3.2	5.1	4.9	2.5	4.6	5.7	4.9	5.6
Germany*	0	−1.0	1.9	3.3	1.9	2.3	1.6	3.7	3.9	4.5
France	1.2	2.5	0.7	1.3	1.9	2.5	2.2	3.8	3.6	2.8
Italy	1.0	0.3	1.1	3.0	2.6	2.5	3.0	4.2	3.2	2.0
United Kingdom	−1.1	1.6	3.6	2.1	3.6	3.9	4.7	4.6	2.2	0.6
Canada	3.4	−3.2	3.2	6.3	4.7	3.3	4.0	4.4	3.0	0.9

Source: OECD, *World Economic Outlook*, December 1990 and July 1991.

Table 11.11 *Standardised unemployment rates in the major industrialised countries, 1981–90 (per cent of total labour force)*

Country	1981	1982	1983	1984	1985	1986	1987	1988	1989	1990
United States	7.5	9.5	9.5	7.4	7.1	6.9	6.1	5.4	5.2	5.4
Japan	2.2	2.4	2.6	2.7	2.6	2.8	2.8	2.5	2.3	2.1
Germany	4.2	5.9	7.7	7.1	7.2	6.4	6.2	6.2	5.6	5.1
France	7.4	8.1	8.3	9.7	10.2	10.4	10.5	10.0	9.4	9.0
Italy	7.8	8.4	8.8	9.4	9.6	10.5	10.9	11.0	10.9	9.9
United Kingdom	9.8	11.3	12.4	11.7	11.2	11.2	10.3	8.5	6.9	7.1
Canada	7.5	10.9	11.8	11.2	10.4	9.5	8.8	7.7	7.5	8.1

Source: OECD, *World Economic Outlook*, December 1990.

Table 11.12 *Current account balances of the major industrialised countries,*
1981–90 (as percentage of GNP*/GDP)

Country	1981	1982	1983	1984	1985	1986	1987	1988	1989	1990
United States*	0.2	−0.2	−1.2	−2.6	−3.0	−3.4	−3.6	−2.6	−2.1	−1.8
Japan*	0.4	0.6	1.8	2.8	3.7	4.4	3.6	2.8	2.0	1.2
Germany*	−0.5	0.8	0.8	1.6	2.6	4.4	4.1	4.2	4.6	3.2
France	−0.8	−2.2	−0.9	−0.2	−0.1	0.3	−0.5	−0.4	−0.4	−0.7
Italy	−2.2	−1.5	0.4	−0.6	−0.9	0.4	−0.2	−0.7	−1.2	−1.3
United Kingdom	2.7	1.7	1.2	0.6	0.8	0	−1.0	−3.2	−3.7	−2.4
Canada	−1.7	0.8	0.8	0.6	−0.4	−2.0	−1.7	−1.7	−2.6	−2.4

Source: OECD, *World Economic Outlook*, December 1990, and July 1991.

appreciated by some 64 per cent and nearly 40 per cent in real terms (see
Figure 11.1). One of the major reasons advanced for the appreciation was
the divergent macroeconomic policy stances pursued by the US, Europeans
and Japanese. The US authorities operated a tight monetary policy but had a
rather relaxed fiscal policy with the US budget deficit rising from $16 billion
in 1979 to $204 billion in 1986. This stood in contrast to the tight monetary
and fiscal policy operated by the Europeans. As US real interest rates rose
relative to rates in Europe, funds were attracted into the US to finance its
growing current account deficit. The US Administration argued that the
appreciation of the dollar reflected the strength of the US economy and that
it was not a policy problem.

However, as the dollar appreciation continued it started to provoke a great
deal of concern. A squeeze on US export and import competing industries
contributed to a rapidly deteriorating balance of payments which in turn led
to persistent calls in Congress for protectionist measures to be adopted
against trading partners especially Japan. Although the Europeans and
Japanese were benefiting from increased exports to the US, they were
concerned about the mounting threat of US protectionism. The Europeans
and Japanese viewed the US budget deficit as the principal cause of the US
current account deficit and argued that the deficit could only be remedied by
policies designed to reduce the US budget deficit. The increasing concern
about the US economy and the strength of the dollar contributed in large
part to the issuing of the Plaza Accord.

■ *11.11* From Plaza to Louvre and beyond

In September 1985 Finance ministers and Central Bank governors from the
so-called G-5 countries (France, West Germany, United States, United

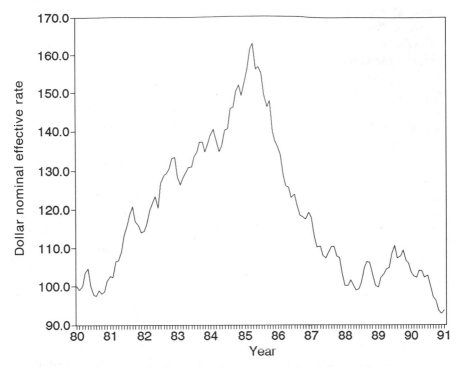

Figure 11.1 *The nominal effective exchange rate of the dollar, 1980–91*

Kingdom and Japan) met at the Plaza hotel and issued a communiqué known as the Plaza Accord. The statement said that the exchange rate of the dollar did not accurately reflect changes in the economic fundamentals notably the US pledge to reduce its budget deficit and measures to stimulate demand in Japan. A further depreciation of the dollar was considered desirable and importantly there was a commitment to 'cooperate more closely to encourage this when to do so would be helpful'. This was followed by purchases of deutschmark and yen. Following the Plaza Accord the dollar depreciated throughout 1986. However, the extent to which the depreciation can be attributed to the Plaza Accord is a matter of conjecture, especially as the dollar had begun to depreciate prior to the Plaza meeting. The depreciation of the dollar was so substantial that the concern by early 1987 switched to stemming the dollar decline.

At a G-7 meeting held at Paris in February 1987 the Finance ministers issued what is known as the Louvre Accord. They made it known that they felt that the dollar had depreciated far enough and that exchange rates were 'broadly consistent with underlying economic fundamentals'. Furthermore, there was agreement to 'cooperate closely to foster exchange rates around current levels'. The Accord was followed by speculation that the authorities had made a secret agreement to keep currencies within specified ranges *vis-à-vis* the dollar.

Exchange rates remained fairly stable following the Louvre Accord but pressure for a further depreciation of the dollar led to large scale purchases of dollars by the Japanese. The dollar remained stable until October 1987 when following the collapse of stock markets around the world it came under renewed pressure. The stock market collapse led to fears that it would be followed by a major worldwide recession as had happened following the stock market collapse in 1929. It was feared that the reduced wealth and US plans to reduce its budget deficit would lead to a cut in expenditure that could herald a worldwide recession.

To reduce the risk of recession there was a significant loosening of monetary policy around the world with Central Banks reducing interest rates. Only in January 1988 with signs that the US trade deficit had started to bottom out did the dollar begin to recover. In 1990 there has been renewed pressure on world inflation as a result of the significant loosening of monetary policy in response to the stock market collapse leading to a series of interest rate rises and recessions for the US and UK economies. The year 1990 also witnessed the reunification of West and East Germany, a heavy decline of the Japanese stock market (some 40 per cent), and the collapse of numerous savings and loans institutions in the United States, which is estimated will cost the US taxpayer in the region of $500 billion. Combined with the after-effects of the war against Iraq following its invasion of Kuwait and the failure of the coup in the Soviet Union, it seems that the 1990s will raise a whole host of new developments.

■ *11.12* The present exchange-rate system

The present exchange-rate system permits countries to adopt whatever exchange-rate policy they wish providing that they do not peg their currencies to the value of gold. In practice, there exists a wide range of exchange-rate policies from completely free floating to various pegging arrangements. **Table 11.13** shows the exchange-rate arrangements of Fund members as at 30 September 1990, which are summarised in **Table 11.14**.

■ *11.13* Reform of the International Monetary System

The present international monetary system has been called a 'non-system' as there are no clear set of exchange rate arrangements among the major

Table 11.13   *Exchange-rate arrangements as at 30 September, 1990*

		Currency pegged to		
US Dollar	*French franc*	*Other currency*	*SDR*	*Other composite*
Afghanistan	Benin	Bhutan (Indian	Burundi	Algeria
Angola	Burkina Faso	Rupee)	Iran, I.R. of	Austria
Antigua and	Cameroon	Kiribati (Australian	Libya	Bangladesh
Barbuda	C. African Rep.	Dollar)	Myanmar	Botswana
Bahamas, The	Chad	Lesotho (South	Rwanda	Bulgaria
Barbados		African Rand)		
	Comoros	Swaziland (South	Seychelles	Cape Verde
Belize	Congo	African Rand)	Zambia	Cyprus
Djibouti	Côte d'Ivoire	Tonga (Austrian		Czechoslovakia
Dominica	Equatorial Guinea	Dollar)		Fiji
Dominican Rep.	Gabon			Finland
Ethiopia				
	Mali			Hungary
Grenada	Niger			Iceland
Guyana	Senegal			Israel
Haiti	Togo			Jordan
Iraq				Kenya
Liberia				
				Kuwait
Oman				Malawi
Panama				Malaysia
St Kitts & Nevis				Malta
St Lucia				Mauritius
St Vincent				
				Morocco
Sudan				Mozambique
Suriname				Nepal
Syrian Arab Rep.				Norway
Trinidad and				Papua New
Tobago				Guinea
Yemen,				
Republic of				Poland
				Romania
				Sao Tome and
				Principe
				Solomon Islands
				Somalia
				Sweden
				Tanzania
				Thailand
				Uganda
				Vanuatu
				Western Samoa
				Zimbabwe

Source: International Financial Statistics.

Table 11.13   *contd*

Flexibility limited in terms of a single currency or group of currencies		More flexible		
Single currency	Cooperative arrangements	Adjusted according to a set of indicators	Other managed floating	Independently floating
Bahrain	Belgium	Chile	China, P.R.	Argentina
Qatar	Denmark	Colombia	Costa Rica	Australia
Saudi Arabia	France	Madagascar	Ecuador	Bolivia
United Arab	Germany		Egypt	Brazil
Emirates	Ireland		Greece	Canada
	Italy		Guinea	El Salvador
	Luxembourg		Guinea-Bissau	Gambia, The
	Netherlands		Honduras	Ghana
	Spain		India	Guatemala
			Indonesia	Jamaica
			Korea	Japan
			Lao P.D. Rep.	Lebanon
			Mauritania	Maldives
			Mexico	Namibia
			Nicaragua	New Zealand
			Pakistan	Nigeria
			Portugal	Paraguay
			Singapore	Peru
			Sri Lanka	Philippines
			Tunisia	Sierra Leone
			Turkey	South Africa
			Viet Nam	United Kingdom
			Yugoslavia	United States
				Uruguay
				Venezuela
				Zaire

Table 11.14 *Summary of exchange-rate arrangements as at 30 September 1990*

Classification Status	
Currency Pegged to	
US dollar	25
French franc	14
Other currency	5
of which: pound sterling	—
SDR	7
Other currency composite	37
Flexibility limited *vis-à-vis* a single currency	4
Co-operative arrangements	9
Adjusted according to a set of indicators	3
Managed floating	23
Independently floating	26
Total	153

international currencies (the dollar, yen, deutschmark and sterling) and as **Table 11.13** shows a whole host of exchange-rate regimes coexist between currencies. The large and dramatic currency swings in the 1970s and 1980s between the major currencies particularly between the dollar and other currencies (see Chapter 6 for plots) have led to a variety of proposals to reform the system. All the proposals are based upon the view that it is desirable to limit the exchange rate swings between the major currencies, but the proposals differ over the best method to achieve this. Three of the best known proposals to bring some stability to the international monetary system have been made by John Williamson, Ronald McKinnon and James Tobin and are worthy of some consideration.

■ *11.14* The Williamson target zone proposal

In a number of papers John Williamson in conjunction with other authors (1983, 1987, 1988) has proposed that the exchange rate between the major international currencies should be managed within a target zone system. For each of the major currencies Williamson has suggested a method to calculate the currency's 'Fundamental Equilibrium Effective Exchange Rate' (FEEER). Broadly speaking the FEEER is a real effective exchange rate that is consistent with a sustainable current account position. The calculated FEEER would be periodically adjusted as the economic fundamentals change, e.g. relative inflation rates, and should not therefore be confused with a fixed central rate. A country's exchange rate would then be allowed to fluctuate within a system of 'soft edged bands' of ± 10 per cent either side of the FEEER. The idea of soft bands is that the authorities will not necessarily be committed to buy or sell the currency if it reaches the upper or lower limit of its band. This it is argued, will prevent creating a one-way bet for speculators who insist on selling a weak currency at the lower limit of its band knowing that the authorities will be obliged to purchase the currency at what will eventually prove to be a high rate once the currency is forced out of its band.

According to Williamson the target zone proposal would have helped prevent the dramatic real appreciation of the dollar during 1980–85 because the US would not have been able to pursue such an expansionary fiscal policy over this period. Furthermore, Miller and Williamson (1987) argue that the target zone proposal can help rule out the possibility of self-fulfilling and destabilising foreign exchange speculation. There has been criticism of the methodology used to calculate FEEERs and that the bands and adjustments of FEEERS will fail to rule out major exchange rate swings. For an extensive review and critique of many issues raised by target zones the reader is referred to Frenkel and Goldstein (1986).

 ## 11.15 The McKinnon global monetary target proposal

Ronald McKinnon (1982, 1984a and 1984b) has argued that much exchange rate volatility is due to the process of currency substitution. McKinnon argues that in a world in which there are few capital controls, multinational corporations and international investors like to hold a portfolio of various national currencies. He argues that demand to hold a portfolio of national currencies is quite stable but that the composition of the total portfolio can be highly volatile. This means that rigid control of the supply of the individual national currencies in the portfolio is inappropriate. He suggests 'that the Friedman rule for smooth monetary growth should be shifted from a national to a carefully defined international level'. For example, if there is a switch in portfolios away from the US dollar to hold the deutschmark and national money supplies are unchanged there will be a depreciation of the dollar and appreciation of the deutschmark. In turn, this will exert effects on the real economies of the two countries.

McKinnon argues that these disruptive real exchange rate changes can be avoided if the German and US authorities peg their exchange rate by contracting the US money supply (thereby eliminating the excess supply of dollars) and expanding the German money supply (thereby eliminating the excess demand for deutschmarks). Such a result would happen if the US and German authorities pursued policies of unsterilised intervention policy in the foreign exchange market purchasing the excess dollars with deutschmarks.

This policy while leading to changes in national money stocks would leave the global money supply and exchange rates unchanged and leave the two economies unaffected by the process of currency substitution.

The McKinnon argument that currency substitution is a widespread phenomenon and therefore a major cause of exchange-rate volatility has been widely challenged (e.g. Dornbusch, 1983). It is more likely that the major source of financial portfolio shifts is not between domestic and foreign currencies but between domestic and foreign bonds. As it happens, the appropriate response to deal with such switches is sterilised intervention to peg the exchange rate. Say there is a decrease in the demand for US bonds and increase in the demand for German bonds. The appropriate response of the US authorities to this would be to sell German bonds and purchase the excess supply of US bonds, which would leave interest rates and exchange rates unchanged.

There are numerous problems with the McKinnon proposal. Many economists dispute his suggestion that currency substitution is a major force in exchange-rate movements. Also by fixing nominal exchange rate at some PPP level the proposal does not allow for the possibility of real exchange-rate changes which some economists believe have been a major force behind large exchange-rate swings. As we saw in Chapter 6, if Japanese tradables productivity growth is higher than US tradables growth, then over time there needs to be a real appreciation of the yen against the dollar. If not, the yen will become undervalued in relation to the dollar and this could lead to serious trade frictions.

11.16 The Tobin foreign exchange tax proposal

James Tobin (1978) has argued that much of the disruptive exchange-rate movements witnessed under floating have been caused by destabilising short-term capital flows. He argues that the highly integrated world capital markets leave very little room for national authorities to pursue independent monetary policies:

> National economies and national governments are not capable of adjusting to massive movements of funds across the foreign exchanges, without real hardship and without significant sacrifice of the objectives of national economic policy with respect to employment, output, and inflation. Specifically, the mobility of financial capital limits viable differences among national interest rates and this severely restricts the ability of central banks and governments to pursue monetary and fiscal policies appropriate to their national economies. (p. 154).

Specifically, a raising of the domestic interest rate can cause a sharp real appreciation while a lowering of interest rates can lead to a sharp real depreciation. To reduce these effects, Tobin has suggested that a tax be imposed on all foreign exchange transactions, 'to throw some sand in the wheels of our excessively efficient international money markets' (p. 154). The tax would reduce the incentives for speculators to suddenly flood money into and out of a currency in response to small interest rate changes. He argues that a small tax of say 1 per cent would especially hit short-term capital movements but not greatly interfere with longer-term capital movements. This would restore some autonomy to domestic monetary authorities.

Tobin acknowledges that in order to be effective and avoid evasion the tax would have to be applied to all foreign exchange transactions and not merely to capital transactions. He acknowledges that there would be a curtailing effect on international trade but argues that the reduced exchange rate movements and extra degree of national monetary autonomy would be worthwhile.

Tobin's proposal differs significantly from those of Williamson and McKinnon because his proposal is motivated by the belief that the exchange-rate regime is not the major problem; rather he traces the problem to excessive capital movements. He displays considerable scepticism over the rationality of foreign exchange market speculation and argues that unlike irrational speculation in innocuous markets like rare coins such speculation in the foreign exchange market has very harmful effects.

There have been numerous criticisms levelled against Tobin's proposal. Clearly not all short-term capital movements are undesirable and the tax would prevent some stabilising movements. Furthermore, some argue that in order to be effective the tax would have to be set at a level that would have a significant curtailing effect on international trade. As for the extra degree of national monetary autonomy that the policy may give, it is not clear that this would be wisely used. It is argued that it is precisely the threat of sudden exchange-rate movements that imposes a degree of discipline on national authorities' conduct of economic policies. Furthermore, in a bid to avoid the tax there could a greater use of barter trade which is notoriously inefficient.

■ *11.17* Conclusions

Since the Second World War the international monetary system has moved from the Bretton Woods system, which represented a cooperative venture between the major industrialised countries with the dollar at the heart of the system, into a far more diversified system. To some extent this reflects the fact that the world economic system has evolved from one which was dominated by the US economy to one in which economic power is increasingly shared between an integrated Europe, Japan and the US and other emerging regions such as South East Asia and Latin America. Nevertheless, the dollar still remains the major reserve currency and this role has to date only been infringed upon at the margins by the SDR and the European Currency Unit (ECU). It is, however, likely that this role will decline during the next decade to more accurately reflect the increased importance and confidence in the stability of other economies notably Japan and Germany.

A greater sharing of economic power has been accompanied by a larger degree of interdependence between economies with respect to both trade and capital flows. The international monetary system has been constantly evolving to cope with these changes (for an excellent review, see Llewellyn, 1990). The move to floating exchange rates was partly motivated by a desire to provide countries with an extra degree of independence in an increasingly interdependent world. However, the policy divergences and real exchange-rate changes of the 1980s have amply demonstrated that floating exchange rates do not provide an escape from this interdependence. This recognition has led to increased discussion among policy makers about policy coordination and the appropriate exchange-rate regime. At times, such as indicated by the Plaza and Louvre Accords, this discussion has led to concerted action.

The major change in the international monetary system was undoubtedly the move to generalised floating in 1973. This move was followed by a more turbulent international economic environment, most notably the two oil shocks, which leaves plenty of scope for discussion about whether the economic performance of the 1970s and early 1980s was primarily a result of floating exchange rates or other factors.

Dissatisfaction with the present system, particularly with the large real exchange-rate changes that have occurred has led to a variety of differing proposals which all seem to have the motivation to limit by one means or another the substantial real exchange rate changes that have occurred.

■ Selected further readings

Argy, V. (1981) *The Postwar International Money Crisis: An Analysis* (London: George Allen & Unwin).

Corden, W.M. (1981) *Inflation, Exchange Rates and the World Economy* (Oxford: Clarendon).

De Grauwe, P. (1989) *International Money* (Oxford: Clarendon Press).

Dornbusch, R. (1983) 'Flexible Exchange Rates and Interdependence'. *IMF Staff Papers*, vol. 30, pp. 3–30.

Dunn, R. (1983) 'The Many Disappointments of Flexible Exchange Rates', *Princeton Essays in International Finance*, No. 154.

Edison, H.J., Miller, M.H. and Williamson, J. (1987) 'On Evaluating and Extending the Target Zone Proposal', *Journal of Policy Modeling*, vol. 9, pp. 199–227.

Frankel, J.A. (1985) 'The Dazzling Dollar', *Brookings Papers on Economic Activity*, vol. 1, pp. 199–217.

Frenkel, J.A. and Goldstein, M. (1986) 'A Guide to Target Zones', *IMF Staff Papers*, vol. 33, pp. 623–73.

Llewellyn, D.T. (1990) 'The International Monetary System', in D.T. Llewellyn and C. Milner (eds), *Current Issues in International Monetary Economics* (London: Macmillan).

McKinnon, R.I. (1981) 'The Exchange Rate and Macroeconomic Policy: Changing Postwar Perceptions', *Journal of Economic Literature*, vol. 19, pp. 531–57.

McKinnon, R.I. (1982) 'Currency Substitution and Instability in the World Dollar Standard', *American Economic Review*, vol. 72, pp. 320–33.

McKinnon, R.I. (1984) *An International Standard for Monetary Stabilization*. Institute for International Economics, Policy Analyses No. 8 (Cambridge, Mass.: MIT Press).

McKinnon, R.I. (1988) 'Monetary and Exchange Rate Policies for Internatioal Financial Stability: a Proposal', *Journal of Economic Perspectives*, vol. 2, pp. 83–103.

Miller, M. and Williamson, J. (1987) 'The International Monetary System: an Analysis of Alternative Regimes', *European Economic Review*, vol. 32, pp. 1031–48.

Milner, C. and Greenaway, D. (1979) *An Introduction to International Economics* (London: Longman).

Niehans, J. (1984) *International Monetary Economics* (Oxford: Philip Allan).

Nurkse, R. (1944) *International Currency Experience* (League of Nations: Columbia University Press).

Scammell, W.M. (1987) *The Stability of the International Monetary System* (London: Macmillan).

Solomon, R. (1982) *The International Monetary System, 1945–81* (New York: Harper & Row).

Tew, B. (1988) *The Evolution of the International Monetary System 1948–88* (London: Hutchinson).

Tobin, J. (1978) 'A Proposal for International Monetary Reform', *Eastern Economic Journal*, vol. 4, pp. 153–9. Reprinted in J. Tobin, *Essays in Economics* (Cambridge, Mass.: MIT Press, 1982).

Triffin, R. (1960) *Gold and the Dollar Crisis* (New Haven, Conn.: Yale University Press).

Williamson, J. (1977) *The Failure of World Monetary Reform* (Sunbury: Nelson).

Williamson, J. (1983) *The Exchange Rate System*. Institute for International Economics, Policy Analyses No. 5 (Cambridge Mass.: MIT Press).

Williamson, J. and Miller, M. (1988) *Targets and Indicators: a Blueprint for the Coordination of Economic Policy* (Washington, Institute for International Economics).

■ *Chapter 12* ■

The Eurocurrency Markets

■ *12.1* Introduction

Eurocurrency markets are defined as banking markets which are conducted outside the legal jurisdiction of the authorities of the currency that is used for banking transactions. Examples of Eurodollar deposits are dollar deposits held in London and Paris, while examples of Euromarks are deutschmarks held in New York, London and Paris. The Eurocurrency market has two sides to it; the receipt of deposits and the loaning out of those deposits. By far the most important Eurocurrency is the Eurodollar which in 1987 accounted for approximately 70 per cent of all Eurocurrency activity, followed by the Euromark, Eurofrancs (Swiss), Eurosterling and Euroyen. The use of the prefix Euro is somewhat misleading because dollar deposits held by banks in Hong Kong or Tokyo are equally outside the legal jurisdiction of the US authorities and also constitute Eurodollar deposits just as deutschmark and yen held in New York constitute Euroyen and Eurodeutschmark. This more widespread geographical base means that Euromarkets are often referred to as 'offshore' markets.

Euromarkets are in many ways a phenomenon of the increasingly open world trading system. There is no reason why deposits and loans in a given currency need be carried out exclusively in the particular country that issues the currency. As we shall see in this chapter, the main reason for the rapid growth of Eurocurrency markets is that they provide better deposit and loan

Table 12.1   *The size of the Eurocurrency market in selected years ($ billions)*

Year	Gross size of Eurocurrency deposits	Proportion of which is the US dollar	Net size of Eurocurrency deposits
1964	19	n.a	14
1966	25	n.a	17
1968	46	79	34
1970	86	79	65
1972	210	78	110
1974	395	76	220
1976	595	80	314
1978	949	74	478
1980	1574	76	797
1982	2164	80	1152
1984	2383	81	1274
1986	3683	72	2076
1987	4509	66	2584

Note:
The gross size of the Eurocurrency market includes interbank deposits.
Source: Morgan Guaranty, *World Financial Markets.*

rates than offered by domestic banks located in the country that issues the currency.

Since the 1960s there has been an astonishing rate of growth of the Eurocurrency market (see **Table 12.1**). In 1958 the gross total value of deposits was approximately $1 billion but by 1987 the Eurodollar market stood at $2976 billion in dollars and some $1533 billion in other currencies.

In this chapter we deal with the origins and reasons for the subsequent rapid growth of Eurocurrency markets over the last three decades. We then consider the role performed by Eurobanks and examine the accusation that they have contributed to an increase in global liquidity and a rise in worldwide inflation. For expository purposes we shall refer to the Eurodollar market but the analysis and arguments extend to the other currencies.

 ## 12.2 The origins and development of the Euromarkets

The origins of the Euromarkets can be traced back to 1957. The Russians having acquired US dollars through their exports of raw materials were, given the strong anti-communist sentiment prevailing in the US and the 'cold war', reluctant to hold these funds with US banks. Instead, they were held in an account with a French bank in Paris, the cable address of which was EURO-BANK. Also in 1957, the Bank of England introduced restrictions on UK banks ability to lend sterling to foreigners and foreigners' ability to borrow sterling. This induced UK banks to turn to the US dollar as a means of retaining London's leading role in the financing of world trade. In 1958 the abolition of the European Payments Union (see Chapter 11) and restoration of convertibility of European currencies meant that European banks could now hold US dollars without being forced to convert these dollar holdings with their central banks for domestic currencies. All these three factors provided the initial demand and supply of Eurodollars.

An important impetus for the rapid growth of the Eurodollars came from the increased regulation of domestic banking activities by the US authorities. Three measures are of particular note in this respect. In 1963 the US government introduced Regulation Q which imposed ceilings on the rate of interest that US banks could pay on savings and time deposit accounts. Since the regulation did not apply to offshore banks this encouraged many US banks to set up subsidiaries abroad in centres such as London. In the same year, the US authorities concerned about the capital outflow on the US balance of payments introduced the Interest Equalization Tax (IET). The IET raised the cost to foreigners of borrowing dollars in New York which encouraged them to borrow funds on the Eurodollar market (the IET was abolished in 1974). A further measure that restricted lending to foreigners by US banks was the Voluntary Foreign Credit Restraint Guidelines which were issued in 1965 and made compulsory in 1968.

This increased regulation of US domestic banks gave a boost to the development of Eurobanking activities to circumvent the effects of these controls. Many US banks decided to set up foreign branches and subsidiaries to escape the banking regulations. More importantly, they gave a competitive edge to Eurobanks which are not subject to such regulations. It is this competitive edge which is the fundamental reason for their rapid and sustained growth. Unlike domestic banks, because Eurobanks are free of regulatory control they are not required to hold reserve assets. This gives them a competitive advantage over domestic banks which are required to hold part of their assets in zero or low interest liquid funds to meet official reserve requirements. The competitive advantage of Eurobanks is illustrated in **Figure 12.1**.

The Eurobanks are generally able to pay a higher rate on deposits and charge a lower rate for loans than US banks can for similar facilities. This implies that the interest rate spread, that is, the difference between the rate paid on deposits and charged for loans is lower for the Eurobanks than US banks. The usual domestic interest rate used for the purposes of comparison with the Euro-interest rate is the interest on certificates of deposit. The

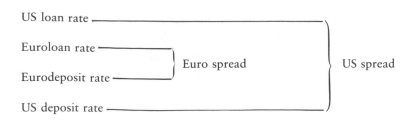

Figure 12.1 *Comparison of US and Eurodollar interest spreads*

difference between deposit rates on certificates of deposit and those on Eurodeposits fluctuates but usually ranges between 1/2 to 1 per cent.

The lower Euro-interest spread can be accounted for by a number of factors. Since Eurobanks are not subject to reserve requirements they are able to hold less money in the form of low interest reserves enabling them to pay a higher interest rate on deposits and charge a lower rate on loans. Another reason for their competitive advantage is that they benefit from economies of scale, the average size of Eurobanks' deposits and loans are generally greater than those of domestic banks, and this makes the operating cost associated with each deposit and loan smaller in relation to the size of the transaction. In addition, Eurobanks avoid much of the personnel and administration costs, and delays associated with complying with domestic banking regulations. Furthermore, the Eurobanking business is highly competitive internationally with relatively easy entrance requirements as compared with domestic banking activity. This encourages greater efficiency on the part of Eurobanks.

Since Eurobanks generally pay higher interest rates on deposits and charge lower interest rates on loans, then it is natural to ask why all borrowing and lending is not carried out via Eurobanks? The answer lies in the transaction costs for the parties involved. It usually pays a US firm to go to its local US bank for a loan because the local bank will have a record and understanding of the business and will be able to assess more easily the risk of lending to the business, secure collateral and monitor the progress of the loan. If the firm were to go to a Eurobank it might prove expensive to convince the Eurobank that it is creditworthy and that the project is soundly based. Similarly, except for substantial sums of money it is not usually worth individuals and small enterprises holding a Eurodeposit.

Following the hike in oil prices in 1973–4 the OPEC countries deposited large amounts of the resulting additional funds on the Euromarkets. The Eurobanks then lent much of the funds to oil importing countries that faced balance-of-payments problems. The Eurobanks played an important intermediary role in recycling funds from the surplus OPEC countries to the deficit oil importing countries. A similar role was performed by the Euro-banks following the second oil price shock at the end of 1978 though on a lesser scale.

In December 1981 the Federal Reserve, recognising that many US Banks had set up offshore branches to avoid US regulations in exotic locations such as the Bahamas and Cayman Islands, decided to legalise so called International Banking Facilities (IBFs). IBFs essentially permit US banks to conduct Eurobanking business, free of US regulations in the United States. Although IBFs can only accept deposits from non US residents and their loan facilities must be used for overseas purposes. Since IBFs are not subject to reserve requirements, interest rate regulations or deposit insurance premiums, their business is maintained on a separate book to the parent bank. IBFs have proved to be popular since their inception and much business that was previously carried out in offshore offices has been relocated back to the US.

12.3 The characteristics of the Eurodollar market

The major centres for Eurobank activity are London, Paris, Luxembourg and Frankfurt which accounted for over 60 per cent of Eurobank activity in 1982. Offshore banking centres in Bahrain, Bahamas, Cayman Islands, Hong Kong, Panama, Netherland Antilles and Singapore accounted for just over 20 per cent with North America and Japan accounting for the remainder. Eurobanks are generally free of government regulation. More especially they do not face compulsory reserve requirements, interest ceilings or deposit insurance.

The main users of the Eurocurrency market facilities are the Eurobanks themselves, non-Eurobank financial institutions, multinational corporations, international institutions and central and local government. Multinationals are attracted by the interest rates paid on their corporate funds and the competitive borrowing rates. International organisations such as the World Bank frequently borrow funds from Eurobanks for lending to developing countries. A large proportion of Eurocurrency transactions are between Eurobanks themselves, those with surplus funds loaning to Eurobanks that have lending possibilities but are short of funds.

The pivotal rate of interest for the Eurocurrency markets is the London Inter-Bank Offer Rate (LIBOR) which is the rate of interest that London clearing banks will charge for loans between themselves on the London interbank market. Non-bank borrowers then pay a spread above LIBOR depending on their credit rating and the bank's transaction costs, while non-bank depositors typically receive a rate of interest on their deposits below LIBOR. In the early days of the Euromarket, the interest paid on deposits and charged for loans was usually fixed for the whole period of the deposit or loan. Increasingly, however, floating interest rates based on LIBOR have become the norm for medium to long-term (above six months) deposits and loans. With floating rates, the interest charged on a medium to long-term loan is adjusted every three or six months to stay at a fixed spread above LIBOR. In effect, many long-term loans are a succession of short-term loans that are automatically 'rolled over', but at interest rates that vary in line with changes in LIBOR. There are usually penalties to be paid if deposits are withdrawn before maturity.

Measuring the actual size of the Eurocurrency market presents some difficulty because a distinction needs to be made between the gross and net size of the Eurocurrency market. The gross measure includes both non-Eurobank and interbank deposits, while the net measure excludes interbank deposits. The gross measure gives an idea about the overall activity in the Euromarkets while the net measure gives a better indication concerning the ability of the Eurobanking system to create credit.

One of the interesting characteristics of the structure of Eurobanks' assets (loans) and liabilities (deposits) is that they are predominately of a short term nature with some deposits being as short as one day (overnight deposit) and the vast majority under six months. Furthermore, there is a close matching of the maturity structure of deposits and liabilities. This is borne out in **Table 12.2**. Such a maturity structure stands in contrast to the balance sheets of domestic banks which usually accept short-term demand and time deposits and then engage in medium to long-term lending.

Eurobanks have to be wary of sudden large withdrawals of short-term funds, for example by the OPEC countries, and this is a major reason for the close matching of claims and liabilities.

Another motivation behind the close matching of assets and liabilities is that it reduces the risks to the banks due to interest fluctuations. Consider a simple example of the risk involved when liabilities and assets are not matched, in the case where a Eurobank receives a $1 million three-month deposit on which it has to pay 9 per cent rate of interest and it loans out the funds at 10 per cent for six months. If at the end of three months a rise in deposit interest rates means that it has to pay 11 per cent to retain the deposit it would effectively be losing money on the remaining three months on the outstanding loan. This would not be the case if the loan was renewable at three months since it could then raise the interest charged on the loan for its remaining three months to say 12 per cent.

Since 1982 the existence of Eurodollar futures markets in Chicago, New York and London has enabled Eurobanks to protect themselves against

Table 12.2 *Maturity structure of Eurocurrency claims and liabilities*

Maturity	Total percent	
	Claims	Liabilities
Less than 8 days	15.6	21.6
8 days to less than 1 month	16.7	20.6
1 month to less than 3 months	23.5	28.2
3 months to less than 6 months	14.8	18.8
6 months to less than 1 year	6.2	5.8
1 year to less than 3 years	7.2	2.7
3 years and over	16.0	2.3
All maturities	100.0	100.0

Source: Bank of England Quarterly Bulletin, December 1983.
Note:
Data are for UK based positions in non-sterling currencies as of 17 August 1983.

interest fluctuations without matching their assets and liabilities. Consider the case where a Eurobank receives a $1 million deposit for three months in March at 9 per cent which it loans out for six months at 10 per cent – it can protect itself by selling in March a $1 million Eurodollar future for June. If in June the Eurodollar interest rate has risen, the value of its Eurodollar future will be lower than sale proceeds it receives on the future (since interest rates and the price of futures are inversely related) – this profit will offset the effects of the higher interest rate it must pay on its deposits. If deposit interest rates have fallen between March and June the Eurodollar future will be worth more than its sale proceeds – while the bank will have lost money on the future; this loss is offset by the lower interest rate it has to pay on its deposits. Hence, Eurofutures provide an important instrument for hedging any mismatches in the maturity structure of Eurobanks' assets and liabilities.

☐ Syndicated loans

The large majority of loans made by the Eurobanks to the developing countries in the 1970s and early 1980s were made by syndicates of Eurobanks. A syndicate is normally led by a 'lead' or 'managing bank' with other banks that wish to participate in a loan contributing to its funding. Such syndicated loans are useful from the perspective of individual Eurobanks because they reduce the exposure of a Eurobank to a given borrower and by participating in a wide range of syndicated loans a Eurobank can diversify and reduce its loan risks far more than by engaging in a limited number of large individual loans.

■ *12.4* The creation of Eurodeposits

Eurobanks are basically financial intermediaries whose function is channelling funds from a non-bank lender to a non-bank borrower. Between the deposit and the lending there may be a series of inter-bank transactions. To enhance the understanding of Eurocurrency markets we examine by means of a hypothetical example how Eurocurrency deposits and loans are created.

In our example, we assume that a multinational corporation SUPER Corp starts off the process by transferring $10 million from its account with Citicorp US into a Eurodollar deposit account with Lloyds UK. The resulting consequences for the balance sheets of the three parties involved are as follows:

SUPER Corp

Change in liabilities	*Change in assets*
	Deposits at Citicorp (US) − $10m
	Deposits at Lloyds (UK) + $10m

Lloyds Bank UK

Change in liabilities	*Change in assets*
Deposit by SUPER Corp + $10m	Reserves held at Citicorp US + $10m

Citicorp Bank US

Change in liabilities	*Change in assets*
Deposit held by SUPER Corp − $10m	
Deposits held by Lloyds UK + $10m	

From these transactions we can see that what has basically occurred is that SUPER Corp has switched a dollar deposit from a US bank to a UK bank. Lloyds UK now has a new deposit liability to SUPER Corp but also now holds increased funds in its account at Citicorp US (its correspondent bank) which it can now utilise for lending purposes. As far as Citicorp is concerned its total deposits are unchanged but the ownership of some $10 million has been transferred from SUPER Corp to Lloyds UK. As far as the

US banking system is concerned, the amount of deposits held by the non bank public has fallen. In large part, the whole process can be viewed as a book-keeping exercise since the dollars have actually remained in the US.

Let us now consider a possible next stage in the Eurocurrency market. Suppose that Lloyds UK does not have any immediate use for its new $10 million of deposits but that Barclays UK does because MINI Corp wishes to raise $10 million for financing purposes. In this case, Barclays UK may borrow funds from Lloyds at fractions of a per cent higher than the interest rate Lloyds is paying SUPER Corp. The effect of these operations on the various parties balance sheets is shown below:

Lloyds Bank UK

Change in liabilities	*Change in assets*
	Deposits at Citicorp (US) −$10m
	Deposits at Barclays (UK) +$10m

Barclays Bank UK

Change in liabilities	*Change in assets*
Deposit by Lloyds Bank UK +$10m	Reserves held at Citicorp US +$10m

Citicorp Bank US

Change in liabilities	*Change in assets*
Deposits held by Lloyds UK −$10m	
Deposits held by Barclays +$10m	

MINI Corp

Change in liabilities	*Change in assets*
Loan from Barclays UK +$10m	Cash balance at Citicorp +$10m

Citicorp Bank US

Change in liabilities	*Change in assets*
Deposits held by Barclays UK −$10m	
Deposits held by MINI Corp +$10m	

The transfer of funds from Lloyds to Barclays bank constitutes an interbank transaction, the effect of which is to raise the total of Eurodollar deposits from $10 million to $20 million. We can now distinguish a difference between the effect on the net size of the Eurodollar market – the original $10 million deposit and the gross effect of $20 million which includes the interbank transaction. With the loan to MINI Corp the funds that were initially deposited by SUPER Corp have been given an ultimate use. Notice that when Barclays extends a loan to MINI Corp, then any drawings by MINI Corp come from the balance of its account held at Citicorp. The Eurobanks are in effect acting as financial intermediaries ensuring that surplus funds from one organisation(SUPER Corp) are transferred to other organisations with borrowing requirements (MINI Corp).

When MINI Corp starts to spend money then the dollars are drawn from Citicorp in the US. Only the US banking system creates dollars; the Eurobanks create deposits which are not a means of payment. Eurobanks are essentially financial intermediaries; they accept deposits and then loan out these funds.

The real question which now arises is what MINI Corp does with its borrowed funds. If it were to just redeposit them with another Eurobank then the whole process could be restarted. However, this is most unlikely to be the case. More likely, MINI Corp will be using the funds to pay various bills due and will redeposit only a small fraction of its $10 million in the Eurobanking system say $1 million with Eurobanks which can be used to create further credit.

This is a highly simplified example of the way the Eurobanking system creates credit. There are some obvious limits to the amount of credit created by the Eurobanking system. In the first instance, Lloyds and Barclays are unlikely to lend out all the deposits they receive and then MINI Corp is likely to redeposit only a fraction of its money with the Eurobanking system. Most of the money received by MINI Corp is likely to be reinjected into the American economy and thereby returned to the US banking system, from which there may be some further leakage back to the Eurocurrency markets. With this example in mind we now proceed to examine in a more formal manner the so called Eurocurrency credit multiplier.

■ *12.5* Eurocurrency multipliers

One of the major concerns expressed about Eurocurrency markets is that they have the potential to create credit and yet remain unregulated. The rapid growth of the Eurocurrency markets in the 1960s and 1970s coincided with a pronounced rise in the inflation rates of the industrialised nations. Some policy makers and economists argued that the growth of the Eurocurrency market was partly responsible for this.

The basis of the argument is that the growth of Eurocurrency markets has had an expansionary effect on national money supplies and thereby helped to fuel inflation rates. Precisely how to model Euromarkets has been an area of considerable controversy in the literature. Friedman (1969) and Mayer (1970) have argued that the Eurodollar market should be seen merely as an extension of the US banking system. Just as a domestic bank's ability to create credit is determined by its cash to deposit ratio and the amount redeposited with the domestic banking system, so too is the ability of Eurobanks. Their initial estimates were that Euromarkets had a very expansionary effect because of their low reserve ratios. However, Klopstock (1968) noted that Eurobanks have very low redeposit ratios which considerably reduced their ability to create credit.

We shall examine the relationship between Eurocurrency markets and national money supplies using the multiplier analysis of McKinnon (1977). His model makes the important point that what is important in deciding whether Eurobanks are responsible for credit creation is their net addition to the supply of dollars, that is, the addition to the global supply of dollars as compared to the supply of dollars in their absence. A survey of various Eurodollar multipliers is contained in Swoboda (1980).

☐ Eurocurrency multipliers

The dollar money supply in the US non-bank public is defined as:

$$M = C + D + E \tag{12.1}$$

where M is the dollar money supply in the hands of the non-bank public, C is the cash in the hands of the public, D is deposits held with the US banking system by the non-bank public, and E is Eurodollar deposits.

It is assumed that the demand for US deposits is a linear function of the global dollar money supply.

$$D = \alpha + mM \tag{12.2}$$

where α reflects the preference for domestic deposits of the non-bank public and m is the fraction of the money supply that is deposited with US banks.

Similarly, the total demand for Eurodeposits is a linear function of the global dollar money supply.

$$E = \beta + eM \tag{12.3}$$

where β reflects the preference for Eurodollar deposits of the non bank public and e is the fraction of the money supply that is deposited on the Eurodollar market.

Eurobanks hold reserves with US banks to meet withdrawals by their depositors. These reserves are assumed to be a proportion to their total deposits:

$$RE = reE \tag{12.4}$$

where RE are total Eurocurrency reserves, and re is the reserve ratio of Eurobanks.

US banks are assumed to hold reserves with the Federal Reserve in proportion to their total deposits which are made up of deposits held by the public and deposits held by Eurobanks. This gives:

$$R = r(D + RE) \tag{12.5}$$

Where R is the reserves of the US banking system and r is the reserve ratio of US banks.

The monetary base of the US is defined as cash in the hands of the public plus banks' reserves held at the Federal Reserve. This gives:

$$B = C + R \tag{12.6}$$

We can now use the above set of relationships to consider the effects of Eurocurrency deposits.

(i)   *The effects of a shift in deposits from the US banking system to the Eurodollar market on total Eurodeposits.* In this instance, $d\beta = -d\alpha$ with the monetary base unchanged, that is, $dB = 0$. The resulting multiplier is given by:

$$\frac{dE}{d\beta} = \frac{1}{1 + \dfrac{er(1 - re)}{(e + m)(1 - r) - 1}} \tag{12.7}$$

Since $(e + m)(1 - r) < 1$ then the multiplier is greater than unity, that is, the Eurodollar market will expand by greater than a dollar for every dollar deposited. If we ignore the possibility of cash holdings, so that $e + m = 1$, then equation (12.7) simplifies to:

$$\frac{dE}{d\beta} = \frac{1}{1 - e(1 - re)} > 1 \tag{12.8}$$

Equation (12.8) is known as the Eurodollar credit multiplier. It shows that the increase in the Eurodollar market will be greater the higher the proportion of money that gets deposited with the Eurobanking system (e) and the lower the reserve ratio of the Eurobanks (re).

The reason why the Eurodollar market expands by more than a dollar for every dollar deposited is fairly straightforward. An additional dollar of Eurodeposits means that Eurobanks have an additional dollar for lending purposes and when most $(1 - re)$ of the dollar is lent out, a fraction (e) gets redeposited with the Eurobanking system.

(ii)   *The effects of a shift in deposits from the US banking system to the Eurodollar market on the money supply.* In this instance, $d\beta = -d\alpha$ with the monetary base unchanged, that is, $dB = 0$. The resulting effect on the US money supply is given by:

$$\frac{dM}{d\beta} - \frac{r(1-re)}{1-m(1-r)-e(1-rre)} > 1 \qquad (12.9)$$

Equation (12.9) is known as the Eurodollar money multiplier and since the multiplier is greater than unity, then the Eurodollar market can be said to have an expansionary effect on the global money supply as defined by equation (12.1). The multiplier will be greater the lower the values of the Eurobank reserve ratio and the lower the domestic reserve ratio. However, even if the Eurodollar reserve ratio is the same as the domestic reserve ratio of US banks ($re = r$) the Eurodollar multiplier still exceeds unity.

The explanation for the expansionary effect of the Eurodollar market on global money supply is as follows: once a dollar deposit is switched from the US money market to the Eurodollar market, the Eurodollar market will expand by more than one dollar. Part of this expansion (m) gets deposited with US banks and part (e) gets redeposited with Eurobanks. US banks will have to hold additional reserves with the Federal Reserve so part of their additional deposits cannot be lent out to the non-bank public, whereas Eurobanks will hold their reserves with US banks who can then lend out part of these Eurobank reserves to the public.

(iii) *The effect of the Eurodollar market on the money supply of an increase in the monetary base.* In this instance, $d\beta = -d\alpha = 0$. Ignoring the fact that some money is held as cash then $e + m = 1$. The effect of an increase in the money base is given by:

$$\frac{dM}{dB} = \frac{1}{r[1 - e(1 - re)]} > \frac{1}{r}$$

If the Eurodollar market did not exist ($e = re = 0$) then the multiplier would be the familiar $1/r$ associated with the domestic banking system. Consequently, the Eurodollar market can be said to have the effect of raising the base multiplier. This follows from the fact that a proportion of the newly created base gets deposited with the Eurocurrency markets which have a greater liquidity effect than the domestic banking system.

12.6 Empirical evidence on the Eurodollar multiplier

The value of the Eurodollar credit multiplier as given by equation (12.8) is dependent upon the values of e and re. Ronald McKinnon (1979) has estimated the cash reserve ratio of Eurobanks(re) to be between 0.01 and 0.05, while the fraction Eurodollar lending that gets redeposited with Eurobanks (e) is generally regarded as being less than 0.2. If we assume a Eurobank reserve ratio of 0.02 and a value for redepositing with the Eurobanks at the upper end of estimates at 0.2 we obtain a value for the Eurocurrency multiplier of 1.24.

$$\frac{dE}{d\beta} = \frac{1}{1-e(1-re)} > 1 = \frac{1}{1-0.2(1-0.02)} = \frac{1}{0.804} = 1.24$$

A Eurocurrency multiplier of 1.24 means that a switch of one dollar from the US banking system to the Eurocurrency markets increases the global dollar money supply by 24 per cent more than would have been the case if the dollar was left in the US banking system. This relatively weak effect does not give much credence to the view that growth of Eurodollar markets is responsible for the rise in world inflation.

It is worth emphasising that the additional liquidity effect of the Eurocurrency market does not rely on the Eurobanks having a lower reserve ratio than US banks; even if their reserve ratio(r) was the same as the Eurobanks (re), there will still be an expansionary effect. Say the Eurobanks also had reserve ratios of 0.10 then the Eurodollar multiplier in our example would be $1/0.82 = 1.22$ which is not greatly different than the 1.24 already mentioned. The crucial reason for the additional expansionary effect of the Eurobanks is that they hold their dollar reserves with US banks and not with the Federal Reserve as US banks are obliged to. This means that much of Eurobanks' reserves gets lent out by the US banking system.

A further issue that arises is what is the effect of rise in the monetary base in the presence of Euromarkets as compared with their absence. Let us again assume a Eurobank reserve ratio of 0.02 and let us assume a reserve ratio for US banks of 0.10.

$$\frac{dM}{dB} = \frac{1}{r[1-e(1-re)]} = \frac{1}{0.1[1-0.2(1-0.02)]} = 12.44 \text{ with euromarkets}$$

$$\frac{dM}{dB} = \frac{1}{r} = \frac{1}{0.1} = 10 \text{ without euromarkets}$$

The effect of a one dollar increase in the money base is to lead to an increase of 10 dollars in the broad money supply in the absence of the Eurodollar market but an increase of 12 dollars 44 cents in the presence of Euromarkets.

Hence, the argument that Eurobanks lead to greater liquidity rests only marginally on the premise that they hold lower level of reserve assets against deposits than domestic US banks. Their lower reserve ratios can be explained by the fact that they do not have to meet official reserve requirements. Also Eurobanks' deposit liabilities, being essentially time deposits, are less liquid than the demand deposits faced by the domestic US banking system. This too enables Eurobanks to hold lower cash reserve ratios. Furthermore, they can hold lower reserves because of their ability to speedily raise funds at competitive interest rates on the Euromarkets, while domestic banks that find themselves short of money raise their funds at penal interest rates from their central bank, which encourages them to hold higher cash reserves.

■ *12.7* Alternative views of the Euromarkets

The more recent literature on Euromarkets has rejected the application of the preceding multiplier analysis to Euromarkets, arguing that they need to be viewed in a very different light. There are a number of recent interpretations that are worth reviewing.

Hewson and Sakakibara (1974 and 1976) have argued that rather than there being a Eurocurrency multiplier there is a Euromarket divider (that is, a multiplier of less than unity)! They argue that Euromarkets need to be treated in a general equilibrium framework that takes account of the effects of Euromarket deposits on interest rates and the demand for loans. An illustration of their basic argument runs as follows: an increase in deposits of $100 million to Euromarkets will depress both Eurodeposits deposit and loan rates. Although the lower interest rates will lead to a rise in the demand for Euroloans, it will also lead to some withdrawal of Eurodeposits of say $20 million. Thus, the maximum the Euromarkets could lend out is $80 million. In other words, the Euromultiplier is less than unity. This argument is depicted in **Figure 12.2**.

Figure 12.2 depicts the supply and demand for Eurodollars. For simplicity, the loan and deposit rates are assumed to be identical and given by $r1$ and that no deposits are held as reserves. At interest rate $r1$ total Eurodeposits and Euroloans are given by $E1$. If there is a shift of US bank deposits to the Euromarket of $E1E2$ there is a shift of the supply schedule from $S1$ to $S2$. The point made by Hewson and Sakakibara is that the increased supply of Euroloans will depress the loan and deposit rates to $r2$. The lower deposit interest rate will lead to some outflow of funds from the Euromarket, the supply of deposits contracts along the $S2$ schedule to $E3$. Hence, an increase in Eurodeposits of $E1E2$ leads to an eventual rise in Euromarket deposits and loans of only $E1 E3$. As $E1E3 < E1E2$ then the Euromultiplier will be less than unity, the precise value being determined by the elasticity of the supply and demand schedules.

Dufey and Giddy (1978) have argued that the Eurodollar market is essentially a substitute for the domestic dollar market on both the deposit and loan side. In the first instance, the deposits they attract are essentially

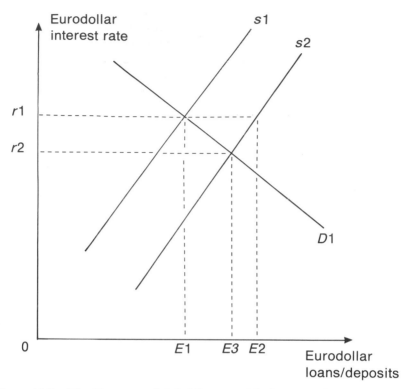

Figure 12.2   *The Hewson and Sakakibara model of Euromarkets*

taken away from the US banking system, while the loans that they make are likewise substitutes for loans by the US banks. This being the case, the Eurodollar multiplier is not a particularly relevant concept.

More recently Hogan and Pearce (1982) have challenged the traditional multiplier analysis of the Eurobanking system. They argue that the rapid growth of Eurocurrency markets is due to one set of countries being in persistent balance of payments surplus and another group in persistent deficit.

Hogan and Pearce's basic argument can be illustrated with a simple example. Imagine that there is a country called Surplusia which has a persistent current account surplus (i.e. it earns more foreign exchange than it spends) and another country called Deficitsia which has a persistent current account deficit (i.e. it spends more foreign exchange than it earns). Say that residents of a third country Balancia which has a current account balance of zero, deposit some of their currency, which is extremely popular on the international money markets (let's call them Balancia dollars), with Surplusia banks. The banks in Surplusia have surplus funds made up of Balancia's currency; these funds are effectively Eurodollars since they are Balancia dollars held in Surplusia. The Eurobanks could lend these funds to Deficitsia to help finance its deficit. By borrowing Balancia's dollars from Surplusia's Eurobanks, Deficitsia has effectively avoided having to take measures to reduce its deficit, such as harsh macroeconomic policies to reduce import expenditure, devaluation or running down its foreign exchange reserves. So long as Surplusia is running a surplus and its Eurobanks are receiving the amount of the surplus in funds of Balancia dollars, its Eurobanks can go on lending money to Deficitsia year after year.

If the cycle goes on for a number of years the outstanding loans to Deficitsia in Balancia's currency will grow and grow. The Eurobanks of Surplusia will have increasing amounts of loans to Defitcitsia (their assets) and similarly increasing deposits of Balancia's currency from Surplusia residents (their liabilities). Hogan and Pearce are very concerned about the fact that Euromarkets enable deficit countries to finance their deficits with relative ease and believe that Euromarkets encourage excessive borrowing. Further, deficit countries can avoid the need to pursue prudent macroeconomic policies. Hogan and Pearce are so concerned about these possibilities that they advocate Euromarket's 'immediate death should be engineered with a maximum of speed and minimum of fuss.' (pp. 127–8).

A number of points follow from Hogan and Pearce's interpretation of the growth of Euromarkets. The rate of growth of Eurobanking activity, i.e. Eurodollar loans and deposits, is determined by the size of the balance of payments deficits of Deficitsia and the willingness of Deficitsia's government to borrow from the Euromarkets to finance these deficits. Another point is that the Surplusia's Eurobanks do not create the Eurodollars; each dollar loan made to Deficitsia is backed by a deposit of Balancia dollars. The role of the Eurobanks is that of a financial intermediary; the rate of growth of the Euromarkets in Surplusia is not dependent upon the creation of new dollars by the central Bank of Balancia as is the case with the Eurodollar multiplier interpretation of Euromarkets. Indeed, the growth of the Eurodollar market did not even require a surplus of deficit on the part of Balancia which had a current account balance of zero.

The Eurobanks of Surplusia are essentially financial intermediaries who receive deposits and make loans. Unlike domestic banks, the liabilities of Surplusia's Eurobanks are time deposits which receive interest rather than sight deposits which do not, that is, they are not part of the narrow definition of the money supply (notes and coins plus sight deposits). Eurobanking activity by Surplusia's Eurobanks does not lead to the creation of new Balancia dollars.

However, there are a number of dangers that could hit Surplusia's Eurobanking system. One might be that after a number of years, Deficitsia has over-borrowed from Surplusia and does not wish to repay: this might provoke a crisis of confidence in Surplusia's banking system. Another problem might be that depositors of dollars in Surplusia's Eurobanks get concerned at the growing size of Surplusia's Eurobanks' exposure to Deficitsia. If they tried to withdraw their dollars deposits from the Eurobanks then two options would be left to Surplusia's Eurobanks: (i) borrow dollars from Balancia's domestic banks or (ii) call in loans from Deficitsia. If Balancia's banks have spare lending capacity then any loans extended to the Eurobanks would lead to the creation of more Balancia dollars; however, it is not Surplusia's Eurobanks that create the dollars, it is Balancia's banking system. If, however, Balancia's banks had no spare lending capacity then Surplusia's Eurobanks would be forced to call in their loans from Deficitsia and the growth of Euromarkets would cease.

Although Hogan and Pearce's views of Euromarkets helps explain the growth of Eurobanking activity, it is not so clear that Eurobanks are doing any harm. It must be emphasised that Eurobanks ultimately act as the intermediaries for the recycling of funds because they are the most efficient institutions for doing this. If they were less efficient than the banking system of Balancia, then Balancia's banks would attract Surplusia's surplus funds and recycle them to Deficitsia, i.e. the real reason for the growth of Surplusia's Eurobanking is the fact that they offer the best return on deposits and charge less for loans. Where Hogan and Pearce's concern is more relevant is if Eurobanks lend money to deficit countries and the money is not wisely used by the deficit countries. In this case, the deficit countries may well have problems repaying and Eurobanks could find themselves in difficulty. However, the problem here is not really Eurobank activity per se but poor bank lending. There is nothing wrong with sound bank lending, be it by Eurobanks or domestic banks.

In the 1970s there was a great deal of recycling of petrodollars by Eurobanks to a number of Latin American countries which had received much of the dollar surpluses of the Oil Petroleum Exporting Countries to finance their deficits. However, a great deal of the financing of these deficits was also carried out by US domestic banks. The fact that much of this lending eventually proved to be unwise (see Chapter 15) is not just a judgement against much Eurobank lending but also against the lending policies of many domestic US banks.

 ## *12.8* Euromarkets and currency and country risks

Another useful function of Eurocurrency markets is that they enable investors to separate out currency and country risks. If dollar funds are deposited on the US money market, then country and currency risks cannot be disentangled. While domestic deposits are secure because of Federal deposit insurance and the fact that the Federal Reserve is unlikely to allow a major US based bank to go into liquidation, this is not so for Eurodollar deposits. If a deposit of Eurodollars is made in London then the investor has the currency risk associated with holding dollars but the country risk associated with England. If the investor prefers the country risk associated with Germany then a Eurodollar deposit can be made in Germany. Eurodeposits may be subject to some degree of liquidity risk in that Eurobanks do maintain lower levels of reserves than domestic banks. However, the close matching of the maturity structure of loans with those of deposits probably makes this risk minimal for Eurobanks.

One particular aspect of Eurobank lending that has come under increasing scrutiny has been the default risk involved. Much of the lending of Eurobanks in the 1970s was to developing country governments, especially to Latin America. The problem with such lending is that there is normally no collateral held as security against the loan and should the foreign government default on its repayments there is no international court to enforce repayment of the loan. As we shall see in Chapter 15, there may have been a problem with much of the Eurocurrency lending of the 1970s in that individual syndicates failed to take into account the increased risk of default to other syndicates when making Euroloans. This is especially the case where a series of interbank transactions have separated the initial Eurobank from the ultimate borrower.

12.9 Euromarkets and government regulation and policy

While domestic banking has remained subject to various regulatory requirements this is not the case with Euromarkets. Examples of two of the most commonly used regulations governing domestic banking activities are reserve requirements imposed by the authorities to limit domestic banks' ability to create credit, and deposit insurance designed to protect depositors should the bank become insolvent.

The lack of regulation governing Eurobanks has often led to calls for some degree of international regulation of their activities. In particular, given the amount of interbank lending on the Euromarkets there has always been a fear that were one Eurobank to fail this could trigger the failure of many Eurobanks. This being the case, the need for effective regulation has been regarded as important in ensuring that Eurobanks conduct their business in a sound manner. However, effective regulation of Eurobanks is fraught with problems. Say the US authorities were to regulate US Eurobanks, all this would be likely to do is to shift Eurobanking activities to non-US Eurobanks. Similarly, if regulation is exercised by a particular Eurobanking centre such as London then all this would be likely to do is to shift Eurobanking business to other non-regulated centres. Unilateral regulation by one particular government or Eurobanking centre is unlikely to lead to greater regulation of Eurobanking activity because it most probably would result in a shift of Eurobanking business to unregulated Eurobanks and centres.

It would seem that effective regulation of Eurobanking activities would require multilateral regulation and guidelines. However, given the high degree of competition for Eurobanking business such multilateral cooperation is unlikely to be forthcoming.

The very fact that Eurobanks have managed to grow rapidly because of the lack of regulation of their activities has probably had the effect of reducing the degree of regulation covering domestic banking activity. Once a regulation is applied to a domestic banking activity, it is often the case that the business is diverted to the Eurobanks where it is free of the constraint. Furthermore, the desire to bring some Eurobank business back to the domestic banking arena has often acted as a stimulus to the relaxation of domestic regulations.

■ *12.10* Conclusions

The growth of Eurobanking activity has been blamed for no end of things ranging from the breakdown of the Bretton Woods system, to the rise in worldwide inflation and the Third World debt crisis. In reality, the Eurobanks provide services that are clearly in demand as is verified by their rapid growth. In particular, their competitive deposit and lending rates prove to be attractive for both investors and borrowers of funds.

Eurobanks have been largely responsible for the increased degree of financial integration between economies and they perform a particularly important role in recycling funds from surplus to deficit countries. While this increased financial integration has made monetary control more difficult for domestic authorities, it must be concluded that the Euromarkets themselves have not had a particularly inflationary impact upon the world economy. Although a switch from domestic to Eurodeposits frees some reserves for additional lending the overall effect on liquidity is not particularly significant and is not necessarily undesirable.

In the end, it is clear that Eurobanks have not had a harmful effect on the way economies work and their overall macroeconomic importance has frequently been exaggerated. Many of the transactions carried out by Eurobanks would be undertaken in their absence by domestic banks only less efficiently so. Eurobanks have expanded rapidly partly because the demand for their services has expanded with the increased degree of trade among nations. Much of this business has ultimately gone to Eurobanks rather than domestic banks because they have a competitive advantage in the provision of the requisite banking services.

■ Selected further readings

Einzig, P.A. (1973) *The Eurodollar System* (New York: St Martin's Press).

Dufey, G. and Giddy, I. (1978) *The International Money Market* (Englewood Cliffs, N.J.: Prentice-Hall).

Friedman, M. (1969) 'The Eurodollar Market: Some First Principles', *Morgan Guaranty Survey* (October), pp. 4–14.

Hewson, J. (1975) *Liquidity Creation and Distribution in the Euro-Currency Markets* (Cambridge, Mass: Lexington Books).

Hewson, J. and Sakakibara, E. (1974) 'The Eurodollar Multiplier: A Portfolio Approach', *IMF Staff Papers*, vol. 21, pp. 307–28.

Hewson, J. and Sakakibara, E. (1976) 'A General Equilibrium Approach to the Euro-Dollar Market', *Journal of Money Credit and Banking*, vol. 8, pp. 297–323.

Hogan, W.P. and Pearce, I.F. (1982) *The Incredible Eurodollar* (London: George Allen and Unwin).

Klopstock, F. (1968) 'The Euro-dollar Market: Some Unresolved Issues', *Princeton Essays in International Finance*, Princeton, No. 65.

Mayer, H.W. (1970) 'Some Theoretical Problems Relating to the Eurodollar Market', *Princeton Essays in International Finance*, Princeton, No. 79.

McKinnon, R.I. (1977) 'The Eurocurrency Market', *Princeton Essays in International Finance* (Princeton, No. 125.

McKinnon, R.I. (1979) *Money in International Exchange* (Oxford: Oxford University Press).

Niehans, J. and Hewson, J. (1976) 'The Eurodollar Market and Monetary Theory', *Journal of Money Credit and Banking* (vol. 8, pp. 1–27:).

Swoboda, A.K. (1968) 'The Eurodollar Market: an Interpretation', *Princeton Essays in International Finance*, Princeton, No. 64.

Swoboda, A.K. (1980) 'Credit Creation in the Euro-Market: Alternative Theories and the Implications for Control', Occasional Paper No. 2 (New York: Group of Thirty).

■ *Chapter 13* ■

International Macroeconomic Policy Coordination

■ *13.1* Introduction

For the majority of this text, we have confined our analysis to the study of a small open economy. By definition the policy measures taken by such an economy have no significant impact upon its trading partners. The small economy assumption is useful in that it makes it plausible to ignore possible reactions to its policies from trading partners. In the real world, however, the actions taken by one country will often have significant effects upon its trading partners. This means that the countries are interdependent and policy measures adopted by one of the economies may provoke a reaction from its trading partners that can reinforce, weaken or even offset its policy. Where such interdependence exists it is frequently argued that countries should consider coordinating their macroeconomic policies to avert the possibility of conflict and improve their positions as compared with pursuing unilateral policies.

In this chapter, we shall look at some of the major issues raised by the topic of international macroeconomic policy coordination. These issues include:

● What is meant by coordination of economic policies?

- Why does the need for international policy coordination arise?
- Is coordination always superior to non coordination?
- What are the obstacles that prevent greater international coordination?

 ## 13.2 What is meant by international policy coordination?

International policy coordination is a very loose term and is sometimes used interchangeably with the word cooperation and the proper distinction between the two terms is not clearly defined in the literature. Perhaps the most useful distinction is that made by Henry Wallich:

> 'Cooperation' falls well short of 'coordination', a concept which implies a significant modification of national policies in recognition of inter-national economic interdependence. But 'cooperation' is more than 'consultation', which may mean little more than that other interested parties will be kept informed.(1984, p. 85)

Notwithstanding this distinction, we shall use the term coordination throughout this chapter although the lower levels of coordination such as the exchange of information might be considered more appropriately as examples of cooperation.

International policy coordination is primarily about some form of co-operative relationship between the policy makers/authorities of two or more nations. Thus, international policy coordination does not *per se* directly involve the private sector. As we shall see, this latter point is important because an arrangement made between national authorities might be undermined by a suspicious private sector. To provide an operational framework for the discussion we shall distinguish between a hierarchy of three types of coordination; the exchange of information; the acceptance of mutually consistent policies and joint action.

☐ *The exchange of information*

A minimal type of coordination is the exchange of information between the authorities of two or more countries. This exchange may be on a limited or quite considerable scale. The type of information that might be exchanged includes the authorities' views about the appropriate value of the exchange rate, the present and future course of their domestic macroeconomic policies and intentions with regard to future exchange market intervention, economic forecasts and principal objectives of economic policies etc. The exchange of information will not by itself lead to agreement on what are the appropriate macroeconomic polices, let alone joint action. As such, it represents a minimal level of coordination. What it is likely to lead to is a better understanding of how conflict can be averted and where the greatest uncertainty lies.

☐ *Mutually consistent policies*

The exchange of information may provide the basis for more active coordination in that the countries concerned accept either formally or informally to adopt consistent macroeconomic policy stances. Each country takes into account the aims and policies stance of other countries when formulating its own policy stance. Coordination at this level means the authorities pursue mutually compatible target values and adjust the selection of policy instruments, their magnitude and timing to avoid conflict with other countries. Such coordination requires an exchange of information with other countries and that account be taken of the policies and objectives being pursued in other countries.

☐ *Joint action*

Having exchanged information and agreed on mutually consistent target values for the objectives of economic policy, the authorities of the two economies could go one step further and agree on joint action to achieve desired targets. For example, if a certain value of the real exchange rate is required to achieve these objectives, joint action would mean that the two authorities act together to manipulate the exchange rate in the desired direction. Joint action means not only an agreement on the appropriate exchange-rate value but also concerted action to achieve that rate. As we shall see, much of the recent literature on macroeconomic policy coordination has focused mainly on two types of joint action. One is when fiscal and monetary policies are adjusted to maximise joint welfare, the other is when the exchange rate is jointly targeted. Some proposals for policy coordination combine fiscal and monetary policies with some form of exchange-rate targeting.

13.3 Why does the need for international policy coordination arise?

Coordination of macroeconomic and exchange rate policies would not be necessary if exchange rate changes truly insulated one country from another as advocates of floating exchange rates had presupposed. In such circumstances, one economy would not be affected by the policy mix pursued in other economies. Experience with floating exchange rates has amply demonstrated that such independence does not exist. In particular, the phenomenon of exchange-rate 'overshooting' (see Chapter 7) means that the monetary policy pursued in one country will have spillover effects on its trading partners. An initial money expansion will lead to a depreciation of the expanding country's real exchange rate conferring on it a competitive advantage. However, the real exchange rate of its trading partners will have appreciated, reducing their exports and thereby their income and employment levels.

Economic policy coordination is only necessary if economic policies themselves have effects upon the real economy. If monetary and fiscal policies have no effect on employment and output levels as some theorists argue, then there would be no benefits to be derived from international coordination of such policies. As Alfred Steinherr puts it:

> In a world where markets for all possible trades exist ('completeness of markets'), where all markets, including the labour market, are competitive and all prices fully flexible, where all agents are rational and adjustment costs of pricing and input decisions negligible there is no need for adjustment policies, and therefore no need for coordination. Each economy would then adjust instantaneously to any surprises ('shocks') and operate at its natural employment level and there would be no overshooting of the exchange rate. Thus the need for policy coordination may from this angle be regarded as due to market imperfections. According to this view reduction of imperfections would reduce the need for policy intervention and coordination, and act as a substitute for coordination. Needless to say, not all imperfections can be eliminated in the real world. As a consequence policies can potentially improve the market outcome and, in interdependent economies, produce spillover effects.(1984, p. 77)

Frenkel (1983) points out that spillover effects that give rise to the need for coordination are the result of two important linkages between the domestic economy and the rest of the world. In the first instance, countries are connected via trade flows; the exports of one country are the imports of another and vice versa. Changes in these volumes will affect the national incomes of the countries concerned and with it employment levels. The second vital linkage is that provided by international capital movements; these permit the transmission of economic disturbances from one economy to another by freeing an economy from the need to keep its current account in balance. In this way, policies that influence the current account position of a country will have spillover effects on its trading partners' current account positions. Capital movements also have the effect of tying international interest rate differentials and expected exchange rate changes via the uncovered interest parity condition. As such, policies that influence the domestic interest rate will have effects on trading partners via induced changes in the real exchange rate.

In effect, the need for coordination is derived from spillover effects associated with interdependence. Cooper (1985) defines structural interdependence as a situation whereby the structures of two or more economies are such, that economic events in one significantly influence economic events in the others. Hence, if economic policies adopted in one country affect its real economy then they will also have spillover effects on other countries. In such circumstances, the optimal course of action for one country will depend upon the course of action taken by other countries. Interdependence means that a country cannot achieve its objectives without these being mutually consistent with those pursued by other countries. Furthermore, the resulting policy interdependence means that a country has to take into account the policies of other countries. This implies the need for a certain degree of international policy coordination if countries wish to achieve their objectives. The need is especially acute where the trade and capital linkages are high such as those which exists between the EEC member states.

As an illustration of the interdependence between economies **Table 13.1** presents the results of the effects of monetary and fiscal expansion by the US and non-US OECD countries according to a variety of well known models of the international economy.

13.4 The benefits from international policy coordination

When one talks about the benefits to be derived from international policy coordination these will be dependent upon the type and degree of coordination undertaken. In general terms coordination is a means of preserving and improving the benefits associated with increased interdependence such as the gains from trade and access to international capital markets. In this section, we examine from a theoretical viewpoint the potential benefits from coordination.

The potential gains from coordination of macroeconomic policies internationally have been conceptually illustrated by Hamada (1974 and 1985) using what has become known as the Hamada diagram. The principles underlying the derivation of the Hamada diagram for the hypothetical case of Europe and America are depicted in **Figure 13.1**.

Table 13.1   Simulation effects of monetary and fiscal policy changes*

International model	Monetary expansion†								Fiscal expansion‡							
	In US				In non-US OECD				In US				In non-US OECD			
	GNP effect (in percent)		CA effect ($billions)		GNP effect (in percent)		CA effect ($billions)		GNP effect (in percent)		CA effect ($billions)		GNP effect (in percent)		CA effect ($billions)	
	D	F	D	F	D	F	D	F	D	F	D	F	D	F	D	F
MCM	+1.5	−0.7	−3.1	−3.5	+1.5	0	+3.5	+0.1	+1.8	+0.7	−16.5	+8.9	+1.4	+0.5	−7.2	+7.9
EEC	+1.0	+0.2	−2.8	+1.2	+0.8	+0.1	−5.2	+1.9	+1.2	+0.3	−11.6	+6.6	+1.3	+0.2	−9.3	+3.0
EPA	+1.2	−0.4	−1.6	−10.1	0	0	−0.1	+0.1	+1.7	+0.9	−20.5	+9.3	+2.3	+0.3	−13.1	+4.7
LINK	+1.0	−0.1	−5.9	+1.5	+0.8	+0.1	−1.4	+3.5	+1.2	+0.1	−6.4	+1.9	+1.2	+0.2	−6.1	+6.3
LIVERPOOL	+0.1	0	−13.0	+0.1	+0.4	+1.6	+7.1	−8.2	+0.6	0	−7.0	+3.4	+0.3	−0.5	−17.2	+11.9
MSG	+0.3	+0.4	+2.6	−4.4	+0.2	+0.3	−15.9	+12.0	+0.9	+0.3	−21.6	+22.7	+1.1	+0.4	−5.3	+10.5
MINIMOD	+1.0	−0.2	+2.8	−4.7	+0.8	−0.3	+3.6	−1.4	+1.0	+0.3	−8.5	+5.5	+1.6	+0.1	−2.2	+3.2
VAR	+3.0	+0.4	+4.9	+5.1	+0.7	+1.2	+5.2	−10.0	+0.4	0	−0.5	−0.2	+0.5	+0.3	+1.7	−2.6
OECD	+1.6	+0.3	−8.4	+3.1	+0.8	+0.1	−1.6	+2.3	+1.1	+0.4	−14.2	+11.4	+1.5	+0.1	−6.9	+3.3
Taylor	+0.6	−0.2	—	—	+0.8	−0.1	—	—	+0.6	+0.4	—	—	+1.6	+0.6	—	—
Wharton	+0.7	+0.4	−5.1	+5.3	+0.2	0	+2.6	+0.5	+1.4	+0.2	−15.4	+5.3	+3.2	0	−5.5	+4.7
DRI	+1.8	−0.6	−1.4	+14.5	—	—	—	—	+2.1	+0.7	−22.0	+0.8	—	—	—	—
Average§	+1.2	0	−2.8	+0.7	+0.6	+0.3	−0.2	+0.1	+1.2	+0.4	−13.1	+6.9	+1.5	+0.2	−7.1	+5.3

*Effects on gross national product (GNP) and current account (CA) of respective domestic (D) and foreign economies (F).
†Increase in the money supply of 4 per cent phased in over four quarters.
‡Increase in government expenditure equal to 1 per cent of GNP.
§Average of the reporting models.

MCM, Federal Reserve Board; EEC, European Commission; EPA, Japanese Economic Planning Agency; LINK, Project Link; LIVERPOOL, Patrick Minford; MSG, McKibbin-Sachs; MINIMOD, Haas-Masson (IMF); VAR, Sims-Litterman; OECD, Interlink; Taylor, Stanford; Wharton, DRI, Data resources.
Source: J.A. Frankel and K.E. Rockett, 'International Policy Coordination when Policymakers Do Not Agree on the True Model', *American Economic Review*, vol. 78, No. 3, pp. 318–340.

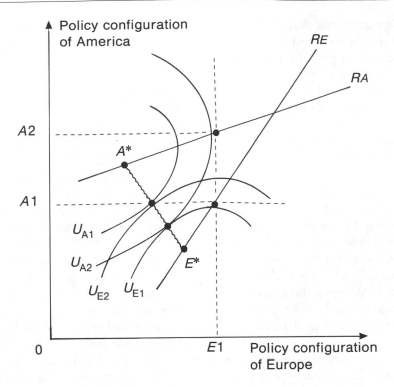

Figure 13.1   *The derivation of the Hamada diagram*

In the Hamada diagram, the macro policy configuration of Europe is shown on the horizontal axis, while the macro policy configuration of America is shown on the vertical axis. For instance, as we move along the horizontal axis the macro policy stance of Europe may be more expansionary, and likewise as we move up the vertical axis for America. Because the two countries are interdependent the optimal policy stance for Europe is dependent upon the policy stance taken by America and vice versa.

Conceptually, there must be a point on the diagram for Europe that gives a combination of its own policy stance and that of America which it prefers to all other possible policy combinations. This point of bliss for Europe is given by point E^*. Likewise, for America there must be a combination of its own policy and that of Europe that it prefers to all other policy combinations and this is given by point A^*.

For both Europe and America we can draw sets of elliptically shaped indifference curves U_E and U_A that denote combinations of European and American policies that yield the same level of utility. From the viewpoint of Europe, the closer the policy configuration of the two economies puts it on a utility curve U_E to point E^* the better off it is. Hence, a combined policy configuration that puts it on utility curve U_{E1} is preferred to U_{E2}. Similarly, from the viewpoint of America, the closer the policy configuration of the two countries puts it on a utility curve to point A^*, the better off it is. A combined policy configuration that puts it on utility curve U_{A1} is preferred to U_{A2}. In the special case where the two countries are totally independent the utility curves for Europe are vertical straight lines and the utility curves for America are horizontal straight lines. Each country could then achieve its optimal level of welfare merely by adjusting its own policy instruments regardless of the policy pursued by the other country.

The problem for each economy is to determine its optimal policy stance for any given policy stance of the other. This yields a policy reaction schedule for each economy. The policy reaction schedule for Europe is found by taking a given policy stance of America and finding a utility curve U_E which is tangential to it. This is the utility closest to point E^*, which means Europe adopts policy stance $E1$ when the US is pursuing policy $A1$. One can find various other optimal policy stances of Europe given a different policy stance by America and joining the points together gives the policy reaction function of Europe as RE. Similarly, the policy reaction schedule for America is found by taking a given policy stance of Europe such as $E1$ and finding a utility curve U_{A2} which is tangential to a vertical line from $E1$. This is the utility curve closest to point A^* which means America's best policy stance is $A2$. In a like manner, one can find various other optimal policy stances of America given a different policy stance by Europe and joining the points together gives the policy reaction function of America as RA.

The locus of points passing between E^* and A^*, where the utility curves U_E and U_A are tangential to one another is known as the Pareto contract curve. Since the indifference curves are tangential to one another along the contract curve this indicates that one country can be made better off only by making the other country worse off. In the region of the contract curve between E^* and A^* the closer we are to point E^* (the further from point A^*) the better off is Europe and the worse off is America. Conversely, the closer we are to point A^* (the further from point E^*) the better off is America and the worse off is Europe.

We can now use the Hamada diagram to illustrate the potential gains from the coordination of macro policies between the two economies. This is illustrated in **Figure 13.2**.

To establish potential gains from international macro policy coordination it is necessary to compare the possible situation under coordination *vis-à-vis* a scenario of non-coordination. The problem is that there is a range of possible coordination scenarios and likewise one could envisage a range of non-coordination scenarios. **Figure 13.2** compares possible coordination scenarios with two popular non-coordination scenarios known as Nash and Stackleberg equilibriums.

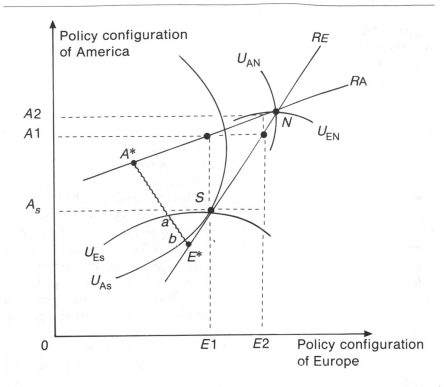

Figure 13.2 *Coordination and non-coordination in the Hamada diagram*

In the Nash non-cooperative scenario each economy takes the policy stance of its partner economy as beyond its influence and adopts its optimal isolationist policy in this belief. If Europe pursues policy $E1$ the optimal policy for America is $A1$, but given the US pursues $A1$ the optimal policy for Europe is $E2$; given Europe pursues $E2$ the optimal policy for America is $A2$ and so on. The economies continue to interact in this manner despite the fact that each economy's policy strategy choice does influence the choice of the other. A Nash equilibrium is finally reached when there is no incentive for either economy to change its policy stance, taking the other's policy as given. In the Hamada diagram the Nash equilibrium is given by point N where the two reaction schedules intersect. At point N there is no incentive for either economy to change its policies. America is on utility curve U_{AN} while Europe is on utility curve U_{EN}.

With the Stackleberg scenario, one of the two countries (the leader) is assumed to be more intelligent than in the Nash scenario and realises that its policy stance influences the choice of the other country, while the other (the follower) ignores the influence of its policy stance on the leader. Consequently, the leader anticipates possible rational reactions of the follower when making its policy choice. In **Figure 13.2** we assume that America is the leader and this leads to a Stackleberg equilibrium at point S. At point S there is a utility curve U_{AS} just tangential to Europe's reaction schedule RE. This is the closest indifference curve to point A^* that America can reach knowing the whole range of possible reactions of Europe. With America pursuing Stackleberg policy AS the best policy for Europe is $E1$.

When comparing the Nash and Stackleberg non cooperative equilibriums the Stackleberg solution is certainly superior for the leader compared with the Nash solution and may or may not prove superior to the Nash solution for the follower. However, both the non cooperative scenarios are Pareto inefficient since they do not lie on the contract curve E^*A^*. In theory, both economies could agree to adopt policy combinations that make them both better off compared with either the Nash or Stackleberg non-cooperative scenarios. For example, between the portion ab on the contract curve A^*E^* both countries would be on higher utility curves compared with the Stackleberg scenario. Hence, with coordination of economic policies the level of welfare of both economies can be raised as compared with non-coordination. If the economies agree to coordinate to get onto the contract curve, the precise position they get to depends upon their relative bargaining strengths. The stronger the relative bargaining power of Europe the closer the position on the contract curve will be to point E^*, while the stronger the bargaining position of America the closer the solution on the contract curve will be to A^*.

In passing, we note that if both countries were to try to become a Stackleberg leader a situation known as 'Stackleberg warfare' would break out. This has no equilibrium solution because the assumptions each country makes are mutually inconsistent.

13.5 A game theory demonstration of the gains from coordination

The Stackleberg and Nash solutions illustrated by the Hamada diagram are demonstrations of the results of traditional game theory. Simple game theory is usually presented as a pay-off matrix, an example of which is set out in **Table 13.2**.

Table 13.2 depicts what is known in game theory as a pay-off matrix. We assume that the pay-off to each economy is measured by a 'misery index' – the misery index is simply the sum of an economy's inflation and unemployment rates. For simplicity of exposition we shall assume that policy makers regard an additional 1 per cent of inflation to be equally as bad as an additional 1 per cent of unemployment. This being the case, the aim of economic policy will be to minimise an economy's misery index. The first

Table 13.2 *A game theory pay-off matrix demonstration of the gains from coordination*

		Europe	
		Policy 1	*Policy 2*
	Policy 3	12,12	15,6
America			
	Policy 4	7,15	8,8

Note:
Read pay-off as; Europe, America.

figure of each of the two figures separated by a comma is the misery index (pay-off) of Europe while the second is the pay-off of America. For example, if Europe pursues policy 1 and America pursues policy 4 the result will be a misery index of 7 for Europe and 15 for America. Similarly, if Europe pursues policy 2 while America pursues policy 3, the pay-off will be a misery index of 15 for Europe and 6 for America.

Using the pay-off matrix it is straightforward to illustrate the potential gains from coordination of policies. Suppose that each economy seeks to minimise its misery index but chooses its policy package in isolation without any coordination. When deciding whether or not to pursue policy 1 or policy 2 Europe does not know what policy will be chosen by America. Hence, the authorities of Europe will consider the consequences if America pursues either policy 3 or policy 4. If America were to pursue policy 3, the best policy for Europe is policy 1 which gives it a misery index of 12 compared with 15 if it pursued policy 2. If America were to pursue policy 4, the best policy for Europe is again policy 1 which gives it a misery index of 7 compared with a misery index of 8 were it to employ policy 2. Hence, no matter what policy is chosen by America the best isolationist policy for Europe to pursue is policy 1. An analogous set of reasoning applies to the policy choice of America. If Europe pursues policy 1, the best policy for America is policy 3 giving a misery index of 12 compared with 15 if it pursues policy 4. Likewise, if Europe pursues policy 2 the best policy for America is again policy 3 which gives a misery index of 6 as opposed to 8 if it pursues policy 4. Hence, no matter what policy is chosen by Europe the best isolationist policy for America to pursue is policy 3.

The result of each making its policy decisions in isolation is that Europe pursues policy 1 while America pursues policy 3. The resulting misery index for both economies is 12. This non-coordination scenario is worse for both economies than if they were to engage in coordination. By coordination Europe could agree to pursue policy 2 and America agree to pursue policy 4. This policy configuration gives both countries a misery index of only 8, which is superior to the 12 of acting in isolation.

One of the problems for such cooperative agreements is that once there is an agreement there may be incentives for one or more parties to renege on the agreement. Suppose Europe and America agree to cooperate and pursue policies 2 and 4 respectively. If Europe is sure that America will adopt the agreed policy 4 then the best policy for Europe to pursue is not policy 2 to which it agreed, but rather policy 1. Similarly, if America is sure that Europe will pursue policy 2 then the best policy for it to pursue is policy 3 rather than policy 4. Hence, it is possible that cooperative agreements will be undermined at times by reneging by one or more parties to the agreement. As such, there may need to be stiff penalties against parties that renege and a monitoring system designed to spot any reneging country.

 ## 13.6 Other potential benefits from coordination

The Hamada diagram and pay-off matrix illustrations provide simple demonstrations of the potential gains to be had from international policy coordination. However, the analysis is simple in that each country is assumed to know the range of potential policies that the other country could pursue and can also calculate the consequences of various policy combinations on its own welfare. In the real world we can expect some gains from coordination that are not well illustrated by traditional game theory. These include:

A reduction of uncertainty – one of the major benefits to be expected from cooperation is that it should help reduce the uncertainty element associated with the implementation of policy. When economies are interdependent, the course of action that a country should take will be difficult to decide in isolation because the optimal policy will depend upon the policy actions taken by the other country. In the real world a country rarely knows the course of action that will be taken by other economies and their probable reactions to changes in its own policy stance. Coordination has the potential to reduce the possibility of serious conflict. An exchange of information improves the information set available to the authorities enabling them to pursue superior policies than could be pursued without such information. In the absence of an information exchange, there may be serious shortcomings in policy design, particularly with regard to miscalculation about the reactions of foreign authorities. Such errors could prove very costly in today's interdependent economies. Furthermore, the reduced possibility of conflict will improve the environment in which international trade is conducted.

Coordination may avoid excessive deflation – Oudiz and Sachs(1985) point out that coordination may prove crucial to improving welfare when the foreign exchange market is forward looking. One way that authorities may be tempted to control inflation in isolation is to announce today that money supply growth will be lower in the future. If such an announcement is believed, the authorities of that country will benefit from an immediate real appreciation of their currency reducing present inflation. The other country, however, will experience a real depreciation of its currency giving a boost to its inflation rate. In the absence of coordination both countries may be tempted to engage in competitive announcements of intentions to control future monetary growth. Only a coordination agreement between the two countries to avoid such a competitive manipulation of the exchange rate can remove the danger of excessive deflation.

 ## *13.7* The potential for coordination to make countries worse off

There is an intuitive inclination to believe that international policy coordination must improve the welfare of each of the countries involved and thereby global welfare as compared with non-coordination scenarios. This intuition runs as follows: since at worse countries could cooperatively agree to pursue similar policies as in a non-coordination scenario then the policies they choose under coordination must be superior or they would have pursued the non-cooperative policies. However, the recent literature has shown that this is not necessarily the case. There are three instances in which coordination between two or more countries may make the participating countries worse off rather than better off. One involves an unfavourable reaction by private agents to coordination between authorities. Another involves an unfavourable reaction by third countries to coordination between a subset of countries. A final instance involves coordination making countries worse off because the policies pursued are based on the wrong economic model.

☐ *The reaction of private agents*

Kenneth Rogoff (1985) pointed out that coordination between national authorities is only potentially superior to non-coordination because it is necessary to take into account the reaction of the private sector. The basic argument put forward by Rogoff is that the behaviour of private agents cannot be considered by the authorities as indifferent to any arrangements that they come to with trading partners. Rogoff argues that an adverse reaction by private agents to a cooperative arrangement between national authorities can make things worse rather than better.

Specifically, Rogoff considers the case where national authorities seek to raise the level of employment in their economies in a model in which there is exchange rate overshooting. Acting in isolation, each country resists the temptation to inflate because they realise that this will lead to a real depreciation of their currencies which will raise import costs and lead to a quick upward adjustment to domestic wages and prices. If, however, the central banks come to an agreement to inflate together to raise employment levels, they can overcome the fear of a depreciation of their real exchange rate. This means that with coordination the incentives to inflate are greater. Rogoff argues that rational private agents will take this additional inflation risk into account when setting their wage contracts and raise their wage demands accordingly. In such circumstances, the authorities may face a higher average inflation rate in a coordination regime than acting in isolation.

The possibility that coordination between authorities may lead to a deterioration in global welfare stems from a credibility problem *vis-à-vis* the private sector. Rogoff suggests that a way out of this credibility problem is for the authorities to make credible institutional commitments not to inflate as part of their coordination. This would then remove private agents' mistrust of the authorities enabling them to coordinate to improve global welfare.

☐ The reaction of third countries

It is conceivable that coordination between two or more countries that would ordinarily raise their joint welfare could provoke an adverse reaction by third countries. If an adverse reaction by third countries has a significant negative impact on the coordinating countries then it is possible that the cooperating countries end up worse off. For example, Europe and America might decide to deflate their economies in their joint interest but because of the adverse effects for Japanese exports this may lead Japan to deflate its economy which then exacerbates the recession in America and Europe above what they anticipated, making them worse off than if they had not agreed to joint deflation.

☐ Coordination based on the wrong model

Frankel and Rockett (1988) argue that cooperation may prove inferior to non-cooperation due to the presence of uncertainty over the true economic model. In a world of uncertainty, the structural parameters and linkages between instruments and targets are not known for sure. Given this, it is possible that if countries agree to coordinate their monetary and fiscal policies based on particular models of their economies and the model(s) used turn out to be the wrong model(s) the agreed cooperative policies may be seriously defective and make one or both countries worse off as compared with non-coordination. The results of the Frankel and Rockett study are considered more fully in Section 13.8.

13.8 Estimates of the benefits and losses from international policy coordination

It is practically impossible to measure the benefits or losses from international policy coordination in the real world because of the perennial problem of estimating what would have happened in the absence of coordination. This has not prevented a number of researchers using economic models to make simulation estimates of the potential gains/losses associated with international macroeconomic policy coordination. One of the most interesting studies is that carried out by Frankel and Rockett(1988).

To estimate the potential benefits from international policy coordination Frankel and Rockett used ten different economic models, the models being the ten listed in **Table 13.1**. These models are representative of a variety of economic methodologies ranging from detailed large-scale structural models to more reduced form models of economies. The models reflect a spectrum of Keynesian, monetarist and neoclassical schools of economic thought.

The basic methodology used by Frankel and Rockett is as follows: each government is assumed to believe that one of the ten models is the correct economic model and may or may not be correct in that assumption. For example, two possible scenarios are that the US may believe in the MCM model while Europe may believe in the OECD model, or the US believe in the OECD model while Europe believes in the EEC model. In some cases, the two parties may believe in the same model. Each party agrees to coordinate with the other party to maximise the perceived joint welfare as compared with the perceived Nash non cooperative outcome. In total there are 100 coordination scenarios to examine. This is because for each of the ten models that the US might believe in, there are ten alternative models that the Europeans could use.

For each of the 100 scenarios Frankel and Rockett examine the welfare effects for both the US and Europe of the coordination scenario as compared with the Nash non-cooperation scenario. To measure the potential welfare gain or loss to each country from coordination under the various scenarios it is necessary to know what the true model is. For each of the 100 scenarios,

Frankel and Rockett examine the welfare gains/losses to the USA and Europe by assuming in turn that each of the ten models is true. For example, in the scenario where the US believes in the MCM model and Europe believes in the OECD model, the potential gains/losses in welfare to each of the two parties are examined by assuming that in turn the MCM model is true, then the EEC model is true, then the EPA model is true and so on. This means that there are 100 times 10, that is, 1000 possible welfare gain/loss scenarios for each party to examine.

Frankel and Rockett discover that out of the 1000 possible combinations of coordination between the two economies, US welfare was improved in 546 cases while it ended up worse off in 321 cases and its welfare was unchanged in 133 cases. Europe's welfare was improved in 539 cases while it ended up worse off in 327 cases and its welfare was unchanged in 134 cases. Hence, although on balance a country is likely to gain from coordination there remains a very significant chance (approximately 32 per cent) that it will end up worse off as a result of coordination because coordination has been based upon the wrong economic model. Even these results are slightly biased in favour of coordination because in instances where at least one of the countries is using the correct model coordination is bound to be beneficial to that country or it would not have agreed to coordinate. By excluding such cases there are 810 combinations where neither country is correct. In these cases, the US has gains in 419 cases, losses in 286 cases and no effect in 105. For Europe there are gains in 408 cases, losses in 298 and no effect in 104.

Frankel and Rockett recognise that the above methodology may underestimate the case for coordination because policy makers do not explicitly take into account the possibility that the model they utilise may be invalid. If policy makers take into account the presence of model uncertainty then the probability of success from coordination is significantly raised, a result that is confirmed by Ghosh and Masson (1988). Holtham and Hughes-Hallett (1987) show that eliminating instances where one of the countries expects the other country to be worse off according to its model considerably enhances the probability of coordination raising the welfare of the countries concerned. They argue that in practice governments will wish to avoid circumstances where they benefit and the other country is made worse off (so called 'weak bargains') from coordination because this would encourage the other country to renege and jeopardise future coordination between the countries.

With regard to the magnitude of gains from international policy coordination, a number of authors such as Oudiz and Sachs (1984 and 1985) and Frankel and Rockett (1988) have shown that the potential welfare gains from macroeconomic coordination are not very high even under conditions very favourable to coordination. These conditions are that both countries use the same model and that model is in fact the true model. In such circumstances cooperation must leave both parties better off or they would not cooperate. Oudiz and Sachs (1984) calculate that even in the case where the US, Japan and West Germany coordinate their fiscal and monetary policies perfectly for the mid-1970s the gains from coordination are approximately $\frac{1}{2}$ per cent of GNP for each country. Marcus Miller and Mark Salmon (1985) argue that in the long run there are no gains from international coordination, since in each country the equilibrium level of output is determined by a vertical Phillips curve and floating exchange rates permit the desired level of inflation to be achieved without the need for international policy coordination. They conclude that, 'What gains there may be from coordination must come therefore, in choosing the path towards equilibrium and not in the final equilibrium'.

Although the gains from international coordination seem to be relatively small, using a somewhat different methodology can substantially raise the gains from coordination. Often coordination is brought about because economies are afflicted by common shocks. Currie, Levine and Vidalis (1987) find that while the gains from cooperation are small in the case of transitory shocks, the estimated gains rise steeply as the persistence of a shock increases. In a similar vein, Holtham and Hughes-Hallett find that the gains from international coordination in the face of permanent shocks can amount to 4–6 per cent of GDP.

Before concluding this section, it is worth remembering that even if the true model were employed by coordinating countries, the rules required to achieve fully optimal policy coordination are likely to prove to be extremely complex, too complex to be implemented in practice. Given this, estimates of the gains from fully optimal coordination, even though not particularly pronounced, probably need to treated as generous estimates of the real world benefits from coordination.

 ## 13.9 Problems and obstacles to international policy coordination

The previous section showed that international policy coordination may have a role in raising global welfare even though the precise gains will be difficult to quantify. Indeed, there are plenty of real world examples of countries involving themselves in some form of international coordination. Membership of the Bretton Woods system, the EMS and the IMF and OECD are all examples of differing types of international macroeconomic cooperation and coordination. However, casual observation suggests that the degree of observed international policy coordination falls far short of the degree of interdependence between economies. For this reason, we need to consider some of the major obstacles that inhibit greater international macroeconomic policy coordination.

☐ Negotiation and reduced flexibility costs

Once a country decides to try and improve its welfare by engaging in international policy coordination an obstacle to it actually achieving a successful coordination package is the negotiation process. Reaching agreement on a successful international macroeconomic policy stance can prove extremely difficult and complex and this complexity will increase exponentially with the number of targets, instruments and countries involved in the process. In addition, it is difficult for many governments to precommit themselves in areas such as fiscal policy. This being the case, international macroeconomic policy coordination is more likely to yield results when the number of countries is small and objectives are limited. Once a coordination package is agreed upon, it is likely that policy makers will find that they have less flexibility and there will be delays when implementing their policies as they have to obtain agreement from other countries when altering their policies.

☐ Disagreement over appropriate macroeconomic policies

One of the major obstacles to greater coordination is not so much an ignorance on the part of policy makers to the potential benefits to be derived but rather disagreement over how to realise them. The debate in macroeconomics over the role, impact and effectiveness of fiscal and monetary policies and major international policy issues such as the desirability of fixed and floating exchange rates is far from settled, as a reading of this book reveals! This disagreement is not restricted to the quantitative effects of given policy mixtures but often concerns the qualitative aspects (see **Table 13.1**). Uncertainty also exists over the appropriate instrument to employ to achieve a given policy objective. This uncertainty over means-ends relationships leaves enormous scope for disagreement between countries that share similar objectives. As Ralph Bryant puts it:

> In real-life discussions among national governments, the most fundamental obstacle to more cooperation is not lack of awareness of the potential gains from coordination. Nor is it merely lack of political will. To be sure,

both those lacunae are important. . . . Yet a still more important obstacle is the tremendous uncertainty about the magnitudes, and even the signs, of cross-border transmissions of economic forces. (1985, p. 216)

The point is that theoreticians who analyse the benefits to be derived from coordination using a game theoretic approach in which the pay-off matrix is known simplify the obstacles to agreement between policy makers who do not know the pay-off matrix or the best policies to pursue to reap gains from coordination. Indeed, this lack of agreement over the best policy exists just as much within as between countries. Such disagreement extends to differences of view over the current state of the economy and what are the appropriate priorities for the economy.

☐ *Not all countries gain from coordination*

If the pay-off matrix is known and means-end relationships are fairly clear it may be possible for policy makers to improve their joint welfare by cooperation. However, designing a cooperative policy that maximises joint welfare does not necessarily mean that each individual country which is party to the agreement necessarily gains. It may be the case that some countries are made worse off when designing a cooperative agreement. In such circumstances, to make it worthwhile for loser countries to engage in policy cooperation it is necessary for some form of compensation to be paid. This is especially the case if the loser countries are the ones that have to make the biggest policy adjustments (from which other countries gain). In the real world, examples of compensation for countries that undertake macroeconomic policies that are beneficial to the rest of the world but harmful to themselves are difficult to cite. In practice, this means that cooperative agreements may be restricted to instances where all countries are made better off which would accordingly reduce the potential gains from coordination.

☐ *Reneging and the problem of time consistency*

Another potential problem with policy coordination is derived by using dynamic game theory. This highlights the problem of time consistency (see Kyland and Prescott, 1977). A policy is said to be time inconsistent if there is an incentive to depart from the policy at any time now or in the future. A time inconsistent coordination arrangement would imply that there are incentives for one or more of the countries that are party to a coordination package to renege, either in the present or sometime in the future. Using advanced game theory, Currie and Levine (1987) have shown that the problem of time consistency can pose a major threat to coordination. The reason is that a country which reneges on a time inconsistent cooperative agreement may retain an advantage in the long run. Moreover, the threat of retaliation by a partner country may not be credible because such retaliation would make the retaliating country worse off.

An associated problem is that making a cooperative agreement time consistent may prove to be markedly inferior compared with a time inconsistent fully optimal cooperative policy. While this may provide a strong incentive for far-sighted governments not to succumb to the temptation of reneging, Currie and Levine suggest the need for innovative punishment clauses as part of cooperative agreements to overcome the threat of countries reneging.

In practice, governments may be very reluctant to renege on coordination agreements and would only rationally do so if the perceived benefits of reneging exceed the perceived costs. By breaking a cooperative agreement the authorities may face penalties from other countries and be excluded from future participation in cooperative agreements. Currie, Levine and Vidalis (1987) argue that in practice these costs will comfortably exceed the benefits, making reneging a fairly rare phenomenon.

■ *13.10* Conclusions

International policy coordination is a very complex issue, posing new issues for policy makers that do not arise if they pursue policies in isolation. These issues are so complex that we should not expect coordination to yield globally optimal solutions. In practice, coordination is likely to remain restricted to certain domains such as the exchange of information, exchange rate policy and monetary policy where means-ends relationships are reasonably clear (avoidance of conflicting policies, preservation of trade flows and inflation control) and the potential gains from coordination greatest. Fiscal policy is probably too complex and politically sensitive a domain for much progress to be expected.

It is noticeable that cooperation has proved easier in the trade arena with such arrangements as the GATT and EEC. There is a large consensus in the trade literature that increased trade is beneficial for all countries. This contrasts with the lack of agreement in the international macroeconomic sphere with arguments over the merits of fixed, floating and managed exchange rates and controversy over the role and effectiveness of fiscal and monetary policy in influencing economic activity.

While uncertainty can prove to be a major obstacle to greater international coordination, this should not be overstated. Uncertainty can at times prove to be an incentive to international coordination; the exchange of information motivated by the desire to avoid policy conflict is one of the most common types of coordination that actually takes place in the real world. In addition, countries have been sufficiently uncertain about the relative merits of over and undervalued exchange rates that they have not become involved in competitive exchange rate manipulations. An overvalued exchange rate in relation to PPP has been viewed as advantageous in the fight against inflation, while an undervalued rate is viewed as useful in giving a boost to exports and employment. This uncertainty may account for the lack of 'exchange rate wars' experienced under floating rates despite the major real exchange rate changes that have occurred.

The move from fixed to floating exchange rates has coincided with a decline in the relative economic influence of the United States. The Bretton Woods system has been analysed as a situation where the US was the leader and Europe and Japan were followers as in a Stackleberg scenario. Since the adoption of floating exchange rates the relative economic dominance of the US has declined, while the economic importance of Europe and Japan has risen that the Stackleberg scenario is no longer an adequate characterisation. In such a tripolar world, the dangers of a Nash type scenario are probably greater especially given the extra degree of freedom associated with floating exchange rates.

A useful distinction can be made between global and sub global coordination. Global coordination involves countries from different regions of the world that have a significant impact on the global economy. The three countries that qualify in this category are the United States, Japan and Germany. Sub-global coordination refers to coordination between countries which are not necessarily important at the global level but which have a high degree of structural interdependence with one another. The Bretton Woods system represented an example of global coordination, whereas the EMS represents an example of sub-global coordination. The move from a US dominated world to a tripolar one has to date increased the importance of the sub-global coordination relative to global coordination though there is no obvious reason for this.

The theoretical and simulation literature has served as a warning that policy makers should not expect substantial gains from the coordination of economic policies internationally. Although this message may sound pessimistic, in many ways it is a reflection of the increasing scepticism concerning the ability of governments to influence the real economy in a desirable and predictable fashion via manipulation of fiscal and monetary policies even in a closed economy framework.

■ Selected further readings

Artis, M. and Ostry, S. (1986) *International Economic Policy Coordination*, Chatham House Papers no. 30 (London: Routledge & Kegan Paul).

Bryant, R.C. (1985) 'Comment' in W.H. Buiter and R.C. Marston (eds), *International Economic Policy Coordination* (Cambridge: Cambridge University Press).

Bryant, R.C., Currie, D.A., Frenkel, J.A., Masson, P.R. and Portes, R. (eds) (1989) *Macroeconomic Policies in an Interdependent World* (Washington: IMF).

Cooper, R.N. (1985) 'Economic Interdependence and Coordination of Economic Policies', in R.W. Jones and P.B. Kenen, *Handbook of International Economics*, vol. II (Amsterdam: Elsevier).

Currie, D. and Levine, P. (1987) 'Does International macroeconomic Policy Coordination Pay and is it Sustainable?' *Oxford Economic Papers*, vol. 39, pp. 38–74.

Currie, D. and Levine, P. (1986) 'Time Inconsistency and Optimal Policies in Deterministic and Stochastic Worlds', *Journal of Economic Dynamics and Control*, vol. 10, pp. 191–9.

Currie, D., Levine, P. and Vidalis, N. (1987) 'International Cooperation and Reputation in an Empirical Two-Bloc Model', in R. Bryant and R. Portes (eds), *Global Macroeconomics: Policy Conflict and Cooperation* (London: Macmillan).

Currie, D.A., Holtham, G. and Hughes-Hallett, A. (1989) 'The Theory and Practice of International Policy Coordination: Does Coordination Pay?' in R.C. Bryant, D.A. Currie, J.A. Frenkel, P.R. Masson and R. Portes (eds), *Macroeconomic Policies in an Interdependent World* (Washington).

Frankel, J.A. and Rockett, K.E. (1988) 'International Policy Coordination When Policymakers Do Not Agree on the True Model', *American Economic Review*, vol. 78, No. 3, pp. 318–340.

Frenkel, J.A. (1983) 'Monetary Policy: Domestic Targets and International Constraints', *American Economic Review Papers and Proceedings*, pp. 48–53.

Ghosh, A.R. and Masson, P. (1988) 'International Policy Coordination in a World with Model Uncertainty', *IMF Staff Papers*, vol. 35, pp. 230–58.

Group of 30 (1988) *International Policy Coordination* (London).

Hamada, K. (1974) 'Alternative Exchange Rate Systems and the Interdependence of Monetary Policies', in R.Z. Aliber, *National Monetary Policies and the International Financial System* (Chicago: University of Chicago Press).

Hamada, K. (1985) *The Political Economy of International Monetary Interdependence* (Cambridge, Mass.: MIT Press).

Holtham, G. and Hughes-Hallett, A. (1987) 'International Policy Cooperation and Model Uncertainty', in R. Bryant and R. Portes (eds), *Global Macroeconomics: Policy Conflict and Cooperation* (London: Macmillan).

International Monetary Fund (1984) 'Exchange Rate Volatility and World Trade', *IMF Occasional Paper*, No. 28 (Washington).

Kyland, F.E. and Prescott, E.C. (1977) 'Rules Rather than Discretion the Inconsistency of Optimal Plans', *Journal of Political Economy*, vol. 85, pp. 473–91.

Miller, M. and Salmon, M. (1985) 'Policy Coordination and Dynamic Games', in W.H. Buiter and R.C. Marston, *International Economic Policy Coordination* (Cambridge: Cambridge University Press).

Oudiz, G. and Sachs, J. (1984) 'Macroeconomic Policy Coordination Among the Industrialised Economies', *Brookings Papers on Economic Activity*, vol. 1, pp. 1–64.

Oudiz, G. and Sachs, J. (1985) 'International Policy Coordination in Dynamic Macroeconomic Models', in W.H. Buiter and R.C. Marston, *International Economic Policy Coordination* (Cambridge: Cambridge University Press).

Rogoff, K. (1985) 'Can International Monetary Policy Cooperation be Counterproductive?' *Journal of International Economics*, vol. 18, pp. 199–217.

Steinherr, A. (1984) 'Convergence and Coordination of Macroeconomic Policies the Basic Issues', *European Economy*, pp. 69–110.

Wallich, H.C. (1984) 'Institutional Cooperation in the World Economy', in J.A. Frenkel and M.L. Mussa (eds), *The World Economic System: Performance and Prospects* (Mass.: Dover).

■ *Chapter 14* ■

European Monetary Union and the European Monetary System

■ *14.1* Introduction

In this chapter, we examine one of the most important current issues on the agenda of the member countries of the European Economic Community (EEC) – European Monetary Union (EMU) and the operation of its European Monetary System (EMS). The EEC at present consists of twelve member countries that have made a commitment to free trade between each other and the adoption of a common commercial policy *vis-à-vis* the rest of the world. More recently, the members have been in the process of tackling non-tariff barriers with the so called 'single market programme' more popularly labelled as the 1992 project. The increasing integration of the member states' economies into a 'single market' has raised the issue of whether this market should be served by a single currency. The EMS commenced operations in March 1979 and it is widely viewed as a potential forerunner to EMU.

Section 14.2 defines what is meant by monetary union and considers both the explicit and implicit requirements. Section 14.3 considers the potential benefits and costs associated with EMU. There is then a brief look at a branch of economic literature known as optimal currency theory. This literature attempts to provide a set of criteria that determine which countries should and should not join together in a monetary union. The chapter then proceeds to describe the EMS and evaluate its performance during its first 11 years of operation. In the final section, we consider some of the specific proposals for achieving EMU, in particular the so called Delors report.

■ *14.2* What is Meant by Monetary Union?

There are two main components to a monetary union between two or more countries; an exchange-rate union and complete capital market integration. By an exchange-rate union we mean that the countries agree to the permanent fixing of their exchange rates with no margin of fluctuation. For all intents and purposes this is equivalent to the creation of a single currency. Indeed, the creation of a single currency would be the logical outcome of such a situation, emphasising the permanency of the arrangement. The second component of a monetary union is complete capital market integration. This means that all obstacles to the free movement of financial capital between the union members are removed. Furthermore, capital market integration also requires that equal treatment be afforded to financial capital throughout the members of the union.

While permanently fixed exchange rates and complete capital market integration are explicit requirements for monetary union these in turn involve some implicit requirements. One is that the members of the union harmonise their monetary policies. Differential monetary growth rates once productivity differentials have been allowed for would lead to differing inflation rates, which would threaten parity changes, undermining the requirement of permanently fixed exchange rates. If a single currency is brought into circulation, it would require a union central bank to control its supply and manage the exchange rate of the currency against third country currencies. Such a central bank would need to be invested with a pool of reserves of third country currencies for this purpose.

Hence, a monetary union differs from a fixed exchange rate system in several fundamental respects. A monetary union is a permanent commitment to peg the exchange rate, logically leading to the creation of a single currency. Fixed exchange systems allow for occasional realignments and usually permit margins of fluctuation around a central rate. A monetary union requires a well developed institutional framework such as a single union central bank. Finally, within a monetary union financial capital must be allowed to move freely between the members of the union. This contrasts with experience of fixed exchange-rate regimes whereby exchange-rate parities are often defended only by resort to capital controls.

The benefits and costs associated with the introduction of a single European currency, legal tender throughout the EEC, are a mixture of political, social and economic. In sections 14.3 and 14.4, we concentrate primarily upon the economic costs and benefits likely to ensue.

■ *14.3* Benefits of European monetary union

□ *Stimulus to intra-EEC trade*

The underlying rationale of the EEC is that the removal of barriers to trade by increasing the volume of intra-EEC trade will lead to corresponding rise in the economic prosperity of its members. To maximise the trade flows between the EEC member states and achieve a truly single market, it is argued that there has to be a common medium of exchange. Differing national currencies that fluctuate against one another inhibit trade flows by increasing uncertainty facing traders which can only be eliminated by hedging techniques that entail additional (though not substantial) costs for small to medium sized companies.

Although short-run exchange-rate uncertainty can be easily hedged and probably has very little adverse effect on trade, e.g. IMF (1984) implying that the benefits from a single currency may be small. More recently, Peree and Steinherr (1989) have argued that the problem is not really short-term uncertainty which can be easily hedged but rather medium to long-term uncertainty (one year plus horizon) for which well developed forward markets do not exist. They find that medium to long-run uncertainty generally exerts a significant adverse effect on international trade. As a monetary union is by definition a long-term arrangement, the adverse effects of medium to long-run exchange rate uncertainty would presumably be eliminated.

A further boost to intra-EEC trade could be expected from the elimination of the transactions costs involved in converting different currencies for intra-EEC trade. These transaction costs involve the time and resources used up by firms acquiring and selling the requisite currencies and banks' commission charges.

A more efficient allocation of factors of production within the EEC

EMU involves not only the creation of a single European currency but also the removal of capital controls and distortions to the treatment of financial capital among EEC countries. There is no doubt that the free movement of capital within the EEC has been distorted by capital controls and differing national treatments of financial capital leading to a sub optimal allocation within the community. Capital controls have typically restricted capital moving from countries where it has a low marginal productivity to countries where it has a high marginal productivity. The permanent abolition of exchange-rate controls and absence of uncertainty created by exchange-rate fluctuations would no doubt lead to a more efficient allocation of capital within the community. Similarly, once wages and salaries are expressed in terms of a common currency EMU should result in a better allocation of labour, as labour moves from areas of low marginal to high productivity regions.

Economising of foreign exchange reserves and seigniorage benefits

Dollar treasury bills held in EEC reserves typically earn low rates of interest and their purchasing power in terms of US goods is eroded over time by US inflation. Economising on the amount of reserves held would reduce the seigniorage benefits accruing to the US (see Chapter 11). EMU would probably reduce the total foreign exchange reserve holdings of EEC countries: there would be no need to hold reserves to manage intra-EEC exchange rates. Furthermore, a single EEC currency would tend to fluctuate less against third country currencies than the individual EEC currencies; this would imply the need for less reserves.

In addition, a single European currency would inevitably become a major world currency. This would lead to an increase in the European currency component of non-EEC countries reserves primarily at the expense of the US dollar resulting in corresponding seigniorage benefits accruing to the EEC.

Cohen and Wyplosz (1989) have estimated that the gains accruing to the EEC from this latter effect could amount to around 0.75 per cent of Community GNP.

Savings in administrative costs for businesses

A potentially significant benefit from EMU is the savings in administrative costs for firms involved in managing their exchange risk and operating their business in many different European currencies. Different European currencies and fluctuations between them mean that firms use up resources in having to monitor their exchange risk exposure and in revising their pricing strategy in the different European markets. A single European currency would considerably reduce these costs – it is not surprising that when asked most businessmen are found to be in favour of a single European currency.

■ 14.4 Costs of European monetary union

Most of the perceived costs of EMU are not so much associated with the final attainment of monetary union but rather with the transitional costs associated in achieving it.

Loss of national macroeconomic policy autonomy

A major argument against EMU is that the acceptance of a single currency would mean that countries are no longer free to determine their own monetary policies and inflation rates. In economics it is widely believed that at least in the short run a trade-off exists between inflation and unemployment known as the Phillips curve. Some countries prefer to have low inflation rates and are prepared to accept relatively high unemployment, while others prefer low unemployment and relatively high inflation. With floating exchange rates these different inflation preferences can be reconciled by an appreciating currency for low inflation countries. Since a monetary union requires common inflation rates, countries with differing preferences with respect to any unemployment–inflation trade-off will lose from monetary union. This argument is depicted in **Figure 14.1**.

Figure 14.1(a) depicts the Phillips curve trade-off for the UK and **Figure 14.1(b)** depicts the German Phillips curve. Assume that UK policy makers

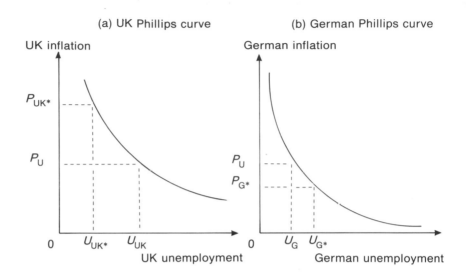

Figure 14.1   *UK and German Phillips curves*

prefer relatively high inflation, while German policy makers prefer less inflation. The optimal inflation–unemployment trade-off for the UK is given by P_{UK*} and U_{UK*}, while the optimal trade-off for Germany is P_{G*} and U_{G*}. In a monetary union both countries have to accept a common inflation rate P_U, which implies higher UK unemployment than UK policy makers prefer and higher German inflation rate than the Germans prefer.

There is much debate in economics over whether Phillips curve trade-off exists. Most economists accept that in the short run such a trade-off usually exists but in the long run no such trade-off exists, with each country having a vertical Phillips curve at its natural rate of unemployment. Hence, the costs associated with the loss of national policy autonomy are probably confined to the short run, the real question being how short is the short run? The loss of national monetary policy autonomy reveals crucially that the achievement of EMU requires an act of political will. Only with differing national governments being prepared to give up their monetary policy autonomy can EMU be achieved.

☐ *Loss of inflation tax*

It is widely accepted that Germany would only agree to EMU if there were guarantees of low inflation rate in the union. For some countries a move to

EMU could prove especially costly because it will be necessary to bring their inflation rates down and into line with the low German rate. This would undermine their implicit inflation tax revenue. In countries where there is a large amount of outstanding public debt and a large holding of the monetary base as opposed to interest earning bank accounts, inflation by reducing the real value of both the outstanding debt and the purchasing power of the authorities' monetary base liability effectively constitutes a tax.

The lower EMU inflation rate would imply smaller inflation tax revenue for high inflation countries meaning that their governments would have to replace the lost inflation tax with explicit direct and indirect taxes. As governments generally perceive such explicit taxes to be politically more costly than the implicit inflation tax they will be reluctant to accept this implication of EMU. In an analysis of this argument, Cohen and Wyplosz (1989) calculate that the taxation of the monetary base effect is far more significant for some countries than others. In particular, assuming a constant 5 per cent inflation rate, the inflation tax as a percentage of GDP is 2.1 per cent for Ireland, 3.9 per cent for Italy and 3.5 per cent for Spain but is only 1 per cent for Germany, 1.1 per cent for France and 0.7 per cent for the UK and the Netherlands. Furthermore, since Ireland, Italy and Spain are among the most heavily indebted countries, the temptation to inflate and reduce the real value of outstanding debt is higher in these countries.

☐ *Regional disparities*

Another concern over EMU is that although it would probably lead to gains for the EEC as a whole, some regions or countries of the community would gain while others would lose. The increased movements of capital and labour associated with EMU, as factors move from low marginal productivity areas towards high productivity areas could manifest itself as a regional problem with undesirable social effects. This effect may be particularly important with respect to labour movements because labour that leaves low productivity areas is usually the most mobile and productive part of a region's workforce. To mitigate such a possibility many proponents of EMU have argued that it needs to be accompanied by an active form of regional policy, with those regions and countries that gain funding compensatory measures in regions that would otherwise lose from EMU.

Although some sort of regional disparities are likely to emerge from EMU, it is very much open to debate as to whether regional policy is the best means of alleviating the problem. Regional policies have fallen out of favour in recent years for a whole host of reasons; these include political manipulation, the diversion of funds to inefficient industries and the delaying of desirable economic adjustments. In practice, it would be difficult to assess whether a region was in decline because of EMU or for other reasons.

☐ *Loss of the exchange rate policy instrument*

Another argument employed against EMU is that the member countries by agreeing to a fixed exchange rate within the union are depriving themselves of both the exchange-rate policy instrument and monetary policy instruments. Tinbergen's instruments-target rule (see Chapter 4) argued that policy makers generally require as many independent instruments as they have targets. The loss of the exchange-rate policy instrument and ability to pursue an independent monetary policy would not matter if the authorities had only one objective, because they could use fiscal policy to achieve internal balance. However, this leaves the problem of external balance.

The question of whether or not the authorities are really losing a policy instrument for dealing with external equilibrium is not clear cut. This is because for the EEC as a whole, there is nothing to prevent a single European currency floating *vis-à-vis* the rest of the world to ensure that the balance of payments of the EEC is kept in equilibrium. Nevertheless overall external equilibrium for the EEC disguises the fact that some member countries of the EEC may experience persistent deficits and others persistent surpluses. What really becomes crucial is whether the surplus countries of the EEC are prepared to finance the deficits of the others. The loss of the exchange-rate policy instrument is therefore applicable to the individual EEC countries.

Overall, it is clear that there are some advantages and some disadvantages attached to EMU. Even if European governments perceive that the overall benefits of EMU exceed the overall costs this does not necessarily imply that they will pursue EMU. One reason is that the benefits may be spread thinly over many millions of people throughout the Community while the losses are heavily concentrated in particular economies. This means that the loser countries may prove more resistant to EMU than the beneficiary countries are to promote the concept.

■ *14.5* Optimal currency area theory

A question that is especially important to any debate on monetary union concerns how large should a monetary union be? Is a single currency optimal only for one country, a group of countries or all countries of the world? Determining a set of criteria to determine which countries should participate in a monetary union has been the subject matter of optimal currency area theory. In the literature on the subject there is no single set of criteria which is generally agreed upon. None the less, it is worthwhile to briefly review some of the criteria that have been suggested for determining which countries should join a monetary union.

☐ *Degree of factor mobility internationally*

Mundell (1961) proposed that the higher the degree of factor mobility between countries then the more beneficial a monetary union would be between them. The rationale behind this criterion is that if a country is in a monetary union and faces a fall in demand for its goods which pushes its balance of payments into deficit, high capital mobility will enable it to finance its deficit more easily without the need for an exchange-rate depreciation. In addition, high labour mobility will mean that deficit regions can deflate their economies without fear of a large increase in unemployment since labour can migrate to other countries within the union. Conversely, if factor mobility is low then an exchange-rate depreciation is required to eliminate the deficit and maintain employment levels, and hence a monetary union would be undesirable.

☐ *Degree of financial integration*

This is connected with the degree of factor mobility mentioned above but is specifically concerned with the ability of a country to gain access to external finance. If a country has a high degree of financial integration with other countries then it will be more able to finance its deficits and less dependent on exchange-rate changes. A small variation in its interest rates will attract the necessary capital flows to finance imbalances. If countries are financially integrated then a single currency is a more feasible option than when countries are not financially integrated.

☐ *Degree of openness*

McKinnon (1963) has argued that the more open the economy as measured by the size of its tradables relative to its non-tradables sector the more profitable it is to join a currency union. The rationale being that if the economy has a large tradables sector it will be much more vulnerable to inflation from a depreciating currency and unemployment from an appreciating currency and therefore the less desirable exchange rate adjustment. Indeed, the more important is trade for the country the more potential it will have to benefit from the introduction of a single currency with its major trading partners. Also, the more open the economy the more the adjustment costs associated with changes in its exchange rate.

☐ *Degree of product diversification*

Kenen (1969) has suggested that the more diversified the country's range of exports and imports the more it will benefit from monetary union. A diversified economy means the less variability in its export earnings and import expenditure and the more stable its balance of payments. Accordingly, the less it will need to resort to exchange-rate changes. If, however, it has only a few export products it may experience much greater variability in its export earnings and will be more dependent upon exchange-rate changes to maintain external equilibrium.

☐ *Degree of similarity of inflation rates*

The idea underlying this criterion is fairly straightforward. If countries have similar inflation rates then PPP theory suggests that there is no need for exchange-rate changes and hence a monetary union is more feasible, whereas if the countries have widely divergent propensities to inflate, then floating exchange rates become necessary to ensure that the relatively high inflation countries maintain their international competitiveness.

Even if we ignore numerous criticisms that can be made of the individual criteria (see the surveys by Tower and Willet (1976) and Ishiyama (1975) and Goodhart (1975, chapter 15)), it is clear that emphasising one particular factor is hardly sufficient grounds for justifying monetary integration. What happens if two countries score well under one of the criteria and poorly on all the others? An index of the various criteria might offer a better solution, but there is plenty of scope for disagreement over the appropriate weight to assign to each of the criteria and then the total index value that would justify membership of a monetary union. Goodhart (1975) emphasises that the need for a high degree of social cohesion appears to be a crucial determinant of the size of a single currency area in the real world rather than any clear-cut economic criteria. In sum, the optimal currency area literature addresses an interesting question but the various criteria that have been suggested are far from conclusive.

14.6 A brief history of European monetary union

The Rome Treaty of 1957 which created the EEC made no explicit mention of monetary union. However, the architects of the treaty no doubt envisaged the EEC eventually developing into a fully-fledged economic union with full monetary integration among its members. At the time of the signing of the Rome Treaty, the priority was the creation of a customs union which involved the adoption of a common tariff policy *vis-à-vis* third countries and the removal of trade barriers (especially tariffs) between the member countries. By 1968 much progress had been made in these areas and it was believed that a means of further increasing trade between the members would be the creation of a single European currency. At the Hague Summit of December 1969 the then six member countries of the EEC agreed in principle to establish complete economic and monetary union in stages, commencing in January 1971 and being completed by the end of 1980. Although in retrospect such a target seems absurdly ambitious, it must be remembered that the Bretton Woods system of fixed exchange rates had been operating with only occasional realignments for two decades.

As a result of the Hague Summit a committee was set up to investigate the subject and in 1972 it delivered the so-called Werner Report on Economic and Monetary Union. The report envisaged a fully-fledged monetary union between the members of the EEC by 1980. In relation to the free movement of factors of production the report argued for the removal of all impediments and distortions to such movements. The report foresaw the conduct of fiscal and monetary policies being carried out at the community level by community institutions invested with the necessary decision taking powers, the main aim of such institutions being to regulate the monetary and credit policies of the union and manage the external exchange rate *vis-à-vis* non EEC currencies, while fiscal policy would be employed to ensure both economic stability and growth. Finally, community institutions would also operate regional and structural policies designed 'to contribute to the balanced development of the community'.

Apart from being over ambitious, there were more fundamental reasons for the failure to achieve EMU by the target date. In the first instance, the six original members were joined by Ireland, the United Kingdom and Denmark in 1973. Their accession negotiations and ensuring their successful integration into the EEC inevitably took precedence. In addition, as we have seen in Chapter 11, the Bretton Woods system of fixed exchange rates broke up in 1971 and this was swiftly followed by the first oil shock of 1973/4. The impact of the oil price rise was not spread evenly and coinciding with the new era of floating exchange rates meant that countries were free to adopt different policy responses. Some countries adopted expansionary policies in a bid to stave off recession, such as the UK and Italy, while others such as Germany were determined to avoid inflation and adopted deflationary policies. With such policy divergences and resulting differential inflation rates any hope of achieving fixed exchange-rate parities between European currencies was soon vanquished. During the period 1971–75 French consumer prices rose by 52 per cent while in Germany they rose by 34.7 per cent and in the UK by 82.5 per cent.

At the end of the day, the principal obstacle to monetary union was that the Heads of State that met at the Hague failed to deliver the political will and commitment necessary for its achievement. To a large extent they misunderstood the full implications required to achieve EMU. Put simply, the declaration to achieve EMU only had a real chance of success if the member states were prepared to sacrifice the macroeconomic control of their national economies to achieve common inflation objectives and the political will to do this was never present.

■ *14.7* The Snake

One direct result of the Werner Report was the setting up of the so called 'Snake in the Tunnel' which subsequently became the plain 'Snake'. The Snake system has sometimes been characterised as a mini Bretton Woods, a description that has subsequently been applied to the EMS. It is worthwhile briefly examining the main features of the system because the EMS owes much of its origins to the Snake.

The Snake in the Tunnel commenced operations on 24 April 1972 and was made up of the original six EEC members (Belgium, France, Italy, Luxembourg, Netherlands and West Germany), on 23 May 1972 the UK and Denmark joined the system and Norway became an associate member. While the member currencies could vary by a maximum of ± 1.125 per cent against each other (the snake) they could float by ± 2.25 per cent against the US dollar (the tunnel) as permitted by the Smithsonian agreement. This smaller margin of fluctuation for the member currencies *vis-à-vis* each other than was permitted against the US dollar gave rise to the term 'snake in a tunnel' to describe the system. In fact, between 1972 and 1976 Belgium and the Netherlands limited the divergence between their currencies to ± 0.75 per cent and this became known as the worm inside the Snake!

The system had a chequered history. The UK abandoned its membership of the system after just six weeks on 23 June 1972 and four days later Denmark withdrew from the Snake only to rejoin in October 1972. Italy withdrew from the Snake in February 1973. The tunnel was demolished in

Table 14.1   *Central parity realignments in the Snake*

Currency	Mar. 1973	June 1973	Sept. 1973	Nov. 1973	Oct. 1976	April 1977	Aug. 1977	Feb. 1978	Oct. 1978
Belg./Lux. fr					−2.0				+2.0
Deutschmark	+3.0	+5.5							+4.0
Dutch guilder			+5.0		−2.0				+2.0
Swedish krone					−3.0	−6.0			
Danish krone					−6.0	−3.0	−5.0		
Norwegian krone				+5.0	−3.0	−3.0	−5.0	−8.0	

+ indicates a revaluation, − indicates a devaluation   Source: European Commission

March 1973 when the Snake currencies decided on a joint float against the dollar. In April 1973 as part of the Snake system the European Monetary Cooperation Fund (EMCF) was set up to provide credits and support for deficit countries. France left the system in January 1974, rejoined in July 1975 and left again in March 1976. Norway left the system in December 1978. Throughout its lifetime the Snake was characterised by a series of devaluations and revaluations which are listed in **Table 14.1**. This coupled with the fact that both Italy and France were out of the system meant that by 1979 the Snake was looking badly mutilated.

In the end, the Snake system failed to produce the necessary degree of coordination of economic policies and convergence of economic performance required for its successful operation.

14.8 The background to the European monetary system

On 17 June 1978, at a conference held in Bremen, six of the community countries committed themselves to the setting up of the European Monetary System to replace the Snake. The EMS aimed to provide a 'zone of currency stability' bringing back into the fold countries like Italy and France which had left the Snake. Before looking at the operation of the EMS it is worthwhile reviewing the motivations behind its formation.

Yao-su-Hu (1981) argues that the formation of the EMS has to be seen in a wider context than simply the setting up of an exchange rate mechanism. He argues that the EMS was based upon a convergence of interests among the EEC countries with regard to a common dollar problem. Under the Bretton Woods system, the dollar was the major international reserve currency, used as a means of settlement between central banks, for exchange market interventions and as a vehicle currency with which to denominate many international transactions. He argues that the US was free to run balance of payments deficits to supply the world with the dollars it required. In return for this freedom from balance-of-payments constraints, the US was expected to avoid undermining the purchasing power of dollars. When President Nixon suspended dollar convertibility into gold in 1971 the US had effectively abdicated its responsibility causing serious economic and financial losses for the Europeans.

The dollar problem had many facets. As the dollar was pegged by foreign central bank purchases of US dollars this led to a rapid growth in the world money supply and thereby contributed to worldwide inflation. Also, the depreciation of the dollar after suspension of its convertibility meant huge losses for central banks who had purchased dollars under the Bretton Woods system and after the adoption of floating exchange rates as they tried to slow down the appreciation of their currencies against the dollar. In sum, it can be argued that central banks' experience of purchasing and holding US dollars in their reserves had not been a happy one. In a similar vein, Robert Triffin has also argued that;

> The Bremen initiative ... reflects, at bottom, a desperate desire of the leaders of the Community to make their countries less dependent on the unpredictable vagaries of a shrinking US dollar.

Another motivation underlying the Bremen initiative was a desire to provide a stable framework for the conduct of European trade. Since the adoption of floating exchange rates in 1973, there had been very divergent inflation rates, economic growth and balance-of-payments performances between the EEC economies. European policy makers were concerned that such divergent economic performances could threaten intra-EEC trade. In particular, there has always been a concern at the Community level that large and sudden changes in international competitiveness associated with exchange-rate movements could undermine the development of the free trade within the Community. It was hoped that stabilising European currencies would lead to a greater convergence of economic performance and ensure the continued growth of European trade.

 ## 14.9 Features of the European monetary system

The EMS commenced operation on 13 March 1979 and despite much initial scepticism is now in its second decade of operation. There are four main features of the system some of which build upon the arrangements of the

Snake; the exchange rate mechanism (ERM), the European currency unit (ECU), financing facilities and the proposed setting up of a European Monetary Fund (EMF). All members the EEC joined the EMS although the UK did not initially participate in the ERM part of the system. After much deliberation, the United Kingdom finally joined the ERM on 8 October 1990.

14.10 The exchange-rate mechanism and the European currency unit

The exchange-rate mechanism (ERM) consists of two parts:

1. A grid of bilateral exchange rate bands between each of the member currencies which defines obligatory intervention.
2. An individual band of fluctuation for each currency against the ECU which if breached by a certain threshold will lead to the expectation that the authorities of that currency will take policy measures designed to bring it back within its ECU threshold.

We shall deal first with the grid of bilateral exchange rates and then examine the definition and role of the ECU in the ERM.

14.11 Bilateral exchange-rate parities

The bilateral exchange-rate aspect of the ERM consists of a grid of central exchange rates between each pair of currencies in the ERM. Each currency can fluctuate a maximum ±2.25 per cent of its bilateral central rate against another member currency of the ERM. On the setting up of the system Italy was allowed to join with a larger band of fluctuation of ±6 per cent; in January 1990 it narrowed its band of fluctuation to ±2.25 per cent. Both the UK and Spain as at 8 October 1990 have a wider 6 per cent margin of fluctuation. **Table 14.2** shows the bilateral grids as at 8 October 1990.

Within the bilateral margins authorities may intervene if they wish but such intervention is not compulsory. **Intra-marginal** intervention can be carried out in either EMS or non-EMS currencies (normally the US dollar). Once two currencies reach a bilateral exchange-rate margin the authorities of the two currencies are obliged to intervene or take economic policy measures to keep the currencies within their bilateral limits. At the outset of the system, the intention was that obligatory intervention should take place in the relevant EMS currencies rather than in US dollars. For example, if the French franc is at the bottom of its bilateral limit against the deutschmark,

Table 14.2 Bilateral central rates and selling and buying rates in the EMS on 8 October 1990

		BFr100=	Dkr100=	FFr100=	DM100=	I£1=	L1000=	DFl100=	Pta100=	£1=
Belg/Lux	S		553.000	628.970	2 109.50	56.511 5	28.193 0	1 872.15	33.693 0	64.605 0
BFr/LFr	C		540.723	614.977	2 062.55	55.254 5	27.566 1	1 830.54	31.731 6	60.845 1
	B		528.700	601.295	2 016.55	54.025 0	26.953 0	1 789.85	29.885 0	57.303 5
Denmark	S	18.914 3		116.320	390.160	10.451 1	5.214 00	346.240	6.231 00	11.947 9
DKr	C	18.493 8		113.732	381.443	10.218 6	5.098 03	338.537	5.868 37	11.252 6
	B	18.083 1		111.200	373.000	9.991 3	4.985 00	331.020	5.526 00	10.597 6
France	S	16.631 0	89.925 0		343.050	9.189 0	4.584 50	304.440	5.478 50	10.505 50
FFr	C	16.260 8	87.925 7		335.386	8.984 8	4.482 47	297.661	5.159 81	9.893 89
	B	15.899 0	85.970 0		327.920	8.785 0	4.383 00	291.040	4.859 50	9.318 00
Germany	S	4.959 00	26.810 0	30.495 0		2.740 00	1.367 00	90.770 0	1.633 00	3.132 00
DM	C	4.848 37	26.216 2	29.816 4		2.678 94	1.336 51	88.752 6	1.538 47	2.950 00
	B	4.740 00	25.630 0	29.150 0		2.619 00	1.306 50	86.780 0	1.449 00	2.778 00
Ireland	S	1.851 00	10.008 70	11.383 0	38.182 5		0.510 246	33.886 8	0.609 772	1.169 20
I£	C	1.809 81	9.786 04	11.129 9	37.328 1		0.498 895	33.129 3	0.574 281	1.101 18
	B	1.769 50	9.568 30	10.882 5	36.496 4		0.487 799	32.393 9	0.540 858	1.037 10
Italy	S	3710.20	20 062.0	22 817.0	76 540.0	2 050.03		67 912.0	1 222.30	2 343.62
L	C	3627.64	19 615.4	22 309.1	74 821.7	2 004.43		66 405.3	1 151.11	2 207.25
	B	3546.90	19 179.0	21 813.0	73 257.0	1 959.84		64 928.0	1 084.10	2 078.79
Holland	S	5.587 00	30.210 0	34.360 0	115.235 0	3.087 00	1.540 00		1.840 50	3.529 50
DFl	C	5.462 86	29.538 9	33.595 3	112.673 0	3.018 48	1.505 90		1.733 45	3.323 89
	B	5.341 50	28.882 5	32.847 5	110.167 5	2.951 00	1.472 50		1.632 50	3.130 50
Spain	S	334.619	1 809.40	2 057.80	6 901.70	184.892	92.240 0	6 125.30		203.600
Peseta	C	315.143	1 704.05	1 938.06	6 500.00	174.131	86.872 6	5 768.83		191.750
	B	296.802	1 604.90	1 825.30	6 121.70	163.997	81.820 0	5 433.10		180.590
UK	S	1.745 10	9.436 10	10.732 0	35.997 0	0.964 240	0.481 050	31.945 0	0.553 740	
£	C	1.643 52	8.886 87	10.107 3	33.898 4	0.908 116	0.453 053	30.085 3	0.521 514	
	B	1.547 90	8.369 70	9.519 0	31.928 0	0.855 260	0.426 690	28.334 0	0.491 160	

Notes:
S is the rate at which the central bank of the currency on the left-hand column must sell its currency.
C is the central rate parity of the currency on the left-hand column.
B is the rate at which the central bank of the currency on the left-hand column must buy its currency.
Source: European Commission.

the French and/or German authorities should sell deutschmarks and purchase French francs rather than the French use dollars to buy francs.

One of the important features of the ERM is that any changes in the grid of central rates require 'mutual agreement'. In practice, this means that parity changes are decided by the Finance Ministers of the currencies participating in the ERM.

■ *14.12* The European currency unit

A key component of the ERM is the ECU which is a weighted basket of the various EEC currencies. The ECU plays an important role in the ERM because it acts as an 'indicator of divergence'. An issue that arises once a bilateral margin is reached which leads to compulsory intervention concerns which authority is responsible for intervention. In the example, when the French franc reaches its bilateral limit against the deutschmark should it be Banque de France that uses its reserves to support the franc or the Bundesbank that sells deutschmarks and accumulates French francs, or a mixture of the two?

The idea underlying the ECU was that it would single out the currency that was diverging from the average agreed parities before obligatory bilateral exchange rate margins were reached. In effect, the ECU is supposed to act as an alarm bell – once a currency crosses its divergence threshold against the ECU the alarm bell is triggered and the authorities of that currency are expected to take measures to bring its currency back into line. Such action may consist of a change in interest rates or in the monetary and/or fiscal policy pursued by the country. Unlike reaching a bilateral exchange rate limit, triggering the ECU alarm bell does not lead to obligatory intervention, only the expectation of a change in policy stance (*presumption d'action*).

□ *Calculation of the ECU*

To clarify the workings of the ECU divergence indicator it is necessary to understand how the ECU basket is defined. Each currency in the EMS is given a central weight in the ECU basket reflecting criteria such a country's economic importance and share of EEC trade. These weights are subject to revision every five years and are depicted in **Table 14.3**.

The precise calculation of the ECU is as follows: the amounts of each of the various currencies in the baskets are defined as:

$$\sim q_1, q_2, \ldots, q_n \sim \text{ is 1 ECU}$$

Table 14.3   *The composition of the ECU and central weights as at 8 October 1990*

Currency	Quantity	ECU central rates	% Weight in ECU
Bel./Lux. franc	3.431	42.403 2	8.09
Danish kroner	0.197 6	7.841 95	2.52
French franc	1.332	6.895 09	19.32
German D-Mark	0.624 2	2.055 86	30.36
Irish punt	0.008 552	0.767 417	1.12
Italian lira	151.8	1 538.24	9.87
Dutch guilder	0.219 8	2.316 43	9.49
Spanish peseta	6.885	133.631	5.15
UK pound	0.087 84	0.696 904	12.60
Portuguese escudo	1.393	178.735	0.78
Greek drachma	1.44	205.311	0.70
			100.00

Notes:
Quantity applied since 21 September 1989.
The Portuguese escudo and Greek drachma have notional central rates against the ECU, although they are not members of the ERM.
Source: European Commission.

where $q_1, q_2, \ldots, q_n$ and are the quantities of the various currencies in the ECU basket listed in Table 14.3.

Given the various bilateral exchange rates in the parity grid, it is possible to work out the value of each currency in terms of the ECU. The formula for calculating the exchange rate of currency j against the ECU is as follows.

$$S_j = \sum_{k=1}^{n} q_k \, sk_j$$

(14.1)

where S_j is the number of units of currency j per ECU, q_k is the quantity of currency k in the ECU, and sk_j is units of currency k per unit of currency j.

Table 14.4 illustrates the calculation of the £ per ECU central rate as of 8 October 1990.

The calculation of the weight of each currency is simply the quantity of currency j in the ECU relative to the quantity of all currencies in the ECU translated into currency j. Algebraically this is denoted as follows:

$$w_j = \frac{q_j}{\sum_{j=1}^{n} q_k \, s_{kj}} \qquad j = 1, 2, \ldots n$$

(14.2)

where the sum of all the weights is equal to unity.

Table 14.4   *Calculation of pound per ECU rate*

Currency	Quantity in ECU	£ per unit of foreign currency	£ value
Bel./Lux. franc	3.431	0.016 435 2	0.056 389
Danish kroner	0.197 6	0.088 868 7	0.017 560
French franc	1.332	0.101 073	0.134 629
German D-Mark	0.624 2	0.338 984	0.211 594
Irish punt	0.008 552	0.908 116	0.007 766
Italian lira	151.8	0.000 453 053	0.068 773
Dutch guilder	0.219 8	0.300 853	0.066 127
Spanish peseta	6.885	0.005 215 14	0.035 906
UK pound	0.087 84	1.0	0.087 840
Portuguese escudo	1.393	0.003 899 09	0.004 084
Greek drachma	1.44	0.003 394 38	0.004 888
		£ per ECU rate	0.696 904

Notes:
Since the £ per ECU rate is 0.696 904 then the ECU per pound rate is 1.434 9.

Given that the quantity of each currency in the ECU (q_j) is fixed, a depreciation of the exchange rate of currency j (rise in s_{kj}) will reduce its weight in the ECU according to equation 14.2. For example, the central weight of the pound in the ECU ($w_£$) is calculated as:

$$w_£ = \frac{0.087\ 84}{0.696\ 904} \times 100 = 12.60\%$$

Clearly, if the pound depreciates against the ECU, its weight will decline. The central weights of all the currencies in the ECU are shown in Table 14.3.

☐ *The ECU as an indicator of divergence*

Having seen how the ECU is defined, we now proceed to see how it is used as an indicator of divergence. The ECU indicator of divergence is defined as the ratio of the percentage deviation of a currency from its central ECU rate compared with its maximum possible divergence.

$$ID_{jt} = \frac{d_{jt}}{\max\ dj} \times 100$$

where ID_{jt} is indicator of divergence of currency j at time t, d_{jt} is the divergence of currency j from its central ECU rate at time t, and max d_j is the maximum allowable divergence spread of currency j from its central ECU rate.

The maximum divergence spread (max d_j) is itself defined as:

$$\max d_j = m_j(1 - w_j^*) \tag{14.3}$$

where m_j is the maximum percentage margin for bilateral parities, which is 2.25 for all currencies except the peseta and pound sterling, which have margins of 6 per cent, and w_j^* is the central weight of the currency in the ECU.

For example, the maximum divergence spread for the pound against the ECU on its entrance to the system with a 6 per cent margin of fluctuation was:

$$\max d_\pounds = 6(1 - 0.126) = 5.244\%$$

Note: the calculation for the other ERM currencies with $\pm 2\frac{1}{4}$ per cent margins of fluctuation is somewhat complicated by the ± 6 per cent margins allowed for the pound and peseta (see Gandolfo, 1987).

Hence, each currency has its own individual divergence threshold against the ECU, dependent upon its weight in the ECU. The greater the currency's weight in the ECU the lower its divergence threshold. The reason for designing the divergence threshold like this is to correct for the fact that currencies with a higher than average weight in the ECU will tend to fluctuate less against the ECU than currencies with a low weight. This is because the higher a currency's weight in the ECU the more the ECU is made up of that currency and since a currency cannot fluctuate against itself the less likely it is to fluctuate against the ECU the greater its weight. To offset this effect, high weight currencies have lower divergence thresholds than low weight currencies.

Once the indicator of divergence ID_j of currency j exceeds 0.75 the alarm bell is triggered and the authorities of currency j are expected to take measures to bring currency j into line. For example, once the pound exceeds $0.75 (5.224) = 3.918$ per cent from its central ECU rate, the UK authorities are expected to take measures to bring the pound back into line. The idea was that this warning bell would lead to action by the responsible country and so avoid reaching bilateral intervention limits which would provoke speculation about parity changes. **Table 14.5** depicts the position of each currency relative to its ECU central rate and the divergence indicator for each currency as at 8 October 1990.

In practice, the divergence indicator does not necessarily work as intended. For example, it is possible that four high weighted currencies in the ECU basket appreciate against weaker currencies in the system but keep their same central rate against each other. In such circumstances, they may reach their bilateral parities against the weaker currencies even though they have not reached their divergence thresholds with respect to the ECU.

Table 14.5   *EMS and the divergence indicator as at 8 October 1990*

Currency	ECU central rates	Currency amounts against ECU on 8 October	Percentage change from central rate	Divergence indicator
Bel./Lux. franc	42.403 2	42.507 6	0.25	− 5
Danish kroner	7.841 95	7.886 43	0.57	− 19
French franc	6.895 09	6.921 68	0.39	− 13
German D-Mark	2.055 86	2.066 94	0.54	− 25
Irish punt	0.767 417	0.770 524	0.40	− 11
Italian lira	1 538.24	1 549.39	0.72	− 28
Dutch guilder	2.316 43	2.330 49	0.61	− 22
Spanish peseta	133.631	129.958	− 2.75	48
UK pound	0.696 904	0.681 891	− 2.15	41
Portuguese escudo	178.735	—	—	—
Greek drachma	205.311	—	—	—

Notes:
(a)   A positive divergence indicator signals a strong currency, a negative divergence indicator signals a weak currency.
(b)   The Portuguese escudo and Greek drachma have notional central rates against the ECU, although they are not members of the ERM.
(c)   The calculation of the divergence indicator is somewhat more complex than in the text because of the non-participation of Portugal and Greece and the wider 6 per cent bilateral margins permitted for the pound and peseta.
Source: Financial Times, 8 October 1990.

■ *14.13* Monetary cooperation

Another key feature of the system is that each member of the EMS deposits 20 per cent of its gold and dollar reserves with the European Monetary Cooperation Fund (EMCF) in exchange for the equivalent value in ECUs. The idea being that authorities use ECUs rather than dollars for their exchange market interventions. Furthermore, since each ECU issued is backed by dollars and gold it was hoped that ECUs would be extensively used for settlements between EEC central banks.

An important feature of the EMS is that members have access to credit facilities enabling deficit countries to defend their exchange rate parities and manage transitory balance of payments problems. These credit facilities consist as follows:

1.   **Very short-term financing (VSTF)** – this is a credit facility which participating central banks grant to one another. Designed predominately to ensure that EMS members who find their currencies under

pressure have the necessary short-term support to intervene to defend their currency. This credit facility is of an unlimited amount with credits and debits denominated in ECUs and the transfers made in the relevant accounts of the EMCF. However, borrowing must be settled within 45 days and the debtor can settle either in the creditor bank's currency or in ECUs. Creditor banks are not obliged to accept repayment in ECUs of more than 50 per cent; the debtor must repay loans made at the relevant money market interest rates.

2. **Short-term monetary support (STMS)** – the funds available under this credit facility are intended to meet financing needs in instances of temporary balance-of-payments problems. The system is based on a system of debtor and creditor quotas which define each central bank's borrowing entitlement and financing obligations. Borrowing is for a duration of three months which is renewable for a further two periods at the request of the borrowing central bank.

3. **Medium-term financial assistance (MTFA)** – this facility provides credits for participating countries experiencing or seriously threatened with difficulties with their balance of payments over the medium term. Each member has an obligation to grant credit up to a predetermined ceiling, but there is no formal ceiling on the amount of borrowing. However, ordinarily no individual country may receive loans of more than 50 per cent of the total committed ceilings. Medium-term loans are for periods of 2–5 years and are conditional upon the borrower taking economic and monetary measures aimed at restoring equilibrium to its balance of payments.

As an inducement for countries with relatively high inflation rates to join the system, the European Investment Bank (EIB) was given the authority to make loans at favourable interest rates to members of the EMS. Such finance was to be used to improve their efficiency and thereby reduce their underlying inflation rates.

☐ *The European Monetary Fund (EMF)*

Under the articles of agreement setting up the EMS, it was planned to replace the EMCF which had been set up under the Snake with a new European Monetary Fund in 1981. The EMCF has no clearly defined role but is empowered to receive monetary reserves from the central banks of the EEC member states and issue ECUs against these deposits. The intention was that the EMF would replace the EMCF and run the ECU credit system and oversee the ERM. While these latter roles are not too controversial, some of the national authorities are very suspicious about more ambitious roles that such an organisation might aspire to. Some plans envisage the EMF becoming an independent European Central Bank with powers to create a single European currency which would mean the loss of member states' monetary autonomy. Given the controversy surrounding its powers and role, the member states have failed to set up the EMF over a decade since it was due to commence operation.

14.14 An assessment of the European monetary system

Despite much initial scepticism many economists have been surprised at the resilience and relatively successful operation of the EMS. Unlike its predecessor the Snake, no countries have left the system and the ERM has become tighter. Monetary cooperation has strengthened and controls on capital movements were largely removed by July 1990.

14.15 Exchange-rate stability

In the early days of its operation some critics of the system as viewed the system as a 'mere crawling peg', a fixed exchange-rate system with bands in which the central parities are frequently realigned. As **Table 14.6** shows, in the first four years of its operation exchange rate realignments were both frequent and quite substantial. Since then realignments have become far less frequent and much smaller. Indeed, there has not been a realignment since January 1987. To a large extent the turbulence of the early years is not surprising given that the second oil shock coincided with the inception of the EMS.

Authors such as Artis and Taylor (1988) have shown that both nominal exchange rates and real effective exchange rates have become less **volatile** for EMS currencies (kroner, Belgian franc, lira, guilder and deutschmark) than for non-EMS currencies(the pound, dollar, yen) since 1979 compared with the first six years of floating. It is not surprising that nominal exchange rates have been more stable, as this is precisely what the ERM is about; the fact that it also holds for real exchange rates is indicative of the fact that as well as providing stability for exchange rates the EMS has also led to a greater convergence of inflation rates.

One of the arguments against adopting exchange-rate targets has always been that countries would be forced to adjust domestic monetary policy and interest rates to the needs of maintaining the exchange-rate target. Hence, exchange-rate stability would be achieved only at the cost of increased domestic instability. Interestingly, Artis and Taylor find that greater stability

Table 14.6 Central parity realignments in the EMS (%)

Currency	Sept. 1979	Nov. 1979	Mar. 1981	Oct. 1981	Feb. 1982	June 1982	Mar. 1983	July 1985	Apr. 1986	Aug. 1986	Jan. 1987
Belg./Lux. fr					−8.5		+1.5	+2.0	+1.0		+2.0
Deutschmark	+2.0			+5.5		+4.25	+5.5	+2.0	+3.0		+3.0
Dutch guilder				+5.5		+4.25	+3.5	+2.0	+3.0		+3.0
French fr				−3.0		−5.75	−2.5	+2.0	−3.0		
Danish krone	−2.9				−3.0		+2.5	+2.0	+1.0		
Lira		−4.8	−6.0	−3.0		−2.75	−2.5	−6.0			
Irish £							−3.5			−8.0	

+ indicates a revaluation, − indicates a devaluation.
Source: European Commission.

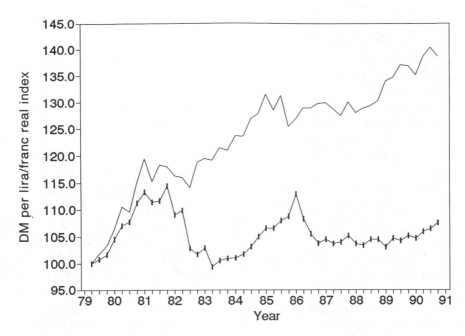

Figure 14.2 *Real exchange rates against the deutschmark. (———) DM/lira,*
(+++) DM/franc.

of exchange rates has been accompanied by increased stability of domestic
short-term interest rates for the ERM countries. It seems that countries have
derived both greater domestic and external financial stability from membership of the ERM.

Although the EMS has resulted in less volatility of real and nominal
exchange rates for its members, there is clear evidence that there have been
significant changes in the **levels** of real exchange rates over time. In
particular, because France, Italy, Denmark and Ireland have had higher
inflation rates than West Germany and the periodic devaluations of their
currencies have on average only partly offset these differentials, they have
experienced real exchange-rate appreciations against the Deutschmark.
These real exchange rates are borne out in **Figure 14.2**.

■ *14.16* The anti-inflation hypothesis

In the way of background, before we consider the anti-inflation hypothesis,
it is a widely held belief that German inflation tends to be lower than that of

other EEC countries because of the independent status of the German Bundesbank. The Bundesbank has a charter (1957) that charges it with the task of ensuring stable prices. The charter enables it to pursue tough monetary policies regardless of political pressures to inflate. Having experienced two periods of hyperinflation in the twentieth century the Germans have a high aversion to inflation. This is not the case for other central banks such as the Banque de France, the Bank of England and Banca d'Italia who have to adopt expansionary monetary policies when instructed to do so by their authorities and this leads to correspondingly higher inflation rates.

A popular interpretation of the advantages of EMS membership to the EMS members has been put forward by Giavazzi and Pagano (1988) and Melitz (1988). According to this interpretation one of the major advantages of ERM membership for relatively high inflation countries such as Italy and France is that participation in the ERM has enabled them to reduce their inflation rates more rapidly, substantially and at lower cost than if they had been non-members. According to this anti-inflation hypothesis, there are two ways that the fight against inflation is assisted by full EMS membership. First, through giving the authorities an incentive to bring inflation under control and secondly by affecting private agents' wage and price behaviour.

With regard to the authorities' incentives, both Italy and France (and other members) by making a commitment to peg their nominal exchange rates against the key low inflation currency in the system – the deutschmark, have in effect pledged to bring their inflation rates down to the German level. If their inflation rates remain higher than Germany then they will be penalised by a loss of international competitiveness. Of course, they could opt for occasional devaluations to maintain their competitiveness but if France and Italy were to do so too frequently this would signal to economic agents that the authorities were not serious in pursuing anti-inflationary policies. By making a commitment to peg their currencies to the deutschmark the authorities have sent a visible signal of their commitment to an anti-inflation strategy. So long as they maintain the peg (tying their hands), they gain some of the anti-inflation credibility that the Bundesbank is renowned for.

The effect on agents' wage and price behaviour is connected with the authorities incentive/credibility effect. Given that their authorities maintain the peg, economic agents in France and Italy soon learn that persisting with high wage and price inflation demands makes their economies uncompetitive. This will ultimately lead to job losses and a recession. Hence, economic agents have an incentive to lower their wage demands which in turn results in lower inflation.

Given the anti-inflation incentives for both the authorities and economic agents' membership of the ERM should assist in the process of bringing down inflation compared with non-ERM membership. The Italian and French authorities by being members of the ERM have been able to bring down their inflation rates more substantially and more quickly than could have been achieved without membership.

While the anti-inflation hypothesis explains what is in ERM membership for traditionally high inflation countries, it does not explain why Germany participates in the ERM. Germany has since the Second World War been a traditionally low inflation country and the Bundesbank already has an anti-inflation credibility. Melitz argues that the main gain for Germany is that while the nominal exchange rates are fixed and other countries still have relatively high inflation rates the Germans experience an improvement in their international competitiveness, due to the resulting real depreciation of the deutschmark.

This interpretation of the EMS suggests that all countries get something out of the EMS but at a cost. The Italians and French have managed to bring down their inflation rates and sustain them at lower rates than had they not joined the system but at the expense of some loss of international competitiveness, whereas the German authorities have probably accepted a marginally higher inflation rate than had they not been EMS members but have been compensated for by increased international competitiveness. Some empirical evidence on the validity of the anti-inflation hypothesis is presented in **Table 14.7**.

While there is no doubt that average rates of inflation have come down in the EMS countries since it commenced operation **Table 14.7** shows that this is not by itself proof of the EMS anti-inflation hypothesis. This is because inflation rates have also fallen in the non-ERM countries such as the United Kingdom and United States. In fact, starting from a similar average inflation rate in 1979, the inflation rate in the non-ERM was lower than in the ERM countries up to 1985. Only since 1986 have the ERM countries had a lower inflation rate.

There have been several more formal empirical studies of the anti-inflation hypothesis. As is usual in these studies, it is not possible to prove the hypothesis that the EMS has helped to reduce inflation because it is impossible to know what would have happened in the absence of the EMS. The most popular method of seeking supporting evidence for the hypothesis has been to compare the EMS countries, inflation performance with the performance of a group of non-EMS countries as opposite. Obviously, such a comparison is not conclusive and the results can prove sensitive to which non-EMS countries are chosen for comparison. Urenger *et al.* (1986) undertook an empirical investigation for the EMS countries up until 1984 and found that the EMS has had a significant negative effect on EMS inflation rates. However, a study by Susan Collins (1988) which compared seven EMS countries' inflation performance with fifteen non-EMS countries

Table 14.7 *Inflation in ERM and non-ERM countries*

ERM countries	1979	1980	1981	1982	1983	1984	1985	1986	1987	1988	1989	1990
Belgium	3.9	6.2	8.7	7.9	7.0	6.0	6.0	0.7	1.7	1.3	3.4	3.4
Denmark	10.5	10.7	12.0	10.3	6.7	6.4	4.3	2.9	4.8	4.0	4.9	2.7
France	10.8	13.3	13.0	11.6	9.7	7.7	5.7	2.7	3.1	2.7	3.3	3.4
Italy	14.5	20.5	18.1	16.9	15.2	11.8	9.0	5.8	5.0	5.2	6.0	6.1
Netherlands	4.4	7.0	6.3	5.3	2.8	2.1	2.2	0.2	-0.1	0.6	1.5	2.5
West Germany	3.9	5.8	6.2	4.8	3.2	2.5	2.1	-0.5	0.6	1.2	3.2	2.7
Average ERM	8.0	10.6	10.7	9.5	7.4	6.1	4.9	2.0	2.5	2.5	3.7	3.5

Non-ERM Countries	1979	1980	1981	1982	1983	1984	1985	1986	1987	1988	1989	1990
Austria	4.5	6.4	7.6	6.0	3.4	5.6	3.3	1.9	0.9	1.6	2.7	3.3
Canada	8.5	10.0	11.2	10.2	6.3	3.9	3.7	3.8	3.9	4.0	4.7	4.8
Japan	3.6	7.1	4.4	2.6	1.9	2.1	2.2	0.6	-0.2	-0.1	1.7	3.1
Norway	5.1	10.0	13.4	11.0	8.4	6.4	5.9	7.6	7.9	6.2	4.4	4.1
United Kingdom	13.6	16.3	11.2	8.8	4.8	5.0	5.4	4.4	4.3	4.9	5.9	9.5
United States	9.2	10.8	9.2	5.7	4.1	3.8	3.3	2.4	4.6	3.9	4.5	5.4
Average non-ERM	7.4	10.1	9.5	7.4	4.8	4.5	4.0	3.5	3.6	3.4	4.0	5.0

Note:
The above inflation rates are based on private consumption deflators.
Source: OECD, *World Economic Outlook*, December 1990.

both during the periods 1974–8 and 1979–86 found only little and inconclusive support for the hypothesis that the inflation rate had come down more significantly for the EMS countries for the whole of the period.

Giavazzi and Giovannini (1988) use a different methodology to test the anti-inflation hypothesis. They exploit the theoretical predictions of what is known as the Lucas critique. In a celebrated paper, Lucas (1976) argued that statistical relationships will change according to the policy regime in force. In the context of the EMS, the change in policy regime represented by the setting up of the EMS means that the statistical parameters governing wage, price and output behaviour in the countries studied (France, Italy, Denmark and Germany) should have changed given the discipline of the EMS. Giavazzi and Giovannini do not find that the statistical relationships change significantly if mid-1979 is taken as the starting point. If the starting point is taken from the beginning of 1982 there is some weak evidence of a change in wage and price behaviour which provides some support for the anti-inflation hypothesis. The authors suggest that because of large real depreciation of the lira and franc in 1978, the French and Italian authorities did not have to accept the EMS discipline in the early stages of the system. Furthermore, it took economic agents time to learn the implications of EMS membership and the authorities time to earn credibility. Only then did agents revise downwards their wage and price behaviour.

Overall, it appears that one of the reasons for the lack of conclusive support for the anti-inflation hypothesis is that in the first three years of its operation it is a seriously defective description of the EMS (see Weber, 1991). The differential effects of the second oil shock made authorities very reluctant to accept the discipline of the system. This is amply illustrated by the frequent realignments and the French dash for growth in 1981. It seems that after 1982 policy makers in France, Denmark, Belgium, and Italy decided to subject their economies to disinflationary policies. For instance, the French government adopted an austerity package in March 1983 and the Italian authorities repealed wage indexation laws in 1984. The resulting disinflation led to both a rapid decline in EMS inflation rates and a greater degree of convergence as compared with the group of non-EMS currencies.

■ *14.17* Intervention in the EMS

Although the EMS was supposed to result in more symmetry with regard to intervention through the mechanism of the divergence indicator, in practice the indicator has not worked particularly well. A study of intervention within the EMS by Mastropasqua, Micossi and Rinaldi (1988) has shown some interesting asymmetries and contrasts with respect to intervention behaviour within the EMS:

The Bundesbank has generally not been very active with regard to non obligatory **intra-marginal** intervention. At times, however, particularly when the system has been on the verge of realignments (such as in January 1987) it has been prepared to engage in heavy obligatory **marginal** intervention. Where the Bundesbank has been far more active is with regard to the dollar exchange rate; it was a large seller of dollars when the dollar was appreciating during 1980–85 and a large purchaser when the dollar subsequently fell.

The other ERM countries have been far more active with regard to **intra-marginal** intervention and keeping their currencies in line with the deutschmark. Increasingly they have used deutschmarks in preference to dollars for such **intra-marginal** intervention.

The other interesting finding is that the Bundesbank typically sterilises its interventions so that they do not affect the West German monetary base. That is, purchases or sales of foreign currency that increase or decrease the West German money supply are typically offset by sales or purchases of domestic bonds so as to neutralise the effect on the monetary base. The other EMS countries studied normally only engage in partial sterilisation (30–40 per cent) so that purchases or sales of foreign currency result in expansion and contraction of their domestic money supplies.

The overall picture that emerges is that the Bundesbank manages the external (*erga-extra*) exchange rate of the ERM currencies against the dollar. While the rest of the ERM members take responsibility for ensuring that they keep their exchange rates in line with the deutschmark managing the internal (*erga-intra*) parities. In addition, the Bundesbank by pursuing a sterilisation policy generally does not allow its exchange-rate policy to influence its money supply and its primary objective of domestic price stability. On the other hand, other ERM countries accept the discipline of the system, by purchasing their currencies when they are weak to keep them in line with the deutschmark and permit this intervention to result in a contraction in their money supplies.

Nevertheless, the authors emphasise that intervention is only one of the means by which countries have maintained their peg to the deutschmark. The most obvious means has been to raise their domestic interest rates when their currencies are under pressure and lower them when the pressure recedes. Here again there is ample evidence that countries other than West Germany have borne most of the adjustment burden, the Bundesbank proving very reluctant to reflate. In practice, far from being a symmetrical system it appears that weak currency members have accepted the discipline of the EMS both with respect to their intervention and domestic economic policies and been prepared to accept the deflationary consequences necessary to maintain their exchange rate parity. In the early years of the system some of the countries found the discipline too much and realigned their currencies.

14.18 The economic performance of ERM and non-ERM countries

While there is widespread agreement that the EMS has succeeded in its aim of becoming a 'zone of currency stability' there is considerable disagreement over the benefits or otherwise of full EMS membership. Even if membership of the ERM does help bring down a country's inflation rate, this may have been at the expense of these countries having to adopt deflationary policies that have led to lower economic growth than non-members. **Table 14.8** shows that economic growth has generally been lower for the ERM countries as compared with the non-ERM countries.

14.19 The private and official usage of the European currency unit

Although it was originally envisaged that the ECU would be used extensively for intervention in the ERM, in practice this has not been the case. Both **marginal** and **intra-marginal** intervention has been primarily conducted in ERM currencies and the US dollar. The ECU has been extensively used by EEC institutions as a means for denominating financial transactions but otherwise the official use of the ECU has been rather limited.

By contrast the ECU proved very popular in private financial markets as a denominator for international bond issues. While private companies were initially responsible for most ECU bond issues, international organisations and some governments (notably France and Italy) have been increasingly keen on ECU bond issues. In 1985 the ECU Eurobond issues amounted to a dollar equivalent value of $6.1 billion and in 1990 the market for new issues was worth $15.9 billion. The attractiveness of ECU lies in the fact that it is made up of a basket of currencies that are closely tied to one another. As such it offers both a diversified portfolio and a good hedge against exchange risk. This popularity in financial markets has not yet extended to commercial transactions; in 1990 less than 2 per cent of trade between Community countries was denominated in ECUs.

■ *14.20* Approaches to EMU

Even if the European heads of government make the necessary political commitment to go ahead with EMU, this still leaves the issue of how to

388 The Post-war International Monetary System

Table 14.8 Economic growth in ERM and non-ERM countries

ERM countries	1979	1980	1981	1982	1983	1984	1985	1986	1987	1988	1989	1990
Belgium	2.2	4.2	-0.9	1.5	0.4	2.0	0.8	1.6	2.3	4.6	4.0	3.5
Denmark	3.5	-0.4	-0.9	3.0	2.5	4.4	4.3	3.6	-0.6	-0.2	1.4	1.6
France	3.2	1.6	1.2	2.5	0.7	1.3	1.9	2.5	2.2	3.8	3.6	2.8
Italy	6.0	4.2	1.0	0.3	1.1	3.0	2.6	2.5	3.0	4.2	3.2	2.0
Netherlands	2.1	1.2	-0.7	-1.4	1.3	2.9	2.4	2.7	0.4	2.7	4.1	3.5
West Germany	4.0	1.5	0	-1.0	1.9	3.3	1.9	2.3	1.6	3.7	3.9	4.5
Average ERM	3.5	2.1	-0.1	0.8	1.3	2.8	2.3	2.5	1.5	3.1	3.4	3.0

Non-ERM countries	1979	1980	1981	1982	1983	1984	1985	1986	1987	1988	1989	1990
Austria	4.7	2.9	-0.3	1.1	2.0	1.4	2.5	1.2	2.0	3.9	4.0	4.6
Canada	3.6	1.1	3.4	-3.2	3.2	6.3	4.7	3.3	4.0	4.4	3.0	0.9
Japan	5.3	4.3	3.7	3.1	3.2	5.1	4.9	2.5	4.6	5.7	4.9	5.6
Norway	5.1	4.2	0.9	0.3	4.6	5.7	5.3	4.2	2.0	-0.5	0.4	1.8
United Kingdom	2.8	-1.9	-1.1	1.6	3.6	2.1	3.6	3.9	4.7	4.6	2.2	0.6
United States	2.5	-0.2	1.9	-2.5	3.6	6.8	3.4	2.7	3.4	4.5	2.5	0.9
Average non-ERM	4.0	1.8	1.4	0.1	3.4	4.6	4.1	3.0	3.5	3.8	2.8	2.4

Source: OECD, *World Economic Outlook*, December 1990 & July 1991.

proceed. In this respect there are two main approaches to EMU, known respectively as the 'monetarist' and 'economist' plans.

☐ The 'monetarist' approach

The monetarist approach to monetary union argues that once countries have made the commitment to achieve monetary union they should immediately agree to fix their exchange rate parities on a permanent basis, the precise exchange rate parities presumably being a topic for discussion. Those advocating the monetary approach accept that it may be necessary in the first instance to impose strict controls on capital movements to defend the exchange-rate parity. However, the idea is that over time authorities will be able to coordinate their monetary policies so as to achieve similar inflation rates. This will eliminate pressures for parity changes enabling the gradual and eventual complete removal of capital controls.

The argument made by the monetarists for fixing exchange rates immediately and coordinating economic policies afterwards is that fixing exchange rates will force countries to coordinate their monetary policies. Monetarists doubt whether countries will ever coordinate enough in the absence of a fixed exchange rate. In addition as the monetary approach to the balance of payments suggests any balance-of-payments problems will be a temporary and self-correcting phenomena.

☐ The 'economists' approach

The essential features of the economists' approach to EMU is that they argue for the coordination and harmonisation of macroeconomic policies prior to EMU and accompanying this with complete freedom of capital movements. Only when countries achieve common underlying inflation rates can exchange rate parities be permanently fixed at realistic rates.

The rationale underlying the economist approach is that members of the EEC are at very different levels of economic development. In such circumstances, to fix exchange rates immediately as suggested by the monetarists would mean that high inflation countries would be forced to adopt deflationary measures to bring their inflation rates in line with low inflation countries. As such, the 'economists' argue that a monetarist approach to EMU is seriously flawed because the deflation necessary in high inflation countries would provoke major regional disparities within the community. The economists argue that to attempt to achieve monetary union without achieving a high degree of convergence of economic performance and the prior strengthening and coordination of macroeconomic policies could prove disastrous.

We now turn to look at two of the most important practical proposals that have been put forward to achieve EMU other than the Werner Report of 1972: the Parallel Currency Proposal and more recently the so-called Delors Report.

■ *14.21* The parallel currency proposal

In 1975 nine leading European economists wrote an article in *The Economist* magazine suggesting the launching of a European currency called the 'Europa' that would be legal tender throughout the community. A centrally issued Europa would co-exist with the various national currencies. Economic agents would have the option of carrying out economic transactions in either their domestic currency or the Europa. The attractiveness of using the Europa would lie in it being 'inflation proof', that is, the general level of prices expressed in terms of the Europa would not rise. The central monetary authority charged with controlling the supply of Europas would adopt a monetary rule to ensure no inflation for prices expressed in Europas.

The proponents of the parallel currency proposal argue that it has several attractive features. National authorities could still continue to supply their national currencies but these would have to compete with the Europa as a means of payment. This would make it essential for national authorities to bring their inflation rates under control. Furthermore, the proponents argued that economic agents would only switch over from using national currencies gradually and voluntarily. Hence, EMU would only be achieved because the citizens of Europe had shown they wanted it by switching away from their national currencies and not because politicians had forced it upon them. Furthermore, since the Europa could be freely used in all EEC countries the acceptance by national authorities of the Europa coexisting with their national currencies would *de facto* mean free mobility of capital within the community.

Attractive as it seems, there are none the less some major problems with the parallel currency proposal. The scheme still does not overcome the problem of obtaining the necessary political commitment on the part of national policy makers. National authorities have to allow the Europa to compete as legal tender in their countries and agree to the setting up of a European Central Bank to control the supply of Europas. Furthermore, if the Europa was a credible inflation proof money which could be used throughout the community, then it is difficult to see why rational economic agents would hold national currencies at all. In other words, far from gradually replacing the various national currencies a Europa could replace them instantly. What makes the parallel currency proposal difficult from a political viewpoint is that it is inflation proof and thereby if national currencies are to survive they too would have to be immune to inflation. This implies a loss of the 'inflation tax' benefit that arises to national governments as inflation reduces the real value of money held by economic agents. This would have to be replaced by a more explicit tax on incomes or goods, which could prove politically unpopular.

■ *14.22* The Delors report

At a meeting of the European Council in June 1988 the Heads of Government of the member countries of the EEC confirmed the long run objective of economic and monetary union. A committee of academics and central bankers was set up 'with the task of studying and proposing concrete stages leading to union' headed by Mr Jacques Delors, President of the European Commission. The result of the deliberations was the so-called Delors report which set out in broad outline a proposal to achieve EMU by three separate stages.

□ *Requirements of EMU*

The report emphasises that member states would have to be prepared to transfer decision-making power to Community institutions in the field of monetary policy and be bound to preset procedures and rules in other areas such as fiscal policy. In particular, it emphasises the need not only for convergent monetary policies but also for convergent fiscal policies.

Further, the report argues that monetary union requires a single currency rather than just irrevocably fixed parities. A single currency would demonstrate the irreversibility of the move to monetary union, considerably facilitate monetary management within the community and avoid the transaction costs of converting currencies. An EEC Central Bank would be a necessity to operate monetary and credit policy and interest policy rather than close coordination between existing central banks. Full liberalisation of capital markets and financial market integration are essential.

Interestingly, the report rejects the parallel currency approach for two main reasons. First, a fear that an additional source of money creation without a precise linkage to economic activity could jeopardize price stability. Second, a feeling that a new currency produced by a community institution would further complicate the task of coordinating different monetary policies.

☐ The three stages to EMU

The report envisages the attainment of EMU in three stages, each stage representing a significant change with respect to the preceding one. Although there is a detailed programme for the first stage, the second and third stages contain more general aims and are less detailed on specifics. Explicit deadlines for all stages were not made, although a deadline for stage 1 was set at July 1991. We now briefly look at the proposals set out for each stage.

Stage 1

The first stage is the initiation of the process aimed at a greater convergence of economic performance and enhancing economic and monetary coordination between member states within the existing institutional framework. The main features of the first stage of the programme are:

(a)   The completion of the internal market project.
(b)   A strengthening of community policies to iron out regional imbalances.
(c)   Greater cooperation and coordination of monetary and fiscal policies.
(d)   Removal of obstacles to financial integration including the removal of all obstacles to the private use of the ECU.
(e)   All members of the EMS joining the ERM.

There was some disagreement in the committee over whether a European Reserve Fund (ERF) should be set up to foreshadow the future European System of Central Banks. The ERF would be invested with some 10 per cent of members' reserves, its task being to manage the reserves, intervene in exchange markets as decided by members and to promote greater coordination of members' monetary policies.

Stage 2

The second stage requires amendments to the Treaty of Rome. In this stage the basic organs and structure of economic and monetary union would be set up involving both the revision of existing community institutions and establishment of new ones.

There would be an evaluation of progress relating to stage 1. In addition, there would be a medium-term framework for key economic objectives, precise but not binding rules as to the size of annual national budget deficits and greater unity of action by the members in the exchange rate and monetary field.

A European System of Central Banks (ESCB) would be set up to absorb the previously existing monetary arrangements (EMCF, Committee of Central Bank governors). The role of the ESCB in the formulation and operation of a common monetary policy would gradually evolve as experience was gained. The key task of the ECSB would be to begin the transition from the coordination of independent national monetary policies to the formulation and implementation of a common monetary policy by the ECSB itself.

Stage 3

The final stage would commence with a move to irrevocably locked exchange-rates and the attribution to Community institutions of the responsibility for the conduct of monetary, fiscal and exchange rate policy. Eventually the national currencies would be replaced by a single Community currency.

Rules and procedures relating to the Community in the macroeconomic and budgetary field would become binding. In particular, the Council of Ministers in cooperation with the European Parliament would have the authority to take directly enforceable decisions. The Council could impose constraints on national budgets and direct Community resources to influence the overall policy stance within the Community.

The ECSB would be given full control over the formulation and implementation of the Community's monetary policy. This would include exclusive power on decisions on exchange market interventions with respect to third currencies.

Remarks on the Delors report

The Delors report takes for granted that the benefits of EMU exceed the costs and it was the remit of the committee to draw up a set of proposals relating to how such a process might be achieved. Although it mentions that there is a need for a degree of fiscal coordination to accompany EMU there is no discussion of what type of coordination is needed and no analysis of the underlying economic rationale. While the report rightly argues that there may be regional imbalances it is not clear that an enhanced community regional policy is a necessary corrective mechanism. On a more fundamental basis the role and status of the proposed ECSB is not fully discussed. Undoubtedly were EMU to proceed the Germans would prefer that it had an independent status similar to the Bundesbank with a priority to ensure price stability. Other EEC members would probably prefer that it had a Board of Governors representing the member countries and was able to adjust monetary policy in the light of the economic conditions in the member states implying a more relaxed policy stance.

■ *14.23* Conclusions

While the EMS differs from a simple agreement to peg exchange rates in a number of important respects such as; the central role of the ECU, the setting up of a common pool of reserves, the individualisation of divergence thresholds and theoretically symmetric responsibilities for surplus and deficit countries, it is far from EMU. The EMS is only a zone of currency stability and even the central rates can be adjusted. There is no European central bank to supply the ECU, which while it has proved popular as a unit of account for private financiers is still far from a medium of exchange. While the EMS may eventually prove to be an important stepping-stone on the path towards EMU it is by no means an automatic step.

The EMS has proved far more resilient and successful than its Snake predecessor. This can be partly explained by the fact that following the experience of the 1970s there has been a greater commitment by governments to control inflation. Furthermore, the associated cost in terms of higher unemployment levels has not proved as politically disastrous as had been previously thought. However, while EMS members do seem to have had a superior inflation performance in recent years, especially in the cases of Italy and France, this does not establish causality. It may well have been the case that Italy and France would have engaged in an anti-inflationary set of policies even if they had not joined the EMS.

If the EEC member states are to achieve full monetary integration it requires a quantum leap in terms of political support. What prevents such a leap is not only that governments jealously guard their macroeconomic autonomy but also the transitional costs associated with the need to bring underlying inflation rates into line and disagreement over what is an appropriate inflation rate for the union. The objections to EMU run much deeper than purely economic issues – many governments are concerned about handing over the responsibilities for the conduct of their monetary and fiscal policies to unelected Community institutions. Institutional reform and greater democratic control of Community institutions will remain an important component of the EMU debate.

In recent years, the balance of benefits and costs has tipped increasingly favourably towards EMU. In large part the main cost associated with EMU, namely the loss of monetary policy sovereignty has already been given up by members of the ERM who accept the monetary discipline of the Bundesbank. For this reason, France and Italy have become increasingly interested in EMU partly because they believe it will give them a greater say in the conduct of monetary policy (as members of the board of the ESCB). In the way of benefits, the single market project by tackling non tariff barriers to trade and requiring the removal of capital controls makes the usage of differing national currencies look increasingly inefficient. The original aim of the EMS was to create a zone of currency stability. It has since evolved as a credible anti-inflation system. It remains to be seen whether it will lead to European Monetary Union.

■ *Selected further readings*

Artis, M.J. and Taylor, M.P. (1988) 'Exchange Rates, Interest Rates, Capital Controls and the European Monetary System: Assessing the Track Record', in F. Giavazzi, S. Micossi, and M. Miller *The European Monetary System* (Cambridge: Cambridge University Press).

Canzoneri, M.B. and Rogers, C.A. (1990) 'Is the European Community an Optimal Currency Area? Optimal Taxation Versus the Cost of Multiple Currencies', *American Economic Review*, vol. 80, pp. 419–33.

Cohen, D. and Wyplosz, C. (1989) 'The European Monetary Union: An Agnostic Evaluation', in R.C. Bryant, D.A. Currie, J.A. Frenkel, P.R. Masson and R. Portes (eds), *Macroeconomic Policies in an Interdependent World* (Washington: IMF).

Collins, S. (1988) 'Inflation and the European Monetary System', in F. Giavazzi, S. Micossi, M. Miller (eds), *The European Monetary System* (Cambridge: Cambridge University Press).

Emerson, M. (1990) 'The Economics of EMU', in *Britain & EMU*, Centre for Economic Performance, London School of Economics, London.

Gandolfo, G. (1987) *International Economics II* (Berlin: Springer-Verlag).

Giavazzi, F. (1989) 'The Exchange Rate Question in Europe', in R.C. Bryant, D.A. Currie, J.A. Frenkel, P.R. Masson and R. Portes (eds), *Macroeconomic Policies in an Interdependent World* (Washington: IMF).

Giavazzi, F. and Pagano, M. (1988) 'The Advantage of Tying One's Hands: EMS Discipline and Central Bank Credibility', *European Economic Review*, vol. 32, pp. 1055–75.

Giavazzi, F. and Giovannini, A. (1988) 'The Role of the Exchange Rate Regime in a Disinflation: Empirical Evidence on the European Monetary System', in F. Giavazzi, S. Micossi, M. Miller (eds), *The European Monetary System* (Cambridge: Cambridge University Press).

Giovannini, A. (1990) 'European Monetary Reform: Progress and Prospects'. Brookings Papers on Economic Activity, vol. 2, pp. 217–91.

Goodhart, C.A.E. (1975) *Money, Information and Uncertainty* (London: Macmillan).

Hu, Y.S. (1981) *Europe Under Stress: Convergence and Divergence in the European Community* (Kent: Butterworth).

Ishiyama, Y. (1975) 'The Theory of Optimum Currency Areas: A Survey', *IMF Staff Papers*, vol. 22, pp. 344–83

Kenen, P.B. (1969) 'The Theory of Optimum Currency Areas: An Eclectic View', in R.A. Mundell and A.K. Swoboda (eds), *Monetary Problems of the International Economy* (Chicago: University of Chicago).

Lucas, R.E. Jnr. (1976) 'Econometric Policy Evaluations: A Critique', in K. Brunner and A.H. Meltzer, *The Phillips Curve and Labour Markets*. Carnegie-Rochester Conference Series on Public Policy No. 1 (Amsterdam: North-Holland) pp. 19–46.

McKinnon, R.I. (1963) 'Optimum Currency Areas', *American Economic Review*, vol. 53, pp. 717–25.

Mastropasqua, C., Micossi, S., and Rinaldi, R. (1988) 'Interventions Sterilisation and Monetary Policy in European Monetary System Countries, 1979–87', in F. Giavazzi, S. Micossi and M. Miller (eds), *The European Monetary System* (Cambridge: Cambridge University Press).

Melitz, J.A. (1988), 'Monetary Discipline and Cooperation in the European Monetary System: A Synthesis', in F. Giavazzi, S. Micossi, M. Miller (eds), *The European Monetary System* (Cambridge: Cambridge University Press).

Mundell, R.A. (1961) 'A Theory of Optimum Currency Areas', *American Economic Review*, vol. 51, pp. 509–17.

Padoa Schioppa, T. (1985) 'Policy Cooperation and the EMS Experience', in W.H. Buiter and R.C. Marston, *International Economic Policy Coordination* (Cambridge: Cambridge University Press).

Peree, E. and Steinherr, A. (1989) 'Exchange Rate Uncertainty and Foreign Trade', *European Economic Review*, vol. 33, pp. 1241–64.

Tower, E. and Willet, T.D. (1976) 'The Theory of Optimum Currency Areas and Exchange Rate Flexibility', *Princeton Special Papers in International Finance* No. 11, Princeton.

Urenger, H., Evans, O., Mayer, T. and Young, P. (1986) 'The European Monetary System: Recent Developments', *IMF Occasional Papers*, No. 48, Washington.

Weber, A. (1991) 'EMS Credibility', *Economic Policy*, vol. 12, pp. 58–102.

■ *Chapter 15* ■

International Debt Crisis

■ *15.1* Introduction

On 12 August 1982, the Mexican government announced that it could not meet its forthcoming debt repayments on its $80 billion of outstanding debt to international banks. This was the first sign of the international debt crisis. Soon after the Mexican announcement a number of other less developed countries (LDCs) announced that they too were facing severe difficulty in meeting forthcoming repayments. Throughout the 1980s the problems faced by the LDCs in servicing their debts have been at the forefront of concerns about the development of the world economy.

The debt crisis encompasses a wide set of countries from low income developing nations to middle income countries. In this chapter, we concentrate upon a group of 19 countries that have been termed by the World Bank in its 1990–91 *World Debt Tables* as Severely Indebted Middle Income Countries (SIMICs). To qualify as a SIMIC a country must be classified as a middle income country and have three of four key ratios above certain critical levels. These ratios are debt to GNP (50 per cent), debt to exports of goods and services (275 per cent), accrued debt service to exports (30 per cent) and accrued interest to exports (20 per cent). Other than the SIMICs there is a group classified Moderately Indebted Middle Income Countries (MIMICs), a group classified as Severely Indebted Low Income Countries (SILICs) and a group of Moderately Indebted Low Income Countries (MILICs).

Although they are both severely indebted there are considerable contrasts between the SIMICs and the SILICs. The 19 SIMICs are especially concentrated in Latin America. In 1989 their combined external debt amounted to $566 billion and 61.8 per cent of their external debt is owed to the private sources made up primarily of Commercial Banks. By contrast, 24 out of the 26 SILICs are to be found in sub-Saharan Africa. In 1989 their combined external debt amounted to $108 billion with only 26.9 per cent owed to private sources and the remainder to official agencies.

The international debt crisis raises many questions. How did the crisis come about? Why did international banks lend so much money to these countries? Why have indebted countries not gone into outright default? How has the debt crisis been managed since the emergence of the problem? What are the various solutions that have been put forward to resolve the crisis? In this chapter we examine possible answers to these questions and a host of other issues associated with the debt crisis.

We pay special attention to the debt problems of the four major SIMICs which are all in Latin America – Mexico, Argentina, Brazil and Venezuela. At the end of 1988 these four accounted for 60 per cent of total SIMICs debt and 71 per cent of SIMIC debt to private sources. The concentration of commercial bank loans in these four economies led to fears that if any of them defaulted – this would undermine the banks that lent to them, especially the US banks that had massive exposures. The resulting knock-on effects would push the world into a major economic recession.

15.2 The low and middle income less developed countries

The less developed countries are traditionally distinguished from the developed economies by their lower per capita GNP. However, developed and less developed countries are far from homogeneous groups. LDCs can be placed into two categories:

1. **Low income LDCs** – typically with incomes of less than $580 per capita at 1989 prices, these include most of sub-Saharan Africa, India and China.

2. **Middle income LDCs** – this group comprises a very wide range of countries with incomes in the region of more than $580 per capita and less than $6000 per capita at 1989 prices. Some of this group can be classified as low middle income countries which includes most countries in Latin America – Argentina ($2520), Brazil ($2160), Mexico ($1760) and Venezuela ($3250) and many richer African countries.

15.3 Characteristics of typical middle income LDCs

Since the debt crisis has been predominately confined to less developed countries especially those in the low middle income group some discussion of the main features of such middle income LDCs is necessary. Although it is difficult to generalise, the following represents a list of the main differences between developed and middle income less developed economies.

☐ *Financial markets*

The financial markets in less developed countries tend to have a relatively limited range of investment opportunities for savers and are normally subject to a high degree of government control. Unlike developed countries that tend to have well developed stock markets, LDCs' stock markets are often rudimentary in nature and companies are therefore heavily reliant on banks for funding. Banks are usually either state owned or subject to heavy government control aimed at maintaining low real interest rates designed to stimulate investment. A major problem that results from these low real interest rate policies is that it tends to further discourage saving which is already low because of their low income levels. Low savings combined with low real interest rates lead to an excess demand for funds requiring credit rationing. Under credit rationing the decisions as to which industries can borrow and how much is largely determined by the government of the day. In addition, the low interest rates stimulate expenditure on imports, contributing to balance-of-payments problems.

☐ *Exchange-rate pegging and exchange controls*

The exchange rates of LDCs are frequently pegged normally to the dollar, pound sterling, French franc or SDR, typically on a 'crawling peg' basis.

Since LDCs tend to have quite high inflation rates pegging their currencies against foreign currencies which have lower inflation rates would be impractical as they would quickly lose competitiveness. For this reason, they frequently devalue the central rate against the currencies to which they are pegged. One of the problems with such crawling peg arrangements is that if the currency to which they are pegged appreciates, such as the strong dollar appreciation between 1980 and 1985, this may prove to be disastrous for the LDC's exports. For this reason, some LDCs prefer to peg to a basket of currencies such as the SDR. A basket of currencies will tend not to appreciate or depreciate as much as an individual currency.

In addition to pegging their exchange rates most LDCs make extensive use of capital controls, with the central bank applying various restrictions on the purchases and sales of foreign currencies. These restrictions serve several purposes as far as the LDC governments are concerned. By restricting the ability of its residents to invest their savings abroad the controls enable the government to borrow funds from its residents at a lower rate of interest than would otherwise be the case. Controls are usually heavily biased against capital outflows, restricting sales of the home currency and reducing the strain on foreign currency reserves which would otherwise be required to defend a pegged exchange rate.

The exchange-rate controls normally require that home residents obtain government permission to purchase foreign currencies. Often the authorities combine the controls with multiple exchange-rate systems. This means that the authorities may offer a different rate of exchange depending upon the nature of the particular transaction. For instance, if the foreign currency is required to pay for imports of capital equipment or essential items, the authorities will usually offer a more favourable rate of exchange than if it is required to pay for the import of luxury consumption goods. This is because capital imports and cheap prices for essentials are considered more favourable to economic development.

☐ *Low degree of diversification*

The output of less developed economies is usually far less diversified than that of developed countries. Agricultural output usually represents a fairly high proportion of GDP and usually their exports are made up of relatively few commodities, such as raw materials and agricultural exports. This means their economic performance can be subject to a wide degree of fluctuation due to bad harvests or changes in the value of their principal exports. The prices of primary products produced and exported by LDCs fluctuate far more than the manufactured products of developed economies. This price variability means that the incomes and trade performances of

LDCs can be subject to large fluctuations from year to year. Recessions in industrialised countries are especially harmful to LDCs as they experience both a fall in the price of their primary products and a decline in their export volumes, meaning large reductions in their export revenues.

☐ *Inflationary environment*

The LDCs tend to have persistent problems with controlling their inflation rates. To a large extent government budget deficits are financed by the government resorting to money creation, partly because the financial markets are too rudimentary to raise the required borrowing from domestic sources, and partly because governments find taxing their citizens to be politically unpopular and often easily evaded. The resulting inflation reduces the real value of money held by domestic residents constituting an 'inflation tax' and reduces the real value of outstanding government debt.

To protect workers' wages from the effects of the inflationary environment there is usually a high degree of wage indexation so that wages rise in line with prices. Wage indexation makes it very difficult for the authorities to bring inflation under control because at the same time as the authorities take measures to slow down future inflation wages are being adjusted upwards on the basis of previous inflation. Indexation also means that real wages are difficult to reduce should an economic shock such as a deterioration in the country's terms of trade require such a fall. Consequently, such shocks normally lead to increased unemployment. A rapidly growing workforce leads to a continuous upward pressure on government expenditure to provide employment in state enterprises.

■ *15.4* The economics of LDC borrowing

A key question relating to the debt problem is why were the middle income LDCs eager to borrow and the commercial banks so willing to supply the funds in the first place?

From the perspective of the LDCs their combinations of low incomes and poorly developed capital markets mean that there is insufficient domestic savings to provide the finance for domestic investment. Their relatively low capital stock means that there are plenty of opportunities for profitable investment. A low capital to labour ratio means that the marginal productivity of capital is high. By borrowing funds from abroad they can raise domestic investment above domestic savings which in turn leads to a higher rate of economic growth than in the absence of such borrowing. The fact that investment then exceeds domestic savings implies that the country is running a current account deficit the counterpart of which is the capital inflow on the capital account. Later on, the LDC will have to repay the principal and interest on the loans extended to it. The hope is that the state of the economy will be such that repayments should present no problems.

As for the developed economies, their relatively high incomes and sophisticated financial markets lead to relatively high savings ratios. Their relatively high capital to labour ratios mean that the marginal productivity of capital is relatively low restricting the amount of profitable investment opportunities. This means that there is an excess of savings looking for appropriate investment opportunities. Such opportunities exist in abundance in LDCs who in turn lack the required funds. Hence, there is the potential for profitable exchange between the developed and developing countries. The LDCs can utilise the excess savings of the developed countries for investment while the lending developed countries have higher prospective returns from investing in the LDCs than domestic investments.

 15.5 **Different types of capital inflows into LDCs**

There are a variety of means available for LDCs to attract capital inflows from the developed economies to finance new investment. An understanding of these different means of raising finance is essential in explaining not only why the debt crisis emerged but also the nature of the debt problem. Many of the proposals for resolving the debt crisis involve converting the liabilities of the indebted nations from one form of obligation into another.

☐ *Bond finance*

The LDC governments can issue bonds to foreign investors with a guaranteed rate of interest on those bonds depending upon the maturity date of the bond and whether or not it is denominated in the domestic or foreign currency. If the bond is issued in the domestic currency it is subject to 'inflation risk' because there is a danger that higher than expected inflation in the issuing country could undermine the real redemption value of the bond. Alternatively, if the bond is issued in a foreign currency it is subject to 'default risk' that is the danger that the LDC will not be able to redeem the bond. While bond finance was an important means of finance for the LDCs up until the 1940s it has not proved to be very significant in the debt crisis as it represented a mere 0.5 per cent of LDC debt in 1988.

☐ *Bank loans*

The LDCs can borrow money from the Commercial banks of the developed countries. Such loans are usually made either at fixed rates of interest or at floating rates of interest and may be of a short term or long term nature. During the 1970s and 1980s this was the major source of finance for LDCs especially for the Latin American countries. The loans extended to the LDCs were predominately 'syndicated loans' that is, loans made by syndicates of international banks. These loans were generally made in US dollars at floating rates of interest, that is, the repayments could be adjusted upwards or downwards in line with changes in international interest rates. The key rate of interest for such loans is the London Inter-Bank Offer Rate (LIBOR), the rate of interest at which London banks lend to one another. Loans to LDCs are normally expressed as a margin over LIBOR.

☐ *Direct investment*

Another means by which the LDCs can raise foreign finance is by attracting direct foreign investment into the country. Such investment can take many forms. It could involve a foreign multinational acquiring equity in a domestically owned business, a multinational expanding an existing subsidiary or foreign investors setting up a completely new enterprise in the LDC. Such direct investment is a popular method of multinationals investing in LDCs since it gives them both ownership and control over the businesses that they set up and acquire.

☐ *Official finance*

In addition to private sources of foreign investment the LDCs are also able to raise money for developmental purposes directly from foreign governments and international institutions. Loans from foreign governments are often made at below market rates of interest to developing countries as part of their foreign aid programmes. Loans from the World Bank come at favourable rates of interest because the World Bank has a top credit rating which enables it to raise large sums of capital from private markets at lower interest rates than the individual LDCs.

Overall, a clear distinction needs to be made between debt finance and equity finance. Debt finance of which bond, bank and official finance are examples, requires the debtor to repay the principal and the rate of interest attached to the loan whatever the economic situation in the debtor nation. If the country faces a worsening of its economic circumstances, it must repay the principal and interest on its outstanding debt regardless. This contrasts with equity finance whereby the foreign investors either own shares or have direct control of LDC companies. In these cases, the repayment for their investment, is in the form of profits and dividends and changes in the value of the companies are directly related to the performance of the companies and the LDC concerned. If the LDC faces adverse economic conditions this will lead to less repayments to foreigners in the form of reduced profits and dividends. Conversely economic prosperity in the LDC will lead to larger profits and dividend payments to foreign investors.

■ *15.6* Measures of indebtedness

When deciding whether to extend a new loan or to make provisions against existing loans or even whether to write off parts of their outstanding loans, private banks will want to know the probability of the existing debt or new loan being repaid. This will enable them to balance the risk and return elements of the loan. The problem is that there is no unique indicator or measure of the burden imposed on a country by its external indebtedness. In order to assess the risks, banks will have to arrive at a view of the economic and political state of a country. In arriving at their decision on risks, banks rely on a range of indicators many of which are reported by the World Bank in its *World Debt Tables*. Some of the most popular statistics employed to assess country risk are:

External debt as a percentage of exports of goods and services – this expresses the country's external debt both private, public and publicly guaranteed as a ratio of its export earnings. The idea is that the export earnings are the means by which the country earns foreign currency to pay off its debt. Problems with this ratio are that exports may be subject to a high degree of fluctuation from year to year and there are alternative measures a country can employ to pay off its external debt other than increasing its export revenues. For example, cutting down import expenditure or running down reserves.

Reserves as a percentage of total external debt – this is a measure showing the reserves that the central bank of the debtor nation could in theory use to pay off its external debt.

External debt as a percentage of Gross Domestic Product – this is a measure that gives an idea of the total debt burden in relation to the GDP of the country. However, it says nothing about the annual burden imposed on the country, the amount of repayments falling due or which section of the community the burden will fall upon.

Box 15.1 *Some debt terminology*

Within the context of the international debt crisis many terms are frequently employed and for this reason are worth defining.

Public and publicly guaranteed debt – most of the loans made to LDCs are loans either directly to the LDC government or to state-owned enterprises. Such debt is known as public debt. Foreign loans to LDCs are frequently made to the private sector but because such lending is regarded as highly risky, it is usually necessary for the LDC government to guarantee to fulfil the loan contract in the case of non-payment by the private borrower. This type of obligation is known as publicly guaranteed debt. The presence of exchange controls in most LDCs means that the LDC government usually gets involved in loan agreements between foreign and domestic residents.

Total external debt – this is the sum of private non guaranteed debt and public and publicly guaranteed debt.

Debt service – this is the sum of principal and interest rate repayments that a country has to make during a given time period.

Default – an LDC is said to be in default when it fails to make the repayments of principal and/or interest specified in its loan contract and has no intention of repaying in the future.

Moratorium – an LDC announces its refusal to make the payments of principal and/or interest specified in its loan contract until it can come to an agreement over future repayments with its creditors. A moratorium differs from default in that the debtor has the intention to continue repayments later on provided it can reach suitable repayment arrangements with its creditors.

Debt rescheduling – this occurs when all or part of the repayments of principal and/or interest due on outstanding debt are postponed to some date in the future. Importantly, when debt is rescheduled interest is payable on the postponed repayments.

Debt provisioning – this is the term used when banks decide to set aside funds into their reserves to cushion themselves against the costs of a debtor nation defaulting on part of its obligations. The provisioning does not alter the contractual obligations of the debtor to repay its borrowing.

Debt forgiveness – this occurs when the creditor is prepared to write off part or all of the principal and/or interest payable on an outstanding loan. Debt forgiveness thereby reduces the contractual obligations of the debtor.

Total debt service as a percentage of exports of goods and services – this measures the public and publicly guaranteed principal and interest repayments that the country has to make as a percentage of its exports of goods and services. This gives an indication of the annual burden facing a debtor in relation to its export earnings. The major problem is the effects of variation in export earnings and this measure only gives the burden for the particular year under consideration.

Total debt service as a percentage of Gross Domestic Product – this figure measures the public and publicly guaranteed principal and interest repayments that the country has to make as a percentage of its GDP.

Of course, other statistics such as the evolution of the current account, unemployment rates and the rate of growth of GDP are usually taken into account when assessing the risk of lending to a given country. Other non economic variables which rely upon judgement are also used, these include the likelihood of internal conflict, degree of religious conflict, wealth disparity measures and so forth. It is apparent that no individual indicator can provide an adequate measure of the complexity of a country's debt problem. For this reason, the various debt measures are usually weighted to provide a formal index measure of the probability of default. None the less, there is plenty of scope for assessments to differ depending upon the list of variables chosen and then the weight attached to each measure.

Even when used in combination the various measures do not necessarily provide an accurate picture of the credit worthiness of different countries. They neglect factors such as the differing degrees of vulnerability to external shocks, differing capacities to increase export earnings and differing future economic prospects of the economies. In addition, there may be a difference between the ability of a country to service its external obligations and its willingness to do so, although the two are usually positively correlated. An understanding of country risk assessment is an essential background to the study of the debt crisis because part of the blame for the crisis is attributable to the inadequacies of the measures used by the banks when extending loans to the debtor nations in the first instance.

■ *15.7* Background to the debt crisis

Although the debt crisis flared up in the early 1980s the LDCs had previously defaulted on loan repayments in the 1930s. Bolivia had defaulted in 1931 and was followed by most other Latin American countries during the next three years. The effect of these defaults was to make developed countries extremely wary of lending to the LDCs on other than a short-term basis right up to the 1970s. Nevertheless, a great deal of direct investment in LDCs took place in the 1950s and 1960s especially with a view to exploiting their raw material resources which were a necessary base for reconstruction and economic growth in the developed countries. The main threat posed to such investment was that of excessive taxation or even nationalisation by the LDC concerned.

☐ *The Paris Club*

In response to Argentina's debt problems and the difficulties being encountered by developing countries in repaying their external debts, creditor governments formed what is known as the Paris Club in 1956. Any creditor government may apply for membership of the Paris Club which conducts negotiations between a debtor government and the creditor governments and meetings are usually chaired by a senior French Treasury official. The purpose of the Paris Club is to provide a framework for rescheduling debt repayments to official creditors. All creditor members of the Club receive equal treatment with regard to debt repayments. Before going to the Paris Club it is usually necessary for the debtor nation to have agreed to an IMF economic stabilisation and adjustment programme. An IMF programme usually requires the debtor to take measures to reduce aggregate demand in its economy by adopting tighter fiscal and monetary policies and accompanying this with a devaluation of its exchange rate, the aim being to reduce imports and expand exports thereby improving the country's current account and its ability to service its debt repayments.

■ *15.8* Origins of the debt crisis

The origins of the debt crisis date back to the oil price shock following the Egypt–Israel war of October 1973. The quadrupling of the oil price was particularly harmful to the non oil producing developing countries. They experienced an enormous increase in their import expenditure and on top of this, the resulting recession in developed countries severely curtailed their export earnings. As a result of this the current account deficits of the LDCs rose from $8.7 billion in 1973 to $42.9 billion in 1974 and $51.3 billion in 1975. The terms of trade of oil importing LDCs deteriorated substantially between 1973 to 1975 from 100 to 40. This meant that in 1975 they needed two and a half times of export volumes for every unit of imports than they had in 1973.

While the oil price rise put the LDCs' and developed countries' current accounts into heavy deficit the counterpart of this was that the OPEC members experienced a massive increase in their current account surplus which rose from $6.2 billion in 1973 to $66.7 billion in 1974. The absorptive capacity of the OPEC economies was such that this enormous increase in their incomes could not all be spent on increased imports of investment and consumption goods. In consequence, they placed much of the so called 'petrodollars' on the London and New York money markets. OPEC members preferred to deposit their money with developed countries' financial centres rather than lend directly to oil importing LDCs because they offered a security and range of investment opportunities for their funds that the LDCs could not compete with.

The enormous funds received by London and US banks raised the issue of how the banks could profitably utilise the money. The rise in inflation resulting from the oil shocks meant that real interest rates in industrialised countries were either low or even negative. By contrast, LDC governments were keen to avoid having to adopt deflationary measures to control their current account deficits. Instead they sought to borrow funds to finance the deficits. The alternative of an IMF adjustment package that would have severely curtailed economic growth was not considered particularly appealing.

The view prevalent among the international banking community that Latin America was set for high rates of economic growth, led to a 'recycling' of the petrodollars in the form of massive lending to the LDCs. Most of the loans made to the LDCs were made in dollars by syndicates of international banks with floating rates of interest based upon a margin over LIBOR. Banks preferred to lend at floating rates of interest because the rates they paid on their deposits were variable. They were keen to protect themselves should the rates of interest they had to pay on deposits rise. The other side of the coin was that it left the developing countries exposed to the risk of a sudden rise in world interest rates. Since the vast majority of LDC borrowing was public or publicly guaranteed the banks regarded the risk of any default on the debt as being negligible. It is of note that at the time the recycling was highly praised by governments and international institutions although the IMF was more cautious.

■ *15.9* The emergence of the debt crisis

Although LDC indebtedness rose substantially from $130 billion in 1973 to $336 billion in 1978, the developing countries were experiencing healthy rates of economic growth and not having any particular difficulties in servicing their debts. However, a number of unfavourable factors led to a rapid deterioration of their indebtedness and ability to service their repayments over the following four years.

In 1979 the OPEC cartel more than doubled the price of oil from $13 per barrel to $32 per barrel. Industrialised countries' response to this second oil shock was more uniform than that following the first oil shock. They were determined to reduce the inflationary consequences even if this meant an

Table 15.1 *Current account balance of the big four debtors, 1972–82 (as percentage of GDP)*

	Argentina	Brazil	Mexico	Venezuela
1972	− 0.5	− 2.9	− 2.0	− 0.7
1973	1.0	− 2.7	− 2.6	5.2
1974	0.1	− 7.3	− 4.0	22.0
1975	− 3.3	− 5.7	− 4.6	7.9
1976	1.2	− 4.3	− 3.8	0.8
1977	2.2	− 2.9	− 2.3	− 8.8
1978	2.8	− 3.5	− 3.1	− 14.6
1979	− 0.5	− 4.7	− 4.1	0.7
1980	− 3.1	− 5.3	− 4.0	8.0
1981	− 3.8	− 4.4	− 5.8	6.0
1982	− 4.1	− 6.1	− 3.7	− 6.3

Source: IMF, *International Financial Statistics*.

increase in their unemployment levels. At the end of 1979 the US authorities adopted a tight monetary policy designed to control its inflation rate, with the UK, Germany, France, Italy and Japan adopting similarly tough policies. By contrast, the LDCs preferred to borrow further funds and their outstanding debt nearly doubled from $336 billion in 1978 to $662 billion in 1982. Cline (1984) has estimated that higher oil prices accounted for some $260 billion increase in non oil producing LDC debt.

In addition to increasing indebtedness there was a substantial rise in interest rates due to a rapid rise in the US budget deficit, the dollar LIBOR interest rate rising from 9.5 per cent to 16.6 per cent between mid-1978 and mid-1981. The rise in interest rates was one of the major factors contributing to the severe world recession of 1981 to 1983. In turn, the recession had a devastating effect on the LDCs because it both dramatically reduced their export volumes and reduced the price of their exports leading to a substantial fall in their export earnings. In addition, the recession induced the developed economies to adopt a more protectionist stance *vis-à-vis* imported goods which further squeezed LDC export earnings. **Table 15.1** shows the evolution of the current accounts of the big four debtor nations.

The high US interest rates and borrowing had two other effects. First, bankers were less willing to lend to the LDCs because of the increased attraction of lending the money to the US. Second, the high interest rates contributed to a rapid real appreciation of the US dollar which in turn meant an increase in the real value of LDC debt service repayments.

The result of all these factors was that in 1982 most LDCs particularly in Latin America found themselves with both record levels of indebtedness and debt service repayments, while their ability to raise revenues to finance the repayments had greatly diminished. Much of the borrowing they had undertaken had not been profitably used for investment purposes but merely wasted on inefficient state enterprises and maintaining artificially high consumption levels. Although we concentrate primarily on the external factors behind the debt crisis there is no doubt that domestic economic policy mismanagement played a major part in the debtors' problems.

■ *15.10* The Mexican moratorium

The debt crisis began with the Mexican moratorium which was announced on 12 August 1982. In the early 1980s the Mexican economy was facing a mixture of external and internal problems. Since the mid-1970s Mexico had been a major oil exporter and for this reason was a beneficiary of the rise in oil prices resulting from the 1973–4 and 1979 oil shocks. As the Mexican state both owned and controlled the oil industry the revenues from oil sales accrued directly to the government. International bankers particularly in the US looking at Mexican oil reserves viewed Mexico as a very safe place to lend money. Given its high oil revenues the Mexican government was keen to adopt a programme of increased public expenditure for improving Mexico's infrastructure and a variety of social programmes. The result was that the government ran a huge fiscal deficit which led to high economic growth. Overall, Mexico experienced a prosperous decade in the 1970s.

Following the second oil shock some major problems began to confront the Mexican economy. In the aftermath of the first oil shock the industrialised countries had taken measures to reduce their dependence on imported oil so that the response of demand to the rise in oil prices following the 1979 price shock was more elastic than was the case in 1974. In addition, the major worldwide recession led to a further decline in the demand for oil. Mexico's relatively high inflation rate made the peso which was pegged to the US dollar increasingly overvalued. The peso overvaluation, combined with the authorities' fiscal deficit and decline in oil export revenues meant that Mexico's current account had moved into large deficit.

The Mexican economy's problems, especially the widely perceived view that its currency was overvalued had for some time led to speculation that the peso would be devalued. Speculation against the peso meant large capital outflows and a fall in the reserve holdings of Banco de Mexico's (Mexico's Central Bank) reserves. In a bid to reduce the current account deficit the peso was devalued in February 1982 but the government failed to adopt other measures to control the deficit such as reducing its fiscal deficit and monetary growth rate. In such circumstances, the main effect of the devaluation was to give an additional boost to Mexico's inflation rate. The

Table 15.2   *Total external debt of the big four debtors, 1972–82 (US$ millions)*

	Argentina	Brazil	Mexico	Venezuela
1972	6 028	10 165	7 028	1 712
1973	6 429	12 939	8 999	1 891
1974	6 789	19 416	11 946	1 784
1975	6 874	23 737	15 609	1 494
1976	8 258	29 031	20 520	3 311
1977	11 445	41 397	31 189	10 727
1978	13 276	53 614	35 732	16 568
1979	20 950	60 419	42 828	23 896
1980	27 157	70 838	57 378	29 310
1981	35 657	80 643	78 215	32 093
1982	43 634	92 812	86 019	32 153

Source: World Debt Tables, Volume 2, *1989–90, p. 59.*

deteriorating position of Mexico's economy and the lack of confidence in its government's resolve to reduce its budget deficit made international bankers increasingly reluctant to extend further new loans Mexico.

With Mexico facing ever increasing debt repayments, its ability to service them was being undermined by its reduced export earnings. This led to further speculation against the peso and a run on the Banco de Mexico's reserves. To stop a crisis developing on 12 August 1982 Mexico announced a moratorium on its debt repayments until a satisfactory arrangement could be drawn up with its creditors. Mexico requested further new loans from foreign governments and a rescheduling of its principal repayments which were falling due. In addition, Mexico made a request for loans from the IMF in return for the adoption of an IMF sponsored stabilisation programme.

■ *15.11* The dimensions of the debt crisis

As a result of the Mexican moratorium international banks began to realise that many other countries were facing similar difficulties in servicing their debt. Table 15.2 shows the rapid growth of external debt for the big four debtors.

The real fear of both the banks and the authorities in the industrialised countries was that if Mexico went into default they would be quickly followed by other major debtors. Many US banks had more loans outstanding in Latin America than the value of their equity as is depicted in Table 15.3. A default by any of the big four debtor nations could easily have set off a chain reaction of banking failures and provoked a collapse of the banking systems in the developed countries. Not surprisingly both the banks and

Table 15.3   *US banks' exposure to five Latin American countries in 1982 (loan exposure as a percentage of bank capital)*

Manufacturers Hanover	262.8
Crocker National	196.0
Citibank	174.5
Chemical	169.7
Bank of America	158.2
Chase Manhattan	154.0
Bankers Trust	141.2
Morgan Guaranty	140.7

Note:
The five countries are Argentina, Brazil, Mexico, Chile and Venezuela.
Source: P. Nunnenkamp, *The International Debt Crisis of the Third World* (Brighton: Wheatsheaf Books, 1986) p. 102.

authorities of the industrialised countries were determined to avert such a scenario.

Precisely how the banks got so heavily exposed with their LDC lending is not easy to explain (see Nunnenkamp 1986, chapter 7 for an extended discussion). In retrospect there were clear flaws in their credit rating procedures and they got somewhat carried away with syndicated loans. As Graham Bird explains, the most simple and convincing explanation was that the banks made major mistakes:

> Certainly, looking back at the 1970s, it appears now that the banks overlent. With the benefit of hindsight, such overlending can be explained in a number of ways. With little recent evidence of country default, the banks probably underestimated the risks of lending. They probably lacked the information necessary to calculate such risks and they may have miscalculated the impact of world recession and rising interest rates on the position of the debtors. Beyond this, a belief that short term lending would enable them to extricate themselves if necessary and a confidence generated by the fact that other banks were also lending, as well as a belief that banks would not be allowed to go bust by national and international regulatory authorities, all had the effect of reducing their perceived risks. (1989, p. 17)

 15.12 A supply and demand framework for analysing the debt crisis

Modelling the debt crisis is an extremely complex task because so many variables influence lending and borrowing decisions. Nevertheless, the

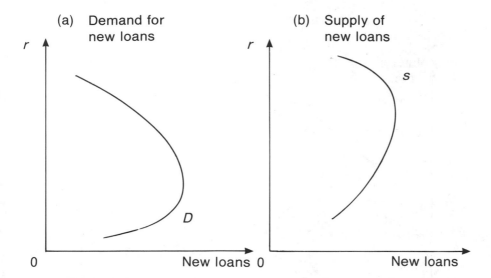

Figure 15.1 *New loans*

explosion of new lending up to 1981 and the fall off after 1982 can be very approximately modelled using a supply and demand for new loans framework.

The supply and demand schedules for new loans to a LDC are depicted in **Figure 15.1**. When determining the slope of the supply and demand for new loans schedules problems are encountered because of the need to distinguish the effects of interest rate changes on the stock of outstanding debt. The demand for new loans comes from the debtor nation and is assumed to be inversely related to the rate of interest as a lower rate of interest makes borrowing more attractive to debtor nations. However, it can be argued that lower interest rate payments, by reducing the debt service payments that a debtor has to make, may actually lead to a fall in its demand for new loans. If this latter effect is strong this may mean an upward sloping demand schedule.

The supply of loans schedule is given by *SS* and has been drawn positively sloped initially but backward sloping once interest rates rise to a certain level. The problem facing the banks is that new lending in the current period will decrease the incentives for debtors to default today while increasing the potential and incentives for the debtor to default in future periods. Hence, the banks will only be prepared to supply new loans in the current period if there is a sufficient rise in the interest rate to compensate. However, beyond a certain rate of interest there is a danger that debtors may be encouraged to default and for this reason above this interest rate the banks may be less willing to make new loans leading to a backward sloping supply of new loans schedule.

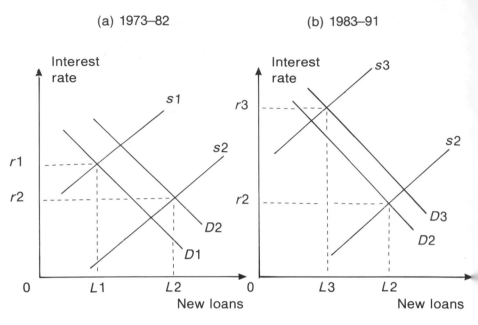

Figure 15.2   *The supply and demand for new loans*

For the purposes of our brief analysis, we shall assume that the supply and demand schedules have their conventional slopes.

Figure 15.2(a) depicts the supply and demand for loans situation in the period 1974 to 1981, while **Figure 15.2(b)** depicts the supply and demand in the period 1983–91.

In **Figure 15.2(a)** the supply and demand situation just prior to the first oil shock are depicted by $S1$ and $D1$ with the corresponding new loans being $L1$. The OPEC oil shock affected both the supply and demand for funds. To finance their current account deficits there was an increase in demand for new loans represented by a rightward shift of the demand schedule from $D1$ to $D2$. The OPEC producers deposited their money balances on the international money markets which greatly increased the supply of funds available for lending to the LDCs. This is represented by a rightward shift of the supply of loans schedule to $S2$. In **Figure 15.2(a)** the shift of the supply schedule is assumed to be greater than the shift of the demand schedule so that the interest rate falls. Overall lending increases from $L1$ per annum to $L2$ while the interest rates remained fairly low.

The situation changed somewhat in 1982. While the demand for funds may still have been increasing from $D2$ to $D3$, there was a large leftward shift of the supply of funds from $S2$ to $S3$. This shift can largely be explained by the dramatic change in the perceived risks of lending to the debtor countries resulting from the Mexican moratorium. Another factor accounting for the supply shift was the increasing attractiveness of lending funds to countries like the US due to the need to finance its increasing budget and current account deficit. As a result the interest rates charged rose while the volume of new lending declined.

▪ *15.13* The economics of default

Once the enormity of debt crisis emerged the main aim of the commercial banks and authorities of the industrialised nations was to avoid one of the major debtor nations declaring default on its debt obligations. Much of the handling of the debt crisis since 1982 can be viewed as the authorities and commercial banks of developed countries adopting strategies designed to avert such a default while at the same time attempting to minimise the financial losses for the banks involved. Since most of the loans taken out by the LDCs were government or publicly guaranteed any default would represent a sovereign default. The most important point about this type of default is that there are no legal remedies available for the creditors to retrieve their money. Nevertheless, debtor nations are normally very reluctant to default on their loans because the savings in the way of repayments are usually less than the perceived costs of declaring default. We now proceed to examine these potential costs of default.

☐ *The costs of default*

Since a debtor government cannot be legally brought to account for a failure to repay its external debts, there must be some perceived costs associated with sovereign default that make countries reluctant to declare default. The three most commonly cited costs of declaring default are:

Exclusion from future borrowing – a country that declares default on its external obligations is likely to be excluded from the possibility of future external borrowing. Those foreign creditors that lose from the default will not be prepared to lend further funds, while prospective lenders will view lending to the country as especially risky. In addition, creditor governments could prevent the IMF and World Bank making further funds available to the defaulting nation. Unable to attract foreign funds for investment purposes, the defaulting nation will be constrained to finance its domestic investment from its relatively low domestic savings which will limit its economic growth. In addition, the country will not be able to smooth out the costs associated with adverse economic shocks by borrowing on world capital markets.

Reduced gains from trade – one of the major costs associated with default would be that the defaulting country would face the increased possibility of protectionist trade measures being adopted against it. There would be a risk that its exports could be subject to seizure when passing through international borders. Gaining trade credit to finance imports will prove difficult in the light of its default. Hence, default is likely to result in a substantial reduction of the defaulting country's volume of trade and with it major welfare losses.

Seizure of overseas assets – although creditors of the defaulting country would be unable to take the debtor governments to court, they might be able to persuade their governments to freeze or seize assets of the defaulting nation held in the creditors' legal jurisdiction. Many LDC governments hold large proportions of their gold and foreign exchange reserves with central banks of the developed nations and they would be worried about the freezing of these assets if they were to default on loans extended by official creditors.

The perceived costs of default are especially worrisome for LDC governments because they are very difficult to quantify and plagued by uncertainty. A debtor government can only guess the extent and duration for which its trade volumes and borrowing capacity would be undermined. The costs of an individual debtor going into default while other debtors do not are likely to be particularly high, especially as creditors would want to demonstrate to other debtors that default is a costly option. If all major debtors were to declare default, the creditor nations would have considerably less scope to adopt penalties. This being the case, the creditor nations will have incentives to avoid the formation of debtors' cartels.

☐ *The benefits of default*

The benefit from the debtor nation's viewpoint of defaulting is that it saves both the repayment of principal due and the interest due on his outstanding debt. Such a sum represents the debt service repayment:

$$DS = P + rD \tag{15.1}$$

where DS is debt service repayment, P is principal and interest due, r is rate of interest, and D is stock of debt remaining.

Equation (15.1) says that the debt service to be paid is the principal and interest due plus the interest payment on the stock of outstanding debt.

Although the debt service ratio represents the payments that the debtor will be expected to make it does not represent the net repayment. The net repayment is the debt service less net new loans received. This is known as the net resource transfer (NRT) from the debtor to the creditor nations.

$$NRT = P + rD - L = DS - L \tag{15.2}$$

where L is the net new loans received by the debtor.

The net resource transfer in this simple model can be thought of as the net saving or benefit from defaulting on the debt. Let us assume that the perceived costs of default are some constant value C. This being the case, the country will not default so long as the net resource transfer is less than the perceived costs of default.

A country will not default on its debt provided:

$$NRT = P + rD - L < C \tag{15.3}$$

While a country will default on its debt if:

$$NRT = P + rD - L > C \tag{15.4}$$

Notice that according to equation (15.4) since the costs of default are positive, a debtor will only consider default if the net resource transfer from the LDC to its creditors is positive. In other words, the debtor's debt service payments exceed the new loans that it receives implying a positive benefit from default that exceeds the positive costs of defaulting.

Equations (15.3) and (15.4) are very important in understanding the various strategies open to the banks to encourage the debtor nations not to default. To avoid default the banks must keep the benefits of default lower than the costs of default and this can be done by either raising the perceived costs of default or reducing the costs of servicing the debt. Commercial banks can persuade debtors not to default by a variety of mechanisms. They can reduce the principal repayments due by restructuring debt repayments over longer time horizons, they could reduce the interest rate repayments due on the stock of outstanding debt, reduce the stock of debt outstanding or engage in new lending. All these methods of reducing the perceived benefits from defaulting have cropped up in one form or another in the management of the debt crisis since its emergence in 1982.

 ## 15.14 The role and viewpoints of the actors in the debt crisis

There have been very divergent views on the nature and extent of the debt crisis and these differences of view have led to different perspectives on how to best manage the crisis. The viewpoint adopted towards the crisis has been partly coloured by the differing interests of the four major actors involved. These are the international banks that have lent the funds, the authorities of the developed nations, international institutions, notably the World Bank and IMF and the debtor nations. We shall briefly overview their perspectives and roles in the crisis although we need to be wary of treating these actors as homogeneous groups. For example, the international banks that lent the money have differing degrees of exposure, face differing regulatory and tax regimes and often have diverse views on the appropriate policy response. Likewise, the debtor nations have differing degrees of indebtedness, differing repayment burdens and prospects with regard to debt repayment. As for the national authorities, their economies have varying degrees of trading links and different historical and strategic relationships with the debtors.

☐ *The commercial banks*

The immediate reaction of international banks to the emergence of the debt problem was to view it as primarily a 'liquidity crisis'. Bankers believed that high interest rates and a large amount of principal repayments falling due combined with adverse economic conditions had meant that the debtor nations were finding themselves in only short-term difficulties. To support this viewpoint it was argued that the debt profile of the debtors was primarily of a short-term horizon and that nations do not go bankrupt. As such, the banks early on sought solutions based upon restructuring debtors' repayments to give the debtors more time to pay. Banks have preferred rescheduling debt repayments and at the same time ensuring that additional interest is paid on the postponed principal repayments.

Bankers have been opposed to granting any debt forgiveness for a number of reasons. They argue that granting debt forgiveness to one country would lead other debtors to seek similar relief. Also debt relief might discourage the debtors from taking the measures necessary to improve their economic performance to ensure they qualify for debt relief. In addition, it is argued that granting a country a degree of debt relief brands it as uncreditworthy so that new loans to the country dry up. In sum, the view of the banking community is that granting debt relief is too costly for banks to contemplate and ultimately harmful to the debtor nations themselves. Banks have argued that any new lending to the Latin American countries should be carried out by the national authorities of the industrialised countries and international institutions. The banks have also been keen to treat each debtor on a 'case by case' approach. This has been motivated not only by a belief that the circumstances facing each debtor are different but also because the different creditor banks have varying degrees of exposure to each debtor. This makes a uniform solution impracticable.

☐ *National authorities*

The national authorities of the industrialised countries have been primarily concerned to avoid a calamitous collapse of their banking systems which could result from a default by one of the major debtors. However, they have been extremely wary of utilising public funds to ease the debtors' plight. Authorities do not wish to be seen to be 'bailing out' the commercial banks whose lending has gone bad. In addition, any significant assistance would be extremely costly and be at the expense of reduced public expenditure or increased taxes. A general feeling is that further loans by the authorities will not help when the problem of the debtors is having too much debt already. Nevertheless, the authorities (especially the US administration) have strategic and economic interests in Latin American debtors, making it impossible for them to be indifferent to the debtors' plight. Rather than get involved in lending new money to the LDCs most authorities have been prepared to allow some tax concessions for provisions banks have made against possible losses on their lending to LDCs. In addition, the authorities have increased the amount of capital available to the World Bank and IMF. Such a method of increasing the funds received by the LDCs is considered useful because the World Bank and IMF can ensure the country is taking appropriate measures to reform its economy and LDCs nearly always ensure repayment of funds to these institutions.

☐ *The IMF and World Bank*

The two main international institutions involved in the debt crisis have played somewhat differing and at times conflicting roles. The World Bank has been very much concerned about the sheer size and extent of the debt crisis and particularly the costs in terms of slower development that debt repayments impose upon the debtor nations. On the other hand, the IMF has seen its main role as ensuring that the debtor nations that come to it for assistance adopt the tough economic measures required to improve their longer-term ability to service their debt. An IMF stabilisation programme can impose high short-term economic costs in the way of reduced living standards and higher unemployment in the debtor nations. Another role played by the IMF has been to ensure that creditor banks continue sufficient new lending to the debtor nations to make it worthwhile for the debtor nations to accept an IMF sponsored adjustment package.

From time to time the two institutions have come into conflict over the handling of the debt crisis, the World Bank criticising the IMF for setting too severe economic adjustment programmes and to some extent infringing upon the Bank's traditional domain. An IMF stabilisation programme often involves a rise in the price of subsidised basic commodities that has been criticised for being inflationary. Overall, the direct impact that the two organisations can have is very much limited by the amount of finance they have. The World Bank has had to be careful not to undermine its AAA credit rating by overextending itself to the SIMICs, while the amount of short-term finance provided by the IMF is very limited compared with the extent of the debt crisis.

☐ *The debtors*

The debtors have to a large extent viewed the crisis they have found themselves in as not of their making but due to a combination of external factors beyond their control. As such, they have felt that the creditor banks should consider the possibility of debt forgiveness which entails them reducing the stock of debt owed by the debtors and/or reduced interest rate repayments below the market rates. Surprisingly, attempts to form a debtors' cartel to improve their bargaining positions *vis-à-vis* the creditor banks have not come to anything. This is partly because the debtors have differing debt problems and so are unable to agree on the way they can best be helped. In addition, the debtors are in competition with one another for whatever new lending is available and creditor banks have been careful to treat them on a case-by-case basis rather than as a group. The debtors have argued that they need some debt forgiveness as an incentive to make economic adjustments in their economies. Without such relief they have little incentive to adjust as all the improved economic performance goes to creditors to pay off their debts.

 ## 15.15 The management of the debt crisis, 1982–91

The debt crisis has been managed largely on a 'case by case' approach, with the creditor banks dealing with each debtor nation on an individual basis rather than collectively as a group. Banks have argued that this is the only realistic option for dealing with the crisis because the problem confronting each of the debtors has its own particular characteristics, requiring its own solutions. Despite this, there are common characteristics in the treatment extended to the debtors.

As bankers initially perceived the crisis as a temporary liquidity problem the main strategy was to reschedule the debt repayments falling due, the aim being to avoid an outright default that would seriously threaten the financial stability of exposed banks and banking community in general. Debt rescheduling packages have not been unconditional; generally the debtor has had to accept an IMF adjustment programme as part of a rescheduling package, particularly where the package has involved new lending. Debt

Table 15.4 *Debt restructuring agreements with commercial banks, 1982–8*

	Average 1982–5	1986	1987	1988
Number of agreements	18	12	19	10
Amount of debt restructured (US$ billions)	42.0	72.7	89.7	79.7
Average consolidation period	2	2.8	4	6.5
Average maturity terms				
Maturity (years)	9	10	15	19
Grace (years)	4	4	5	7
Spread over LIBOR (per cent)	1.8	1.3	1.0	0.8

Source: World Debt Tables, 1989–90, p. 59.

rescheduling has usually been accompanied by further, often reluctant, new lending by the creditor banks that has been termed 'involuntary lending'. **Table 15.4** draws out some of the main trends in restructuring packages during the period 1982–9.

Some clear trends in the rescheduling packages emerge from Table 15.4. Predictably the number of rescheduling packages has remained high over the years reflecting the scale of the debt crisis. Over time the actual value of rescheduling packages has grown if somewhat unevenly, revealing that the debt crisis is far from the temporary phenomenon that it was first perceived to be. The terms of the rescheduling packages have become somewhat less onerous with the maturity and grace periods before payments on the rescheduled debt have to be made lengthened, while the interest rate margin over LIBOR on the rescheduled debt has been gradually reduced. In other words, the debt profile of the debtors has to a large extent been restructured and the terms attached to the debt made less exacting.

Despite their heavy degrees of indebtedness, the debtors' need for new funds has not been greatly diminished by the crisis. New funds are required for investment purposes and in helping to meet their debt service commitments. The banks have been very reluctant to extend new funds to the debtors given the precarious position of their outstanding loans. Many bankers have taken the view that extending new loans to the debtors is 'throwing good money after bad'. Despite this, the banks have realised that without new loans the incentives for the debtors to default rise and so some new lending has been an essential part of restructuring packages designed to avert default by the debtors.

Another notable feature of the management of the debt crisis has been the increasing involvement of the official sector in the way of governments and international institutions. The share of the official sector in the outstanding debt of the SIMICs has increased from 14 per cent in 1982 to 30 per cent in 1988. This reflects in large part the lack of new funds made available by the commercial banks since 1982.

Banks have usually made new loans conditional upon the debtor accepting an IMF adjustment programme, there being no point in extending new money to the debtors unless there are improved prospects of debt service repayments being made. An IMF adjustment package has generally involved the setting of tight monetary and fiscal targets designed to deflate the debtor's economies and a devaluation of its real exchange rate to improve its international competitiveness. Overall the combination of reduced aggregate demand and improved competitiveness should improve the debtor's current account balance and thereby its ability to finance its debt service commitments.

There is little doubt that the debtor nations have undergone considerable adjustment as reflected in their improved current account positions (see **Table 15.5**). None the less, there has been increasing concern that much of the improvement in the current account performance of the debtors has been at the expense of reduced imports of capital and investment goods which does not bode well for the future development of the debtors. A further problem for the debtor countries is that while they did much to stimulate their export volumes this has to a large extent proved self-defeating, in that the increased volumes have depressed their export prices keeping the value of export earnings stagnant. For instance, between 1981–5 Latin American export volumes rose 25 per cent but the deterioration in their terms of trade meant their export earnings remained stagnant.

Table 15.5 shows that the external indebtedness of the SIMICS in 1989 has actually grown since 1983, although their various debt ratios generally exhibit some marginal improvement. As for the big four debtors **Table 15.6** shows that while some of their debt ratios have improved the improvement is not particularly marked and some of the ratios have actually deteriorated since 1982. On the other hand, the restructuring of debt repayments has had the effect of significantly lowering the total debt service to exports of goods and services ratio for Argentina, Mexico and Brazil. However, even the 1989 ratios still represent an enormous burden for the countries concerned.

An important point that needs to be borne in mind is that the marginal improvement in the big four debtors' position has required them to adopt quite tough macroeconomic policies. **Table 15.7** shows that economic growth in the 1980s has been significantly lower in the big four debtors than in the 1970s. This stands in marked contrast to the relative prosperity of the industrialised countries in the 1980s as compared with the 1970s.

The considerable difficulties faced by the debtors in having to meet their debt service repayments leaving less money to finance government expenditure has led many of the debtor governments to resort to printing money. The result of excessive money creation has been very high inflation rates as is depicted in **Table 15.8**. Of the big four debtors only Venezuela has managed to keep its inflation rate under control.

A final worrying aspect of the debt crisis in recent years has been a dramatic increase in the stock of debtors' arrears not only to private creditors but also to official institutions like the World Bank and IMF. This is illustrated in **Table 15.9**.

The growth in arrears is an indication of the considerable difficulties that debtor nations are having in repaying their debt. The failure to repay funds to official creditors is potentially very serious as these institutions are normally the last line of credit for the debtors.

■ *15.16* Provisioning

When a bank makes provisions this is purely an accounting exercise and involves the bank putting aside reserves against outstanding loans in low earning but risk-free assets. The reported profit figures will be reduced by the amount of the provisions and thereby implies a lower dividend to bank shareholders. In May 1987 Citicorp – the major US bank – announced that it was setting aside $3 billion to its loan-loss reserves against its lending to developing countries. Its decision was quickly followed by provisioning by other major banks both in the US and Europe. Provisioning has since become a regular feature in the annual accounts of the major international commercial banks with exposure to the debtor nations. While provisioning prepares the banks for any eventual losses on their outstanding debts it does not reduce the contractual obligations of the debtors to repay their debt. In other words, provisioning is quite distinct from 'writing down' debt which means that the banks reassess the book value of their outstanding loans, or 'writing off' loans whereby the bank reduces the contractual obligations of the debtor. While reducing the provisioning bank's profitability provisioning has the advantage of reducing risk exposure were a debtor to default.

The motivations behind provisioning are varied, but since 1985 it has become increasingly apparent that the initial appraisal of the debt crisis as a

Table 15.5   *Debt statistics of the SIMICs, 1980–90 ($millions)*

	1980	1983	1984	1985	1986	1987	1988	1989	Projected 1990
Total external debt	298 629	442 656	463 432	499 627	531 471	586 562	567 812	565 729	587 614
Current account	−39 539	−11 880	−3 149	−5 352	−23 024	−13 399	−11 922	−11 680	−8 132
Net transfers	13 780	−8 078	−13 379	−17 091	−19 430	−14 980	−20 282	−17 787	n.a.
Principal ratios (%)									
EDT/XGS	195.8	318.3	284.1	317.5	374.8	374.9	319.7	294.3	283.0
EDT/GNP	37.7	62.0	63.1	67.0	68.2	72.3	61.4	54.9	58.9
TDS/XGS	36.0	42.4	37.1	36.8	41.5	35.7	36.2	28.6	26.1
INT/XGS	18.6	28.4	24.8	25.4	24.6	20.9	21.6	16.4	13.9
INT/GNP	3.6	5.5	5.5	5.4	4.5	4.0	4.2	3.0	2.9
RES/EDT	17.8	8.5	10.5	10.3	8.7	9.4	8.3	8.5	11.7

EDT, total external debt; XGS, exports of goods and services; GNP, gross national product; INT, interest repayments; TDS, total debt service.
Source: World Debt Tables, 1990–91, Volume 1, p. 158.

Table 15.6   *External debt statistics of big four debtors 1982–9 (US$millions)*

	1982	1983	1984	1985	1986	1987	1988	1989
Argentina	43 634	45 920	48 857	50 945	52 450	58 425	58 706	64 745
Brazil	92 812	98 095	105 015	105 526	113 043	123 560	115 646	111 290
Mexico	86 019	92 964	94 822	96 865	100 872	109 447	101 752	95 641
Venezuela	32 153	38 297	36 881	35 332	34 637	35 275	34 473	33 144

Argentina Principal Ratios (%)

	1982	1983	1984	1985	1986	1987	1988	1989
EDT/XGS	447.3	470.3	493.1	493.2	593.3	695.5	520.3	537.0
EDT/GNP	83.8	77.3	67.5	84.2	70.5	76.6	66.2	119.7
TDS/XGS	50.0	69.7	52.4	58.9	76.2	74.3	44.8	36.1
INT/XGS	36.7	55.7	44.1	49.1	48.7	48.3	27.9	17.7
INT/GNP	6.9	9.2	6.0	8.4	5.8	5.3	3.5	3.9

Brazil Principal Ratios (%)

EDT/XGS	395.4	403.0	347.6	360.0	449.8	430.1	316.8	301.6
EDT/GNP	36.1	50.4	52.6	48.7	42.1	42.3	33.8	24.1
TDS/XGS	81.3	55.1	46.3	38.6	46.9	41.9	48.6	31.3
INT/XGS	49.2	39.8	31.3	31.5	31.3	26.3	36.4	15.5
INT/GNP	4.5	5.0	4.7	4.3	2.9	2.6	3.9	1.2

Mexico Principal Ratios (%)

EDT/XGS	311.5	324.0	291.3	326.0	422.7	363.0	312.2	262.9
EDT/GNP	52.5	66.4	57.1	55.2	82.6	82.3	60.9	51.2
TDS/XGS	56.8	51.7	52.1	51.5	54.2	40.1	47.9	39.5
INT/XGS	40.4	34.8	34.7	34.4	35.1	27.7	27.0	25.5
INT/GNP	6.8	7.1	6.8	5.8	6.9	6.3	5.3	5.0

Venezuela Principal Ratios (%)

EDT/XGS	159.8	220.8	195.6	205.6	307.8	273.8	279.2	211.5
EDT/GNP	41.4	48.4	63.8	59.1	58.7	75.6	60.5	79.9
TDS/XGS	29.5	26.8	25.2	25.0	45.3	37.8	43.7	25.0
INT/XGS	17.5	17.4	15.2	19.2	27.4	21.3	24.6	20.3
INT/GNP	4.5	3.8	5.0	5.5	5.2	5.9	5.3	7.7

Notes:
EDT, total external debt; XGS, exports of goods and services; GNP, gross national product; INT, interest repayments; TDS, total debt service.
Source: World Bank, *World Debt Tables, 1990–1*, volumes 1 & 2.

liquidity problem was somewhat erroneous. Increasingly, bankers began to realise that they were unlikely to recoup a substantial proportion of their loans to the SIMICs. This realisation has come about due to a combination of factors:

1.   The deteriorating economic performance of the SIMICs. Although their current account performance has stabilised their rates of economic

Table 15.7   *Economic growth of the big four debtor countries, 1973–89 (per cent per annum of GDP)*

	Argentina	Brazil	Mexico	Venezuela
1973	5.9	13.5	8.4	6.3
1974	5.6	9.7	6.1	6.1
1975	0	4.2	5.6	6.1
1976	−5.3	9.8	4.2	8.8
1977	5.6	4.6	3.4	6.7
1978	−5.3	4.8	8.3	2.1
1979	11.1	7.2	9.2	1.3
1980	1.5	9.1	8.3	−2.0
1981	−6.7	−3.3	7.9	−0.3
1982	−4.9	0.7	−0.6	0.7
1983	3.0	−3.4	−5.3	−5.6
1984	2.6	5.0	3.7	−1.4
1985	−4.3	8.3	2.7	0.2
1986	5.6	7.5	−3.7	6.5
1987	2.2	3.6	n.a.	3.6
1988	−2.7	0.0	n.a.	5.8
1989	−4.6	n.a.	n.a.	−8.3

Source: IMF, *International Financial Statistics.*

Table 15.8   *Inflation rates of the big four debtor countries, 1982–9 (per cent per annum)*

	Argentina	Brazil	Mexico	Venezuela
1982	164.8	97.8	58.9	9.6
1983	343.8	142.1	101.8	6.3
1984	626.7	197.0	65.5	12.2
1985	672.1	226.9	57.7	11.4
1986	90.1	145.2	86.2	11.5
1987	131.3	229.7	131.8	28.1
1988	343.0	682.3	114.2	29.5
1989	3079.2	1286.9	20.1	138.6

Source: IMF, *International Financial Statistics.*

growth, levels of investment to GDP and trade volumes have shown a significant slowdown.

2.   The overall levels of indebtedness and many of the debt service ratios and other indicators have actually deteriorated since 1982 as is shown in **Tables 15.5** and **15.6**.

Table 15.9   *Stock of SIMICs arrears, 1985–9 ($billions)*

	1985		1987		1989	
	Interest	*Total*	*Interest*	*Total*	*Interest*	*Total*
Official	2.8	9.8	7.7	20.8	12.4	24.4
Private	2.9	11.2	7.5	19.4	15.1	30.8

Source: World Bank, *World Debt Tables*, 1990–1, volume 1.

3. Signs of a deteriorating world economic environment. The 1980s witnessed one of the longest sustained periods of economic growth for most of the major industrialised countries. Without such a cushion the debt crisis might well have proved unmanageable. However, the stock market collapse in October 1987 and the rising trend of world interest rates at the end of the 1980s raised the risk of a world recession which would adversely affect debtor countries' export volumes and terms of trade.

4. The rising discount on secondary market debt. Since the emergence of the debt crisis there has developed a secondary market for developing country debt on which the creditor banks can sell their outstanding loan assets to third parties (mainly other commercial banks) at a discount to its face value. Part of the secondary market is made up of swaps between banks which enable them to reshuffle their loan exposure portfolios. The size of the secondary market was estimated by the IMF (1990) to be approximately $5 billion in 1985 and $30–40 billion in 1988. As Table 15.10 shows this discount has gradually risen over the years reflecting the increasing probability that much of the debt will eventually have to be written off.

5. A slowdown in economic growth in the debtor countries and falling per capita incomes. This was combined with a continued deterioration in non-oil producing LDCs' terms of trade that were at their lowest point in 1986 compared with manufacturing prices since the Second World War.

The discount on debt rose substantially between April 1987 and March 1989 reflecting a perceived deterioration in the debt crisis, one of the factors being the Brazilian moratorium announced in February 1987. Worsening market valuations made it increasingly untenable for banks not to make provisions against the loans. Once Citicorp had made its provisions, provisioning by other banks became inevitable.

The ratio of provisions as compared with outstanding loans made by banks has varied considerably both within and between countries. Different

Table 15.10 *The secondary market price of debt for the big four debtors,*
1985–91 (cents per dollar)

	October 1985	October 1986	April 1987	March 1988	March 1989	January 1991
Brazil	78	76	64	48	28	22
Mexico	80	57	59	49	33	44
Argentina	65	66	60	29	18	18
Venezuela	82	74	74	54	33	49

Notes:
The secondary market can at times exhibit quite substantial changes in prices, particularly
for countries where the market is rather thin. Markets for the above countries, debt are
fairly well developed.
Source: Salomon Bros, New York.

provisions by banks within the same country can be accounted for by the differing degrees of overall exposure, those banks most heavily exposed generally making the lowest provisions. In addition, some banks are more exposed to countries where the secondary price of debt is relatively low as compared with other banks. Differences in provision levels between banks of different countries can to a large extent be explained by the different regulatory and tax treatments accorded to provisioning. This is borne out by the fact that in the UK, Germany and France where the regulatory and tax regime is favourable to provisioning the level of provisions in mid 1990 were, UK 50–70 per cent, France 56–61 per cent and Germany 50–78 per cent. While in Japan, where the regime is much tougher the level of provisions was only 25–30 per cent. The major US banks generally had provision levels of 30–50 per cent in 1990(although a couple had much higher provisions).

One of the most disturbing trends in the debt crisis is the gradual drying up of new loans to the debtor nations as banks try to reduce their exposure and extricate themselves from further involvement in the debtor nations. In the immediate future, the prospects for new lending to the debtors are bleak and are likely to remain so until problems posed by the enormous debt overhang are substantially reduced. It seems likely that banks will remain reluctant to extend new loans to debtors so that their best hopes for new development finance will lie in direct foreign investment. Although the World Bank has shown some interest in co-financing new investment in the debtors, such projects are unlikely to make more than a marginal impact. The World Bank does not have sufficient funds to make significant investments and the commercial banks are wary of its bureaucratic involvement.

An overall evaluation of the management of the debt crisis is hard to arrive at since the crisis is still nowhere near resolution and very much in a state of flux. From the perspective of the banks the strategy pursued has so far avoided pushing the debtors into to default and because of provisioning the banks are much better placed should some defaulting occur. In this sense the management of the debt crisis can be regarded as a success. However, the overall levels of indebtedness of the debtors and their debt service ratios have continued to worsen despite considerable hardship and the large economic adjustment programmes that have been undertaken. In many respects, the debt problem at the beginning of the 1990s is still as serious as at the beginning of the 1980s. A variety of solutions have been put forward to ameliorate the crisis. In the next section we consider some of the proposals that have been put forward.

■ *15.17* Solutions for resolving the debt crisis

The differing solutions put forward to resolve the debt crisis have largely been determined by the differing views on the nature and extent of the crisis and interests of those making the proposals. The sets of proposals can be categorised into three broad strategies, although most proposals combine elements of all three:

1. Alter the structure and nature of the debt.
2. Economic reform in the debtor countries.
3. Some degree of forgiveness on the debt owed.

Alter the structure and nature of the debt – this is the type of proposal that the banks generally support being loath to write off any debt. Banks argue that by lengthening the time horizon for repayments of the debt, the debt service repayments become more manageable. For example, much of the floating rate debt could be converted into bonds carrying a fixed rate of interest enabling debtors to be more certain of their future debt service commitments. To a large extent this has been how the debt crisis has been managed since 1982 with various rescheduling packages.

More recently, it has become popular to consider various means of converting the debt assets of the creditors into a form that reduces the debt servicing commitments of the debtors. One popular example of this is 'debt-equity' swaps. A typical debt-equity swap operates as follows: a commercial bank sells some of its debt at a discount to its face value to a third party who buys the debt with dollars. This third party may be a domestic resident of the debtor country with foreign exchange or a foreign resident wishing to invest in the debtor country. The third party then has the right to exchange the debt with the authorities of the debtor country for local currency which can then be exchanged for equity in debtor country enterprises. Sometimes, the creditor banks convert some of the debt owed by enterprises they have lent into shares in the enterprise. This means that the creditor banks still manage to maintain the book value of their assets but they receive funds only if the enterprises they have equity in make profits and pay out dividends.

Although subject to much hype 'debt-equity' swaps are likely to make only a marginal contribution to alleviating the debt crisis although they amounted to $13 billion in 1988 and $12 billion in 1989. There are regulations which limit bank ownership of enterprises that have reduced the appeal of debt-equity swaps. A further problem is that arbitrage forces come into play; if such conversions prove very attractive, the sales of debt increase the discount on the debt while the purchases of equity push up equity prices reducing the return on equity. These effects reduce the attractiveness of switching from debt to equity. In addition, it might be the case that converting a large amount of bonds into equity would merely change the nature of risks from default risk into expropriation and tax risk should debtors find the dividend and profit transfers excessive. More recently, there have been concerns about the potential inflationary impact of the consequent increase in the money supply when the debt is exchanged for local currency.

Economic reform in debtor nations – the banks and international institutions such as the IMF have been keen to promote economic reforms in the debtor nations which they believe will improve their ability to service their debts in the short term and their economic performance in the medium to long run. These measures include at the macroeconomic level an exchange-rate devaluation to make the economies more competitive, a tight fiscal policy based primarily on reducing government expenditure and a tight monetary policy to stabilise inflation. These measures often need to be supplemented by market based reforms such as reducing food subsidies that distort the allocation of resources, and reduced protectionism. Overall the measures have been aptly summed up as 'devaluation, deflation and deregulation'. The problem with such measures is that in the short term they often result in increased unemployment and rises in the prices of basic commodities such as food making them politically destabilising for the debtor nations to implement.

Debt forgiveness – the advocates of some debt forgiveness view the plight of the debtor nations as so serious that the best means of helping them is to actually write off part of the debts that they owe. They argue that most banks now realise that they are unlikely to recover a large proportion of the loans they have made and they should recognise this by formally writing off part of the debt. Proponents of debt forgiveness argue that writing off part of the debt now, will reduce the amount of write offs the banks would have to make in the long run, particularly if debt forgiveness is linked to economic

---

Box 15.2   *The Baker and Brady plans*

The Baker Plan

In October 1985 the US Treasury Secretary James Baker announced a major three-year initiative for managing the debt crisis. The Baker Plan was launched against a background of increasing disenchantment on the part of debtor nations over the recessionary impact of adjustment programmes and the drying up of voluntary bank lending. The Plan endorsed the 'case by case' approach to dealing with the debt crisis, that is, treating each debtor nation in a manner appropriate to its individual circumstances. Baker envisaged debtor nations growing out of their debt problems by undertaking market based structural reforms, including trade liberalisation, cuts in government expenditure and a relaxation of regulations relating to inward foreign investment. An enhanced role for the IMF and World Bank in the process of economic growth was envisaged via increased and more effective structural adjustment lending. In addition, a target of $7 billion annually was set for new lending by the commercial banks to the 15 major debtor nations, such additional lending by private banks being supported by a $3 billion annual increase in Multilateral Development Banks' (mainly the World Bank and Inter American Development Bank) net disbursements.

Overall the implementation of the plan was not considered a success. Voluntary bank lending did not resume on the scale envisaged by the plan and even official lending fell short of its target (see Cline, 1990). The price of secondary debt of the 15 debtor nations plummeted from an average 70 cents to 35 cents per dollar over the following three-year period, while economic growth in Mexico, Brazil and Argentina stagnated and inflation rocketed (see Tables 15.7 and 15.8). However, the poor economic performance can be attributed as much to domestic economic policy mismanagement as the continuation of the debt crisis.

The Brady Plan

A reformulation of the strategy for dealing with the debt crisis was signalled by the new US Treasury Secretary Nicholas Brady in March 1989. The 'case-by-case' approach, encouraging debtors to undertake market based reforms and the adoption of stable macroeconomic policies continued to be viewed as essential components for resolving the debt crisis. However, in addition to emphasising the need for additional new bank lending the Brady plan also explicitly recognised the contribution that voluntary debt forgiveness may make in resolving the crisis. He argued that the path to creditworthiness for many SIMICs required some debt and debt service reduction on a case-by-case basis. The major innovation of the Brady initiative was its inclusion of official support for debt and debt service reduction. Both the World Bank and IMF were asked to set aside funds for this purpose for SIMICs with high external debt problems and undertaking appropriate adjustment programmes. Subsequently, US Treasury Under Secretary David Mulford set a target of $60 billion in debt forgiveness for 39 of the leading

Box 15.2   *contd*

debtor nations over three years with the IMF and World Bank expected to provide some $20 billion for lending purposes designed to support debt and debt service reduction.

Note: The so-called 'Baker 15 Counties' are: Argentina, Bolivia, Brazil, Chile, Columbia, Ecuador, Ivory Coast, Mexico, Morocco, Nigeria, Peru, Philippines, Uruguay, Venezuela, and Yugoslavia.

reform in the debtor nations. Indeed, without debt relief the incentives for the debtors to default will grow as they struggle to meet their obligations.

There have been a variety of different schemes put forward involving debt forgiveness. Some involve reducing the principal owed by the debtors either by direct write downs of the debt or allowing debtors to buy back debt at a discount to its face value. Other schemes involve reducing the interest repayments below market rates. Most schemes involve a mixture of the two elements. An example would be a scheme allowing a debtor to convert $100 million of debt with a maturity date of five years and a variable current rate of interest of 13 per cent into long-term bonds of 20 years worth $80 million at a fixed 8 per cent interest.

A key stumbling-block to debt forgiveness proposals is a dispute between banks and the governments of the creditor nations over who bears the cost. The banks have been reluctant to consider debt forgiveness in case the debtors were to become economically viable in the future. In addition, they argue that debt relief might encourage debtors to pursue profligate economic policies to ensure that they qualify for debt relief or discourage them from taking measures to meet debt service commitments. As such they have made debt provisions but sought to gain tax relief on these potential losses from their tax authorities. Governments have been reluctant to grant tax concessions because of the loss of revenue and the fear that bailing out the banks would only encourage them to engage in further risky/reckless lending in the future.

Most approaches to resolving the debt crisis combine elements of the above proposals. What is clear is that there are no easy solutions and that any solution will have to involve a bit of give and take by each of the major actors involved in the crisis.

■ *15.18* Conclusions

The debt crisis arose through a mixture of domestic and external circumstances which varied from debtor to debtor. Nevertheless, the extent and close timing of debtors' problems suggests that common external factors played a significant part in the crisis. It is too simplistic to apportion the crisis solely to excessive borrowing by the debtor nations. In large part the crisis reflected excessive lending by the commercial banks.

Although the crisis was in great part due to a combination of events outside the debtor countries' control most of the adjustment burden for managing the crisis has fallen on the debtor nations. There is some justification in the criticism that the management of the crisis has been biased towards the requirements of the creditor nations rather than the needs of the debtor nations. For instance, real per capita GNP was 10 per cent lower in Latin America in 1985 than in 1980.

The role of the IMF and World Bank in the debt crisis has often been criticised as being too biased in favour of the creditors and requiring too heavy an adjustment by the debtors. To some extent this criticism is unfair because the IMF often recommends policy measures that the debtor would have to undertake anyhow. It merely provides a convenient scapegoat for the debtor government to implement necessary adjustment packages. The IMF and World Bank simply do not have the resources to make more than a marginal impact on debtors' financial positions.

It is also a mistake to make generalisations about the best method to tackle the debt crisis. The circumstances and prospects of the debtor nations are immensely varied. In this respect, the 'case by case' approach taken to manage the crisis is almost certainly justified. Nevertheless, the recognition of the fact that debtors' circumstances differ should also mean that IMF stabilisation programmes exhibit a greater degree of variety than the almost standard package of deflation, devaluation and deregulation. Furthermore, when proposing solutions there needs to be a recognition that there is a large degree of interdependence among the debtor nations. It is no use encouraging export led growth by a number of debtors if such measures merely depress their export prices on world markets leaving their export revenues stagnant.

A final point that needs to be remembered in connection with the debt crisis is that it is not just a major problem for the debtor countries' economies and the financial community of the industrialised countries. The stagnation in debtors' economies also limits the employment and export prospects, that is, the real economy in the industrialised nations. A solution will be in the interests of all parties.

■ Selected further readings

Bird, G. (1989) *Commercial Bank Lending and Third World Debt* (London: Macmillan).

Cline, W. (1984) *International Debt: Systematic Risk and Policy Response* (Cambridge, Mass: MIT Press).

Cline, W. (1990) 'From Baker to Brady: Managing International Debt', in R. O'Brien and I. Iversen (eds), *Finance and the International Economy: 3* (Oxford: Oxford University Press).

Dornbusch, R. (1985) 'Policy and Performance Links Between LDC Debtors and Industrial Countries', *Brookings Papers on Economic Activity*, vol. 2, pp. 303–56.

Griffith-Jones, S. (ed) (1988) *Managing World Debt* (Hemel-Hempstead: Harvester-Wheatsheaf).

Kuczynski, P. (1988) *Latin American Debt* (Baltimore: Johns Hopkins University Press).

Nunnenkamp, P. (1986) *The International Debt Crisis of the Third World* (Brighton: Wheatsheaf Books).

Sachs, J. (1984) 'Theoretical Issues in International Borrowing', *Princeton Studies in International Finance*, No. 54.

Sachs, J. (1986) 'Managing the LDC Debt Crisis', *Brookings Papers on Economic Activity*, vol. 2, pp. 397–431.

Sachs, J. and Huizinga, H. (1987) 'US Commercial Banks and the Developing Debt Crisis', *Brookings Papers on Economic Activity*, vol. 2, pp. 555–601.

General Texts in the Field of International Finance

Argy, V. (1981) *The Postwar International Money Crisis: An Analysis* (London: George Allen & Unwin).

Batchelor, R.A. and Wood, G.E. (1982) *Exchange Rate Policy* (London: Macmillan).

Bhandari, J.S. (1985) *Exchange Rate Management Under Uncertainty* (Cambridge, Mass.: MIT Press).

Bhandari, J.S. and Putnam, B.H. (1983) *Economic Interdependence and Flexible Exchange Rates* (Cambridge, Mass.: MIT Press).

Bigman, D. and Taya, T. (1982) *The Functioning of Floating Exchange Rates; Theory, Evidence and Policy Implications* (Cambridge, Mass.: Ballinger).

Bilson, J.F.O. and Marston, R.C. (1984) *Exchange Rate Theory and Practice* (Chicago: University of Chicago Press).

Brooks, S., Cuthbertson, K. and Mayes, D.G. (1986) *The Exchange Rate Environment* (Beckenham: Croom Helm).

Bryant, R.C., Currie, D.A., Frenkel, J.A., Masson, P.R. and Portes, R. (1989) (eds), *Macroeconomic Policies in an Interdependent World* (Washington: IMF).

Buiter, W.H. and Marston, R.C. (1985) *International Economic Policy Coordination* (Cambridge: Cambridge University Press).

Chipman, J.S. and Kindleberger, C.P. (1980) *Flexible Exchange Rates and the Balance of Payments* (Amsterdam: North-Holland).

Claassen, E.M. and Salin, P. (1983) *Recent Issues in the Theory of Flexible Exchange Rates* (Amsterdam: North-Holland).

Cooper, R.N., Kenen, P.B., Macedo, J.B. and Ypersele, J.V. (1982) *The International Monetary System Under Flexible Exchange Rates.* (Cambridge, Mass.: Ballinger).

Copeland, L.S. (1989), *Exchange Rates and International Finance* (Kent: Addison-Wesley).

Corden, W.M. (1985) *Inflation, Exchange Rates and the World Economy.* 3rd edition (Oxford: Clarendon).

De Grauwe, P. (1983) *Macroeconomic Theory for the Open Economy* (London: Gower).

De Grauwe, P. (1989) *International Money* (Oxford: Clarendon Press).

De Grauwe, P., Fratiani, M. and Nabli, M. (1985) *Exchange Rates, Money and Output. The European Experience* (London: Macmillan).

Dòrnbusch, R. (1980) *Open Economy Macroeconomics* (New York: Basic Books).

Dornbusch, R. and Frenkel, J.A. (1979) *International Economic Policy* (Baltimore: Johns Hopkins University).

Eltis, W.A. and Sinclair, P.J.N. (1981) *The Money Supply and the Exchange Rate* (Oxford: Clarendon).

Frenkel, J.A. (1983) *Exchange Rates and International Economics* (Chicago: University of Chicago Press).

Frenkel, J.A. and Johnson, H.G. (1978) *The Economics of Exchange Rates* (Reading: Addison-Wesley).

Gandolfo, G. (1987) *International Economics*, vol. 2 (New York: Springer-Verlag).

Hallwood, P. and MacDonald, R. (1986). *International Money: Theory Evidence and Institutions* (Oxford: Basil Blackwell).

Jones, R.W and Kenen, P.B. (1985) (eds) *Handbook of International Economics*, vol. II (Amsterdam: Elsevier).

Kane, D.R. (1988) *Principles of International Finance* (Beckenham: Croom Helm).

Kenen, P.B. (1988) *Managing Exchange Rates* (London: Routledge).

Kenen, P.B. (1989) *International Economy* (New York: Prentice-Hall).

Krueger, A.O. (1983) *Exchange Rate Determination* (Cambridge: Cambridge University Press).

Krugman, P.R. and Obstfeld, M.(1988) *International Economics* (Boston: Scott Foresman).

Levi, M. (1990) *International Finance* (New York: McGraw-Hill).

Llewellyn, D.T. and Milner, C. (1990) (eds) *Current Issues in International Monetary Economics* (London: Macmillan).

MacDonald, R. (1988) *Floating Exchange Rates: Theories and Evidence* (London: Unwin Hyman).

MacDonald, R. and Taylor, M.P. (1989) *Innovations in Open Economy Macroeconomics* (Oxford: Basil Blackwell).

McKinnon, R.I. (1979) *Money in International Exchange* (Oxford: Oxford University Press).

Miller, M., Eichengreen, B. and Portes, R. (eds) (1989) *Blueprints for Exchange Rate Management* (London: Academic Press).

Niehans, J. (1984) *International Monetary Economics* (Oxford: Philip Allan).

Pilbeam, K.S. (1991) *Exchange Rate Management: Theory and Evidence* (London: Macmillan).

Rivera-Batiz, F.L. and Rivera-Batiz, L. (1985) *International Finance and Open Economy Macroeconomics* (West Drayton: Collier Macmillan).

Salvatore, D. (1990) *International Economics*, 3rd edn (London: Maxwell Macmillan).

Shone, R. (1989) *Open Economy Macroeconomics.* (Hemel Hempstead: Harvester Wheatsheaf).

Yeager, L.B. (1976) *International Monetary Relations: Theory, History and Policy* (New York: Harper & Row).

Williamson, J. and Milner, C. (1991). *The Open Economy and the World Economy.* 2nd edn (New York: Basic Books).

■ Useful journals for international finance

American Economic Review
Brookings Papers on Economic Activity
European Economic Review

IMF Staff Papers
Journal of Money Credit and Banking
Journal of International Economics
Journal of International Money and Finance
Journal of Political Economy
Scandinavian Journal of Economics

 # Useful theory and policy analysis publications

Bank for International Settlements, Economic Papers, Basle.
Group of Thirty Occasional Papers, New York.
IMF Occasional Papers, Washington.
Institute for International Economics, Policy Analyses. MIT Press, Cambridge, Mass.
Princeton Essays in International Finance, Princeton University, Princeton.
Princeton Studies in International Finance, Princeton University, Princeton.
The Economist Magazine.

Sources of statistical information

Country Studies, Organisation for Economic Cooperation and Development, Paris, published bi-annually.
Main Economic Indicators, Organisation for Economic Cooperation and Development, published monthly.
International Financial Statistics, International Financial Statistics, Washington, published monthly.
Economic Outlook, Organisation for Economic Cooperation and Development, Paris, published bi-annually.
World Debt Tables, World Bank, Washington, published annually.
World Development Report, World Bank, Washington, published annually.
World Economic Outlook, International Monetary Fund, Washington, published bi-annually.

Author Index

Subject Index